OTHERS SAY ...

"Victor Shane's *Book of Life* offers intriguing prescriptions for society's problems. In an audacious feat of virtuosity he blends the physical and the spiritual into a seamless solution that is persuasive and compelling."

—Rabbi Daniel Lapin, *Toward Tradition*

"An immense and worthy Biblical-philosophical work; soundly based in the timeless truth, yet relevantly addressing the contemporary confusion—the 'strife of tongues' that stand against ultimate realities."

—Pastor Jack Hayford, *The King's Seminary*

"Though I disagreed with some aspects of this book (the theory of Satan), I found this to be a profound contribution and worthy to be published. It is a fascinating read."

—Daniel Juster, *Tikkun Ministries International*

"I can not say that I agree with all that Victor Shane presents in his *Book of Life*, but I did find considerable material that sparked my thinking."

—Gerald L. Schroeder, Ph.D., Jerusalem

"I Think this book will heighten the religious-scientific world outlook of the average person."

—Joseph Davydov, Ph.D.

Book of Life

סֵפֶר הַחַיִּים

God, Cosmos and Man:
A New Understanding of Human Nature

Victor Shane

PARA-ANCHORS INTERNATIONAL

Scripture quotations are either from the King James Version of the Holy Bible, or the author's own interpretation derived from Hebrew and Greek texts. Hebrew Tanach and Mishna texts courtesy of Davka Corporation's *DavkaWriter* program.

First paperback edition published 2003.

Publisher's Cataloging-in-Publication
(Provided by *Quality Books, Inc.*)

Shane, Victor.
Book of life : God, cosmos and man : a new understanding of human nature / Victor Shane.
p.cm.
Includes bibliographical references and index.
LCCN 2003103920
ISBN 1-878832-04-2

1. Religion and science. 2. Consciousness.
3. Cosmology. 4. Philosophy of nature. I. Title.

BL240.3.S53 2003 191
QBI33-1152

זָכְרֵנוּ לְחַיִּים, מֶלֶךְ חָפֵץ בַּחַיִּים,
וְכָתְבֵנוּ בְּסֵפֶר הַחַיִּים,
לְמַעַנְךָ אֱלֹהִים חַיִּים.

Remember us unto life,
O King who delights in life,
and inscribe us in the Book of Life,
for Your sake, O God of life.

Contents

And if the blind lead the blind, both shall fall into the pit.
(Matthew 15:14)

Author's Introduction
Classical Boundary Conditions

On 11 September 2001 terrorists under the direction of Osama Bin Laden hijacked and crashed four passenger jets, two into the World Trade Center in New York, and one into the edifice of the Pentagon, killing thousands, changing the New York skyline, creating havoc, pandemonium, destruction, chaos and disorder of unprecedented proportions. They killed innocent civilians—fathers, mothers, sons, daughters, uncles, aunts, grandmothers, grandfathers, butchers, bakers, physicians, accountants, janitors, firemen and peace officers. They caused economic losses amounting to tens of trillions of dollars, stock market closures and wholesale layoffs, not to mention the compromise of national and civil liberties.

What was "911" all about? Religion? Politics? Ideology? In truth what happened in New York on 9/11/2001 was nothing new. The history of the world is full of violence, terrorism, war, reduction, destruction, pogrom, genocide, holocaust and ethnic cleansing. It has been said, for example, that from the dawn of recorded history until today, a period of almost 6000 years, the world has known only three days of uninterrupted peace! That is, only three days in which man's inhumanity to man was taking a holiday on earth—only three days in which members of one faction were not murdering members of another. Only three days of peace in 6000 years? Something is wrong here. Something fundamental. Something systemic. Something that goes to the core of human nature itself. What might it be, and why can't we recognize it for what it is? Is there something wrong with us? If so, why are we so blind that we can't see it?

The contradictions that abound in the world and history would seem to be telling us that there is indeed something wrong with us. What is it? What devil is there in us that would drag us down into disorder? We had better find out before we fill the next millennium with violence and destruction. But this is where we run into a paradox and a *catch-22*. In order to arrive at the truth about our own irrational nature we would have to engage in rational thought. But if we could engage in rational thought, how could our nature be irrational? We are like blind men trying to set up a double-blind experiment.

In his work *A Brief History of Time* the scientist Stephen Hawking speculates about the nature of this *catch-22* :

> Now, if you believe that the universe is not arbitrary, but is governed by definite laws, you ultimately have to combine the partial theories into a complete unified theory that will describe everything in the universe. But there is a fundamental paradox in the search for such a complete unified theory. The ideas about scientific theories outlined above assume we are rational beings who are free to observe the universe as we want and to draw logical deductions from what we see.... Yet if there really is a complete unified theory, it would also presumably determine our own actions. And so the theory itself would determine the outcome of our search for it! [1]

If an individual is born with eyesight and then loses his sight, he is then able to comprehend the meaning of "blindness." But individuals who are *born* blind are not capable of comprehending the idea of "blindness" by themselves. Those who are born blind are up against a similar catch-22 situation. To recognize their blindness, they would need "sight," in which case they would not be blind. But being blind, they do not possess the means of recognizing "blindness." Many individuals are born blind in this world. If they realize that they are "blind," it is only because they have been informed by family members who can "see." And it is no small miracle when they recognize and acknowledge their "blindness," having never known such a thing as "sight" in the first place.

But what if all men were born blind? A troubling question. Who would inform them of their blindness? Having never known such a thing as "sight," they would stumble about unaware of their handicap. They would eventually learn to find their way about with the use of canes, for instance. Their building tools would be the tools of the blind. Their institutions would be the institutions of the blind.

They would develop their own systems of sightless communications. All of their books and their writings would be in braille. Some of them would periodically fall into this and that "pit," but they would get used to that. This dilemma, "falling into a pit," would provoke some philosophical discussion among their wise and learned, but in time they would blame the whole thing on "fate," or "human nature," or something like that. After a while their entire blind race would condition itself to the business of "falling into a pit." In the end they would merely shrug their shoulders and say, "ah well, that's life I guess! We will just have to learn to live with it."

Perhaps we should stop at this eleventh hour and ask if we are suffering from some such "blindness." Some deep intuition would seem to be warning us that this may in fact be the case. Certainly the Bible has been warning us about something similar for thousands of years. And if the warnings of God were not enough, there's the evidence of history itself. The evidence is all around us even today. In our own day we see that all men, all cultures, all races and all nations desire peace and prosperity. But alas there doesn't seem to be any end to war and poverty. Somewhere in the world children are starving to death. Somewhere in the world the "shelling" continues and the death toll keeps rising. Somewhere in the world an unsuspecting farmer is stepping on an old landmine. Somewhere in the world human beings are needlessly suffering. Somewhere in the world people are dying violent deaths.

Our God-given conscience bears witness, for example, that injustice, prejudice, hatred, racism and antisemitism are irrational and injurious. But these demons continue to flourish here and abroad. And the same may be said of the seven thousand vices that have attached themselves, leech-like, to the human condition. Deceit, iniquity, murder, larceny, graft, corruption, perversion and obscenity have become fixtures of our existence, or so it seems. Why does it *have* to be this way?

Science and technology have all but harnessed the forces of nature to the service of man. Every technological ingredient necessary for the arrival of global peace and prosperity is at hand, but the harvest does not come! The vintage of true civilization fails! In spite of every advance, every improvement, every breakthrough in science and industry, we keep sliding closer and closer to the abyss. We now know, for example, that the entire human race can be sustained at the highest standard of living on its daily quota of solar energy alone. But alas nations continue to sink deeper and deeper in the quagmire of pollution, congestion, waste and want. And although deep down we know that our very survival depends on earth's vital resources, we find ourselves destroying them as though we had no control over the situation.

What is the efficiency of our so-called "civilization" presently? How much is being spent on the munitions of war and destruction? How much is now wasted that would allow the highest standard of living for every man, woman and child on earth? Whence this monstrous contradiction between reality and hope? Why does it *have* to be this way? Whence this veil of tears? Why is there so much evil in the world? Why can't we replace it with good? Why should that be so difficult? What exactly is the stumbling block?

The contradictions are all around us. The most powerful and resourceful institutions on earth are those that underwrite fear, debt, disease and pollution. There are now more people employed by the cancer industry than actually dying from the disease. And someone has calculated that nations have stockpiled enough weapons of mass destruction to allocate fifteen tons of TNT for the destruction of every man, woman and child living. What does this say about our race? What manner of madness is this that we have become accustomed to, accepting it with a wave and a shrug?

Where is the *caput nili*? Where is the source and origin of this deeply irrational component in human nature? And why should it be so inclined towards everything that is unproductive, ruinous, injurious and destructive? Why should it defy every attempt at explanation? Are we ourselves? Do we choose freely? Or are the choices and decisions being made for us by some unknown principle or principality? Are we acting on our own "free will?" Or are we under the influence of something that remains hidden from us? Is there a rational, scientific explanation for the root of depravity in human nature? Is there a rational, scientific explanation for the pattern of failure observed in the laboratory of human history?

Why do men continue to practice what they despise in others? And what about man's inhumanity to man? Do holocausts, atrocities, genocides, pogroms, massacres and other acts of mayhem transpire arbitrarily? Or is there some underlying imperative, order or principle directing them? Do these destructive traits exist arbitrarily? Or are they the outworkings of some underlying principle, nature, property or orientation? Are we rational beings? If we are, we would be behaving rationally. But is this the case? No it is not. And what can we infer from this? We can infer the existence of some contrary principle at work within our material nature.

How are the contradictions in our nature to be explained? Do these contradictions exist because we are not yet "educated" enough? Would they go away if every human being on earth had a college degree? Would they go away if everyone had lots of money, a mansion, a swimming pool and two cadillacs in the garage? What is the answer? Where does the solution lie? In the prescriptions of secular humanism? In a pretense of tolerance and consanguinity? In an Orwellian paradigm of conformity and homogeneity? In a United Nations inquisition to enforce uniformity? In the structural adjustment programs of the IMF and World Bank? In privatization? In junk commercialism and "market morality?" In so-called "rational design?" Will the perfectly-designed city produce utopia on earth? Will technological advances improve the morality of mankind?

Are we to believe that there is no answer? Are we to believe that the human gene is inherently defective? What then? Does the answer lie in the science of genetic manipulation? In behavior control? In "paradise pills?" In resignation and escape? In virtual reality, neural implants and the seven thousand vices that mankind is still innocent of?

Living in our modern era, we pride ourselves in our civilization. We like to say that we are not like our barbaric ancestors. Yet our own age is rife with barbarities and blood-lettings that put the mayhem of our ancestors to shame. As Will Rogers once said, "You can't say civilization isn't advancing: in every war they kill you in a new way!" Where does the problem lie? Does it have something to do with "religion?" Does it have something to do with "politics?" Does it have something to do with "money?" Does it have something to do with "ideology?" Does it have something to do with "nationalism?" Does it have something to do with "social conditioning?" The philosophers of our age are not in agreement as to what the problem might be. Their models of human nature reveal as great a confusion of ideas and thoughts on the parts of their authors as one can imagine.

What a fond hope it was that welled up in us when the Berlin Wall came down, when communism began to collapse and Vaclav Havel stood on the balcony in Prague's Wenceslas Square to face cheering crowds. We all thought that those happy events would herald a new age of peace and democracy. How wrong we were! Even before the echoes of the cheering crowds could die down, seven thousand repressed demons came out of their closets to demand a ransom in wholesale new bloodletting. And as the Bosnian demon was massacring innocent men, women and children, we stood in silence, dumfounded, stunned and paralyzed by the deficit of rational explanation. And even as the scenario repeated itself in Rwanda, we did nothing but throw up our hands and make the old excuse—"Ah well, that's human nature for you!"

Let us pause and take inventory of our own record. Let us consider something written by the distinguished British journalist Michael Ignatieff in his book entitled *Blood and Belonging*. Ignatieff went rummaging through the burned down rubble of the former Yugoslavia, trying to find some sort of rational explanation for all the destruction and killings going on over there. Here are Ignatieff's words in regards to the city of Vukovar, for example, reduced to a heap of ruins by the Serb militia:

> Some quite uncontrolled adolescent lust was at work here. The tank and artillery commanders could not have seen what they were hitting. It was all abstract and as satisfying as playing machines in a video arcade.[2]

Ignatieff tried to find some sort of rational explanation for all the mayhem and disorder. After looking at the enigma from every possible angle, after exploring all of the issues of "religion," "past history," "bad blood," "an eye for an eye," "nationalist delusion," etc., after rummaging through all the debris, ruin and destruction, after visiting all the mass graves, he writes the following:

> There are puzzles which no theory of nationalism, no theory of narcissism of minor difference, can resolve. After you have been to the wastelands of the new world order, particularly to those fields of graves marked with numberless wooden crosses, you feel stunned into silence by a deficit of moral explanation.[3]

How often have we seen this same spirit of resignation? Great philosophers, poets, writers and thinkers agonize over the human condition, only to run into the same brick wall and resign themselves to despair. This element of despair can be found in the lamentations of all the great authors of mankind from Homer to Shakespeare, from Omar Khayyam to Yevgeny Yevtushenko. Even the eminent William Faulkner, having agonized over the nature of man, seems to be telling us that we will never know the answer to the human condition.

With all of their pretensions of mind and power the politicians of the world don't seem to know the answer either. They too grapple with the same ineffable "blindness." They may propose this and that "solution," and some may even succeed in producing spasms of social reform. But the spasm is all too soon replaced by the familiar regression into disorder.

CLASSICAL BOUNDARY CONDITIONS

The human race seems to be up against some sort of *classical boundary condition*. Perhaps we can define the condition as follows:

> You can't fix something that's broken on the basis of the same set of assumptions that broke it in the first place—you will just bounce off the same walls and end up right back where you started.

What exactly are the boundary conditions of human failure and disorder? What are the fundamental assumptions that need to be changed? Whatever they may be, we need to discover and overcome them soon. It is now very late and "business as usual" won't cut it any more. It is time for another tectonic shift. The old model of human nature is now a bankrupt enterprise. Any continuance of the old model would spell ruination. The conventions of the past are inadequate for the present. Whatever is wrong with us must be discovered and fixed, otherwise we will continue to bounce off the same walls with devastating results—more war, more terrorism, more biological warfare, more destruction, more hate, more genocide, more holocausts, more ethnic cleansing, more reduction, more degradation, more global warming, more disease, more pollution, more congestion, more waste, more perversion, more obscenity, more banality, more crime, more imbecility, more poverty, more famine, more starvation and more mass misery with no end in sight.

The ignorance of man may have been sufferable in ages past when the world was such a big place and the partitions of time and distance working insulators. But the world has grown small suddenly. The differentiations that were yesterday insulated from one another are now rubbing raw against some imperative that does not allow peaceful coexistence or harmonious multiplicity. If the nature of this imperative is not understood, and compensated for, we can only guess at the field day that the devil is going to have among the dissimilar factions of the human race. The lateness of the hour and the unprecedented distress of mankind now render the former ignorance deadly. It is time to lay the axe to the root. It is time for another tectonic shift in the collective consciousness of Man. It is time for a Great Awakening, a Sea Change. It is time for an Exegesis and a Revelation that can relate God, Man and Cosmos in a rational and holistic formula.

THE IMPORTANCE OF TRUTH

Truth is the guiding principle of all inquiries. God who desires man to be *truthful*, has endowed him with the capacity to mirror reality with the use of words. Truth is an honest representation of reality by means of words, allowing mankind to perceive entities and relationships as they really are. This honest reproduction of reality, by means of *words*, is the foundation on which all inquiry and justice depend. For only according to a truthful description of things can we understand their relationships with one another, and behave justly. Truth must be consistent with reality—a faithful description of reality by means of words. If this description is carelessly or deliberately falsified, the fabric of "right" and "justice" will be pulled out from under the feet of mankind. For then, given a false reality, human behavior will be falsified as well, along with the whole gamut of human existence.

God has knitted together the community of man with the golden threads of truth. Truth is the fabric on which religion, philosophy, science, law, government and justice, depend. Distort the truth and you will tear the very fabric of human existence. Truth is the basis of all good on earth, falsehood the basis of all evil. He who misuses words to distort reality communicates a falsehood to his brother, who may then stumble and fall. He who denies truth to his brother violates the most basic of human trusts, calling down a curse on his brother and all mankind. Every violation of truth is not only a curse on the violator, but an attack on the health of society. The liar steals the most precious thing on earth—truth. The liar is more dangerous than a thief. The thief steals only the material means of life, whereas the liar and the propagandist steal from life itself. Just as God links the supreme good of all men to truth, so also He links the greatest of all evils to lies, even calling the devil "the father of lies" (John 8:44).

The liar and the propagandist extinguish the Divine spark, not only in themselves, but also in those who are gullible enough to believe the falsehood. Deceit and propaganda are contagious. One falsehood leads to another, and another, and before you know it truth has fallen in the public forum and society is no longer capable of discriminating between reality and delusion. This is why we are made to swear that we will tell the truth, the whole truth, and nothing but the truth in a court of law.

In an irrational age in which society has rejected all absolutes and jettisoned all frames of reference, in a postmodern age in which mankind has rendered all moralities "relative" and all truths "subjective," we should begin our inquiry by providing some guidelines about the absolute nature of truth:

> Truth is non-contradiction.
> Truth is consistent with reality.
> Truth is the essence of successful prediction.

Throughout history great thinkers have looked for some underlying truth that will enable them to make sense of it all. The milestones in this process of rationalization have produced tectonic shifts in the collective consciousness of Man, allowing successive abrogations of the institutions that were built on wrong knowledge. Every tectonic shift in Man's understanding of the universe has shed one more layer of error from his mind and one more demon from his soul. Whereas each shift has brought the mind of Man a little closer to an understanding of the nature of Reality, it is now time to press for the goal itself. Half-measures won't do any more. Our goal in this publication will not be to perform superficial patchwork on existing models of human nature. What we have in mind is a new model that is fully grounded in Reality. One with universal truth-anchoring.

בָּרוּךְ אַתָּה יְיָ אֱלֹהֵינוּ מֶלֶךְ הָעוֹלָם...

Blessed are You, Eternal our God, Sovereign of the universe...

(Ancient Hebrew Invocation)

SECTION 1

God, Cosmos and Man

Presuppositions

In inquiries of every kind there are certain presuppositions on which subsequent reasoning must depend. Much of science, for example, has to begin with certain presuppositions about the universe, which in themselves cannot be proven or falsified, but are necessary in that they provide a *frame of reference* for what follows. Beginning with a hypothetical frame of reference, scientists can then proceed by way of experimentation, observation and investigation towards template approximations of reality, known as *theories*. We must now list some of the presuppositions that will provide our inquiry with a crucial frame of reference and lay the foundation for a new theory of human nature. What follows in this publication is based on a number of presuppositions, among them the following:

A sample size of one (closed) universe
The Causality Principle
The Cosmological Principle
The Thermodynamic Assumptions

Cosmos, (the world, the sum of physical reality), is the frame of reference used by philosophers, scientists, theologians, and the Bible itself. All the belief systems of the world base themselves on some model of the universe. One might describe these belief systems in terms of a triangle, at the apex of which lies *cosmos*, at one corner of the base the *self*, and at the other *society*. It may be said that all belief-systems, even atheistic ones, "back-engineer" themselves from certain models of cosmos and reality. And if the model is flawed, then the entire frame of reference—the entire foundation of human existence—may be flawed as well.

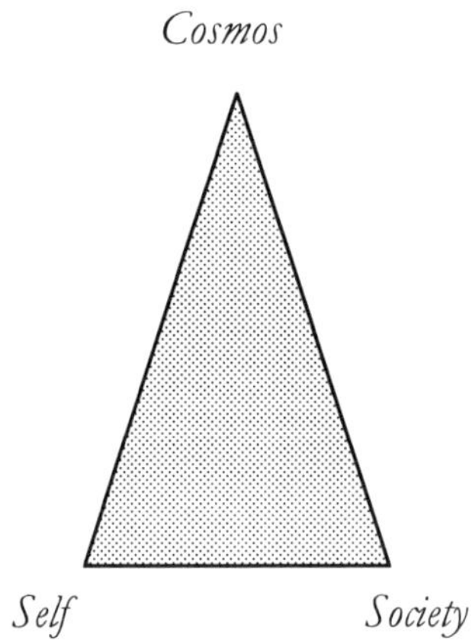

So then we would do well to ground our inquiry in an accurate model of cosmos furnished by modern science. Let us now take a look at some of these presuppositions.

SAMPLE SIZE OF ONE (CLOSED) UNIVERSE

The universe needs to be treated as a single *closed* system, otherwise there may be no clear distinction between physics and metaphysics. This may sound odd but it is an important presupposition nevertheless. Granted it can't be "proven" or "falsified" per se, but it provides a necessary frame of reference. A closed universe would afford containment for the conservation of energy, for example, underwriting the first and second laws of thermodynamics, whereas an open universe might not. A closed universe that is billions of years old would still be "warm"—you would expect it to contain something similar to the cosmic background radiation that we find in this universe. An open universe would likely be cold—devoid of any "afterglow."

Some scientists are now leaning in the direction of metaphysics, appealing to *infinity issues* and positing such things as *parallel universes*. Unfortunately these approaches tend to lie outside the methodology of investigation. For all we know the cosmos may be an avocado balanced on the back of a turtle. For all we know our entire universe may be just one atom in a higher level universe of unimaginable proportions. Although "possible," these ideas would find little support among rational scientists. Those who wish to toy with metaphysics run into another obstacle as well, one set up by Sir William of Ockham in the 14th century. Nowadays referred to as *Occam's Razor*, it goes something like this:

> Terms, concepts and assumptions must not be multiplied beyond necessity.

Occam's Razor cautions scientists not take too many liberties with their theories. They may not resort to unnecessary, unwarranted and extravagant assumptions in order to explain unknowns. Everything else being equal, the simplest and most rational explanation should suffice until something more substantial comes along. So then at least for here and now we will refrain from going off on wild goose chases, tempting as they may be, and confine ourselves to the solid ground afforded by a sample size of *one closed universe*. As the saying goes, "a bird in the hand is worth two in the bush."

CAUSAL PRINCIPLE

The Causal Principle posits the non-separation of cause and effect, implying that effects do not exist unless causes exist, and vice versa. The relationship between cause and effect does not have to be instantaneous, linear, Newtonian or deterministic. It can, for example, be probabilistic (statistical/quantum). Either way, cause and effect cannot be fully separated, else we would be living in chaos instead of cosmos. Cause and effect have to be conjoined, the cause the antecedent of the effect, the effect an "extension" of the cause. Any talk about separation of cause and effect, or the non-existence of cause and effect, would amount to contradiction. We began this inquiry by making a statement to the effect that *truth is non-contradiction*. Reality cannot contradict truth. The Causality Principle is the foundation of the physical sciences because it denies contradictions. Without truth (non-contradiction) we would be living in a chaos of unknown things—science would have no ground to stand on.

One UNItary principle or imperative must underlie the entire universe, otherwise it would not be a UNIverse. And if one principle or imperative underlies every stratum of the UNIverse, then it is plausible to assume that some representation of it would be found in all physical systems, binding them together physically and informationally. Furthermore, since what we really want to do is to investigate our own relationship with the cosmos, we must not exclude our own *human* condition from the Causal Principle. If one unitary principle underlies every stratum of the cosmos, then some aspect of it must be internalized in human nature as well. If we are living in a unified creation governed by law, we must not treat ourselves with privilege, as though we were living in a zone of exclusion. If everything in the universe is wired together non-locally, then *we* must be wired into the cosmos as well.

Physically, (ignoring any and all spiritual considerations for the time being), it is not possible to exclude the human condition from the cosmic process. We are made from the physics of this universe. We cannot fully disassociate our own behavior from the behavior of matter and energy. It is not possible to investigate human nature independently of the nature of the cosmos. The laws that rule on the behaviors of matter and energy have to be factored into human behavior.

In order to investigate the nature of reality we must first take stock of our human instruments, because our awareness of reality, and our ability to relate to it, depend on the energy-driven instruments of our five senses. The thing that connects our sense experiences with the universe is *energy*. Without energy the ear could not function as an instrument of hearing, nor the eye as an instrument of seeing, nor the brain as an instrument of thinking. A computer will not work without power. Neither will the human brain. And note that some of the largest arteries in the body are the ones that deliver fuel and oxygen to the organ of the brain.

For example, the "colors" that we perceive are actually different wavelengths of energy. For the eye itself there are no reds, no oranges, no yellows, no greens, no blues, no magentas, no violets, only invisible quanta of light which are converted into chemical reactions and tiny electric currents travelling through nerve fibers. It is only when these impulses reach the brain that light and color come into being. The scientist Johannes Dogigli explains this in his book *Magic of Rays*:

> [T]he many millions of nerve fibers would be virtually superfluous if there were not certain areas in the brain specially designed to respond to chemical and electrical reactions of these fibers. It is here that the impression produced by the photons...first becomes *light* and *color*.... Light and color are therefore not outside us: we carry them within ourselves, for the world around us is blacker than the most stygian night.[1]

The operation of the brain itself depends on the physics of the universe. In which case even "thinking" would have to be a product of an energetically regulated matrix determined by the way in which our neurons are "wired" into the realms of matter and energy. From a purely physical point of view, everything that we think or do is the result of a chemical or electrical reaction occurring somewhere in the body. These chemical and electrical reactions have to conform to universal imperatives—we can't even "think" without conforming to the laws that govern the disposition of matter and energy.

In order to "think," we have to use energy. But to use energy we have to let the cosmos regulate the way in which we use it. In which case some of our "thoughts" may be cosmos-driven and cosmos-derived as well, skewing our entire existence in the direction of some universal imperative, say, towards the conservation of energy, or towards the acquisition of lower energy states. How then do we know if our thought processes are our own? We don't. For all we know the energetic requirement of the thinking process may be making some of our "decisions" for us— making selections in favor of familiar information that has been processed already and does not require additional energy for reprocessing.

So from the onset we would like the reader to understand that we cannot exclude human history and the human condition from the Causal Principle. There is no earthly reason to exclude the human condition from the cosmic process. Evidence for the cosmic process can be found in human history as well as in a scientific laboratory. History is in fact the greatest "laboratory" of them all, containing the largest sample of human elements and reactions, and it is not as though we enjoy some sort of "privilege" or "exemption" in the universe.

Absent the *spiritual* worth and value that God places on us we are nothing but physical systems—"just a bunch of neurons." The attempt to claim "cosmic exemption" may in fact be a large part of the overall problem. The human condition, or rather the *reprobate* human condition, has always moved from low to high entropy states just like any other physical system in the universe. It is time to smash this last pedestal of human arrogance and come out of denial. It is time that scientists started looking at the human condition in terms of a *physical system*, because that is exactly what it is. A complicated system perhaps, but in principle no different from any other energy-driven system in the universe.

Likely those who would claim exemption for human behavior would do so by appealing to "quantum uncertainty." But quantum uncertainty does not imply that we are living in a chaos of unknown things. Quantum uncertainty does not imply stochastic chaos, it never has. While it may be true that individual quantum events may—from a human perspective—appear to behave in arbitrary ways, it is also true that sufficiently large collections of quantum events will always move in the direction of increasing entropy. This has to do with a principle called *decoherence*, as the scientist Ian Stewart explains in his book *Nature's Numbers*:

> [E]ven if quantum mechanics is correct about indeterminacy on the smallest scales, on macroscopic scales of space and time the universe obeys deterministic laws. This results from an effect called *decoherence*, which causes sufficiently large quantum systems to lose nearly all of their indeterminacy and behave much more like Newtonian systems.[2]

Cosmos does not imply chaos. Relativity does not imply chaos. Quantum mechanics does not imply chaos. The universe is not a chaos of arbitrary things.

Granted, reality is "fluid." Granted, open systems should not be confused with closed systems. Granted, increasing entropy does not translate into local determinism. However, these arguments which are quite valid in context, have little to do with the question that we are now asking about relationship between the *nature* of the cosmos and the *nature* of human beings. Human beings do not live in a zone of exclusion.

Ultimately there is only one "closed system" to speak of, and that is the UNIverse itself. Meaning non-separation. Meaning that there is no discontinuity between the behavioral field of the cosmos and the behavior of the natural man. We are made from the physics of this universe. We cannot bat an eyelid without degrading energy, which results in an instantaneous increase in the entropy of the entire universe. Yes, we may enjoy a measure of God-given free will in a *spiritual* sense, (depending on how one would define that word), but otherwise we are *physical systems* wired into the fabric of the universe.

The first pedestal of human arrogance had to do with the notion that we were the center of the universe. Happily that pedestal was smashed by the likes of Galileo. The second pedestal of human arrogance had to do with the notion that evolution had granted us "privileged status" on the tree of life, and that pedestal was smashed by the likes of Stephen Jay Gould. The last pedestal of human arrogance has to do with this business of trying to claim exemption for human behavior. The evidence found in the large sample of history would seem to be telling us that we enjoy no such exemption. Absent the influence of God in our lives, we are nothing but physical systems moving from ordered to disordered states, just like any other physical system in the universe.

We say again: apart from any *special* worth and value bestowed on us by God, and apart from any *spiritual* Liberty and free will that He may have invested in our earthly existence, we are nothing but physical systems whose behaviors are essentially cosmos-derived and cosmos-driven, no different from any other physical system in the universe. The sooner we swallow our pride, come out of denial, admit this and smash this last pedestal of human arrogance, the sooner will we be able to break free of the boundary conditions of error and failure.

COSMOLOGICAL PRINCIPLE

In essence the Cosmological Principle says that the laws of physics operate UNIformly throughout a UNIverse. These laws are indeed universal. A law that only works some of the time, or only in one place, is no good. Mysticism and superstition may posit chaotic laws and arbitrary events, but within the scientific discipline the laws of the universe are taken to apply uniformly and unfailingly everywhere throughout space and time. No exceptions and no exemptions.

Meaning that we are indeed living in a UNIverse, and not some BIverse, or TRIverse or OMNIverse. Meaning, for example, that the electron charge on your monitor screen is identical to the electron charge on a quasar at the edge of the universe. Meaning that the speed of light is constant throughout the universe. Meaning that the gravitational constant is the same throughout the universe. Meaning that the "basic numbers" are the same everywhere. Meaning again that there are no *zones of exclusion*—places where the laws of physics do not apply uniformly. One cannot posit zones of exclusion without throwing out the Cosmological Principle, and one cannot throw out the Cosmological Principle without transforming cosmos into chaos and physics into metaphysics. Look up at the night sky: do you see all those pinpoints of light? They are all laboring under the duress of the same universal imperative as you and I.

THERMODYNAMIC ASSUMPTIONS

In essence the Thermodynamic Assumptions say that energy cannot be created or destroyed—only changed. All universal "activity" results in a net conservation of energy (first law of thermodynamics) and a net increase of universal entropy (second law of thermodynamics); implying that everything in the universe is informationally "wired" on some existential balance sheet. In physical terms we humans are not merely *in* the universe but *of* the universe. We cannot even blink an eye without degrading energy, which reduces the amount of graded energy in the universe, which results in a net increase in the entropy of the entire universe. We are energy-driven systems made from the physics of this universe. Our material existence and behavior are "wired" into the fabric of the cosmos in ways that may yet take centuries to fully understand.

At the heart of thermodynamics is the *second law* which invests the cosmos with a sort of one-way "ratchet" mechanism. Albert Einstein once said that the second law of thermodynamics was the premier law of all of science, and the great physicist Sir Arthur Eddington described it as the supreme metaphysical law of the entire universe. The second law of thermodynamics—the law of increasing entropy—stamps the universe with an arrow of time, identifying the greater order of change. It invests the entire cosmos with a nature, a property and an orientation. Scientists were quick to draw the conclusion that the cosmos is engaged in a one-way slide towards disorder, hence the loose definition of entropy as *the inexorable tendency of the universe and every closed system in it to move towards disorder.* The French have a simpler explanation:

> *Tout lasse, tout casse, tout passe!*
> (Everything wears out, everything breaks, everything passes away!)

Although the word "entropy" describes degraded energy, ("the energy in a closed system that has been degraded and is no longer available to perform work"), in the broader context of this publication we will use it to describe degradation in general. *Environmental entropy*, for example, might describe the degree to which rivers and oceans have been polluted. *Nutritional entropy* might describe the degree to which foodstuffs have been degraded before ending up on supermarket shelves. *Urban entropy* might describe the degree in which streets have been degraded by garbage and graffiti. Slums, ghettos and prisons might provide future historians with measures of *national entropy*. Vices such as addiction, perversion and pornography might provide them with measures of *moral entropy*. Derivatives, junk bonds and junk financial instruments might provide them with measures of *economic entropy*. One could make a general statement to the effect that we are now living in an "entropic society," one that is degrading the very environment that it needs to stay alive; whereby the city dump (a repository of garbage, useless waste and degraded things) might represent a measure of *societal entropy*. Or in an even broader philosophical context, such things as debt, poverty, war, destruction, disease and crime might be described as various forms of *global entropy*.

There are many other useful analogies. Signal to noise ratio, for example, where the "noise" (the unwanted "snow" that you might see on your TV screen) would be analogous to entropy. The interest accumulated for the duration of a 30-year mortgage might be analogous to entropy. Junk mail, or junk e-mail would be other forms of "entropy." Junk entertainment. Junk medicine. Junk science. Junk in general, would equate with what we are now calling "entropy."

Question: If entropy is degraded energy, then what is graded energy? Generally it is what scientists call *Gibbs free energy*. Granted that Gibbs free energy is measured in units called *joules*, whereas entropy is measured in *joules/Kelvin* (joules of energy per degree of temperature). However entropy may also be represented as a *ratio* of joules of degraded energy to the total joules of energy in a system. If this is a little confusing to the lay reader, just remember that energy has to be measured in some unit, usually *joules* (after the great physicist James Prescott Joule). Remember also, although energy cannot be created or destroyed, it can be graded or degraded, so we need to be able to measure the difference.

Just look at what happens to the energy in a battery. If you leave the battery on a shelf for a few years it will run down. What happened to its energy? Assuming that the battery is a closed system, the energy could not have escaped, and it could not have been destroyed. So then why won't it start the car now? Well, it has to do with the universal law that says *entropy must increase in closed systems.* The battery will not start your car because the graded energy that it once contained has been degraded into entropy.

If the battery is an *open system*, it can be hooked up to an external source and recharged (re-graded). However, in order to recharge the battery, other cosmic energies must be degraded. The cosmic energy degraded by the battery charger itself is coming from a wall socket, which is coming from a powerplant, which is in the final analysis coming from the earth or the sun—the cosmos. The quantity of the energy degraded by the battery charger will *always* exceed the quantity that has been upgraded in the battery, producing an increase in the entropy of the universe in the manner described by the second law of thermodynamics. And that is why scientist keep telling us that universal entropy is *always* increasing. There is nothing in all heaven and earth that you or I could do that could ever bring about a *decrease* in the entropy of the universe.

In essence, the second law of thermodynamics describes a cosmic ratchet that can turn in one direction only—in the direction of increasing entropy. What does this mean? It means that in the universe at large, the greater order of change is flowing down the gradient that leads from low to high probability. Think of it in terms of the "motion" of a huge river, a river of time, a river of change. Locally there may be low-probability redistributions, anomalies and eddies, but the river as whole can only move "downhill"—towards the high-probability state of the sea. Likewise, the cosmos itself can only move in the high-probability direction of *increasing entropy.*

ORDER VS DISORDER

Since most discussions about "entropy" have something to say about order and disorder, perhaps we should clarify a few things. Any definition of *order* must begin by specifying a frame of reference. For purposes of this publication we will specify a purely *human* frame of reference. But is there another frame of reference? Yes there is, the *cosmic* one. The cosmic frame is opposed to the human frame. Why should these two frames be opposed? Because our human definition of "stability" is somewhat the reverse of the cosmic one. Using the *cosmic frame*, the cosmos becomes more "stable" as universal entropy increases, gradually moving towards a final "equilibrium state" in which no life would be possible. (Cosmic "stability" and "equilibrium" should not be confused with what we humans understand by those terms.) Universal systems achieve maximum "stability" at their respective equilibrium states, but using the cosmic definition, human beings achieve maximum "stability" in their respective graves. (Going by a purely *cosmic* convention, the equilibrium state reached at maximum entropy would be the most stable and ordered state in the universe. But to us it would mean chaos and death.)

What do we humans mean by a "stable" or "ordered" society? Well, we don't mean a dead society, do we? No, we mean something quite the reverse, some living condition that on the whole depends on low entropy states. We mean local states that abound with enough graded (unstable) energy to underwrite and sustain such things as structure, organization, life, and *complexity*. The human definition is not to be confused with what physicists and chemists call "equilibrium state" (the point at which systems die and no more change is possible).

Let us look at the universe from a non-human perspective. As universal entropy increases, the cosmos becomes more "stable." In this context, increasing entropy translates into increasing stability, which translates into "increasing order." And if the entropy of the universe were to reach a maximum (at what is commonly referred to as "the heat death of the universe,") the cosmos would reduce down to pure undifferentiated energy, at which time it would be perfectly "organized," perfectly "homogeneous," and perfectly "ordered."

Unfortunately we would all be dead. So what do we *humans* mean by "order," what do we mean by "disorder," and how are we supposed to define these terms? Again, the answer is that you can't define them without specifying a frame of reference. Given a *cosmic* frame of reference, increasing entropy would be the essence of "order" and "stability." Given a *human* frame of reference, increasing entropy would be the essence of "disorder" and "death." The conventions of order and disorder are reversed between man and cosmos.

Human order (decreasing entropy) runs deeply against the grain of cosmic order (increasing entropy). Granted, human order cannot articulate itself independently of cosmic order, but in principle the two are reversed, standing, as it were, in contempt of one another. And this is where we need to pry them apart, because very often they are superimposed and conflated. Hitler's definition of "order" wasn't the same as Mother Teresa's. Yet both these individuals were trying to "order" the world.

What do we mortals mean by "order?" In trying to answer the question we need to take a look at the conventions that were laid down by God in those six "days" (six stages) of creation. God started with disorder, and finished with order. What God did in those six stages was to lay down rudimentary order, and then progressively work towards the superlative order of Life, laying on various levels of refinement up to the point where the superlative order of Adam became possible locally.

Genesis is the first book of the Bible, containing the premises from which the rest of the Bible flow. We can assume that it contains God's own *preferences*, as it were—His own conventions of order and disorder. This being the case, we must strive to understand those conventions or we may never understand the rest of the Bible. God weaves a complex thread of meaning in the 66 books of the Bible, but the Rosetta Stone is in the Genesis narrative. In the very first act of creation—"Let there be light!"—God supplants the "darkness" of chaos with the rudimentary order of "light," orienting and aligning the universe with a uniform convention throughout. Having thus established rudimentary order, the Creator then sets about the business of establishing higher level orders.

Although the directive "let there be light" may also mean "let there be order," the concomitant emergence of physical light (photons) would not present an insurmountable hurdle of exegesis.

We just have to be careful not to confuse what God means by "light," with physical photons. If we can avoid such confusion, the creation of photons may in fact be a byproduct of that initial ordering activity. There is no order in darkness—darkness implies chaos. That the creation of rudimentary order might go hand-in hand with the emergence of light (the opposite of darkness) would be understandable.

In his commentary on the Book of Genesis, Derek Kidner writes the following:

> *Light*, which has lent its name to all that is life-giving (Jn. 1:4), truth-giving (2 Cor. 4:6), gladdening (Ec. 11:7), and pure (1 Jn. 1:5-7), appropriately marks the first step from chaos to order. [3]

In trying to ascertain what God Himself would want to call "order," Scripture provides us with a clue in the fourth verse of Genesis:

וַיַּרְא אֱלֹהִים אֶת־הָאוֹר כִּי־טוֹב
And God saw the light, that it was good.
(Genesis 1:4)

This is the very first occurrence of the word *good* in the Bible, significant in that it provides us with a clue as to what God Himself might call "order" or "good," as opposed to "disorder" or "evil." If God calls the ordered state of light "good," then we can reasonably infer that He calls the disordered state of darkness "evil." And we find a confirmation of this in the next half of the same verse, where the Creator is *dividing* the light from the darkness—separating the order from the disorder:

וַיַּבְדֵּל אֱלֹהִים בֵּין הָאוֹר וּבֵין הַחֹשֶׁךְ
And God divided the light from the darkness.
(Genesis 1:4)

What God might call "disorder" is here identified with the "darkness" wherein there is no separation and distinction. What God might call "order" is here identified with the "light" that is productive of illumination, articulation, separation and distinction.

Throughout the opening verses of Genesis we are given a

measure of understanding in expressions such as "God created," "God divided," "God saw that it was good." At the same time we are given to understand that only the Creator of the universe has the final say-so as to what is "order" or "disorder," "good" or "evil." This description of the Supreme Judge of the universe, as the One who separates good from evil and order from disorder, is prominent throughout the rest of the Bible. As Moses declares:

רְאֵה אָנֹכִי נֹתֵן לִפְנֵיכֶם הַיּוֹם בְּרָכָה וּקְלָלָה
Behold, I set before you this day a blessing and a curse.
(Deuteronomy 11:26)

It is as though the Creator is saying: "This way leads to order, that way to disorder." Throughout the Bible, the Divine Activity is nearly always associated with the transformations of chaos into order, darkness into light.

Only five verses into Genesis and we can already see the outlines of what might be called a *preference* on the part of the Creator. God has written separation and distinction into the order of Man. Howbeit separation and distinction presuppose low entropy states. In which case we can make a statement in regard to what we humans might mean by *order*, and what we might mean by *disorder*. Everything else being equal, by *order* we mean decreasing entropy in general and low entropy states in particular; i.e., conditions that are supportive of life, *complexity*, structure, organization, separation and distinction. Whereas by *disorder* we mean the opposite: increasing entropy in general and high entropy states in particular; i.e., conditions that are detrimental to life and *complexity*. So for the purposes of this publication we define *order* and *disorder* as general functions of decreasing and increasing entropy respectively.

"Entropy" was one of the subjects discussed in the celebrated lectures of the brilliant scientist Richard Feynman. In those lectures Feynman showed the difference between thermodynamic entropy and what he called *logical entropy*. He then showed how *logical entropy* increases when two different gasses at the same temperature are mixed, and then went on to define what we humans might mean by *order* and *disorder*. Feynman, along with other rational scientists, equates higher entropy states with higher levels of *disorder*, and vice versa. Everything else being equal, the following would be representative of *human* definition of local order and local disorder:

Order: decreasing entropy in general, and low entropy states in particular.
Disorder: increasing entropy in general, and high entropy states in particular.

The scientist will no doubt say: "Well yes, but you can't build human order without *creating* entropy!" True, but this has little to do with the *principle* that we are trying to unveil. We all produce entropy just in the course of breathing—we could not live without producing entropy. Every thought, every blink of an eye, every movement of a muscle requires graded energy, which is degraded into entropy on use. No disagreement there. Howbeit this does not change the fact that the survival of our species depends on ordered (low entropy) states. We are equating what we call *order* with the desirable state in which mankind is able to survive as a species by stemming the tide of increasing entropy locally. In which case *disorder* would be the opposite—an undesirable state in which mankind is facing extinction because of an inability to stem the rising tide of increasing entropy locally. Generally speaking, where entropy increases locally, it can only do so at the expense of life and *complexity*.

God made us from the physics of this universe. We are energy-driven creatures. If graded energy is available, we survive as a species. If not, we face extinction. The mindset that would divorce the human condition from the availability of graded energy needs to be replaced by a more realistic view. Science can no longer afford to play the part of the idiot savant who is too wrapped up in "method" to care about the human condition. The ultimate goal of science has been to slice away layers of nescience and error, bringing mankind nearer to a rational and holistic understanding of his relationship to the universe. The words of scientist Stephen Hawking:

> We already know the laws that govern the behavior of matter under all but the most extreme conditions.... Yet we have certainly not reduced these subjects to the status of solved problems; we have, as yet, had little success in predicting human behavior from mathematical equations.... A complete, consistent, unified theory is only the first step: our goal is a complete *understanding* of the events around us, and of our own existence.[4]

From Aristotle to Kant there was no schism between philosophy, religion and science. In the eighteenth century, philosophers and theologians considered the whole of human knowledge to be their field, discussing questions that are now discussed by modern scientists. Only in the nineteenth century do we see the beginning of a fracture between the spiritual and material disciplines of man.

Some of the greatest pillars of science were believers in God, among them Lister, Pasteur, Boyle, Cuvier, Babbage, Rayleigh, Fleming, Maxwell, Faraday, Kelvin, Herschel, Mendel, Agassiz and Reinmann. Johannes Kepler considered astronomers like himself to be "priests of the highest God in regard to the book of nature." The celebrated French mathematician Blaise Pascal described God as the "Author of mathematical truths and the order of the elements." Sir Isaac Newton, one of the greatest scientists of the world, wrote volumes on theology, including *Observations on the Prophecies of Daniel and the Apocalypse of St. John* in which he undertook the laborious task of deciphering the symbolic language of the Book of Revelation. It is no sin for a scientist to believe in God. Neither is it a sin for a scientist to provide mankind with rational definitions of "order" and "disorder."

DEFINING "COSMOS"

The Greek term *kosmos* implies *order of arrangement*. For the purposes of this publication we would define "cosmos" as a *process* that is constantly arranging and rearranging universal systems in deference to the imperative of increasing entropy; i.e., the vast *processes* of space and time, or the aggregate thereof. The sum of all universal "activity," or the great river of change taken as a whole. A gigantic behavioral field that is moving towards increasing entropy, sliding down the gradient that leads from low probability to high probability.

The term *universe*, on the other hand, we would apply to the sum of physical things, all the wonderful things that we see when we look up at the night sky—galaxies, nebulae, clusters, stars, solar systems and planets. Following the argument of St. Augustine, we could say that the material *universe* was "good," but undergoing corruption. In Augustine's day the Manichaeans were implying that the material universe was "evil." Augustine opposed them, saying that the material universe had to be "good," otherwise it could not undergo corruption; i.e., the ontology of "evil" is not rooted in the physical universe itself, but in the *process* whereby it is being corrupted. In Augustine's own words:

> It was obvious to me that all things are good even if they are corrupted. They could not be corrupted if they were supremely good; but unless they were good they could not be corrupted. If they were supremely good, they would be incorruptible; if they were not good at all, there would be nothing in them to be corrupted.... Therefore, whatever exists, is good. Evil, then, the origin of which I had been seeking, has no substance at all [is not a material substance]; for if it were a substance, it would be good. I understood, therefore, and it was made clear to me that Thou [God] madest all things good, nor is there any substance at all not made by Thee.[5]

Going by Augustine's line of reasoning, the material universe could not be said to be the "supreme good," for then it would be incorruptible like God. Howbeit it could be said to be "good," since it is capable of undergoing corruption, which would not be the case if it were "evil"—fully corrupted and incapable of further corruption.

While the distinction between "cosmos" and "universe" might seem trivial to some readers, it can make all the difference between correct and incorrect exegesis. New Testament Greek is a precise language. Several terms may render "world" in the course of translation into English. For example, *oikoumene*, translated as "world" in many New Testament passages, might imply the earth, the physical globe, parts thereof, or the Roman empire. *Thalassa* might imply the chaotic masses of humanity—the "sea" of men mentioned in Revelation 13:1. These and other Greek terms, translated into the English "world," should not be confused with *kosmos*, which has a different meaning rooted in the ontology of physical reality. An illustration might be sought in one of the most misinterpreted passages of the New Testament. This is the passage in which Christ makes the statement that is so often quoted by those who would try to exclude the principles of the Kingdom of God from civil government and human society:

> My Kingdom is not of this *world* [< Greek *kosmos*].
> (John 18:36)

Christ is not saying that the Kingdom of God is not of this *universe*, or of this *earth*. He is merely saying that the organizational principles of the Kingdom of God are not patterned after the organizational principles of the cosmos. The organizational principles of the cosmos are oriented towards increasing entropy (disorder), whereas the organizational principles of the Kingdom of God are oriented towards decreasing entropy (order).

Scofield's Reference Bible (Authorized King James with introductions and annotations) provides a footnote to John 18:36 which reads as follows:

> This verse has erroneously been taken to mean that Christ was disavowing that His kingdom would be established on earth. Apart from the incompatibility of such a view with the entire testimony of Scripture (cp. Lk. 1:33; Rev. 11:15), it conflicts with the remainder of the verse.

Concerning the New Testament's use of the Greek term *kosmos*, Scofield's footnote to Revelation 13:8 reads as follows:

> World (Gk.*kosmos*), Summary: In the sense of the present world system, the ethically bad sense of the word refers to the order or arrangement under which Satan has organized the world of unbelieving mankind upon his cosmic principles of force, greed, selfishness, ambition, and pleasure.... This world system is imposing and powerful with military might; it is often outwardly religious, scientific, cultured, and elegant; but, seething with national and commercial rivalries and ambitions, is upheld in any real crisis only by armed force, and is dominated by satanic principles.

(Concerning the "fall," and how the cosmic process of corruption came to attach itself to the *spirit* of man, we will pursue that subject in a later place in this publication.)

DEFINING "NATURE"

While we are sorting out our definitions, we should perhaps try to clarify what we mean by "nature," because this is where we run into another insidious mixup and conflation. What do scientists mean by "nature?" What do philosophers mean by "nature?" What do theologians mean by "nature?" Ask a dozen of them and you may get a dozen different answers. Most scientists, for example, tend to go by the generalization provided by Darwin in *The Origin of Species* :

> It has been said that I speak of natural selection as an active power or Deity; but who objects to an author speaking of the attraction of gravity as ruling the movements of the planets? Every one knows what is meant and is implied by such metaphorical expressions; and they are almost necessary for brevity. So again it is difficult to avoid personifying the word Nature; but I mean by Nature, only the aggregate action and product of many natural laws, and by laws the sequence of events as ascertained by us. [6]

The astute reader may see the problem with Darwin's definition. We have already pointed out a discrepancy between the human and the cosmic definitions of *order*, indicating the necessity of specifying a frame of reference. To the extent that *order* may become *disorder* depending on the frame of reference, so also *natural* may become *unnatural* depending on the frame of reference. Given a purely cosmic frame of reference, the increase of entropy would be the most *natural* thing in the universe, but it could also be the most *unnatural* and destructive thing here on earth. So then the "natural" process of increasing entropy should not be confused with the labor of the Providential agency that we loosely refer to as *Mother Nature*, whose agenda and mandate is to maintain the low entropy states associated with various habitats and ecosystems found on earth.

What do we mean by "nature?" In his time Darwin might have assumed that life could have arisen spontaneously and *naturally*. However Darwin never claimed to know how life got started on earth, so it remains altogether unintelligible how he might have assumed it "natural." Even to this day scientists don't know how life got started on earth. So here also it remains unintelligible how they might assume it "natural." For all we know life could be the most *unnatural* thing in the universe.

For the purposes of this publication we will take the expression *Mother Nature* to represent the Providential agency which is supportive of living things here on earth—grass, flowers, trees, forests, babies, creatures great and small. But we will take the term *nature* to represent the cold and indifferent force that underpins the material and elemental order of the cosmos, i.e., the force associated with universal imperative of increasing entropy. Thus by "nature" we generally mean the imperative that underlies, governs and directs the greater order of universal change within the cold and indifferent realms of matter and energy. Whereas by "Mother Nature" we generally mean the opposite—some local, benign and benevolent anthropomorphization. Like the Providential agency referred to by the Founding Fathers of America:

> When in the course of human events, it becomes necessary for one people to dissolve the political bands which have connected them with another, and to assume among the powers of the earth, the separate and equal station to which the laws of *Nature* and *Nature's* God entitle them, a decent respect to the opinions of mankind requires that they should declare the causes which impel them to the separation.
>
> (U.S. Declaration of Independence, emphasis added.)

What did these Founders mean by "the laws of Nature and Nature's God?" Likely what we are now calling Mother Nature. Living 200 years ago they were referring to the *local* creation of God—the pristine forests of the New World, the untrodden hills, valleys, meadows, unspoiled rivers, lakes and living things that they were privileged to observe at that time.

Perhaps we should point out that by "Mother Nature" we do not mean some representation of *Ishtar* or *Gaia*, or even some angelic being. The term "Mother Nature" as used in this publication is just a useful metaphor—an anthropomorphization of the Providence of God. In which case it wouldn't hurt to use the usual imagery of the beautiful lady in the flowing white robe, wearing flowers in her wind-blown hair. Metaphorically speaking, Mother Nature may indeed be invested with certain human characteristics—a benevolent nature, a beautiful countenance, a stern disposition and an emotional and sympathetic character. Not to be confused with the "nature" of the cosmos itself, which would have no capacity for "sympathy" or "emotion," knowing no more good from evil than mercy from vengeance, being nothing more than a discriminating principle—a cold and indifferent number-cruncher.

DEFINING *COMPLEXITY*

Trying to define *complexity* is very difficult, but make no mistake, the science of the new Millennium will be the science of *complexity*. God is the Zenith, Source, Author and Creator of the magnitude of *complexity* we see on earth. To draw near to God is to draw near to *complexity*. Not in the spirit of idolatry, as though to venerate *complexity* itself, but in the spirit of awe, humility, thanksgiving, knowledge and understanding.

What is *complexity*? The reader should understand that *complexity*—underlined three times in red ink—is not to be confused with "complication" or "convolution." We will put the word in italics throughout the rest of this publication to remind the reader that we are not going by a dictionary definition. As things now stand even the crowned heads of the Santa Fe Institute do not have a rigorous definition of *complexity*, let alone a way of measuring it.

What is *complexity*? We may not know, but by asking the question we sense deeply and instinctively that we are drawing near to something larger than life. Certainly we will have to improve our understanding of *complexity* if we are to break free of the tethers that keep us earthbound. The Space Shuttle, for example, is a complex creation of man. The crew of the Space Shuttle deal with *complexity* on an hourly basis—their lives depend on it. The age of *complexity* has already overtaken us. If our mission in the universe is to replace non-life with life, then the key to the undiscovered country lies in understanding *complexity*. Be it terra-forming on Mars, or establishing human colonies in regions beyond, the science that will pave the way to such auspicious and limitless horizons will be the science of *complexity*. If any would understand the full measure of the destiny of mankind, let them inquire into the meaning of *complexity*, which is what we will try to do in the remainder of this publication, though we may stumble here and there, as though walking on an unmarked road.

The reader will find the word *complexity* cropping up throughout this book. As for a definition, we have very little to offer:

Complexity is the logical opposite of entropy, intuitively understood. Complexity is a measure of the quality of information.

Of course this is where we run into a problem. Present day scientists feel comfortable investigating and measuring *quantities*. But just mention the word *quality* and they suffer apoplectic fits of evasion. Notwithstanding the difficulty, science is on the verge of taking the quantum leap from *quantities* to *qualities*. The science of the Millennium stands to be the science of *qualities*, and happily a few brave scientists are well on their way in this respect. Some, like William Dembski, have all but resigned themselves to make the difficult jump come hell or high water. Dembski has already made great strides when it comes to an understanding of what he calls *complex specified information.*

Perhaps the way to understanding *complexity*, is by first understanding what we mean by *information*. For even as the flood-tide of the information age rises to drown us without mercy, we have yet to fully define the term. We should emphasize that in referring to *in-form-ation*, we are appealing to the broadest of possible meanings, i.e., something that goes much, much deeper than mere bytes and megabytes.

The acts of creation undertaken by God in those six "days" must have involved a great deal of *in-forming*. The Spirit of God in-formed the whole universe with rudimentary order, later in-forming the earth with the potential to bring forth the exuberant variety of living things. We are living in an *in-formed* creation it seems:

בְּרֵאשִׁית בָּרָא אֱלֹהִים אֵת הַשָּׁמַיִם וְאֵת הָאָרֶץ:
וְהָאָרֶץ הָיְתָה תֹהוּ וָבֹהוּ

In the beginning God created the heavens and the earth:
and the earth was *formless and void.*
(Genesis 1:1-2, emphasis added)

How did God create the magnitude of the *complexity* associated with living things? Perhaps by *in-forming* the earth. By in-putting the quantum events, that produced the space-time events, that transformed formlessness into form, void into substance, non-information into information, simplicity in to *complexity*. We may not know how God did all this, but by using the intellect that He gave us we can certainly try to speculate about the general principles. Certainly it does not appear that God has tried to conceal those principles from us. There is ample evidence to show that He Himself had to fine-tune and *in-form* the universe with mathematical precision.

Notwithstanding the unknowns of Intelligent Design, we can infer that those acts of Design and Creation must have involved investments on the part of God, which transformed non-formation into in-formation, and non-specified information into *complex specified information*. What scientists are now edging towards in terms of *information theory* may very well be the essence of Intelligent Design, the whole universe being a unified field wired together *informationally*. And if one uses entropy as a measure of *information*, then it is a relatively small step to the Millennial science of *complexity*.

In the Millennium we will need accurate measures of *complexity*. An illustration will show why. Currently we don't know how much *complexity* is being destroyed in the cutting down of the Brazilian rainforest. Is the cost/benefit ratio positive or negative? Is the sum of that which is being destroyed trivial, or is it astronomical? We don't know, because we don't have a way of measuring *complexity*. If we did, we could calculate the sum and use it a basis for rational and holistic judgments.

Let us exercise the imagination. Let us fast-forward to the 23rd century, and let us imagine that there are now twelve Justices sitting on the bench of the Supreme Court of Federation Earth in Jerusalem. And let us imagine that a certain nation, instead of going to war, has brought suit against a neighboring nation, accusing it of destroying regional *complexity* shared by both nations. How will those twelve Justices be able to hand down a just decision if there is no way of measuring *complexity*? They will not.

What is the magnitude of the *complexity* that is being destroyed in the cutting down of each hectare of rainforest, and to what benefit? Presently we can't answer the question because we have no way of measuring *complexity*. We are hamstrung and stymied, deprived of such a vital scientific tool, even as the chain saws rip and the bulldozers level.

A hundred years from now the Justices of the Supreme Court of Federation Earth will have access to accurate measurements of *complexity*, say in units called *avigdors*. No doubt those Justices will have a vast array of accurate numbers to work with, perhaps provided by the scientists at an *Institute of Planetary Complexity* in Jerusalem. Armed with empirical evidence, the Justices will then be in a better position to judge between nations and hand down fair rulings, fulfilling the Divine mandate given in the book Deuteronomy:

צֶדֶק צֶדֶק תִּרְדֹּף!
Justice, justice shall you pursue!
(Deuteronomy 16:20)

But justice cannot be pursued without knowing the whole truth about the actual amount of *complexity* at issue. This sort of empirical truth must be available before those Justices can perform their God-given—hallowed—duties.

We don't have a way of measuring *complexity* today. And even at the dawn of the Millennium scientists seem reluctant to take that all-important first step, finding all sorts of excuses and alibis to delay. What is the magnitude of the irreplaceable *complexity* that is being destroyed on the planet earth daily? We don't know. We don't have a clue, because scientists have yet to get their act together in this respect.

וַיֹּאמֶר יְהוָה אֶל־הַשָּׂטָן מֵאַיִן תָּבֹא?
וַיַּעַן הַשָּׂטָן אֶת־יְהוָה וַיֹּאמַר מִשּׁוּט בָּאָרֶץ וּמֵהִתְהַלֵּךְ בָּהּ

And the LORD said unto Satan, Whence come you?
And Satan answered the LORD and said, From going to and fro
in the earth, and from walking up and down upon it.
(Job 1:7)

SECTION 2

God, Cosmos and Devil

Cosmic Constable

While we would not be so foolish as to try to define God, thereby subjecting the Creator of the universe to human judgment, we would nevertheless identify Him as the God of Abraham, Isaac and Jacob—the God and Father of *Yeshua* (Jesus Christ). As such, an Augustinian God who is *external* to space and time. Augustine recognized that time is a creation of God, and so placed the Creator outside its stream. A key feature of the Judeo-Christian world view is that the existence of the Creator is not dependent on the existence of space and time. The eternal and incorruptible Nature of God does not imply an eternal or incorruptible universe, as in some pagan and pantheistic schemes where the created universe is believed to be indistinguishable from and identical to its creator.

But what does it mean for a God who is external to space and time to "cause" something to happen within space and time? The difficulty is not insurmountable. A temporal god would have to be *of* the cosmos, bound by the same limiting adjuncts as we mortals. A temporal god would have to be physically "over here" or "over there," in "the past," or in "the present," or in "the future." Not so an Augustinian God, there being no "limitation," "restraint," "hindrance," "here," "there," "past," "present" or "future." An Augustinian God would enjoy unrestricted Liberty with respect to the dominions of space, time, matter and energy, being unaffected by any limitations contained in or imposed by His own creation. Such a God would be free to "move" within any or all points in space and time at will, there being nothing to prevent Him from doing so. How is this possible? We cannot know, being ourselves defined by the limitations of space and time. We would have to shed our own spacial and temporal dimensions—our mortality—to even get a glimpse of the Mind of the Eternal.

וַיֹּאמֶר אֱלֹהִים אֶל־מֹשֶׁה אֶהְיֶה אֲשֶׁר אֶהְיֶה,
וַיֹּאמֶר כֹּה תֹאמַר לִבְנֵי יִשְׂרָאֵל אֶהְיֶה שְׁלָחַנִי אֲלֵיכֶם
And God said to Moses, I AM THAT I AM: and He said,
Thus shall you say to the children of Israel, I AM has sent me to you.
(Exodus 3:14, emphasis added.)

God does not change, He is the great "I AM." We cannot treat the Existence of God as a temporal "event"—He is the *Creator* of all events. The events that constitute our own mortal lives begin and end in time. God does not. About mortal events we might say, "John Smith accomplished such and such before he died," but such eventualities do not apply to an Augustinian God. The directive I AM THAT I AM tells us that the God of the Bible is what He is in spite all else. He is not touched by the nature of the changing universe. He never changes. His existence is not related to or dependent upon the adjuncts of space, time, nature, necessity, entropy, corruption. He is timeless and unchanging, as Scripture affirms:

כִּי אֲנִי יְהֹוָה לֹא שָׁנִיתִי וְאַתֶּם בְּנֵי־יַעֲקֹב לֹא כְלִיתֶם
For I the LORD do not change,
therefore you, O sons of Jacob, are not consumed.
(Malachi 3:6)

There is a paradox in the idea of vested bodies saving themselves, (analogous to a man trying to lift himself up by his own bootstraps). A temporal god could not secure the salvation of mankind, because he would be bound by the same limitations as mankind, subject to the same boundary conditions and "catch-22" that we spoke about. The salvation of man requires a Savior-God who is *external* to space and time. Only an Augustinian God would be in a position to deliver man from the spiritual pitfalls of space, time, entropy and corruption.

The God that we appeal to throughout this publication is not some New Age (pantheistic) god who is internal to time. He is not some deification of cosmos according to the New Age perversion whereby we are asked to believe that the universe is "waking up to self-awareness" through intelligent life-forms like ourselves, or that "the universe is trying to express itself through us," (to quote the words of one New Age guru). Although the God of the Bible can and does have intercourse with His own creation, He is Himself non-material and non-temporal.

The scientist Joseph Davydov has this to say in his work entitled *God Exists* :

> "*In the beginning God created the heavens and the earth*".... The significance of the first verse of the Bible lies in its emphasis on the absolute primacy of God, and the relative subordinacy of the entire world, both the physical and nonphysical. According to the Bible "In the beginning God created" space, time, and everything that exists in space and time. This means that God Himself existed outside of any space and outside of any time even when there was no time, no space, no physical bodies, no earth, no sun, no galaxies, no Universe, and no world whatsoever. This leads to the unambiguous conclusion that the Bible portrays God as an absolute category instead of a material category.... God is an eternal, bodiless, and absolutely perfect category which has no physical attributes and no biological organs. God is not a biological being. God is the creator of living beings. Even space and time are a product of the creative endeavors of the Absolute God, not the realm of God's own existence.[1]

So then this is what we mean by *an Augustinian God.* Not some mystical invention of St. Augustine himself, but a quasi-scientific description of the Creator of the universe. The expression *Augustinian God* does pop up in the scientist-philosopher's lexicon now and then. For example, in his book *Time's Arrow and Archimedes' Point,* scientist and philosopher Huw Price has this to say about how an Augustinian God might perceive or view the creation from a window *outside* of time :

> From the inside, as it were, we perceive a difference between (what in the standard temporal frame will be described as) the inputs and the outputs. The inputs appear as fixed, or given, while the outputs are what is open, or potentially subject to our control. It is important to stress the subjectivity of this, for the point was that no such difference between inputs and outputs is apparent from the atemporal [timeless] perspective—an Augustinian god just sees a nexus for a complicated structure of correlations. The difference between the fixity of the inputs from the past and the openness of the outputs to the future is a feature of the experience *from the inside...* [2]

For purposes of this publication, when we refer to the God of the Bible we are referring to an Augustinian God who is fundamentally *external* to space and time.

BIBLICAL "DEVIL"

Before attempting to treat a disease a physician has to obtain a correct diagnosis. Before attempting to dispose of the "devil," we have to obtain a correct diagnosis as well. What is the Biblical devil? Is he something outside us? Is he something in our physical constitution? Is he a Manichaean monster with horns and hooves? A poltergeist? A metaphor? Whatever the devil may be, he/it plays a prominent role in the Biblical narrative, very much portrayed as the nemesis, adversary and accuser of mankind—very much a plague on living things in general. But what exactly is the devil?

The Bible uses the language of accommodation, metaphor, and anthropomorphism to make the incomprehensible understandable to man. Where there is a *principle*, the Bible may posit a corresponding *principality* (principle-enforcer). We do the same thing ourselves. An illustration may be found in the way in which we personify the law, for example. We say, "here comes the law!" when we see a uniformed policeman approaching. The policeman's name may be John, he may be a son, a father, a husband or an uncle, but when he puts on the uniform of the law he puts on the nature of the law, becoming a personification (anthropomorphization) of the law. We do not say, "here comes John," or "here comes so and so's son," or "here comes so and so's father," or "here comes so and so's husband." We say "here comes the law!" We say this because, in context, the principle and the principality are inseparable.

Is there a universal principle to speak of? Yes, and we have already identified it as *increasing entropy* (increasing disorder, from a human point of view). Can we posit a corresponding *principality* or *principle-enforcer* in this case as well? The Bible does just that, calling it הַשָּׂטָן (*ha-satan*, "the adversary"). Is the Bible justified in humanizing the universal imperative of disorder? Yes, because the context of the Biblical narrative is personal and human. Had that context been non-personal and scientific, say, dealing with thermodynamics, gravity, relativity or quantum physics, the personification would not have been necessary. Whatever the Biblical "devil" may be, there is reason to believe that he assumes this "devilish" characteristic in the human sphere. As the Bible suggests:

וַיֹּאמֶר יְהוָה אֶל־הַשָּׂטָן מֵאַיִן תָּבֹא?
וַיַּעַן הַשָּׂטָן אֶת־יְהוָה וַיֹּאמַר מִשּׁוּט בָּאָרֶץ וּמֵהִתְהַלֵּךְ בָּהּ.
And the LORD said unto Satan, Whence come you?
And Satan answered the LORD and said, From going to and fro
in the earth, and from walking up and down upon it.
(Job 1:7)

Here the devil is described as "going to and fro in the earth, and *walking up and down upon it*," suggesting a local personification; i.e., whatever principle the devil may enforce in the universe at large, he takes on the form of הַשָּׂטָן (*ha-satan*) in a local and earthly context, suggesting an *anthropomorphization*.

What are we to understand by "anthropomorphization?" The cosmos is vast beyond our imaginings, our little planet not even a speck of dust by comparison. Nevertheless we are proud anthropocentric creatures, determined to interpret the universe in terms of our own humanity. The word *anthropomorphization* implies just that—a *personification* or *humanization* of something non-personal and non-human. Knowing that we would try to interpret the universe in our own terms, knowing our foolish pride, our hubris, our vanity, our arrogance, and our anthropocentrism, God responds with all of the familiar anthropomorphizations found in the Bible—"serpent," "devil," "Satan," "Beelzebub," "waster," "plague," "thief," "god of this world," "principality," "prince of the power of the air," "beast," "dragon," etc.. Knowing that we would anthropomorphize the whole universe, God bends the human vice to His own advantage, so as to warn us about the spiritual hazard that we face as mortals. Our Heavenly Father gives that spiritual hazard a man-like face and character that we can identify with, calling it "devil" and "Satan." God uses the power of myth to burn the reality of the hazard into our collective consciousness like a brand.

Mankind is a complacent creature, hard of hearing and quick to forget. In trying to warn mankind of the hazard, God had to chose a stratagem that would penetrate the fog of time and stick fast throughout all generations. The discourse of the Biblical "devil" is the Creator's way of warning us about that hazard by giving it a dreadful face and identity, one that would penetrate our collective consciousness and remain there until such a time when there would be enough science to untooth and demystify it. Thanks be to God we now have enough science to do just that. In this publication we will try to unmask and untooth the monster. And since much of this unmasking and untoothing will deal with *anthropomorphization*, we should perhaps take a look at that word derived from the Greek *anthropo-*, a combining form meaning *man* or *human*. As in *anthropo-logy*, for example, which means "the study of man." The reader is encouraged to look up some of these terms in various dictionaries:

Anthropocentric—the regarding of man as the central fact of the universe.
Anthropomorphize—to ascribe human characteristics to.
Anthropomorphism—the attribution of human motivation, personality, characteristics or behavior to non-human events, laws, principles, or natural phenomena.
Anthropomorphization—an interpretation of something impersonal and non-human in personal or human terms.
Anthropomorphosis—transformation into human form of something non-human.

The anthropomorphisms that abound in all civilizations seem to be telling us something. Whence, for example, the dreadful imagery found in pagan legends? Or the dreadful expressions on the faces of ancient carvings? Or the apprehension invested in the megaliths of Easter Island? Or the grimacing icons of the Incas and Aztecs? Since the beginning of history it seems something deep in the psyche of man has been trying to pay homage and blood-sacrifice to the universal devil of disorder.

What then can we say about the Biblical devil? Is he a "fallen angel," as many believe? The Bible itself has this to say concerning the fallen angels:

> And the angels which kept not their first estate, but left their posts, God has reserved in everlasting chains under darkness, unto the judgment of the great day.
>
> (Jude 1:6)

If God has bound the fallen angels "in everlasting chains," pending the judgment of the great day, what is this fallen angel doing running loose on earth? Does the construct of a Manichaean fallen angel have any Biblical basis? Such a fiend could not run around for a single hour without defying the Sovereignty of God.

The Manichaean construct of a personal devil—a diabolical, grotesque, misshapen creature of refined evil who can defy God—can be traced all the way back to Zoroaster. The prophet Zoroaster, thought to have come on the Persian scene around 660 B.C., conceived of a dualism that pitted the forces of the good god *Ahura Mazda* against those of the evil god *Ahriman.* Regardless of what Zoroaster had in mind when he modelled the universe after a struggle between these two "primal spirits," in the centuries that followed his dualism grew into a bogeyman of world-wide proportions. Human nature, looking for an excuse to demonize "others," found what it was looking for in the dualism of Zoroaster.

Zoroaster's dualism posits three stages of creation; a beginning stage in which good and evil were completely separate, a middle stage in which these radically opposed elements became "mixed," and a future stage when the two will be disentangled and the original duality restored. Naturally this scheme does not allow for any *reconciliation* between elements held to be radically different—it does not, for example, allow for the redemption and *transformation* of evil elements into good.

It is said that Zoroaster's dualism has exerted more subtle influence on the history of the world than many other religions combined. His dualism was the spiritual underpinning of the Persian Empire that at one time spread all the way to India on the east and Greece on the west. Circa 510 B.C. the Jews of the southern kingdom of Judah were taken captive into Babylon/Persia, where some of them assimilated the dualism and later brought it back with them to Jerusalem under Ezra and Nehemiah. In the time of Christ the faction known as the *Essenes* was an extension thereof, mixing the Persian dualism with Hebrew traditions to embrace a fundamentally *apocalyptic* world view. These fatalistic world views, extant even today, deny any possibility of the transformation of the forces of evil by the forces of good, positing the annihilation of the former by the latter in fiery events that bring the world to an end.

Zoroaster's religion grew many branches, one of which came to be known as *Mithraism*. Mithras was said to have been created by Ahura Mazda to act as mediator between the forces of good and evil. At one time Mithraism provided a spiritual underpinning for Roman paganism, the emperor Diocletian reputed to have proclaimed Mithras protector of Rome. Many Roman emperors imagined themselves to be keepers of the ancient wisdom of the East, whereby Mithraism gained prominence throughout the Empire, being the chief rival of Christianity in the second and third centuries. Mithraic legacy conceived numerous customs we observe even today, among them the handshake, the wearing of crowns by monarchs and the observance of pagan holidays.

In the third century came the Babylonian prince *Mani*, who considered himself the successor of Mithras. Mani mixed Zoroaster's dualism with elements of Judaism and Christianity to develop *Manichaeism*, which then spread throughout the Greek and Roman worlds like wildfire. Mani's teaching exerted a powerful influence in the world long after the fall of Imperial Rome. At its zenith the Manichaean world view was embraced throughout Asia and the Mediterranean, reaching to China on the east, North Africa on the south and Spain on the west. Manichaeism remained a major religion in the East until the 14th century, though it waned in the West by the 6th. Augustine himself was a staunch Manichaean before his conversion. Even today, many of the fundamentalist and futurist doctrines of the Christian religion have Manichaean undercurrents.

Mercifully Judaism, having more or less gone "underground" after the destruction of the Second Temple, was spared wholesale Manichaean engraftations. Today, for example, most Jews do not believe in a Manichaean devil, whereas most Christians do. Our sister religion Islam seems to have suffered the greatest degree of engraftation, believing in a Manichaean *Shaytan* that is more or less identical to Zoroaster's *Ahriman*. That entire region of the world—Arabia, Palestine, Turkey, Syria, Iraq, Iran, Uzbekhestan, Afghanistan, Pakistan and parts of India—was at one time the breeding ground of Zoroastrian dualism, the strong residue of which can still be found in many places today.

Christianity itself has nothing to boast about. The "falling away" predicted by Rav Shaul (St. Paul) plunged Europe into the paganism, superstition and Manichaeism of the Dark Ages. Circa A.D. 776, for example, the medieval abbot Beatus wrote his so-called "masterpiece" describing the apocalyptic end of the world. This doomsday scenario was very popular in the Dark Ages, used by pagan pontiffs to terrify the common folk into submission and conformity. There are many artistic renditions of *The Apocalypse of Beatus*, in spirit not too different from paintings found in ancient Persian manuscripts. There is a famous rendition of *The Apocalypse of Beatus* in the Bridgeman Art Library in London. Created by the monks Martino and Petrus, it portrays the apocalyptic doom of sinners—hellfire, damnation, emaciated bodies dangling over the pit of hell and a serpent-monster crawling out of the inferno. Sadly, this is the Manichaean scenario that so many Christians embrace even today. The fiery tragedy that took place in Waco, Texas, for example, was instigated by an apocalyptic cult-leader calling himself David Koresh. *Koresh* is a transliteration of the name of the Persian emperor *Cyrus*.

In a supposedly "Christian" frame, the diabolical sinners of the world stand to be destroyed in the Apocalypse of Beatus. In a supposedly "Islamic" frame, the diabolical infidels of the world stand to be destroyed in the jihad of Osama Bin Laden. Going by a Manichaean expedient, there is no redemption possible for those diabolical "others" who have somehow managed to mix themselves with the children of light. In a Manichaean frame, those who are "different" are much more than sinners who can be redeemed and transformed by God; they are diabolical extensions of *Ahriman* himself, deserving merciless extermination.

Curiously enough there seems to have been some strange connection between Zoroaster's dualism and the holocaust as well. We know, for example, that the Nazis were obsessed with separating the Aryan race from the "inferior" peoples of the world. What was Hitler reading when he was in prison composing the text of *Mein Kampf*? What was the bible of the cutthroat HJ and the Nazi SS?

What was the spiritual underpinning of the holocaust? It was a tome written by Friedrich Nietzsche entitled *Also Sprach Zarathustra* ("Thus Spake Zoroaster.") We know that Hitler himself set up monuments in honor of Nietzsche and ordered respect for the Aryan peoples of the Middle East. In essence Nietzsche's *Zarathustra* gave Hitler the green light to embark on the merciless extermination of "those evil others who have gotten themselves mixed up with our kind." We are perhaps looking at the most internecine combination in the history of the human race: Nazi paganism + Zoroastrian dualism.

One needs to see the fundamental difference between St. Paul's Gospel and Zoroaster's dualism to understand why the Christian Gospel embodies such "Good News." There is no earthly hope in dualism—the forces of "good" can only condemn and annihilate the forces of "evil," which is what Hitler imagined himself doing. If one models the universe after a Manichaean struggle between good and evil, the forces of light and the forces of darkness must be segregated, as though they were matter and anti-matter. The dualism that began with Zoroaster preaches an apocalyptic segregation such as this. The Gospel that began with Rav Shaul (St. Paul) uses the light of God's truth to redeem and transform the so-called "forces of evil." The former preaches dualism, fatalism, scapegoating, demonization, hate, segregation, doomsday, destruction, apocalypse and death. The latter preaches unity, hope, love, peace, reconciliation, construction and life. The fiction of a Manichaean devil has no Biblical basis.

MODELLING THE UNIVERSE

In this publication we do not model the universe after a Manichaean struggle between good and evil. The contest does not pit God against a Manichaean Anti-God, Christ against a Manichaean Anti-Christ, "our gang" against "those evil others who are different from us." The contest pits all men against an evil tendency internalized in their flesh. The struggle also pits the survival of enclaves of *complexity* (of which earth and its living things would be supreme examples) against the rising tide of simplicity, or what scientists are calling "increasing entropy." Within the frame and context of a universal struggle such as this, the devil would be a "plain vanilla" anthropomorphization. What do we mean by this? An illustration might help. A mother goes to comfort her child who is crying in the night. "What's the matter, dear?" she asks. The child says, "Mommy, mommy, there is a horrible monster over there looking at me, he has horns and terrible eyes!" The mother smiles and tells her child that there is a *plain vanilla* explanation for that monster. She turns on the light and the "monster" turns out to be a coat draped over a chair, the "horns" formed by the upturned collar, the "terrible eyes" the buttons.

Perhaps a more germane illustration might be found in the emancipation that followed the discoveries of the great scientist Louis Pasteur. Before Pasteur came along the causes of diseases were thought to be Manichaean—poltergeists, unearthly manifestations, gremlins, demons and malevolent spirits. Because of this, the practice of medicine remained a macabre art for centuries, thousands perishing horribly from simple infections mistaken for "demons." Pasteur's discoveries exorcised those "demons." In essence Pasteur said this: "These diseases are not caused by Manichaean demons. There is a *plain vanilla* explanation for what is going on here: germs and microbes!"

We will attempt to achieve a similar emancipation with respect to the Manichaean bogeyman in this publication, reducing the monster to a plain vanilla principle of physics.

Throughout this publication, where we refer to "devil" we mean an anthropomorphization of the statistical tendency to disorder internalized in all flesh. Thus internalized, this "devil" can acquire all the personal qualities and subtleties of men, but those qualities and subtleties are not his own—they are appropriated from human hosts by way of superimposition. And although the Biblical devil can be said to have many human agents ready to oppose God, those human agents are not diabolical "others" as in the Manichaean fiction. They are fallible human beings just like ourselves who may be redeemed and transformed by the mercy and grace of God.

"COSMIC CONSTABLE"

Where there is a principle, the Bible may posit a corresponding *principality*, or *authority*. The authority invested in this *principality* is derived from the *principle* that he is enforcing. Rav Shaul alludes to *principalities* and *authorities* in may of his letters:

> Put on the whole armour of God, that you may be able to withstand the wiles of the devil. For we wrestle not against flesh and blood, but against *archas*, (principalities), against *exousias* (authorities), against *kosmocratoras* (cosmos-rulers)...
> (Ephesians 6:12, emphasis added)

Most religious folks would read passages like this in a Manichaean frame, assuming that the Bible is referring to diabolical entities, demons and poltergeists. The truth may be much plainer than that, as indeed the plain truth nearly always is. The Greek term *archas*, translated as "principalities" in most Bibles, hails from a primitive verb meaning "chief, fundamental, primary, princely, principle, dominant, predominant," i.e., first in various applications of order, time, nature, necessity, rank, or authority, as though having been around longer than anything else. From which we derive such words as *archaic, archangel, archbishop, archduke, archetype, archetypal, architect, archive* and *archivist*. The Oxford Companion to Philosophy has this to say about the Greek term *arkhe* :

> *arkhe*: A "first thing from which something is, or comes to be, or is known".... Applied to materials which do not arise out of anything more primitive, to causes of change, to propositions fundamental in deductive systems, by teleologists to benefits and beneficiaries, and, colloquially, since they are sources of initiatives in states, to governments.... [3]

Where there is a principle, the Bible posits a corresponding *principality* or *authority*. Is there a universal principle? Yes, scientists call it "increasing entropy." Let us now posit a corresponding principality. And having done so, let us give him a descriptive nickname as well. What shall we call the *Prince* or *Archon* that enforces the archetypal order of increasing entropy? We could call him *Entropy Demon*, for example, or *Entropy Archon*, or *Energy Archon*, or *Cosmic Archon*, or *Cosmic Dictator*.

Let us make the learning process fun by calling him *Cosmic Constable* instead. And since people find it easy to remember pictures, let us draw an appropriate cartoon, say, that of some cosmic character reminiscent of a Victorian police constable. Surely the reader will have no difficulty in conjuring up the image of a portly

Victorian constable in traditional attire, helmet with strap under the chin, stiff upper lip, brass buttons, whistle, polished black boots, swinging his truncheon as he enforces the rudiments of cosmic correctness. And let us say that he is now directing traffic on a cosmic one-way street, making sure that things are moving in the direction of increasing entropy—towards higher states of disorder.

Cosmic Constable, directing the course of universal change from low entropy states to high entropy states, from low probability to high probability, from complexity to simplicity, from heterogeneity to homogeneity.

Let us try to describe what we have just created. Who or what is this Cosmic Constable? Out there in the cold and indifferent reaches of space and time he is top dog when it comes to the dispositions of matter and energy. It is his job to direct all the "cosmic traffic" in the general direction of increasing entropy. Are there limits to his authority? Yes there are. Just as the Victorian constable had to work within a framework of laws, likewise our Cosmic Constable has to work within the framework of laws, among them the four major forces of the universe. Out there, in the unimaginably vast expanses of space and time, God gives the Cosmic Constable a great deal of leeway when it comes to moving universal systems towards higher entropy states. But not unlimited freedom. Doubtless the Constable would prefer to take short cuts to maximum entropy. No doubt he would even like to reduce the entire universe to pure undifferentiated energy in one cataclysmic event. But he is restrained from doing so by the higher principles of physics instituted by God, which act as cosmic "resistors," placing limits and restraints on his activity. The Constable may be top-dog in the realms of matter and energy, but he cannot direct the cosmic traffic towards equilibrium states arbitrarily. He has to conform to the "rules of the road" laid down by the Creator of the universe. He has to honor all of the Divine "road blocks."

These "rules of the road" include the four major forces—gravity, electromagnetism, weak and strong nuclear force. These forces embody higher level order-processings in that they regulate, structure and limit the universal activity of the Cosmic Constable. Gravity, for example, is the glue of large-scale structure. The Constable may take a dim view of structure in general, but the "road block" was put there by the Creator and he must honor it. Gravity restrains the Constable from reducing universal structures along paths of least resistance.

Without gravity the cosmos would be one gigantic, diffuse, indistinct, homogeneous cloud of hydrogen or plasma. Gravity changed all that, bringing about separation and distinction. The force of gravity transformed homogeneity into heterogeneity, non-structure into structure. It ordered, articulated, collapsed and concentrated what was hydrogen plasma into discrete structures associated with galaxies, clusters, stars, solar systems and planets. The structure of the earth is held together by gravity. What would happen if gravity were to fail? The Constable would unravel the structured bundle of matter that we call home. Our atmosphere would explode and diffuse out into space, our oceans would evaporate overnight, the planet would fly apart into a randomized cloud of debris and we'd all be dead in short order. But the force of gravity "keeps things together."

Gravity is not the only force that prevents the Constable from unravelling the knot of cosmic structure. The other major forces play crucial roles as well. Nuclear forces hold together the building blocks of matter. How strong is the strong nuclear force? Try splitting an atom and you will find out. The energy that is released in splitting the atom (nuclear explosion) is the energy that is holding the atomic structure together. Without weak and strong nuclear forces there would be no organized atoms or molecules. These forces provide structure at the level of the microcosm, ruling on such things as crystallization, molecule formation, production and polymerization, underwriting the whole of the "chemistry" on which our biological existence depends. One might say that the four major forces behave as cosmic glue, gravity being the glue that holds galaxies together, strong nuclear force the glue that holds atoms together, etc..

All the physical laws established by God have this sort of higher-level ordering effect, regulating the universal activity of the Cosmic Constable, setting up the "roadblocks," "resistors" and "dams" that afford the structures of atoms and planets alike, providing a material basis on which God can evolve the superlative order of Man.

The Constable has to honor other fences, hedges and restraints erected by God as well, though he doesn't have to like them. Naturally he would like to be able to reduce the superlative order of Man to the diminutive order of dust. But he is restrained from doing so by *local* fences erected by God:

וַיַּעַן הַשָּׂטָן אֶת־יְהוָה וַיֹּאמַר הַחִנָּם יָרֵא אִיּוֹב אֱלֹהִים׃
הֲלֹא אַתָּה שַׂכְתָּ בַעֲדוֹ וּבְעַד־בֵּיתוֹ וּבְעַד כָּל־אֲשֶׁר־לוֹ מִסָּבִיב
מַעֲשֵׂה יָדָיו בֵּרַכְתָּ וּמִקְנֵהוּ פָּרַץ בָּאָרֶץ׃

Then Satan answered the LORD and said, "Does Job fear God for nought? Have You not made an hedge about him, and his house, and all that he has, on every side? You have blessed the work of his hands, and his substance is increased in the land."
(Job 1:9-10)

The blessings of God accrue within "sanctuaries" that protect local *complexity* from the universal activity of the Cosmic Constable. Living cells, the basis of all biological life, represent miniature "sanctuaries." Eden was a fenced off sanctuary. The desert tabernacle that the Israelites carried with them was a sanctuary. The walled city of Jerusalem was a sanctuary. The earth itself is a sanctuary. God places a protective enclosure around the earth—our atmosphere acts as a giant cell wall, protecting living things from lethal doses of ultraviolet radiation. From the simplest to the highest life form, if the protective enclosure fails the organism dies. So whether we are dealing with the protective hedge that God places around the earth, or the protective hedge that God places around biological cells, or the protective hedge that God places around the Judeo-Christian family, or the protective hedge that God places around sovereign nations, this principle of *enclosure* is fundamental in that it shelters *complexity* and prevents it from being reduced to simplicity by the Cosmic Constable.

Tell me then, is the Cosmic Constable "good," or "evil?" The answer of course is that he is neither. In the cosmos at large there is no "morality," only matter, energy, number and entropy. The picture may change here on earth, however. Here on earth the Constable would be pushing for higher entropy states—higher states of disorder. Meaning that any human expression of the Cosmic Constable would be a "devil" like Hitler himself—a practitioner and purveyor of disorder. We will be sure to dissect and expose the motives of the Fuhrer elsewhere in this publication, but for now we must lay a proper groundwork by obtaining a holistic understanding of the constitution, character, and modus operandi of what we are calling "Cosmic Constable."

What can we say about our Constable? What sort of body does he inhabit? What is his trademark? And how might scientists and philosophers conceive of him? Let us begin by describing all the things that the Constable is not, starting with the obvious—he is not God. The Constable is a principle. God is a Person. Edith Schaeffer explains the Personal nature of God in her book *Christianity is Jewish*:

> "In the beginning God." That is to say, in the beginning a Person—an Infinite Person, but truly a person. In the beginning thinking, acting, feeling, love, communication, ideas, choice, creativity. Yes, in the beginning this God who made man in His image. Personality already existing. A personal universe created by a Person. A "people-oriented universe" created by a Person. A universe with fulfillment in it for the aspirations of artists, poets, musicians, landscape gardeners, because it has been created by an Artist, Poet, Musician, Landscape Gardener.[4]

From the onset let us make it clear that the Cosmic Constable is not some "aspect" of God, or "the bad side of God," or some Gnostic superstition. You may recall that Plato was obliged to invent two gods in order to reconcile some schism that he saw in creation. We are doing no such thing—we are not inventing the Cosmic Constable to have someone to blame all the evil of the world on. What we are now calling "Cosmic Constable" is a metaphor, a caricature, a cartoon, a gestalt that describes the universe's statistical tendency to disorder. What we are calling "Cosmic Constable" is not Plato's *Demiurge*, or Anaximander's *Apeiron*, or Heraclitus' *Cosmic Fire*, or the Brahmin's *Pradhana*, or the mystic's *World Soul*, or any other first-principle invented by Greek, Gnostic, Hindu, or any other school of philosophy.

We should also stress that the Cosmic Constable is not some fallen angel, though he may be described as the "god" of the idolatrous world, in the figurative sense that one applies to such things as money, power and materialism. And needless to say the Cosmic Constable should not be confused with the benevolent principality that we have nicknamed "Mother Nature," the beautiful lady with flowers in her windblown hair. Granted the Constable may rule it over Mother Nature in demanding that she show deference to the universal imperative of increasing entropy, but God can overrule the Constable in favor of Mother Nature *locally*. So we could say that there is no love lost between Mother Nature and the Constable, even though their activities have to mesh and dovetail somehow. The default of Man in Eden rendered Mother Nature vulnerable to the activity of the Constable, and she has been suffering ever since, groaning under duress, laboring in bitterness and frustration:

> For the *creation* awaits with eager anticipation for the manifestation of the children of God... because the *creation* herself will be set free from her bondage to decay and obtain the glorious liberty of the children of God. We know that the whole *creation* has been groaning in travail together until now....
>
> (Romans 8:19-22, emphasis added)

The Greek word translated "creation" is *ktisis*—creatures, living things, ecosystems. The "groaning" described in this passage is local, not cosmic. It is the groaning of Mother Nature. Scripture is describing the consequences of human failure and default in terms of the planet-wide degradation of living *complexity*. In reverting to the ways of the Constable, mankind is now laying the beautiful face of Mother Nature to waste, plowing cruel furrows on her back, furrows from which her lifeblood pours profusely. Mother Nature's wonderful menagerie is now under two-fold attack, the Constable from without, back-slidding man from within. Our spiritual default is now overtaking Mother Nature's capacity to recover. That beautiful Lady is now fighting for her life, all the decks stacked against her. Even she is no match for the unholy alliance between Cosmic Constable and reprobate man. Entropy is increasing all around and she knows it. She is now fighting to keep her head above the rising waters, gasping for air, going down for the last time. The ignorance of man has become a blight on all living things.

Mother Nature labors to maintain low entropy states. She labors to sustain, nourish and protect the exuberant variety of living things on earth. The Constable labors to increase entropy. Don't be surprised if the two eye each other with a great deal of suspicion and mistrust. The Constable cannot be expected to have any sympathy for the beautiful lady who has been empowered by God to reverse the conventions of order and disorder locally. Don't be surprised to find the Constable harboring a great deal of contempt for Mother Nature, despising her beautiful countenance and abominating the *complexities* that have been entrusted to her care by the Creator of the universe.

What other characteristics might we attribute to something as abstract, cold, and indifferent as the Cosmic Constable? Well, we might say that he lives on the non-human side of the interface, or "on the interior of the computer screen." On the human side of the interface we discern colors, shapes, forms, meanings, expressions, music, poetry, literature, and such things that inspire and evoke emotions. On his side of the interface the Constable sees only zeroes and ones, as it were. The world in which the Constable exists consists of numbers and entropy.

The Cosmic Constable does not "think" as we do. The expression *cognito, ergo sum* ("I think, therefore I am") cannot be applied to the Cosmic Constable, any more than it could be applied to a computer. Because we are human, and because our inquiry has to be undertaken from a human point of view, we may refer to the Constable as "him" or "he." But we should always bear in mind that we are dealing with an "it." The world in which the Constable exists does not allow human considerations. Unlike the Person of God, the Constable cannot see things as we humans see them. He is utterly incapable of comprehending such things as beauty, love, inspiration, joy, hope or fear. The Constable does not speak a human language. He could not appreciate our "poetry." He speaks the language of pure *mathematics*. And the fact that his activity can be observed and investigated in terms of "numbers" has profound significance. It means that mathematicians can "converse" with the Cosmic Constable, though they might find the conversation a trifle one-sided. When Galileo said that the book of nature was written in a mathematical language he wasn't far from the truth. As far as the Constable is concerned, "number is the measure of all things," (to quote Pythagoras). One needs to be a mathematician to understand the language of the Cosmic Constable. One does not need to be a mathematician to understand the Language of God, one only needs to be human.

This raises another question. Is God a mathematician? Yes, and one "of a very high order," to quote the physicist Paul Dirac. God would have to be a mathematician in order to tell the Constable what he can or cannot do. He would have to be a mathematician in order to customize all the default settings of the universe. He would have to be a mathematician in order to be able to input the quantum events that jumpstarted life, or produced "miracles." Yes, in so far as God launched the universe with mathematical precision, He Himself is Sovereign Mathematician.

כִּי לֹא מַחְשְׁבוֹתַי מַחְשְׁבוֹתֵיכֶם וְלֹא דַרְכֵיכֶם דְּרָכָי נְאֻם יְהוָה:
כִּי־גָבְהוּ שָׁמַיִם מֵאָרֶץ כֵּן גָּבְהוּ דְרָכַי מִדַּרְכֵיכֶם וּמַחְשְׁבֹתַי מִמַּחְשְׁבֹתֵיכֶם

For My thoughts are not your thoughts, neither are your ways My ways, says the LORD. For as the heavens are higher than the earth, so are My ways higher than your ways, and My thoughts than your thoughts.
(Isaiah 55:8-9)

The Mind of God is simultaneously aware of everything that is going on in the universe. Even a sparrow cannot fall without His knowledge. He is able to number each and every hair on our heads, each and every grain of sand on every sea shore, and even measure the velocity and position of each and every elementary particle in the universe. How can He do this? We cannot answer that question from our frame. We can't think without using up energy, and even that is limited by the number and efficacy of the neurons in our brains. We cannot even conceive of an Intelligence who is capable of processing all information simultaneously without the use of energy or neurons.

Nothing is hidden from the Mind of God. He has the capacity to "know" all things simultaneously, see past, present and future as one continuum. However from the circumstance of His omniscience it does not follow that He is subject to the knowledge of everything that is going on under the sun. God cannot be Sovereign and subject at the same time—He cannot be *subjected* to knowledge and knowing. A Sovereign God does not have to be permanently engaged in the cognition of everything—that would imply a lack of Sovereignty on His part. By the same token we cannot consider the cognition of God to be "non-permanent" either, for that would imply a cessation of omniscience. So then much caution is due when it comes to assumption and oversimplification. Perhaps the omniscience of God should be understood in the sense of a *capacity for all knowledge.*

Perhaps God can open and close any "window" of knowledge at will. At any rate we know that He is not subject to anything under the sun, and that He can come and go as He pleases. He can choose to "hang out," as young people might say. Or He can choose to turn His back and walk away. Either way, there are no causes that can compel God to do anything. He is Sovereign Person, existing beyond causality, free to come and go, choose or reject, love or hate, raise up or let fall. During the Exodus, God wanted to personally accompany the Israelites in their journey to the Promised Land. This He did much of the time, except when they provoked Him to wrath, as at Taberah, at Massah, and at Kibrothhattaavah, (refer to Deuteronomy 9:22). For reasons of their stubbornness, hardness of heart, and deafness of ear, God parted company with them at that time, as He did on other occasions. The Sovereign of the universe can do as He pleases.

The Constable, on the other hand, has no choice when it comes to the "knowledge" of what is going on in the realms of matter and energy. His cognition and assessment of all the "numbers" of the universe is continuous. His mind is like a cosmic balance sheet that is getting updated continually. It is like the "mind" of a super computer that has to correlate all the numbers in the universe simultaneously, a "left-brain" analytical automaton and number-cruncher that provides physical reality with accounting checks and balances. In some infinitesimal way every event in the universe increases the entropy of the universe, which affects everything else in the universe. Even the energy degraded by the blink of a human eye registers a change on the cosmic balance sheet. Does the Constable detect the change? He would have to. Does God see the change? He could, but that is besides the point. And what is the point? The point is that God has better things to concern Himself with—the well-being and happiness of His children here on earth.

What do we humans see when we look at a work of art hanging in a gallery? We see an expression of the human spirit. The Cosmic Constable sees only the "numbers" associated with whatever was layered onto the canvas—chemical properties governed by the dispositions of electrons and atoms. That's what he "sees," a universe filled with the dervish dance of elementary particles. He sees numbers where we see galaxies, numbers where we see the sun and moon, numbers where we see hill and dale, numbers where we see forests and rivers, numbers where we see vineyards and orchards, numbers where we hear the sound of music. Are these numbers real? Indeed they are. Today it is possible to convert music into numbers. The Constable doesn't hear the music recorded on a CD, he "sees" the numbers associated with the digitization (the elemental patterns that the digital recorder has burned on the CD). It is now even possible to treat a painting, a song, or a poem as having entropy. And that is the sort of thing the Constable sees—number and entropy.

Composers may express the human spirit in terms of musical notes and symphonies. The Constable is altogether deaf, dumb and blind with respect to things of the human spirit. On his side of the interface every shade, color, sound, word, note, tone, structure, pattern, chord and melody is detected as number and entropy state. A human being may listen to the works of a great composer and draw inspiration. The Constable cannot. In Beethoven's Fifth Symphony he detects nothing but numbers, the aggregate of which describe a very low entropy state. Naturally the Constable would prefer to re-write Beethoven's Fifth along lines of repetition and noise instead. Noise would have a higher entropy state than the music of Beethoven's Fifth.

In attempting to describe the nature of the Cosmic Constable a useful analogy can be found in the computer. Some scientists are now describing the universe in terms of a gigantic computation process wherein the laws of nature can be thought of as "programs." If the cosmos was a gigantic computer, then the Constable's universal activity would amount to a default operating system. In computer jargon *default* stands for a particular setting or value for a variable that is assigned automatically and remains in effect unless overriden.

Default also implies a rudimentary state to which things will revert in case of higher-level failure. Perhaps in some sense the Constable's activity can be said to be the *modal default* of physical reality.

An illustration may be found in the default settings of an electric typewriter. When you first purchased that old typewriter and turned it on, right away you noticed that it came with certain default settings such as preset margins and tabs. Later on you discovered that you could change or *customize* those settings to suit your own particular needs—wider margins and different tabs. A month later there was a power failure, and when the lights came back on you noticed that your electric typewriter had reverted to its default settings.

It is a matter of general experience that things will revert to disorder if left to themselves, suggesting something about human nature. If higher level order fails, human nature will revert to disorder. In the absence of the spiritual imperatives of God the behavior of man will default to the material imperative of the Cosmic Constable. God made us from the "dust" of the earth—the physics of this universe. We are all born with the *factory setting* of the cosmos internalized. Divested of the Spirit of God, the human condition will revert to the rudiments of the perishable universe. Much of human history is a catalog of such backsliding. The Bible puts it bluntly:

> It is happened to them according to the true proverb:"The dog returns to his own vomit, and the sow that was washed to her wallowing in the mire."
>
> (2 Peter 2:22)

This tendency to revert to barbarism has been the subject of many poems, among them William Butler Yeats's *The Second Coming*, describing a world that is falling apart at the seams. It has been the subject of many novels, among them William Golding's *Lord of the Flies*. Golding's epic is a harrowing tale about well-bred English schoolboys who get shipwrecked on a desert island and in no time revert to savagery and barbarism. Many of Shakespeare's plays are about historical figures who, unable to hold on to a higher order, fell back to the modal defaults of disorder and mayhem. It is as though the human condition is making a quantum jump to lower energy states in times of stress.

The history of the human race is a catalog of such backslidings. Abraham himself was tempted to revert to the pagan default. Sodom and Gomorrah wholly reverted and paid the price. When God destroyed the twin cities, He ordered Lot and his household not to "look back"—not to even think about reverting to such degradation. Lot's wife did, and was turned into a pillar of salt. Later "Egypt" became a Biblical type of backsliding. The physical Exodus out of Egypt was also a spiritual Exodus out of the derivative modes of existence. The Exodus was in some sense the beginning of a quantum jump towards authentic modes of existence. Yet no sooner had Moses gone up into the mountain than the children of Israel reverted to the derivative. While Moshe was up in the mountain receiving the Ten Commandments, the children of Israel were reverting to the pagan default whence God had just extricated them.

וַיְדַבֵּר יְהוָה אֶל־מֹשֶׁה לֶךְ־רֵד כִּי שִׁחֵת עַמְּךָ אֲשֶׁר הֶעֱלֵיתָ מֵאֶרֶץ מִצְרָיִם:
סָרוּ מַהֵר מִן־הַדֶּרֶךְ אֲשֶׁר צִוִּיתִם...

And the LORD said to Moses, "Get down there,
for your people which you brought our of the land of Egypt
have corrupted themselves [reverted]: They have turned aside quickly
out of the way which I commanded them..."
(Exodus 32:6-8)

Thereafter some were continually wanting to "go back to Egypt," murmuring against Moses. Korah and his mob backslid and were buried alive by God. Centuries later we find the same backsliding in the Promised Land. All we in our flesh resonate the nature, property and orientation of the cosmos, bedeviled by its statistical tendency to disorder. All we like foolish sheep tend to go astray.

Increasing entropy is the *natural orientation* of the greater physical reality that surrounds and penetrates us from cradle to grave. Universal entropy is increasing as we speak. Our consciousness is continually recording the entropy changes in the world around us. We see friends get old and die. We see things wear out. We see things decay. We see things degrade and deteriorate—tell-tale signs of the Constable's incessant activity.

What then? Can the Constable be said to be "a necessary evil?" Perhaps. Were it not for his universal activity we might find ourselves alongside Alice in Wonderland, watching water flow uphill, old men grow young, balls turn into hedgehogs, hoops turn into marching soldiers and the rules of the game changed from minute to minute by the infernal Queen. Were the Constable to fall asleep on the job all the principles of physics might go topsy turvey—electricity might refuse to flow from high to low potential, all of the engines and powerplants of man could freeze, our brain neurons could stop functioning.

The business of the Constable is all wrapped up with the consummation of potential differences and stabilization of energy. Within the narrow confines of his agenda he has an aversion towards any sort of differentiation. He sees "order" in homogeneity and "disorder" in heterogeneity. He is like a cosmic cookie-cutter man, preferring isotropism, repetition and sameness. He takes a dim view of *complexity* and will bring pressure to bear to try to reduce it to simplicity—with Blitzkrieg and Panzer division if necessary. He is never satisfied with status quo reduction. Just because he has reduced something today doesn't mean that he will take a break. The Cosmic Constable doesn't takes breaks. His appetite for increasing entropy is like Hades—insatiable. He will not be satisfied until he has done away with all the gradients of the universe. When there is no more differentiation to be found anywhere, when the universe has been reduced to pure undifferentiated energy, then and only then will the Constable be able to retire on his policeman's pension.

The Constable is trying to consummate all the potential differences of the universe and he will exert pressure to accomplish that goal. If he meets with resistance he may lose his temper, and the final consummation may be quite violent. Perhaps we could describe the Constable as a cosmic demolition man, his wrecking ball and steamroller fueled by *energy*. All the energy in the universe is at his disposal, though God can overrule what he might do with it locally. The energy that we human beings have learned to harness is in fact the strength of the Cosmic Constable. In a sense we have been empowered by our Heavenly Father to tame the Cosmic beast, restrain him with bit and bridle, and use his strength, for example, to power our cities. By the same token we have also learned that we have to pay a premium in terms of "insulation," knowing that the Constable will not hesitate to consummate potential differences along paths of least resistance. The "short circuit" is one of his favorite ploys. He would short-circuit every grid and burst every energy dam in the universe if he could.

Energy can be said to be the strength of the Cosmic Constable, the power that levels the gradients of the universe, transforming itself into entropy in the process; the power that moves universal systems from low to high probability states. In order for us to utilize this power we must build resistance against the Constable's activity. But this makes him mad as a hatter. When we humans dam up the flow of a river we had better be sure that the structure is strong enough, otherwise the Constable will breach it. In order to harness cosmic energy, we must construct gradients, potential differences, resistors, dams and engines. And to do that we must avail ourselves of every ounce of spiritual resolve, creative ingenuity and grim determination that God gives us, otherwise the Constable will wreck the whole thing in no time. He is demolition man and dam buster rolled into one. Give him half a chance he will breach every dam in creation, looking on with pleasure as the ensuing flood takes the path of least resistance to consummation, devastating every pattern of human *complexity* in its path. He is just like Murphy, always looking for a flaw, always looking for the weakest link, always trying to make complex things fall apart—"Houston we have a problem!" And the more complex a thing is, the more vigorously will he attack it to try to reduce it to simplicity.

In trying to consummate potential differences, and in trying to level all things, the Constable will abide little resistance to his activity. He desires to see general movement towards higher entropy states, and will get upset if the flow is restricted locally. He will not tolerate excessive blockage and damming up of energy. Not for long he won't, and not without demanding an exorbitant price for his tolerance. He imposes severe penalties on all energy dams and is constantly looking for opportunities to breach them and restore free flow. He is directing the greater order of universal change from low to high probability states. Don't be surprised to find him trying to level and reduce every low probability pattern of *complexity* found on earth. It is his duty to identify, stamp, file, index, regulate, reduce and level every gradient and potential difference in the universe. He has jurisdiction over the aggregate of universal gradients, and takes that jurisdiction very seriously.

We might say that the Cosmic Constable has an aversion towards potential differences and gradients. He takes a dim view of anything "standing upright," for example. He would rather level and reduce everything to a flat-line of simplicity and homogeneity. We might say that the Constable is intolerant of differentiation and heterogeneity. We could in fact describe him as a narrow-minded "control freak" obsessed with homogenization and assimilation. Like Hitler himself, the Constable likes to see everything levelled down and the same. All the chickens in the cosmic coop must be white clones, and woe betide any black or speckled bird wandering inside. A coop full of identical white clones would be the Constable's notion of "order." The order of simplicity and sameness. The order of conformity, uniformity and homogeneity.

The conventions of order and disorder are reversed between Man and Constable. What we perceive as "order" becomes "disorder" when viewed from the perspective of the Constable. An illustration might be sought in how we and the Constable might view a work of art, say, a magnificent vase. The vase, created by a human artist, represents a low entropy, low probability pattern of *complexity* in the universe. Let us say that someone accidentally drops it and it breaks into a thousand pieces on the floor. The question is this: how does the Cosmic Constable see the vase before and after the accident?

While the vase was standing on the table it embodied the sort of low probability state that the Constable equates with "disorder"—a tight knot in the fabric of space and time. When the vase fell and broke into a thousand piece, the tight knot of "disorder" became unravelled into the high probability state that the Constable prefers. The broken shards on the floor may represent "disorder" from our human point of view, but "order" from the Constable's point of view. *Complexity*, that is, highly specified combinations of matter, energy and information, is an accursed thing to the Constable. His agenda is to reduce *complexity* into simplicity. He prefers the reduced, rundown, corrupted, and degraded version of everything.

That extraordinary beautiful Mediterranean villa overlooking the sea may embody "order" from a human perspective, but it represents "disorder" from the Constable's. He would prefer the broken down slum. The patterns of simplicity and degradation he sees in Skid Row are much more to his liking. He would prefer to see the whole world reduced to shard and rubble. He would prefer to see pollution, congestion and waste. He would prefer to see cities teetering on the edge of bankruptcy, streets overrun by garbage and graffiti, run-down neighborhoods ruled by gangbangers and drug pushers. These patterns of reduction, degradation, and disorder are seen by him as *affirmations* of the universal imperative of increasing entropy. Life, structure, organization and complexity are seen by him as *violations* of the universal imperative of increasing entropy.

And so it would appear that the old saw about cleanliness being next to Godliness wasn't far from the truth. But there is much caution due here as well. Let us be very careful to understand what we mean by "cleanliness," because the Constable has his own definition for that as well. When we say "cleanliness is next to Godliness," we do not mean Hitler's "racial hygiene." We do not mean psychotic and neurotic obsession with sterility, uniformity and homogeneity. We do not mean the scapegoating of heterogeneity, or the labelling of those born different as "unclean." We do not mean rampant paranoia and the hysterical appeal to "order" that has been the siren song of every demagogue and dictator in history. We do not mean the compulsive addiction to "perfection" that is a characteristic of disturbed minds, or the repeated hand washings associated with the behavior of the mentally ill. And we most certainly do not mean that other form of insanity referred to as "ethnic cleansing." These definitions of "cleanliness" are not of human origin; they are cosmos-derivative.

When the city of Man has been reduced by famine, sword, and pestilence, when the entire continent of Europe has been reduced to a bombed-out rubble, that is when the Constable will be happy. And when he looks down at all the destruction, he does not see the wreckage of human lives either. That too is "order" from his perspective. In the spectacle of death and destruction he sees *affirmations* of the universal imperative of increasing entropy.

It goes without saying that the Cosmic Constable would prefer war to peace. Not only does war bring out the worst in man, not only does it saddle nations with soul-consuming debts and financial liabilities, it also produces massive increases of local entropy. The Constable would definitely encourage war and discourage peace. The cities, structures, organizations and patterns of *complexity* that man is able to build during brief periods of peace are as insults to his power and authority. The leveling of cities, the plunder, the mayhem, the ruin, the death and destruction associated with war are *affirmations* of his power and authority.

A house divided against itself, an institution in disarray, a society in shambles, a nation ruled by the law of the jungle, a state drowning in revolution, political chaos, debt, currency inflation, social upheaval and economic disintegration—all these things are affirmations of the "order" of which the Constable is choreographer.

If the Constable were endowed with the gift of human speech his decree would be heard bellowing throughout the cosmos:

> Order! Order! Order in the universe! Consummate all the gradients! Reduce patterns of complexity to patterns of simplicity! Level down! Level down! Level down! Homogenize! Homogenize! Homogenize! Reduce, assimilate and absorb! Render everything isotropic and the same! Arrest and prosecute all heterogeneity! Resistance is futile. You will be assimilated. Order! Order! Order in the universe!

Let us sum up the devil whose teeth we have just pulled. The "Cosmic Constable" is not some Manichaean fiend with horns and hooves. He is a plain vanilla anthropomorphization of the universe's tendency to disorder resonating in human nature. Which brings us to the two foundational premises of this publication:

1) Material reality is statistically oriented towards disorder (increasing entropy).
2) Material human nature is governed by the same orientation.

We will explore the moral and ethical ramifications of the Cosmic Constable later, but for now we must digress briefly to address the controversy surrounding "evolution."

בְּרֵאשִׁית בָּרָא אֱלֹהִים אֵת הַשָּׁמַיִם וְאֵת הָאָרֶץ

In the beginning God created the heavens and the earth.

(Genesis 1:1)

SECTION 3

Cosmos and Evolution

The Fundamental Darwin

I dare say that 99% of the folks who take pleasure in cursing Darwin haven't bothered to read *The Origin of Species*. Alas many religious folks seem to have gotten themselves mired down in an irrational hatred of the man, rejecting everything he said without investigation. Many are intimidated by the word *evolution*, presumably because they see in it a threat to everything they believe in. This is a deplorable condition for any believer to be in. If one's faith can be upset so easily it is not worth the paper it is written on.

Darwin wasn't perfect by any stretch of the imagination, (who is perfect in this world?) And there is no denying that certain godless factions have made him their poster boy. Notwithstanding, we would have believers engage in clear and rational thought. Truth is the guiding principle of the Kingdom of God. Truth does not stand or fall because of cultural or religious animus. Theological arguments based on a faulty understanding of natural science or the Bible are counterproductive to a search for truth. Darwin didn't create the geological column or the fossil record: God did.

What scientists call *evolution* is nothing more than the outworking of the Divine program that has "brought forth" the exuberant variety of living things on earth. Believers who get into heated debates about evolution without knowing what they are talking about are not doing God a favor. Zeal for God is no excuse for ignorance. Zeal has to be grounded in knowledge to amount to something. We understand theological concerns about allowing science too much control over exegesis, but truth has to be consistent with reality. True science helps us honor the Creator and wrestle with the task of interpreting

His ways of speaking to us. While science can never replace faith, it can be a most faithful friend and ally when it comes to separating fact from fiction.

Science deals with that which has been created by God. All "knowledge" can therefore be traced to God. Some of the world's greatest scientists have been believers in God. Even those who do not believe in God are helping the cause of God by engaging in true inquiry. And if God should use the wrath of man to praise Him, who are we to question Him? So let us start with a clean slate and pursue our own inquiry with an open mind of God-given wisdom. Whatever Darwin was, or wasn't, his methodology and his science were impeccable. Read *The Origin of Species* for yourself and you will agree that the fundamental Darwin takes great pains to describe, faithfully and laboriously, the efficient mechanisms whereby the Creator may have caused the exuberant variety of living things to be brought forth on earth. Here are his own words:

> There is grandeur in this [evolutionary] view of life, with its several powers, having been originally breathed by the Creator into a few forms or into one; and that, whilst this planet has gone cycling on according to the fixed law of gravity, from so simple a beginning endless forms most beautiful and most wonderful have been, and are being evolved.[1]

ABIOGENESIS vs EVOLUTION

In science, *abiogenesis* and *evolution* represent two related but different branches of inquiry. Most of the problems, misunderstandings, strife and contention result from a mixing of the two. Let us try to pry them apart.

Abiogenesis—the branch of science that inquires into processes and mechanisms whereby ordinary matter was transformed into the simplest of life forms. Specifically, abiogenesis deals with the creation or "jump-starting" of life, beginning with inanimate matter and ending with the first viable living organism. Perhaps the scientist who could be said to embody this branch of the discipline would be Stanley Miller.

Evolution—the branch of science that inquires into the processes and mechanisms whereby living organisms have undergone variation and modification subsequent to abiogenesis. Evolution begins where abiogenesis leaves off, investigating the flowerings and branchings of the tree of life and the full range of its variations. Perhaps the scientist who could be said to embody this branch of the discipline would be Stephen Jay Gould.

While the origins of life remain a mystery, the mechanisms that have brought about evolution are by now fairly well understood. In so far as evolution is concerned, scientists have a fairly good handle on the subject. Their knowledge may not be whole, and they may be in error in other respects, but what they do know is substantial and should be respected. Religious folk are not doing God any favors by putting up and then shooting down their own straw models of evolution. Evolution is God's most excellent way of filling every nook and cranny of the blue planet with the exuberant variety of living things.

Let us investigate the dichotomy between abiogenesis and evolution a little further. Just as a constitution is a thing antecedent to government, so and likewise abiogenesis is a thing antecedent to evolution. Abiogenesis covers the processes that transformed non-life into life. How did that happen? Those of us who worship the God of Abraham believe that the Creator inputted the quantum events that jump-started life *locally*. Not "random permutations," not some "glorious accident," but God manipulating reality at the quantum level.

There is not enough space in this publication to go into all the problems that scientists encounter when they try to reduce abiogenesis to "natural" or "spontaneous" processes. Suffice it to say that the statistical resources of the universe are limited—the number of "possibilities" are not infinite. The universe may be vast, but it is finite. Cosmos can only supply so many "bits" of information, and the laws of physics limit the speed with which they can be "switched." These and other considerations all but rule against the probability of spontaneous abiogenesis—the notion that atoms can organize themselves into living cells accidentally. As for appeals to "infinity issues," or "parallel universes," these too are problematic in that they assume the benefit of an infinite sample size without supporting evidence.

Avoiding infinity issues, and appeals to metaphysics, we are dealing with a sample size of one finite universe which had a beginning many billions of years ago and is still cooling down. This places a huge question mark next to the subject of abiogenesis. Stanley Miller:

> The problem of the origin of life has turned out to be much more difficult than I, and most other people, envisioned.[2]

Darwin himself never pretended to know how life began on earth. He limited his own field of research to the domain of evolution, i.e., what happened *after* life got its initial start. Here are his own words:

> Many instincts are so wonderful that their development will probably appear to the reader a difficulty sufficient to overthrow my whole theory. I may here premise that I have nothing to do with the origin of the mental powers, any more than I have with that of life itself.[3]

No doubt Darwin thought that science would shortly discover how life got started. But that has not been the case. Even today the origin of life remains a mystery. Like Darwin himself, the late Stephen Jay Gould also focused on evolution, starting with what he called *the left wall of minimal complexity*—the first viable living organism. Note Gould's use of the adverb "presumably" in the statement below:

> The earth is 4.5 billion years old. Life, as recorded in the fossil record, originated at least 3.5 billion years ago, and probably not much earlier because the earth passed through a molten period that ended about 3.8 billion years ago (the age of the oldest rocks). Life presumably began in primeval oceans...[4]

The mystery surrounding the origin of life has caused a number of famous scientists to posit a theory of *directed panspermia.* Those who subscribe to this theory reason that since life could not have risen "spontaneously" on earth, it must have been transported or "seeded" by extra-terrestrials hailing from advanced civilizations located elsewhere. But this raises a question as to how these extra-terrestrials themselves came into being. The associated paradox goes something like this: If life arose spontaneously on *Planet Mongo* (the place where those extra-terrestrial came from), why couldn't it have arisen spontaneously on earth as well? Confronted with this question, the proponents of *directed panspermia* might suggest that conditions in that part of the universe could have been sufficiently different to skew the laws of nature in favor of accidental abiogenesis. But that creates an entirely new set of problems, not the least of which would be a violation of the Cosmological Principle, (the principle that requires natural laws to operate uniformly throughout the universe).

Physicists recognize the essential similarity between universal phenomena and have developed the theory of quantum mechanics to explain it. Statistical theory is one of the pillars of quantum mechanics. If statistical theory functions differently on Planet Mongo, then it can't be relied on as a basis for quantum theory here on earth. In which case most of modern science would have to be judged unreliable as well, there being no longer any basis to analyze the relationship between probable and improbable.

It does not appear that life could have been "seeded" here by benevolent extra-terrestrials hailing from Planet Mongo. In which case we are right back where we started, asking the same question—how did life start on earth? The question is so troubling that some of the world's most famous scientists are now participating in a "contest" to offer a huge monetary reward for a major breakthrough in abiogenesis. Scientists don't know how life got started on earth. But they do know a great deal about the evolutionary mechanisms that took hold *after* life got its initial start.

UNDERSTANDING EVOLUTION

God could have spent all day and all night creating a single species. Instead He spent six "days" writing the *biologos* that would automatically bring forth the exuberant variety of living things. Concerning which, we have the testimony of Scripture:

> And God said, *let the earth bring forth* vegetation, and herb yielding seed, and the fruit tree yielding fruit after its kind.
> (Genesis 1:11, emphasis added)

> And God said, *let the waters bring forth* abundantly, the moving creature that hath life, and foul that may fly above the earth... and God blessed them saying, be fruitful and multiply, and fill the waters in the seas, and *let the fowl multiply in the earth.*
>
> (Genesis 1:20, emphasis added)

> And God said, *let the earth bring forth* the living creature after its kind, cattle, and creeping things, and beast of the earth after its kind.
>
> (Genesis 1:24, emphasis added)

Nowhere in the Genesis narrative do we find God creating millions of species one at a time. Only in the case of man is there a suggestion of *special* labor on the part of God:

> And God said, *let us* make man in our own image.
>
> (Genesis 1:26, emphasis added)

A distinction must be made between the autonomous activity of Mother Nature, signified by the words *let the earth bring forth*, and the special activity of God, signified by the words *let us create man in our own image.* Mother Nature's business limits itself to the evolution of animals. God's business centers around the evolution of Adam.

God's instructions to Mother Nature might read something like this:

> *Fill the earth with the exuberant variety of living things!*

That is exactly what Mother Nature has done through evolution in terms of what Stephen Jay Gould called *Full House.* Mother Nature has filled every nook and cranny of the blue planet with the exuberant variety of living things. The fact that many scientists reduce evolution to an autonomous and directionless process is understandable. If God set into motion a mechanism that would *automatically* fill every nook and cranny of the planet with living things, you would expect some scientist to come along and describe the result as an outcome of "chance" or "contingency." This would, on the surface, be a valid observation, if God had in fact invested the earth with a potential to *bring forth* the exuberant variety of living things. And if God initially shaped man by a process of evolution, the Genesis narrative would by no means disallow the considerable stock of near-humans that must have preceded *Adam*. There is nothing in the Genesis narrative that requires *Adam* not to have been of a species prepared for God's personal touch by evolution.

In order to understand the difference between Man and other living things a distinction must be made between primary and secondary causation. Primary causation would relate to God's *special* actions. Secondary causation would relate to God's *non-special* way of operating, by which He sustains His creation not through personal intervention, but through principles and natural laws. But would primary causation violate those natural laws? Not necessarily. The special acts of God might cause *redistributions* only. As long as those special acts were accompanied by (A) a net conservation of energy, and (B) a net increase in universal entropy, there would be no fundamental violation of the laws of the universe.

What do we mean by *redistribution*? An illustration might be sought in the Divine act that raised Lazarus from the dead. Did the "miracle" violate the laws of the universe? Not necessarily. This is what could have happened:

> Something local became more complex.
> Something non-local became less complex.
> There was *redistribution.*
> There was a net conservation of energy.
> There was a net increase of universal entropy.

Lazarus' body had been dead for days—and already undergone significant degradation. The act of restoring it to living *complexity* would have required, among other things, a massive decrease of local entropy. Did this amount to a violation of the laws of the universe? Not necessarily. The local decrease could have been offset by a non-local increase. When Lazarus was raised from the dead, highly specific combinations of matter, energy, and information were *redistributed* within the universe. Something local became more complex at the expense of something non-local. We know that Lazarus' body was brought back to life, but we don't know what might have happened elsewhere by way of compensation. Perhaps there was a minor solar flare. Perhaps there was a reciprocal increase of entropy on the surface of Jupiter, or Saturn, or Pluto, or elsewhere in the galaxy. Who knows, and what difference would it make? The universe is vast and *redistributions* would not pose a problem for an Augustinian God. An Augustinian God would have no difficulty inputting the quantum events that would jump-start life by primary causation—*abiogenesis*. Furthermore, He would have no difficulty writing the biologos that would fill every nook and cranny of the earth with living things through secondary causation—*evolution.*

Today we see the full range of variation on earth. As far as size is concerned, Mother Nature has filled every nook and cranny of the spectrum with the exuberant variety of living things. The blue planet may not accommodate a mile-long whale, but it will accommodate the blue whale, which is quite big by any standard. How big or heavy can a creature get before its legs get crushed by its own weight? Fifty feet tall and weighing in at around eighty tons, Brachiosaurus was probably a land-based limit. How small can a living thing get before it is too small to house the minimal functions and fixtures of life? Whatever the answer, between Brachiosaurus and bacteria every nook and cranny of the size spectrum has been filled.

What about the shape spectrum? That has been filled too. Ditto color. Ditto skin texture. Ditto everything else you might think of. One could play a science game where one player conjures up some strange creature, and the other tries to find an approximation in earth's *Full House*. What's your pleasure? A bird with gray feathers and gaudy blue feet? You'll find it in the blue-footed booby. A fish with scales arranged like the colors of the rainbow? You'll find it. A creature with black and white racing stripes? The zebra. Something big, with a rounded stony shell, living on both land and sea? The Galapagos turtle. Something very tiny, very angular, with striped purple, orange and black sticks for legs and large green eyes? It's there somewhere. A beetle capable of delivering a broadside that would put Napoleon's canons to shame? The Bombardier. A creature that can live at the volcanic depths of the sea? It's there somewhere. There really isn't much that you could imagine, or wish for, no matter how outlandish, or gaudy, or strange, or bizarre, that could not be found in earth's *Full House.*

GENESIS AND EVOLUTION

Can we reconcile the Genesis narrative with the aeon-long processes of evolution? Not if we assume the Creator to be internal to time. Only by comprehending the Creator to be an Augustinian God external to time, can we reconcile evolution with the six "days" of Genesis. An Augustinian Creator would not "see" things as we do. An Augustinian God would have a *block-view* of what we call "time," seeing past, present and future as a unified whole; i.e., an Augustinian God would not have to "wait" for aeons to see the earth bring forth living things. Such a God would be able to "see" the end from the beginning in all cases.

זִכְרוּ רִאשֹׁנוֹת מֵעוֹלָם כִּי אָנֹכִי אֵל וְאֵין עוֹד אֱלֹהִים וְאֶפֶס כָּמוֹנִי
מַגִּיד מֵרֵאשִׁית אַחֲרִית וּמִקֶּדֶם אֲשֶׁר לֹא־נַעֲשׂוּ

Remember the former things [I predicted] of old: for I am God, and there are no other gods, and there is none like me: declaring the end from the beginning, and from ancient times the things that are not yet done...
(Isaiah 46:9)

The stumbling block has to do with our own misconceptions about God. We imagine that God's frame of reference is temporal, just like our own. But it is not. The Creator of time is transcendent of time. From God's perspective, past, present, and future merge into a single continuum with movable foci. In paradoxically human terms, an Augustinian God would be able to "see" end results by moving His focus forward on the continuum of space and time.

An analogy is required to illustrate the perspective of an Augustinian God. Let us imagine that we are in a News Media helicopter high over a yellow school bus that has stalled on the railroad tracks. The school children have been taken off and moved to safety, and the driver is in the bus, frantically trying to restart the engine. There is a freight train coming. From our perspective in the helicopter we can see both the school bus and the approaching train. What will happen? Will the bus driver be able to start the engine and drive the bus off the tracks in time? Or will he have to get out and run for his life before the train demolishes the bus? We mortals have to sit and "wait" for our temporal focus to advance along the continuum to the point where we see the outcome. An Augustinian God would not have to.

From our temporal perspective we would have to consider two "possibilities," one in which the driver succeeds in driving the bus off the tracks, another in which there is a terrible wreck. Would an Augustinian God have to consider similar "possibilities?" The answer, of course, is no. Being external to space and time, an Augustinian God would be able to see all outcomes in terms of *certainties*. There would be no "possibilities" from His atemporal perspective, only certainties. God would see the outcome. If it is actually the case that the driver succeeds in driving the bus off the tracks, that is what God would "see," and vice versa. What then? Does this imply determinism? Does this mean that the future is fixed and can't be changed? No, because an Augustinian God would also have the capacity to "interfere" or "manually override" the normal course of events through primary causation. An Augustinian God could, if He so chose, input the quantum events that start the engine of the bus supernaturally ("supernaturally," from a human perspective). There is therefore no determinism in that sense—the future is not "fixed." By tweaking the knobs of our "present," an Augustinian God could change our "future" to bring His own plan to fruition.

{ Sidebar: By right an Augustinian God would also be Supreme Law-Giver and Judge, precisely because He does see all outcomes ahead of time. In looking down at the wicked Canaanites, for example, God was able to see their final state of degradation, seeing them sacrificing their own children on the fires of Moloch. An Augustinian God would therefore be in a position to *preempt* such outcomes. Just as a physician may need to amputate a gangrene-infested limb, likewise God may need to amputate evil before it achieves critical mass. There is of course a caveat in all this: *only* God can see all the certainties of the future, hence *only* God can issue preemptive directives like the ones He issued to Joshua. }

So as far as evolution is concerned, "time" is not a Biblical issue, seeing that it has no meaning from the perspective of an Augustinian God. From God's perspective each "day" may have been millions or billions of years long. Up to the establishment of *Adam* the Genesis narrative assumes the external frame of an Augustinian God. There is no human convention of time before *Adam*. Only with the emergence of *Adam* does the temporal frame of the Bible narrow down to a human frame of reference.

In his book *Genesis and the Big Bang* Israeli nuclear physicist Gerald L. Schroeder has this to say about the temporal link between man and God:

> Until Adam appeared on day six, God alone was watching the clock. *And that is the key*....For the first one or two days of the six days of Genesis, the Earth didn't even exist.... Because there was no Earth in the early universe, and no possibility of an intimate tie or blending of the reference frames, there was no common calendar between God and the Earth.... Instead, a compromise had to be made to describe the sequential development of the universe. This compromise was to choose, for the time preceding Adam, the Creator's own reference frame that viewed all the universe as a single entity.... It is only at the instant when God places in Adam his breath (in Hebrew the *neshamah*), that both the created and the Creator become inseparably linked. [5]

God would not have to "wait" to see the earth bring forth the exuberant variety of living things. Apply the perspective of an Augustinian God to the Genesis narrative and the controversy between creation and evolution disappears. Apply it to the following passages for example:

> ...and the earth brought forth..*and God saw that it was good.*
> (Genesis 1:12, emphasis added)

> ...and God created the great whales and every living creature that moves, which the waters brought forth abundantly, after their kind, and every winged fowl after his kind: *and God saw that it was good.*
> (Genesis 1:21, emphasis added)

> ... and God made the beast of the earth after his kind, and cattle after their kind, and every thing that creeps upon the earth after his kind: *and God saw that it was good.*
> (Genesis 1:25, emphasis added)

Do these passages assume the temporal frame of man? No, because *Adam* had yet to emerge. Apply God's atemporal frame to them and there is no contradiction because God would not have to sit around for millions of years waiting to "see" the earth bring forth the exuberant variety of living things. If we understand God to be internal to time, there is a contradiction between Genesis and the fossil record. If we understand God to be external to time, there is no contradiction. An Augustinian God would be able to "see" all the end points of phylogenesis from a window outside of time, and therefrom declare them "good."

Theologians fall into the error of assuming a temporal Deity, and then run into a problem. And how do they dispose of the problem? By positing a *Gap Theory*. By claiming that there is a fantastic gap between Genesis 1:1 and Genesis 1:2. They claim that Genesis 1:1 refers to a *first creation*, which was destroyed by God in Genesis 1:2 to make way for a *second creation*. The proponents of the Gap Theory reinterpret the words of Genesis 1:2 to read "the earth *became* formless and void," instead of "the earth *was* formless and void." It is interesting to note that the proponents of the Gap Theory also tend to blame all of the evils of the world on the "spirits" of the diabolical creatures that inhabited the *first creation*. Some even claim that these primal spirits are now roaming the earth as invisible "demons." It should come as no surprise to find that these are the same folks who are now waiting for the apocalyptic events that will bring the world to an end and segregate evil from good.

Many years ago theologians could dismiss the evidence of the fossil record with the wave of a hand. But as the volume of evidence increased it became more difficult to do that. The upshot was the *Gap Theory*—a convenient way of shoe-horning the Genesis narrative to the fossil record. The Christian version of the Gap Theory was not introduced until the late 1870's. For almost 4000 years of history, from the time of the patriarch Abraham to the time of Abraham Lincoln, no one spoke about a *gap* between Genesis 1:1 and 1:2, until scientists presented evidence about the age of the geological column. That was when the Gap Theory emerged, killing two birds with one stone. Not only was the Gap Theory a convenient way of papering over the "contradictions" found in the fossil record, but it was also an excuse to revive the Manichaean dualism.

At the beginning of this publication we emphasized the importance of truth, saying that it must at all times be the guiding principle of the Kingdom of God. The salt of the earth and the light of the world must now show deference to the truth and nothing but the truth. Anon, we have wasted enough time on vain controversy. Let us be about our Father's business, educating ourselves about the way in which He filled every nook and cranny of the blue planet with the exuberant variety of living things.

EVOLUTIONARY CLASSIFICATIONS

Classification has to do with the ordering of the living things created by God into groups on the basis of their relationships. Groups may be referred as *taxa*, for example, or *kingdom*, or *phylum* (in animals), or *division* (in plants), or *class*, or *order*, or *family*, or *genus*, or *species*.

We don't want to get too bogged down in scientific jargon, but in order to educate ourselves we need to understand a few basic terms:

Taxonomy—the study of the classification of created organisms, based on certain physical features, genetic relationships, etc.
Phylogeny—the entire evolutionary history of a species or other taxonomic group of created organisms.
Phylogenetic Tree—a diagram showing lines of descent derived from the fossil record and other evidence.

There are 7 levels of classification, as follows:

Kingdom—the lowest and most basic level.

Phylum—a major grouping (taxon) into which kingdoms (the animal kingdom, for example) are divided and which contains a number of classes.

Class—a taxon (classification) between phylum and order. Related classes make up a phylum, just as related orders make up a class.

Order—a taxon that occurs at a level of classification between a class (which may contain several orders) and a family, several of which may in turn be found in an order.

Family—a taxon between order and genus that normally contains more than one genus. The family names of animals usually end in *-idae*, (e.g., Ursidae, the bear family), and the family names of plants usually end in *-aceae*, (e.g., Rosaceae, the rose family).

Genus—a taxon immediately above that of species and usually containing a group of closely related species. The name of the genus (the generic name) is usually written with an initial capital letter, followed by the specific name of the species, which invariably has a small initial letter. As in *Homo sapiens*. Or as in *Erithacus rubecula* (the scientific name for Old World robins).

Species—the lowest and most important grouping.

Do you see the narrowing down of the evolutionary stream, which becomes more *specific* as we go from kingdom to species?

kingdom▸ phylum▸ class▸ order▸ family▸ genus ▸ species.

Each kingdom branches into different phyla. Each phylum branches into different classes in broad areas of the earth, then narrows down to families in smaller areas, then narrows down to genera in more restricted areas, and finally ends with some species in a very tight environment or niche. Members of a kingdom or phylum will be much more stable—able to survive in the broadest of areas, like the oldest bacteria which have hardly changed in aeons. Members of a species will be far more vulnerable, able to survive only in the restrictive niches to which they have specified themselves. Look at it another way. As we go from phylum to species, the labor of Mother Nature becomes more difficult and the labor of the Cosmic Constable more easy.

The word *species* implies specification. What is evolution if not a process of *specification*? Evolutionary streams become more specified to the point of maximum specificity, and then stop. They must stop, because they can't become any more specific. Species do not specify themselves to abstractions: they specify themselves to niches, being defined by their particular environment. A species would represent the maximum degree of *specification* afforded by a particular environment at any one time. As evolutionary streams move forward in time one would see more adaptation, more specialization, more specification, more narrowing down, to an end-point where one would find a *species*. Think of a phylum as the base of a giant pyramid, getting narrower and narrower, ending with a species at the top. A species would be analogous to the singularity that can only exist at the tip of the pyramid—*the end-point of phylogenesis*.

Species are regarded by scientists to be "the one and only natural unit of classification." But there may be a problem with this view because many scientists don't agree on a precise definition. It has always been difficult to define *species* rigorously. Darwin ran into the difficulty himself:

> Many years ago, when comparing, and seeing others compare, the birds from the closely neighboring islands of the Galapagos archipelago, one with another, and with those from the American mainland, I was much struck how entirely vague and arbitrary is the distinction between species and varieties. [6]

DEFINING SPECIES

In science a great deal depends on precise definitions. Most scientists tend to define a species by its inability to reproduce with members of other species. In as much as one species cannot physically join to reproduce with other species, this would seem a good definition. But is it good enough? If species are to be defined by nothing more than their incapacity to breed with other species, modern geneticists could "create" new species merely by altering genes to make it impossible for one *variety* to reproduce with another.

In seeking a more concise definition of "species," perhaps the most important thing to bear in mind is that they occur at the *closure* of evolutionary streams. They are singularities that occur at end-points of phylogenesis. So for the purposes of this publication we offer the following definition:

Defined retroactively, species are end-points of phylogenesis.

Why do we need to define species *retroactively*? Because end-points of phylogenesis need to be distinguished from end-points in time, or what we call "the present." We can clearly identify certain species now extinct—the Hybodont shark, for example, which lived in the Early Jurassic period. But what about some existing sharks? Are we looking at a bonafide species, an end-point in phylogenesis? Or are we looking at a genus that is still evolving? To answer the question we would have to jump on a time machine, go thousand of years forward, and then look back to see if the particular shark had stopped evolving at the turn of the millennium.

How then are we to understand all the creatures that we see presently? Are they bonafide species because our own "present" happens to be the end-point of all that came in the past? Surely the reader can grasp the difficulty. Is *Homo sapiens* a bonafide species? Well, again, we would need a time-machine to go forward from here and try to see if our own particular evolutionary track (genus) had ended at the turn of the millennium.

We need to belabor the point because science depends on good definitions. Here is the nature of the problem. The stream of time has moved forward from the past to the terminus of the present. We find ourselves situated in the "present," which, from our temporal perspective, is the end-point of all of the evolution that came before. What does this mean? Does it mean that every creature living today is a bonafide species? The cladistician would answer, "Yes! Yes! Every group living today is a bonafide species!" But is this good science? No, because it may conflate two different taxa—genera that are still evolving today, and bonafide species that long ago stopped evolving but continue to survive.

This can be likened to a man walking on a railroad track found in episodes of *The Twilight Zone*. He can see the tracks behind him, but if he tries to look forward he will see a blurred quantum field. Are we, *Homo sapiens*, at an end-point in phylogenesis? Unknown. The tracks may continue forward for miles. Or we may indeed have reached the end of our line. We don't know, because our view of the future is obstructed. This is why we need to define species retroactively. This may also call for some additional fine-tuning. Perhaps we can talk about *bonafide species* and *tentative species*, as follows:

Bonafide Species—those whose end-points can be seen in the fossil record.
Tentative Species—those whose end-points cannot be seen in the record.

Species are not starting points. They are the end-points of all that came before. A species can only be found at the *end of the line*, being itself that terminal. An evolutionary stream doesn't yield a "species" until it has reached the end of the line. Each and every bonafide species is the end of a line.

An illustration. You want to go from point "A" to point "B" in London, England. You take the Underground subway train, knowing that you will have to get off at a certain station to change trains. But you fall asleep and miss your connection. An hour later you are awakened by the voice of the conductor—"End of the line! End of the line!" What are you going to do now? Well, there isn't much you can do. It is impossible to go *forward* or *sideways* from there to anywhere else. The only thing you can do is *go back* to the hub or junction, get off this track, get onto the right track, and then go *forward* again to your intended destination.

This train analogy is useful because we can describe the phylogenetic tree as a complicated system of tracks as well, each headed to a particular end-point or species. There are no bridges or missing links between bonafide species, because species only occur at the ends of the lines. You can only go *back* from a species to its genus, family or order, "change tracks," and then move forward again until you reach another species. You cannot crossover or transit "sideways" from species to species. There are no "missing links" between end-points.

It is said that the human mind has difficulty relating to abstract concepts, but can easily relate to pictures. Let us provide a picture in terms of the evolution of automobiles, where Volkswagen would be one species, and Chevrolet another. There are no "missing links" between Volkswagen and Chevrolet. Why not? Because they are *species* of automobiles. The only way in which you could "link" the Volkswagen species with the Chevrolet species would be to go back to their common genus, family, order, etc., say, back to the internal combustion engine, or even the Industrial Revolution itself. Likewise, there are no "missing links" between bonafide species. Bonafide species cannot "evolve" into other bonafide species—any more than a Volkswagen can "evolve" into a Chevy. End-points of phylogenesis cannot "evolve" into other end-points.

Species of whales and dolphins may have evolved from the same order, but not from one another. Chimps and people may have evolved from the same family, but not from one another. There are no forward or sideways links or bridges between species, each species being in a sense "sovereign." To transit from one bonafide species (end-point) to another bonafide species (end-point) you must retrace your steps on the tracks, get onto another track, and then go forward until you reach the very end. Obviously the hub or junction that you have to go back to will depend on the phylogenetic "distance" between the species. If the species are close—e.g., two similar mammals—you may only have to go back to the level of the genus. If the species are wider apart—birds and reptiles—you will have to go further back. Only by going back far enough and getting on a different "track" will you be able to move among the species.

Refer to the following representation again and use your imagination to explode it into a circle with *kingdom* at the center. Remember, each kingdom might lead to a multiplicity of phyla, each phylum to a multiplicity of classes, each class to a multiplicity of orders, each order to a multiplicity of families, each family to a multiplicity of genera, each genus to a multiplicity of species.

kingdom▸ phylum▸ class▸ order▸ family▸ genus ▸ species.

EXTINCTIONS AND "MISSING LINKS"

One problem that Darwin himself wrestled with had to do with the question of extinctions. Isn't Mother Nature supposed to be economical and parsimonious? Wouldn't she be better off dipping into the existing gene pool and resurrecting an old species—a tried and true design—instead of going into all the trouble of evolving a new species? The awkward question may be asked as to how species could ever become "extinct?" How could anything become "extinct" if all it had to do was to "evolve" into something else? Is there in fact such a thing as natural extinction, or are we merely looking at shape shifters? And if shape-shifters, then why do scientists keep telling us that 99% of all the species that ever lived are now extinct?

Whether we are talking about individual extinctions, or periodic mass extinctions, on the ordinary view the issue is problematic. On the sensible view that *bonafide species* are nothing but end-points of phylogenesis, the issue is elegant and clear. Extinct species don't come back to life because they are ends of lines. The absence of bonafide missing links confirms this. There are no missing links because bonafide species cannot "evolve" any further.

Darwin himself understood that if species were capable of evolving into other species, the number of intermediate links between them would have to be unimaginably large. But where are these intermediate links? There are none because bonafide species only occur only at the end of a line. Intermediate links can be found, but only back on the same track—between a species and its genus, for example. Here is Darwin wrestling with the same conundrum:

> I have found it difficult, when looking at any two species, to avoid picturing to myself forms *directly* intermediate between them. But this is a wholly false view; we should always look for forms intermediate between each species and a common but unknown progenitor; and the progenitor will generally have differed in some respects from all its modified descendants.[7]

Here is another useful analogy. Have you ever visited England and travelled on British Railways? If so you may recall the names of a few terminals in London. Paddington Station is one of them. Go to this station and you will see where the tracks actually end. Not to be confused with Piccadilly Circus, for example, which is just a stopping place, the tracks continue from there. Now imagine that both Piccadilly Circus and Paddington Station had been heavily damaged by bombs during World War II, and later rebuilt. When Paddington was rebuilt it was still the end of the line. When Piccadilly was rebuilt it was still the middle of the line. So then perhaps we can liken natural extinctions to Paddington Station and man-made extinctions to Piccadilly Circus. Perhaps dinosaurs didn't come back to life because their position on the phylogenetic tree was similar to that of Paddington Station—end of the line. Or perhaps the creatures forced into premature extinction by man *can* be brought back to life because their positions on the phylogenetic tree is similar to that of Piccadilly Circus.

This brings us to the *Jurassic Park* assumption. Can certain dinosaurs or other long-extinct species be resurrected if we obtain their DNA? This is like saying "give me the blueprint for Paddington Station and I will rebuild it on the surface of Mars." Paddington Station is a terminal within the integrated context of the myriad other tracks, branches and junctions that constitute British Railways. You can't rebuild Paddington Station independently of the entire British Railway System. Likewise you can't rebuild extinct dinosaurs independently of the entire phylogenetic tree.

Some species become extinct when the environments to which they had adapted suddenly change. Other creatures in similar circumstances do not become extinct but re-adapt, because they were not *bonafide species* to begin with—they were genera capable of further evolution. A genus can evolve into a species, but a species cannot evolve into a genus. It goes without saying, therefore, that a bonafide species is for all intents and purposes already extinct, even though, like some species of nautilus or shark, it may continue to survive for millions of years if nothing drastic happens to its environment.

NATURAL SELECTION

While the Constable is trying to make universal selections in favor of *increasing* entropy, Mother Nature is trying to make local selections in favor of *decreasing* entropy. The selections that she makes on behalf of living things are not "natural" from a cosmic point of view. So perhaps it would be better to refer to the evolutionary process as *genetic selection.* Likely that is what Darwin would have called it had he known what we now know about genes. But he called it *natural selection* and we will honor that for the time being.

What then are we to understand by "natural selection?" First we need to understand what Darwin described as *unnatural* or *man-made* selection, the sort of selections that are made by botanists, farmers, ranchers, cattle breeders, horse breeders, dog breeders, cat breeders and bird breeders.

An illustration. A cattle rancher is accidentally gored by a mean-spirited bull with exceptionally large and sharp horns, putting the rancher in the hospital for two weeks. Lying on his back in the hospital, the rancher vows to breed kindlier bulls with smaller, more innocuous horns. How would he do this? Simple, come breeding season he would "select-out" the bulls with the big sharp horns and "select-in" the ones with smaller, more blunt horns, not to mention kindlier dispositions. Presto, a few generations down the line his bulls have shorter, more benign horns. This would be "man-made," "artificial," or "unnatural selection." It is going on all over the world—farmers making selections in favor of healthier stock or more robust crops, grandma working in her garden making selections in favor of her favorite variety of rose, dog breeders making selections in favor their favorite Australian shepherd, cat breeders making selections in favor of their favorite Siamese, etc.. In principle, Darwinian natural selection is similar to the above, only it describes what will "naturally" survive in the wild, given a general environment in which entropy is increasing.

Take natural selection to be the mandate of the providential agency that we are now calling Mother Nature—the beautiful lady with the flowers in her hair. She has a duty to fill every nook and cranny of the planet with the exuberant variety of living things, in spite of every effort of the Constable to the contrary. In which case you can understand why she would want to make general selections in favor of healthiest and most robust genes—the bull with the strongest and sharpest horns, the horse with the strongest legs, the eagle with the most powerful wings, etc.. That the fittest, most durable, most resilient and most adaptable of creatures would have a better chance of withstanding the shenanigans of the Cosmic Constable is a foregone conclusion. That Mother Nature would want to equip all creatures for *survival* should come as no surprise.

But what are we to understand by the *struggle for survival*? If entropy were not increasing there would be no such struggle. But because entropy is always increasing, (because graded energy gets de-graded upon use and can never be fully re-graded), there must eventually arise the principles of competition that Darwin describes as "struggle for existence," or "survival of the fittest." Otherwise why should survival be an issue at all? Exactly what is it that living things are trying to survive? What is the contrary principle that would drive them into extinction?

The contrary principle is of course increasing entropy. The graded energy required to sustain *complexity* gets degraded into entropy upon use and cannot always be recycled. There is competition because living resources are limited. Granted Mother Nature has a marvelous way of squeezing every ounce of biological *complexity* out of every joule of graded energy, but there are limits to what she can do without violating the fundamental laws of the universe. And these are precisely the limits that trigger the mechanisms of natural selection. Evolution requires living things to make the most efficient use of available resources. Those that do will be selected for survival. Those that don't, for extinction. The ontology of survival is rooted in the principle of increasing entropy. The entropy tax must be paid to the Cosmic Constable, leaving something over to survive on. Those that use what's left over efficiently will survive. Those that don't won't.

Granted that the earth is an open system receiving massive infusions of generic energy from the sun, but unless Mother Nature can up-grade generic energy into something that creatures can "eat," it won't amount to a hill of beans (pun intended). Green things upgrade sunlight into complex carbon compounds suitable for consumption by higher life forms, but those higher life-forms degrade it upon use. Mother Nature is clever, economical, efficient and resourceful, but her hands are tied by the cosmic imperative.

Life is not a function of energy alone. Had that been the case we'd be looking for abiogenesis at the receiving end of the accelerator at Fermilab. Life is a function of a highly specific combination of matter, energy, and information—*complexity*. Life requires a specific grade of energy, just as an automobile or aircraft may require a specific grade of fuel. The more complex life forms require higher grades, and vice versa. The phylogenetic tree had to start with organisms that could grade the energy of the sun or the energy of the earth itself. The earliest deep sea organisms, or surface algae-like organisms may have started this "grading" process, aided by general photosynthesis later on. Photosynthesis is fundamental to earthly life, up-grading the generic energy arriving from the sun into complex carbon molecules that can serve as "food" for higher life forms.

For each species the supply of specifically graded energy is limited. This limits the extent to which that species can prosper and multiply; granted Mother Nature makes sure nothing gets wasted; granted one creature's degraded energy ("waste") may provide a feast for a lower life form. But the living order overseen by Mother Nature assumes an ongoing degradation of graded energy ("food") in its various forms. This can only lead to the struggle for existence that is the basis of natural selection. The whole economy of Mother Nature is energy-driven. She makes selections in favor of those creatures that *make the most efficient use of energy in a general environment in which entropy is increasing.*

Although the universal imperative of increasing entropy was either unknown or unclear to Darwin himself, the great naturalist was nevertheless keenly aware of its implications in terms of what he himself called *the struggle for existence*:

> Before entering on the subject of this chapter, I must make a few preliminary remarks, to show how the struggle for existence bears on Natural Selection.... All these results, as we shall more fully see in the next chapter, follow from the struggle for life. Owing to this struggle, variations, however slight and from whatever cause proceeding, if they be in any degree profitable to the individuals of a species... will generally be inherited by the offspring.... I have called this principle, by which each slight variation, if useful, is preserved, by the term Natural selection, in order to mark its relation to man's power of [unnatural] selection....
>
> We will now discuss in a little more detail the struggle for existence.... Nothing is easier than to admit in words the truth of the universal struggle for life, or more difficult—at least I have found it so—than constantly to bear this conclusion in mind. Yet unless it be thoroughly engrained in the mind, the whole economy of nature, with every fact on distribution, rarity, abundance, extinction, and variation, will be dimly seen or quite misunderstood.[8]

The whole economy of Mother Nature—the whole evolutionary process—presupposes a frame of reference in which entropy is increasing and there is only so much graded energy to go around. That Mother Nature would want to make selections in favor of the creatures that are most efficient in the use of graded energy is a foregone conclusion, because even Mother Nature has to obey the fundamental laws of the universe. Graded energy is everything. If it is available species will survive. If not they will perish. Generally, those that make efficient use of what is available will be selected for survival, and those that don't will be selected for extinction. (All things considered, and everything else being equal.)

VARIATION

As the reader can readily see, *variation* is the other half of natural selection. There must be some genetic variety for Mother Nature to pick and choose from. Natural selection will not work without variation. If all bulls are genetically identical no natural selection would be possible. As Darwin explains:

> As many more individuals of each species are born that can possibly survive; and as, consequently, there is a frequently recurring struggle for existence, it follows that any being, if it vary however slightly in any manner profitable to itself, under the complex and sometimes varying conditions of life, will have a better chance of surviving, and thus be *naturally selected.* [9]

We can assume that God's *biologos* provides for variation, but how? A difficult question, in answer to which scientists make do with something they call "random mutations." Perhaps a century from now scientists will be able to provide a more detailed answer. Darwin himself was quick to admit his own ignorance of what he called *laws of variation*:

> Our ignorance of the laws of variation is profound. Not in one case out of a hundred can we pretend to assign any reason why this or that part has varied. [10]

DNA was unknown in Darwin's day. How many DNA replications have there been since the beginning of creation? The number must be mind-boggling! The copying process involves splitting the DNA strand. In principle it can be likened to copying information from one floppy disk to another, and another, and another. Imagine doing that billions of times without errors cropping up. Assume that errors would crop up, likely a few bits of information missing here and there. Given the gazillion-trillion DNA copies that must have been made since the beginning of creation, copying errors would be inevitable. Say, simple mechanical errors caused by environmental factors. They would be very rare, but they would happen. Scientists assume that these errors might have provided Mother Nature with something to pick and choose from. But can *errors* provide a basis for beneficial selections? Errors, and accumulations of errors, would tend to be injurious to evolution. Think of it. Can you see Mother Nature trying to make selections between this or that "error?" Think of it in terms of our floppy disk analogy. Can you see Mother Nature trying to improve the quality of her software by picking and choosing from floppy disks containing errors?

Let us assume that the Creator of the universe anticipated these errors, and in fact used them as the very basis of natural selection. How would that work? It might work something like this. When a copy of DNA is missing a few bits of information, an internal program will detect the error and try to repair it by way of logical "splice-ins." Is this so far fetched? No, even today's computer utilities perform such tasks routinely, automatically "fixing" a corrupted file structure, or using some sort of logic to "fill in" what might be missing, or at the very least providing the user with prompts to the effect that the file was not copied properly.

You would expect the quality of the *biologos* written by the Creator of the universe to be infinitely higher than that of the computer software written by mortal programmers. If fallible human beings can write programs that can "check and fix" copying errors, the Creator of the universe can do the same thing on a far higher order of magnitude and perfection. Assume that the quality of the information contained in DNA is so high that it will detect and try to "fix" copying errors. How? Presently unknown. We are only just now beginning to understand the human genome. Notwithstanding our ignorance, perhaps the blueprint of God forces the DNA to splice in a few additional bits of information along lines of a given logic structure.

And so we might speculate that DNA is capable of detecting copying errors, and repairing them by logical "fill-ins" or "add-ons." These add-ons, fill-ins, or splice-ins, may in fact be identical to what's missing. OR, they may be ever so slightly different. Those slightly different bytes of information would then afford the *variation* that could serve as a basis for natural selection. The tiny little bit that is different in the copied DNA would give Mother Nature something to "select" if she thought it beneficial to the survival and improvement of the stock. Notwithstanding, there must at all times be *reproduction and variation*, otherwise there will be no evolution possible. Darwin's own words:

> Natural selection acts solely through the preservation of variations in some way advantageous, which consequently endure. [11]
>
> Slow though the process of selection may be, if feeble man can do much by artificial selection, I can see no limit to the amount of change, to the beauty and complexity of the coadaptations between all organic beings, one with another and with their physical conditions of life, which may have been effected in the long course of time through nature's power of selection, that is by the survival of the fittest.[12]
>
> Natural Selection acts exclusively by the preservation and accumulation of variations, which are beneficial under the organic and inorganic conditions to which each creature is exposed at all periods of life. [13]
>
> The mind cannot possibly grasp the full meaning of the term of even a million years; it cannot add up and perceive the full effects of many slight variations, accumulated during an almost infinite number of generations.[14]

Unless blinded by religious animus, the reader will marvel at the elegance and perfection of the *automatic* and *efficient* process whereby the Creator has invested the earth with the potential to bring forth the exuberant variety of living things through the mechanism of evolution. Truly, He has made the cup of life to run over everywhere on earth.

THE FUNDAMENTAL DARWIN

Scientists posit "theories" in the hope that they can be refined, improved, modified, falsified or shot down. This is the nature of the scientific discipline—float a trial balloon and see what comes of it. Granted that the evolutionary balloon has run into many problems. "Gradualism," for example, has been replaced by something called "punctuated equilibrium." Notwithstanding, Darwin's fundamental theory of *evolution* is a scientific description of the principles, laws and mechanisms whereby the Creator has filled every nook and cranny of the blue planet earth with the exuberant variety of living things. At this point we would ask the reader to turn to the opening verses of Genesis once again, where the Creator is found investing the earth with a potential to "bring forth" the exuberant variety of living things. The words *let the earth bring forth* are clear and unambiguous. Nowhere does the Bible describe God as saying, "Let Me create millions of species one at a time!" No, those opening passages describe God as investing the earth with the potential to bring forth the exuberant variety of living things *automatically*, (without further manual input on the part of the Creator). Does the Fundamental Darwin try to repudiate this? No he does not. The Fundamental Darwin tries to repudiate what might be called *A Theory of Special Creation.*

To help the reader to understand what we mean by *A Theory of Special Creation* we offer the following analogy. Let us imagine that we are in the Potter's house, and there, sitting at the wheel, is the Creator of the universe, thumping away at the clay, working it, shaping it, the wheel spinning, spinning, spinning. He labors unceasingly, and finally creates a single species. He takes the species, puts it away in the closet, comes back to the wheel, takes a new lump of clay, throws it on the wheel, and goes to work again to create another species. He labors and labors, thumping away at the clay, working it, shaping it and fashioning it, the wheel spinning, spinning. Finally He creates a second species. He takes the second work, puts it away in the closet, comes back to the wheel, takes a new lump of clay, throws it on the wheel and, starting from scratch, goes to work to create the third species.

There are said to be some 200,000 species of beetles on the planet earth. What then? Did God create them one at a time? This is the question that the Fundamental Darwin is asking. Those who answer "yes," subscribe to *A Theory of Special Creation.* Are they right? Common sense would indicate that God would not have to repeat the same mundane labor 200,000 times in order to create 200,000 species of bugs. He could write the *biologos* that would bring forth the exuberant variety *automatically* and without special input on His own part. Isn't this how we would do it?

Granted that "automatically" does not imply the absence of a Creator, as some atheists might imagine. Granted that those who want to "un-God" the universe would also want to view the fossil record through rose-colored glasses, seeing an automated process and crying, "Ah ha! You see, there is no God!" (This is like someone seeing a computer performing automated tasks and imagining that the computer had created itself.) But this is not what the Fundamental Darwin is saying—Darwin was not an atheist. In essence the Fundamental Darwin is saying that the creation of millions of species need not have required millions of insulated, separate and *special* acts of God. An omnipotent God could just as easily have caused the *aggregate* of living things to be brought forth via secondary causation—the principles and mechanisms of "evolution." Here are Darwin's own words, (emphasis added):

> Until recently the great majority of naturalists believed that species were immutable productions, and had been *separately* created. [15]

> Where many species of a genus have been formed through variation, circumstances have been favourable for variation; and hence we might expect that the circumstances would generally be still favourable to variation. On the other hand, if we look at each species as a *special* act of creation, there is no apparent reason why more varieties should occur in a group having many species, than in one having few. [16]

> It is a truly wonderful fact—the wonder of which we are apt to overlook from familiarity—that all animals and all plants throughout all time and space should be related to each other in groups, subordinate to groups, in the manner which we everywhere behold.... If species had been *independently* created, no explanation would have been possible of this kind of classification; but it is explained through inheritance and the complex action of natural selection, entailing extinction and divergence of character....[17]

> When we see any part of organ developed in a remarkable degree or manner in a species, the fair presumption is that it is of high importance to that species: nevertheless it is in this case eminently liable to variation. Why would this be so? On the view that each species has been *independently* created, with all its parts as we now see them, I can see no explanation. But on the view that groups of species are

descended from some other species, and have been modified through natural selection, I think we can obtain some light. [18]

He who believes that each equine species was *independently* created will, I presume, assert that each species has been created with a tendency to vary, both under nature and under domestication, in this particular manner, so as often to become striped like the other species of the genus.... To admit this view is, as it seems to me, to reject a real for an unreal, or at least for an unknown cause. It makes the works of God a mere mockery and deception; [19]

He who believes in *separate* and innumerable acts of creation may say, that in these cases it has pleased the Creator to cause a being of one type to take the place of one being to another type; but this seems to me only re-stating the fact in dignified language. He who believes in the struggle for existence and in the principle of natural selection will acknowledge that every organic being is constantly endeavouring to increase its numbers; and that if any one being varies ever so little, either in habits or structure, and thus gains an advantage over some other inhabitant of the same country, it will seize on the place of the inhabitant, however different that may be from its own place. Hence it will cause him no surprise that there should be geese and frigate birds with webbed feet, living on the dry land and rarely alighting on the water, that there should be long-toed corncrakes, living in meadows instead of in swamps; that there should be woodpeckers where hardly a tree grows; that there should be diving thrushes and diving Hymenoptera, and petrels with the habits of auks.[20]

A volcanic island, for instance, upheaved and formed at the distance of a few hundreds of miles from a continent, would probably receive from it in the course of time a few colonists, and their descendants, though modified, would still be related by inheritance to the inhabitants of that continent. Cases of this nature are common, and are, as we shall hereafter see, inexplicable on the theory of *independent* creation. [21]

Why, it may be asked, has the supposed creative force produced bats and no other mammals on remote islands? On my view this question can easily be answered; for no terrestrial mammal can be transported across a wide space of sea, but bats can fly across. Bats have been seen wondering by day far over the Atlantic Ocean; and two North American species either regularly or occasionally visit Bermuda, at the distance of 600 miles from the mainland.... Hence we have only to suppose that such wandering species have been modified in their new homes in relation to their new position...[22]

Rudimentary organs may be compared with the letters in a word, still retained in the spelling, but become useless in the pronunciation, but which serve as a clue for its derivation. On the view of descent with modification, we may conclude that the existence of organs in a rudimentary, imperfect and useless condition, or quite aborted, far from presenting a strange difficulty, as they assuredly do on the old doctrine of creation, might even have been anticipated in accordance with the view here explained. [23]

How inexplicable on the theory of [*special*] creation is the occasional appearance of stripes on the shoulders and legs of the several species of the horse-genus and of their hybrids! How simply is this fact explained if we believe that these species are all descended from a striped progenitor, in the same manner as the several domestic breeds of pigeon are descended from the blue and barred rock-pigeon! [24]

On this view of each organism with all its parts having been *specially* created, how utterly inexplicable is it that organs bearing the plain stamp of inutility, such as the teeth in the embryonic calf or the shrivelled wings under the soldered wing-covers of many beetles, should so frequently occur. [25]

I see no good reason why the view given in this volume should shock the religious feelings of any one.... A celebrated author and divine has written to me that "he has gradually learnt to see that it is just as noble a conception

> of the Deity to believe that He created a few original forms capable of self-development into other and needed forms, as to believe that He required a fresh act of creation to supply the voids caused by the action of His laws." [26]

What then is the Fundamental Darwin trying to tell us? Perhaps he is trying to tell us something like this:

> Do you believe that the Creator caused the exuberant variety of living things to be brought forth on earth? If so, don't insult Him by your ignorance of the mechanisms by which He caused them to be brought forth!

Much of the force of the theological objection to the Fundamental Darwin rests on something other than evidence or truth. There is presently an unhealthy tendency among many religious folks to engage in what the British call "picking up fag-ends," (picking up cigarette butts left by others and smoking them). Someone picks up religious gossip on the internet, puts his own twist on it, and before you know it misinformation has assumed the stature of religious dogma. This is known as "hearsay"—something based on gossip and innuendo.

Speaking of gossip and innuendo, much fuss has been made, for example, of the complex organ of the eye. Or rather, something that someone else said about the "irreducible complexity" of the eye. In closing let us take a look at what Darwin has to say about it:

> To suppose that the eye with all its inimitable contrivances for adjusting the focus to different distances, for admitting different amounts of light, and for the correction of spherical and chromatic aberration, could have been formed by natural selection, seems, I freely confess, absurd in the highest degree. When it was first said that the sun stood still and the world turned around, the common sense of mankind declared the doctrine false; but the old saying of *Vox populi, vox Dei*, as every philosopher knows, cannot be trusted in science. Reason tells me, that if numerous gradations from a simple and imperfect eye to one complex and perfect can be shown to exist, each grade being useful to its possessor, as is certainly the case; if

> further, the eye ever varies and the variations be inherited, as is likewise certainly the case; and if such variations should be useful to any animal under changing conditions of life, then the difficulty of believing that a perfect and complex eye could be formed by natural selection, though insuperable by our imagination, should not be considered as subversive of the theory.[27]

There are millions of eye configurations on our planet, embodying different levels of *complexity*, having differing functions, different structures, different purposes, different shapes, etc.. From simple membrane-blobs on micro-organisms that do nothing but react to light, to the more purposeful eyes found on primitive insects, to the magnificent faceted eye of a common house fly, to the "perfect" eye of a human being, there are millions of different configurations. What then? Did God create all of them one at a time? Or did He encode an ideally efficient program that would produce the entire range as necessary? And how are we to explain the non-functioning eyes of creatures that have adapted themselves to living in dark caves? Or the perfectly formed but useless eyes found on fish living in dark depths thousands of feet below the surface of the sea? Did God create these by *special* acts of creation as well? Did He do so absentmindedly, putting eyes on creatures that have absolutely no need for them?

To say that God created all eyes one at a time by special acts of creation is to mock the wisdom of the Creator. If God can call the universe into existence out of nothing, He can also write the *biologos* that can yield something as complex as a human eye in due season. Darwin came close to discovering the superlative order and economy that might underlie that *biologos*. The fact that some devil in human nature has tried to pervert Darwin's legacy is no excuse to throw the baby out with the bathwater. Believers need to stop making irrational judgments based on gossip, animus, emotion and prejudice. Granted that we all want to strike a blow for the Bible, but unless we know what we are talking about we may end up shooting ourselves in the foot, not to mention making Christianity and Judaism the laughing stock of the world.

וַיֹּאמֶר יְהוָה אֶל־אַבְרָם לֶךְ־לְךָ מֵאַרְצְךָ וּמִמּוֹלַדְתְּךָ
וּמִבֵּית אָבִיךָ אֶל־הָאָרֶץ אֲשֶׁר אַרְאֶךָּ׃ וְאֶעֶשְׂךָ לְגוֹי גָּדוֹל
וַאֲבָרֶכְךָ וַאֲגַדְּלָה שְׁמֶךָ וֶהְיֵה בְּרָכָה...וַיֵּלֶךְ אַבְרָם
כַּאֲשֶׁר דִּבֶּר אֵלָיו יְהוָה.

Now the LORD said unto Abram, "Go from your country, and from your kindred and your father's house to the land that I will show you. And I will make of you a great nation, and I will bless you, and make your name great, and you will be a blessing..." And Abram went forth, as the LORD had told him.

(Genesis 12:1-4)

SECTION 4

Cosmos and Idolatry

Babylon the Great

The Ten Commandments of God begin with two prohibitions against gross idolatry and end with eight that warn against subtle forms of idolatry. The command against idolatry is the one most repeated in the Bible. Rav Shaul equates any sin with idolatry in Colossians 3:5. But what are we to understand by "idolatry?" We can break the word down into its components: idol + *latry*, from a Greek term meaning "to serve." What does God mean when He says "you shall not *serve* idols"?

לְֹא־תִשְׁתַּחֲוֶה לָהֶם וְלֹא תָעָבְדֵם

You shall not bow down to them, and you shall not serve them.
(Exodus 20:5)

Let us use the magnifying glass of the New Testament to try to understand what the Holy Spirit is saying. Here are the words of Rav Shaul, addressed to the formative church in Rome:

> Do you not know that to whatever you yield yourselves as slaves to obey, his slaves you are to whom you serve, whether of sin unto death, or of obedience unto righteousness?
>
> (Romans 6:16)

On reflection it can be seen that the Holy Spirit is warning against some form of conformity. But what is it that God does not want us to conform to? The answer would have to be something existential. Something "natural," universal and derivative. It would make no sense to find God cautioning us not to conform to something imaginary or unreal. It would make all the sense in the world to find God cautioning us not to conform to something existent and real, some hazard to which we ourselves remain blind by reason of the "catch-22" that we mentioned in the beginning of this publication.

It is one thing for material things to conform to the directive of the Constable. It is another thing for the spirit of Man to conform to the directive of the Constable. It is one thing when matter and energy "bow down and serve" the universal imperative of increasing entropy. It is another thing when the spirit of Man does the same thing. It is one thing for the material universe to undergo corruption. It is another when the spirit of Man undergoes corruption. God will not suffer the spirit of Man to conform to the rudiments of the perishable universe.

Come with me to the surface of the moon where we can obtain a better perspective. Here we are, standing on the surface of the moon, just like Neil Armstrong. Look at the cold and indifferent behavioral field of the cosmos all around you: do you see all the planets, stars and galaxies being slowly and inexorably eroded by the Cosmic Constable? Now look at that tiny blue planet housing mankind. Do you see the Constable trying to do the same thing to the human condition? Look beyond all the surface clamor and confusion of history and you will see the Constable trying to move the human condition towards higher entropy states, just like everything else in the universe. Has he had any success? The magnitude of the disorder cataloged in history bears witness to his success. This is what happens when the spirit of Man conforms to the rudiments of the perishable universe. This is what God warns against. This is what the Bible calls "idolatry."

The derivative and pagan frame of existence that predates the Judeo-Christian frame is an anthropomorphization of the universal imperative of increasing entropy. We need to understand that the Judeo-Christian frame is not the existential norm. That classification belongs to the much older, derivative, idolatrous, pagan, materialistic, elemental, pantheistic and atheistic models of existence. The Judeo-Christian frame is the *exception* to the universal rule. The guiding principles of Judeo-Christian morality run deeply against the grain of the cosmos, urging mankind to apply the spiritual brakes and resist the temptation to go with the flow. The guiding principles of paganism conform to the grain of cosmos, urging mankind to throw off all restraint and go with the flow. Even the present culture war pits those who would go with the cosmic flow against those who would resist it. Predictably those who refuse to go with the flow are once again being cursed by those who would. But we must remind ourselves that the present culture war is as old as history itself.

AVRAM

It is unthinkable that an omnipotent and all-knowing God would bring Man into a cosmos such as this without making provision for his deliverance and salvation. God's plan of salvation began with the election of the patriarch *Avram*. Most Biblical names have profound meanings. *Avram* is the noun form of a Hebrew verb meaning "to pass over," or in this case, "to walk on the opposite side of conformity." This is how the Bible describes the patriarch of the three sister religions, *Avram*, the one who walked on the opposite side of conformity. The wandering Aramean who made his exodus from the derivative orders of existence and went looking for the superlative order of the Kingdom of God. One might say that Avram was the first "revolutionary" or "non-conformist" to try to break free of the boundary conditions of cosmos and pass over into the sanctuary of the Kingdom of God.

Avram made his exodus out of a Sumerian city-state founded on the worship of cosmos—sun, moon and stars. Scripture tells us that he went looking for "a city which hath foundations whose builder and maker is God," (Hebrews 11:10). Sumerian civilization was patterned after the rudiments of the perishable universe, deriving its nature, orientation, spirit and mind from all things cosmic. Life in Ur was wholly cosmos-derivative, nothing like the Judeo-Christian civilization we know. Ur conformed itself to the cycles of the sun, moon and stars, transforming "cosmos" into every form of idolatry imaginable. Sumerian life took the form of one repetition after another. Individuality was unknown. The whole of human existence was some banal and wretched anthropomorphization of cosmos. In a sense men and women were worshipping the Cosmic Constable, paying homage and blood sacrifice to him via pagan rituals carried out by temple prostitute-priests. Sexual perversion was a way of life. Every activity was a glorification of the "cosmic man" imbecility—the fertility machine operated by capricious, narcisstic, psychotic and oversexed "gods."

It was in this context that the Word of God came to Avram commanding him to make his exodus out of the derivative forms of existence. Avram obeyed God. The Hebrew words **וַיֵּלֶךְ אַבְרָם** ("and Avram went forth") signal a complete departure from everything that was done in the corporate history of the human race. What happened to the patriarch Abraham was unique, and history has never been the same since. His exodus out of Ur was the beginning of the spiritual exodus of mankind out of elemental conformity. It marked the beginning of the end of the Constable's dominion over the human spirit. It marked the beginning of the end of derivative civilizations.

In the Biblical story of Abraham we are looking at one of the greatest turning points in the history of mankind. An enormous value shift. Up to the time of Abraham the spiritual underpinnings of human civilization were derived from the rudiments of the perishable universe, or what might be called "the great cosmic wheel." In essence, pagan civilizations had "cosmic" foundations. One might say that all of them went round and round that cosmic wheel. However in the first two books of the Bible a new value system emerges whereby mankind is no longer the hamster in the cosmic wheel. Avram makes his exodus out of Sumer and there is a spiritual bifurcation. A sea change, a tectonic shift. Formerly human civilization was derivative. Now it is *authentic*. Formerly man went round and round the cosmic wheel. Now, he is endowed with a measure of spiritual independence, autonomy and authenticity.

Avram's non-conformist life was the archetype of everything that is authentic and human, as opposed to everything that is banal, elemental, derivative, mindless and mechanical. What Avram did was very significant indeed. We have to remember that there was no Bible at the time, no spiritual chart or compass to rely on, nothing to use as a reference for navigation other than *trust* in the Person of God. And that is precisely the *faith* that God credited to Avram as "righteousness." That is why God made His covenant with him and changed his name to *Avraham*—father of many nations.

By faith Avram obeyed God, turning away from the derivative towards the authentic. He broke free of the cosmic wheel and passed over into the dominion of the Kingdom of God. Centuries later his descendants would do the same thing on that terrible night of the *Passover* in Egypt. Centuries later still, *Yeshua* would break bread on the night of a later *Passover*, preparatory to another exodus leading to a New Covenant.

The non-conformity of the patriarch Abraham was the archetype of Judeo-Christian morality. However the derivative order of existence did not get extinguished when Avram left Ur of the Chaldees; it did not get extinguished when Israel broke free of Egyptian bondage; it did not even cease to exist with the advent of Christianity. It is, even today, the existential "default" that lies just below the surface of any society, looking for an excuse or opportunity to come out of the closet. The temptation is always there for societies to revert to the rudiments of the perishable universe. Postmodern society is reverting as we speak.

ARETZ ISRAEL (LAND OF ISRAEL)

In establishing the children of Israel in their own land, God sanctified and separated them, cautioning them not to revert to the pagan conventions of the nations round about. For a little while they obeyed God, but then began backsliding. God sent His prophets and seers to warn them not to revert to the derivative modes of existence. But they stoned His prophets and broke His Covenant. Later when they had fallen into hopeless apostasy God divorced the northern kingdom of Israel in the Diaspora of 721 B.C. The southern kingdom of Judah lasted a little while longer, but also backslid and was taken captive into Babylon circa 510 B.C. Thus the *two witnesses* of the Kingdom of God (Israel and Judah) were separated, the former sown among the nations and disappeared from history, the latter in exile and in Babylon. At that time God permitted the rise of a wholesale derivative order that is referred to in the Bible as *Babylon the Great*—a descriptive name for a world system patterned after the rudiments of the perishable universe. The generic term *Babylon* has since come to describe the succession of derivative empires that we can now identify as Babylon, Medo-Persia, Greece, Imperial Rome, and the Holy Roman Empire.

In the seed of Abraham, God chose and set aside a Kingdom of His own, to begin man's arduous climb out of the derivative order of existence. He chose the twelve tribes of Israel and entered into a covenant with them, spelling out the terms of His contract in the 26th chapter of Leviticus. Israel was to champion the cause of Man against the Cosmic Constable. Israel was to serve as a beacon for mankind, a clear demonstration—an exemplar—of the blessings that would accrue to a nation if it conformed to the superlative order of God. Circa 721 B.C. Israel was divorced of God in accordance with the terms of the covenant. Circa 510 B.C. Judah was taken into exile into Babylon. At that time the Kingdom of God went "underground," where it would remain for many centuries before re-emerging. With the Kingdom of God underground, the ball ended up in the Constable's court by default, and the world began to bow down to him in earnest. Thus did the devil of disorder lay claim to the kingdoms of the world, setting up his idol over the human race to demand a ransom in elemental conformity. A succession of derivative empires came to wax and wane on earth, each one conquering and homogenizing the known world. This succession was the subject of the dream that God visited on the Babylonian emperor Nebuchadnezzar.

The great king Nebuchadnezzar, "brother of the sun and conqueror of the nations," had a terrible dream one night. A frightful dream, full of omen and foreboding. He was so disturbed by it that he could hardly eat or drink for many days. None of his diviners could recall the dream, let alone interpret it. He was about to put all of them to death when the exiled Jew, Daniel, came forward with a Providential interpretation. Daniel informed the king that the dream was a revelation of the empires that would wax and wane on earth. He told the king that he, Nebuchadnezzar, would be the ruler of the first such world governing empire, but that his would not be the last—Imperial Babylon would be followed by a succession of other world-homogenizing powers.

The image that the king had seen in his dream was that of a dreadful statue with a head of gold, breast and arms of silver, belly and thighs of bronze, legs of iron, and feet made of a mixture of iron and clay. Biblical scholars now agree that the various elements were representative of the derivative empires that would wax and wane in the absence of God's authentic Kingdom. The head of gold was Babylon itself. The breast and arms of silver were Medo-Persia. The belly and thighs of bronze were Greece. The legs of iron were Imperial Rome, and the feet of part iron and part clay were the Holy Roman Empire.

The transition from gold to clay is surely significant, describing a principle of devaluation that is the essence of increasing entropy:

$$\text{gold} \mapsto \text{silver} \mapsto \text{bronze} \mapsto \text{iron} \mapsto \text{clay}$$

Through Nebuchadnezzar's dream, the prophet Daniel was given a vision of the derivative nature of the empires that would rule the earth, having for their head one prototype referred to as *Babylon the Great.* One idol would describe their character, constitution and modus operandi. One elemental impetus would underlie all of them. They would all have the same "family tree," cut from the same elemental cloth. Although layered upon one another, and seemingly different in appearance, these empires would be integral components of one world system standing on feet of clay, symbolic of the weak and beggarly rudiments of the perishable universe.

With proper hindsight we can now see that the statue was representative of what we are now calling "Cosmic Constable." Nebuchadnezzar's dream heralded the arrival of the Constable's rule on earth, the hidden and mysterious power to which all state authorities would be subject, drawing from it their characteristic marks of idolatry, paganism, injustice, tyranny and oppression. Many empires but one orientation. Many powers but a uniformity of purpose and agenda rooted in the universal imperative of increasing entropy.

Babylon levelled and homogenized all the regions it conquered, crushing any who would not conform. Ditto Persia. Ditto Greece. Imperial Rome was a meatgrinder with "teeth of iron," (Daniel 7:19; Revelation 9:8), homogenizing all the regions it conquered on pain of torture and crucifixion. The latter Rome forced spiritual conformity on pain of anathema, imprisonment, torture, and excommunication. All of these world-governing empires lived and died by the sword.

Regardless of their aspirations to liberty, regardless of their pomp and circumstance, regardless of their pious follies and noble vanities, all of them were homogenization machines. All were cosmos-derivative. All spread their oppressive yokes throughout the existing world like plagues. All were ruthless practitioners of ethnic cleansing. It was their policy to level ethnic differences, if not by sword and fagot, then by wholesale depopulation. All behaved like the Constable himself, leveling and reducing the cultural gradients of the human race in utter disregard of human rights. Though determined not to be slaves themselves, they used every barbaric measure to enslave and reduce others. One might say that all of these empires had stony hearts. All behaved like "beasts," and are described as such in the Book of Revelation.

This was to be *Babylon the Great*, supreme anthropomorphization of the universal imperative of increasing entropy. A succession of derivative civilizations conforming to the nature of the cosmos in heart, in mind, and in spirit. *Yeshua* refers to this 2500-year succession as "the times of the gentiles":

> And they shall fall by the edge of the sword, and shall be led away captive into all nations: and Jerusalem shall be trodden down of the Gentiles, until *the times of the Gentiles* be fulfilled.
>
> (Luke 21:24, emphasis added)

This is the Great Controversy that we see throughout history, the constant tug of war between two radically opposed modes of existence, one derivative, the other authentic. Two radically opposed factions, one trying to revert to the derivative modes of existence, the other trying to make the quantum jump to the Kingdom of God. Babylon the Great vs the Kingdom of God.

Even today the Great Controversy pits the ideal of the Kingdom of God against the idol of the cosmos itself. Many atheists, for example, venerate cosmos, claiming that "cosmos is all that there ever was, is, or ever will be." Predictably "cosmos" has also become the great idol of the New Age Movement. Some of the adherents of New Age believe that "the universe is trying to express itself through us." Many New Age cults are looking for ways of achieving "cosmic consciousness," or becoming seamlessly integrated with cosmos, not realizing that this is what happens in the course of physical death. Some New Age cults have reputedly committed mass suicide in the effort to become one with the universe.

MACCABEEAN REVOLT

The tensions that led to the Maccabeean Revolt were rooted in the same Great Controversy, the Jews of Jerusalem representing the Abrahamic order, the pagans of Antiochus IV Epiphanes the derivative order. Circa 168 B.C. these idolators occupied Jerusalem and began insinuating themselves into the affairs of the Second Temple. They set up idols and began offering sacrifices to Heracles (Hercules). By their sacrificing, feasting, debauchery, immorality and perversion, these idolators tried to reduce the Temple of God into a pagan brothel. The final insult, for which Antiochus IV Epiphanes deserves the pun *abomination*, was the sacrifice of a pig on the Temple Altar.

At that time a group of courageous men banded together under the leadership of Judah Maccabee. In the epic revolt that followed, the Rebel Alliance defeated the pagans, drove them out of Jerusalem, and restored the convention of the Kingdom of God. Having done so, the Maccabeeans then undertook the sacred task of cleansing the Temple and re-lighting the Temple Menorah, the many-branched lampstand that has since become a symbol of Liberty for believers throughout the world. At that time God also smiled upon the occasion by a sign and a wonder: only one cruse of pure olive oil could be found for the Menorah, but that small quantity burned miraculously for eight days.

Jews celebrate the triumph of the Rebel Alliance by way of a joyous festival called *Hanukkah*. Also known as *Festival of Lights*, Hanukkah commemorates the restoration of the convention of the Kingdom of God and the re-dedication of the Temple in 165 B.C., after it had been profaned by Antiochus IV Epiphanes. Curiously, the restoration took place on a date corresponding to December 25 on the Gregorian calendar. That Christians and Jews celebrate superlative affirmations of Liberty about the same time is surely significant—the Maccabeean Revolt restored the convention that would later evolve into the moral character of Christendom.

Notwithstanding, the derivative order that began with Imperial

Babylon continued to wax and wane uninterrupted, Imperial Rome re-inventing the old idols and sinking to new lows. Baal became Zeus and the elemental imperative resurfaced with a vengeance, figuring prominently in all of Rome's infamous cruelties, perversions and debaucheries. Thousands of innocent Jews and Christians suffered unimaginable tortures at the hands of perverse, sadistic, psychotic, neurotic, mattoid and lunatic emperors like Nero. About that time the Cosmic Constable set about the business of trying to corrupt the new religion as well.

The Great Apostasy began with the nominal "conversion" of Constantine in the 4th century, at which time a flood of paganism entered the church, bringing with it customs, practices and idols which were merely changed into the icons of Jesus and Mary. Precedent by precedent the backsliding gained strength, paving the way for pagan doctrines, rites, observances, vain ceremonies, cabalism, spiritism and priestcraft, corrupting the Great Commission beyond recognition. The dictatorship of the *anthropos* (translated "man of sin" in 2 Thessalonians 2:3) began in the sixth century when a powerbase was established in the imperial city of Rome and the bishop of Rome was declared supreme pontiff over the entire world. In the figurative language of Revelation, *the dragon gave to the beast his power, and his seat and great authority* (Revelation 13:2). Here, the *dragon* would be a figure of the Cosmic Constable, and the *beast* would be a figure of his derivative order.

And so entered Europe into the Dark Ages foretold in the prophecies of Daniel and John—1260 years of religious oppression under the yoke of a system wearing the disguise of "Christianity." In Revelation 13:17 this system is described as stamping the foreheads and hands of all men with the *mark of the beast*, signifying plenary domination of thought (forehead) and labor (forehand) by the Cosmic Constable. There was no freedom of thought in the Dark Ages. The Bible was held in obscurity and any who dared read it for themselves were hunted down, tortured, imprisoned, burned at the stake. There was no freedom of labor or free enterprise either. Beginning with the decrees of Pope Damasus around 370 A.D., all men were required to pay tithes and tenths *on pain of anathema.*

In the thirteenth century came the abomination referred to as the *Inquisition*, leaving on the pages of history a stain too foul to be recorded. This was when Babylon the Great became "drunk" with the blood of the saints, (Revelation 17:6). It was as though the whole world had been immersed in thick darkness. The palaces of pontiffs became places of vilest sexual excess and debauchery. Progress ceased throughout Europe. Science, inquiry, medicine, the arts, literature, everything ground to a complete halt.

John Adams, second President of the United States, described the whole sordid business in his *Dissertation on the Canon and the Feudal Law*:

> Numberless have been the systems of iniquity contrived by the great for the gratification of this passion in themselves; but in none of them were they ever more successful than in the invention and establishment of the canon and feudal law. By the former of these (canon law), the most refined, sublime, extensive, and astonishing constitution of policy that ever was conceived by the mind of man was framed by the Romish clergy for the aggrandizement of their own order. They even persuaded mankind to believe, faithfully and undoubtingly, that God almighty had entrusted them with the keys of heaven, whose gates they might open and close at pleasure; with a power of dispensation over all the rules and obligations of morality; with authority to license all sorts of sins and crimes; with a power of deposing princes and absolving subjects from allegiance; with a power of procuring or withholding the rain of heaven and the beams of the sun.... All these opinions they were enabled to spread and rivet among the people by reducing their minds to a state of sordid ignorance and staring timidity, and by infusing into them a religious horror of letters and knowledge. Thus was human nature chained fast for ages in a cruel, shameful, and deplorable servitude to him, and his subordinate tyrants, who, it was foretold, would exalt himself above all that was called God, and that was worshipped. [1]

The religious stranglehold of the Cosmic Constable was broken in the Reformation of the sixteenth century. John Wycliffe (1324-1384) who popularized the expression *government of the people, by the people, for the people*, was among the first to reckon that the best way of breaking the grip of Rome would be to translate the Bible and put it into the hands of the people themselves. William Tyndale was among the first to try to do that in earnest. He met with bitter opposition, was accused of blasphemy, hunted down, caught, and publicly burned at the stake in October 1536. But Tyndale's work became the basis of subsequent versions until finally under Henry VIII the Bible was translated into English and placed in to the hands of the common folks. The effect was immediate.

When the people of Western Europe read the Scripture for themselves their eyes were opened and they saw the sham and error of the existing forms of State Religion. Whereupon they stood up in protest. This protest, or *Protestant* movement for the reformation of the institutions and doctrines of the Church, was itself the greatest promotional factor that flung open the gates of Europe to bring awakened peoples to the shores of the New World. In a very real sense America was born in the wake of an historical protest against the Constable's interventions in human affairs. America was wrought in the wake of a great Protestant Awakening, in the spirit of a great and religious Reformation, which then led to a sweeping political reformation, which gave form to the Constitution and Bill of Rights. This was the historical context in which America's Founding Fathers, "with a firm reliance on the protection of Divine Providence," declared their independence from the Old Order, and framed the Constitution of the New Order. Like *Avram* himself, these Founding Fathers walked on the opposite side of conformity.

We do not wish to dwell on the contradiction between the authentic intent of the Founding Fathers and the derivative agenda of those who are now trying to make America revert to idolatry, paganism, and immorality. For here and now we wish to draw near to an understanding of the truth that is consistent with history—the ancient tug of war between the derivative order patterned after the rudiments of the perishable universe, and the authentic order that the Bible refers to as *The Kingdom of God.*

THE DEVIL IN ADOLPH HITLER

Given the homogenizing activity of the Cosmic Constable, it is easy to see the potential for havoc in a world that is full of racial, cultural and ethnic heterogeneity. Nowhere in the pages of history is the Constable's obsession with homogeneity more visible than in the handiwork of that monster of arrogance and cruelty, Adolph Hitler. Nowhere in the blood stained records of human history are the fangs of the Cosmic Archon more shamelessly exposed and more ruthlessly employed than in the rise and fall of the Third Reich. To understand the Constable's directive is to understand the Nazi mentality. To understand the Constable's aversion towards heterogeneity is to understand Hitler's hatred of culture and diversity. (To quote the words of Goering himself, "When I hear the word 'culture,' I reach for my revolver.")

Historians and psychologists have yet to resolve the enigma of Adolph Hitler. Instead they keep asking the same old question: how could such an instrument of havoc and destruction have succeeded in seducing millions of otherwise intelligent people? The question demands an answer because the Fuhrer's ghost does not seem to want to retire to the realm of the dead. Even today the unclean spirit lives on in the minds of thousands of closet fascists, skinheads and "respectable" Neo-Nazis throughout Europe, the Middle East, Asia, Russia, North America, South America, and everywhere else in the world.

How could this madman have succeeded in seducing an entire nation? In order to answer the question we need to go back to the foundational premises of this publication:

1) Material reality is oriented towards disorder (increasing entropy).
2) Material human nature is governed by the same orientation.

In this publication we have anthropomorphized (personified and humanized) the universe's statistical tendency to disorder and given it the nickname of "Cosmic Constable." It goes without saying that if this "Cosmic Constable" were to assume the shape of a human pedagogue, that pedagogue would naturally move towards a policy of antisemitism. Indeed for the millennia in which this "Cosmic Constable" has been oppressing mankind, the Jew has been his favorite target. What the Constable sees when he looks at a Jew is an obstinate "gradient" that he cannot homogenize or assimilate. A stubborn "rebel" that has evaded all of his historical attempts at homogenization. Sharply distinguished from all other peoples, the Jew has been the scapegoat of tyrants, demagogues, kings, emperors, caesars and pontiffs alike.

If we may quote words from a Jewish *Passover Seder*:

> Not in one country alone or in one age did evil men rise up against us. In every generation oppressors have attempted to destroy us. But the Holy One of Israel, blessed be He, delivers us from their hands.

The children of Israel were the first *authentic* civilization on earth, deriving their modes of existence from the Spirit of the Creator. In as much as derivative civilizations were in the majority, the children of Israel were the proverbial thorn in the side of paganism. Chosen, consecrated, sanctified, separated and set apart by God, forbidden to conform to the ways of the idolatrous world, handed an entirely different set of rules and customs to live by, the Jew has remained ever insoluble, ever impossible to assimilate. Egypt, Assyria, Babylon, Persia, Greece and Rome tried to assimilate the Jew, and failed. In the words of Claudius himself, "As for the Jews, there is no place for them in Rome: they will not assimilate!"

Pharaoh was driven half mad trying to assimilate the children of Israel. Failing that, he tried to destroy them, and would have succeeded, had not God intervened with terrible signs and wonders. When the twelve tribes finally arrived in the Promised Land the pagan king Zippor made little effort to negotiate or compromise with them, instinctively sensing that Israel was walking on a different path than the rest of the world. So he hired Balaam to curse them instead. But Balaam could not curse Israel, declaring them to be "a people who have been set apart and shall not be reckoned as those of other nations," (Numbers 23:8-9).

The gulf between the derivative consciousness of the pagan world (the majority) and the authentic consciousness of the children of Israel (the minority) was wide indeed, isolating them from a world that came to hate them for being "different." Centuries later Jews continued to remain insoluble, refusing to relinquish their God-given authenticity. The Judahites that were exiled to Babylon, for example, were not assimilated there. This is not to say that the Babylonians did not try to assimilate them. Emperor Nebuchadnezzar tried to assimilate all the peoples that he had conquered by setting up a 90-ft. image of gold in the Plain of Dura and ordering them to bow down before it. Some Jews, among them Shadrakh, Meshakh and Abednego, refused. Furious, the king ordered them to comply or else. Daniel respectfully informed the king that they would not bow down to any idol. Preferring to die rather than be assimilated, these Jews were then thrown into the infamous fiery furnace, to be miraculously delivered by God.

When Babylon was conquered by Medo-Persia, the Persian emperor Ahasuerus didn't know what to do with the Jews that he had inherited. His ministers tried to trick him into exterminating them. To quote the words of the wicked Haman:

וַיֹּאמֶר הָמָן לַמֶּלֶךְ אֲחַשְׁוֵרוֹשׁ יֶשְׁנוֹ עַם־אֶחָד מְפֻזָּר
וּמְפֹרָד בֵּין הָעַמִּים בְּכֹל מְדִינוֹת מַלְכוּתֶךָ
וְדָתֵיהֶם שֹׁנוֹת מִכָּל־עָם וְאֶת־דָּתֵי הַמֶּלֶךְ אֵינָם עֹשִׂים.

And Haman said to king Ahasuerus, "There is a unique people scattered and dispersed among other peoples in all the provinces of thy kingdom, whose customs are different from all other people, neither will they conform they the king's laws!"
(Esther 3:8)

Haman, the consummate propagandist, succeeded in forcing the hand of the king, and a decree was then issued to all the provinces of the Persian Empire "to destroy, kill and annihilate all the Jews, young and old, women and little children, on a single day, the thirteenth day of the month of Adar," (Esther 3:13). The evil plot would have succeeded, had it not been for the Providential intervention of Mordecai through the beautiful queen Esther.

The rulers and governors of Imperial Rome had standing orders to homogenize and assimilate indigenous peoples throughout the Empire. And homogenize they did, crucifying all who would resist. During the time of Christ the highways and byways of the Eastern Region were littered with crucifixes on which hung in agony the tortured bodies of "Jewish rebels." Notwithstanding, Jews continued to remain insoluble, preferring to die in places like Massada rather than be assimilated. Two millennia later we find the same elemental agenda in Hitler's "final solution." The obscenities of the Third Reich, undertaken in mindless conformity to the Constable's directive, are among the most heinous of the failures of mankind as a whole. The atrocities of the Third Reich prick the conscience of entire humanity.

Of what does the human spirit despair most, making its muffled protests in the lamentations of poets and composers? Of what does the Polish composer Gorecki despair in his *Symphony of Sorrowful*

Songs, for example, and whence the inconsolable grief expressed in his *Miserere Nobis*? Of what does Yevtushenko despair in *Babiy Yar*?† Of the same spiritual default. Of the same failure to act as authentic human beings. Of the same betrayal of human trust. Of the ease with which we revert to derivative and elemental modes of existence. We get used to things, even though we know them to be evil. We take the easy way out. We put on the blinders, yielding to the inertia that Hannah Arendt referred to as *the banality of evil.*

As evidenced by his own writings, Hitler's mind and conscience were showing signs of failure even from the onset of his mercifully brief career. At a crucial juncture his mind and conscience seem to have deserted him utterly, causing him to revert to the directive of the Cosmic Constable. Let us review that directive:

> Order! Order! Order in the universe! Consummate all the gradients! Reduce patterns of complexity to patterns of simplicity! Level down! Level down! Level down! Homogenize! Homogenize! Homogenize! Reduce, assimilate and absorb! Render everything the same! Arrest and prosecute all heterogeneity! Resistance is futile. You will be assimilated. Order! Order! Order in the universe!

Thus seduced, Hitler set up the idol of the Third Reich through the bludgeon of the National Socialist Workers Party, paving the way for the holocaust. But how did the transformation take place? What finally clinched it? What exactly triggered the holocaust? If we are to say "never again," we must answer these questions.

We have already mentioned the Manichaean ingredient in the agenda of the Third Reich. We know, for example, that much of the Nazi mentality was derived from Nietzsche's *Also Sprach Zarathustra* ("Thus Spake Zoroaster"). Putting two and two together, it isn't too difficult to show causality for the Nazi obsession with mayhem and destruction. But there is more to it than that. There had to be some other catalyst. What was it? We find some answers in Hitler's *Mein Kampf*, where he chronicles his own Faust-like transformation of soul.

---

† *Babiy Yar* is the name of a valley near the city of Kiev, the sight of a massacre by German troops of thousands of Jews, Russians and Ukrainians. The Russian author Yevgeny Yevtushenko composed a haunting poem in memorium, which was then set to music by the composer Dimitri Shostakovich (Symphony #13, *Babiy Yar*).

Mein Kampf means "my struggle," and the question has to be asked as to what it was that Hitler was struggling against? Was he struggling against something unique and personal? Or was he struggling against something universal and existential? As mortal and fallible human beings we all struggle with the "evil tendency" in our flesh, and manage for the most part not to be overcome by it. Hitler struggled with the same devil and was wholly overcome by it. We can see the whole sordid process unfold in the pages of *Mein Kampf*, where he writes the following:

> It cost me the greatest inner soul struggles, and only after months of battle between my reason and my sentiments did my reason begin to emerge victorious.[2]

In this passage, as elsewhere, one need only substitute the word "compulsion" in place of "reason" to get a clear picture of how Hitler resolved the struggle within himself. It was only after he had subordinated his soul to elemental compulsion (or "elemental impetus," as he himself calls it), that he came to forfeit his own humanity and become the mouthpiece of the Cosmic Constable. As the Constable has a pathological aversion towards heterogeneity, so also Hitler found that he could not abide the spectacle of racial, cultural and ethnic heterogeneity. He said it made him sick to his stomach:

> I grew sick to my stomach when I even thought back on this Babylon of races.[3]

At a certain stage Hitler began to see all of creation through the eyes of the Cosmic Constable:

> Vienna appeared to me in a different light than before. Wherever I went, I began to see Jews and more Jews, and the more I saw, the more sharply they became distinguished in my eyes from the rest of humanity.[4]
>
> I was repelled by the conglomeration of races which the capital showed me, repelled by this whole mixture of Czechs, Poles, Hungarians, Ruthenians, Serbs, and Croats, and everywhere, the eternal mushroom of humanity—Jews and more Jews.[5]

At some level, *Mein Kampf* seems to be the diary of the Cosmic Constable himself! A catalog of his fears, his concerns, his anxieties, his phobias, his neuroses. One can hardly read a single page without detecting the oppressive presence of some elemental demon yearning to come out of the closet. The hysterical tirades and paranoid fits that we see in old film clips seem to be directed at the whole spectacle of human *complexity*. The shrill voice that we hear blaring over the loudspeakers seems to be coming from the outer reaches of the cosmos—"Zeig Heil! Zeig Heil! Zeig Heil! Order! Order! Order in the universe!"

To understand the nature of what we have been calling "Cosmic Constable" is to understand the nature of fascist rituals, fascist salutes, fascist chants, fascist demonstrations, rallies and marches. As well might the slogan of Mussolini's *Fasci di Combattimento* (shock troops of Italy's first Fascist Party) have been the slogan of the Constable himself:

> *Credere! Obbedire! Combattere!* Believe! Obey! Fight! Arrest the foreign element! Crush and destroy all who are different! Wipe out, kill and annihilate heterogeneity! Sanitize, purge and cleanse the chicken coop of all but the white clones! Render the coop smooth and homogeneous! Order! Order! Order in the universe!

By deceit and propaganda Hitler succeeded in silencing the voice of his own conscience; and by making his sanction to the elemental he succeeded in silencing the conscience of an entire nation. The rest, as they say, is history. But where exactly is the *catalyst* that we are looking for? What exactly was the turning point? What belief, what sort of mindset provided the final green light for the holocaust? The Fuhrer provides the answer himself. In the passage below let us bear in mind that Hitler's use of the term "nature" corresponds with what we have been calling "Cosmic Constable." He is not talking about Mother Nature here, he is talking about the nature of the cosmos. Here it is, straight from the horse's mouth:

> The ultimate wisdom is always the understanding of the instinctive causes—that is: a man must never fall into the lunacy of believing that he has really risen to be lord and master of Nature...he must understand the fundamental

> necessity of Nature's rule, and realize how much his existence is subjected to these laws of eternal fight and upward struggle. Then he will feel that in a cosmos in which planets revolve around suns, and moons turn about planets, where force alone forever masters weakness, compelling it to be an obedient slave or else crushing it, there can be no special laws for man.[6]

Here is the *caput nili*—the source and origin of Nazi atrocities. These are the words that laid the foundations of Auschwitz, Buchenwald, Belzec, Sobibor, Dachau, Treblinka, Chelmno, Mauthausen, Bergen-Belsen, Majdanek Lublin, Stutthof and Westerbork. What is the Fuhrer saying? Read between the lines and he is saying "my kingdom is of this cosmos!"

It should come as no surprise to find *Yeshua*, the Prince of Peace, making a contrary statement to Pontius Pilate:

> My kingdom is not of this cosmos. (John 18:36)

What sort of propaganda is Hitler peddling when he says "there can be no special laws for man?" The same propaganda that the serpent was peddling in Eden—"never you mind any *special* laws of God, just do what comes naturally!" The serpent and the Fuhrer are saying the same thing—"the laws that govern the behavior of mankind should be no different from the laws that govern the behavior of matter and energy in the cosmos." One can understand why a devil like Hitler would want to pattern his kingdom after the rudiments of the perishable universe, and why Jesus Christ would not.

Hereby it can be seen that man's ignorance of the nature of the cosmos is fraught with grave consequences. Hitler's view of "nature" was as ruinous as it was false, as immoral as it was absurd, as corrupting as it was contemptible. The mind of Hitler was steeped in falsehood, and that falsehood reduced an entire continent to a rubble of simplicity. The rise and fall of the Third Reich was based on a derivative error such as this. The Nazis made their appeal to the lowest common denominator of existence, using deceit and propaganda to encourage men and women to revert to the rudiments of the perishable universe. The result was a massive increase of local entropy on earth—death, degradation, destruction and reduction of unprecedented proportions throughout Europe and elsewhere.

The appeal to the elemental has been the siren song of every demagogue from Nimrod onward. Nimrod, son of Cush, son of Ham, son of Noah, was a carnal man given to excessive leaning on material trust. In a sense, he was the first tyrant to make his appeal to the Cosmic Constable. Whereas Jacob dreamt of a ladder that would unite Man with God, Nimrod conceived of a Tower that would unite man with the Cosmic Constable. Nimrod wanted to bring "cosmos" down to earth, so to speak. He wanted to build a plenary edifice of domination and control patterned after the rudiments of the perishable universe.

The story of Nimrod and the infamous Tower of Babel provides us with important insights into the Mind of God. Before Babel, mankind was homogeneous and homologous. It took an act of God to diversify the languages and cultures of Man. In the story of Babel we are thus given to understand that the best interests of man do not lie in the rudiments of sameness and homogeneity. In the story of Babel we are made to appreciate, respect, honor and value the heterogeneity and *complexity* of the human race.

In some respects the *Hitler Jugend* (Hitler's youth brigade, referred to as the *H.J.*), and its Italian equivalent, the *Batilla*, represent the epitome of the mayhem that the devil of homogeneity can produce when men revert to the derivative modes of existence. The Hitler youth were in all respects encouraged to venerate homogeneity and despise heterogeneity. To wit the guiding principle of the Nazi Party became the law of the chicken coop, which one might state as follows:

> All the chickens in the coop must be white clones. No exceptions allowed. Any speckled bird or any chick with black feathers must be pecked to death immediately. Order! Order! Order in the chicken coop!

On the night of November 9, 1938, referred to as *Kristallnacht* ("night of breaking glass"), the deadly pecking began in earnest, and before it was over millions of Jews lay dead and bloodied on the floor of the glorified chicken coop of the Third Reich. Nazi thugs and perverts, wholly governed by elemental impetus, took onto themselves the nature of demons, committing unspeakable atrocities. In no time the Cosmic Constable came to assume a human form, trampling over all the rights of man, levelling, reducing and destroying any pattern of *complexity* he could lay his hands on. Elemental decrees were then issued by the Nazis, mirroring the Constable's decree. Germany was to be sanitized and rendered *Auslanderfrie* (free of foreigners). The fatherland was to be cleansed and rendered *Judenrein* (purged of Jews). "Zeig Heil! Order! Order! Order in the universe!"

At a certain stage the Nazis divested themselves of all traces of humanity and became unobstructed media through which the Cosmic Constable could bring about massive increases of local entropy here on earth. One can actually see the increase of "entropy" in US War Department animations showing the Nazi menace as a growing black spot that eventually chokes the whole of the map of Europe. Austria overrun. Czechoslovakia absorbed. Poland obliterated. Hungary annihilated. Denmark crushed. Holland reduced. France assimilated.

This pattern of transformation, from *complexity* to simplicity, from heterogeneity to homogeneity, is the very essence of what we have been calling *increasing entropy*. One should not look at the surface appearances. One should look at the underlying principle, as though with the eyes of an impassionate scientist or mathematician. It matters not that the increase of local entropy involved the use of tanks and guns and soldiers and planes and bombs: the underlying transformation is taking place along the cosmic gradient that leads from low entropy states to high entropy states. The destructive changes wrought by the Nazis fully qualify as *anthropomorphizations* of the universal imperative of increasing entropy. If one looks beneath the surface of WWII one will see the cold, indifferent, and impersonal elements of increasing entropy, mistaken for authentic human behavior and agenda.

Seeking affirmation in the cosmic imperative, the Nazi war machine reduced European nations into vassal states, crushing any who would resist. Churchill's England would not yield, so Hitler set his sights on that ancient island as well, swearing that he would annihilate Britain—"I shall wipe out their towns and cities…Britain is no longer an island…she shall be a camp for my soldiers, and I shall go to Buckingham Palace in August!" To which Dr. Goebbels added his tuppence, saying, "England shall be erased from history…it will be over in a few weeks!" To which Reichsmarshall Hermann Goering added, "The end of Britain is near. In a few days London will no longer be a town. Over the desolation made by my beloved Luftwaffe, German soldiers will tower over history's greatest triumph: we shall parade in White Hall in August."

But for the grace of God—and a few brave RAF pilots—the devil might have assimilated England as well, forever altering the history of the world as we know it. The story of the *Battle of Britain* is well known—an epic of Biblical proportions. 15,000 River barges loaded with Nazi troops and weapons, ready to cross the English Channel, waiting for Goering's Luftwaffe (airforce) to clear the way. Picture the scene on that fateful summer of 1940. Hear the air raid sirens blare as thousands of Heinkel 111 bombers and Messerschmitt 109 fighters swarm over the green fields of England like locusts, literally darkening the skies, the roar of their engines drowning all else. Only to be met, picked off, shot down and repulsed by a few squadrons of RAF fighter planes. Six crucial weeks that would define human history for generations to come. Touch and go every inch of the way, pushing the limits of men and machines, minute by minute standing on the ragged edge of victory or defeat, the angels of God looking down anxiously.

Here we should perhaps say something about a unique and legendary fighter plane, brainchild of British aircraft designer R.J. Mitchell who was referred to by RAF pilots as "good old Mitch!" We are, of course, speaking about the eminently elegant, efficient, and deadly Supermarine-Vickers *Spitfire*, screaming to the rescue at 400 miles per hour, 1000 hp Rolls Royce *Merlin* engine growling, eight wing-mounted Browning machine guns blazing defiance at Goering's Luftwaffe. At times outnumbered five-to-one, those brave *Spitfire* and *Hurricane* pilots were able to prevail against everything that Goering could dish out in those six weeks. In the words of Winston Churchill, "Never in the field of human conflict has so much been owed by so many, to so few." It was largely thanks to the valiant efforts and selfless sacrifices of these RAF pilots that those 15,000 Nazi barges never did get to cross the English Channel. Hitler never did get to parade in White Hall. By October of 1940 he had given up on England and gone to try to destroy Russia instead.

The most extreme expression of this mania for destroying things was Hitler's scorched earth decree for Germany itself in September of 1944. Everything, simply everything, was to be utterly destroyed, leaving nothing to the Allies. Buildings were to be dynamited. Food supplies were to be poisoned. Farms were to be burned and cattle killed. All works of art were to be vandalized. Historical treasures, monuments, palaces, ancient castles and churches, everything was to be reduced to rubble—maximum entropy.

Many a demagogue has condemned himself to hell by mouthing the name of God. And in this the Fuhrer condemned himself to hell as well. The "god" whose dirty work Hitler performed in the liquidation of Jews was none other than what we have been calling "Cosmic Constable." And in all this the Fuhrer tried to consecrate the black lie into the hallowed Truth of God! In trying to make Heaven his personal accomplice, Hitler brought condign judgment on his own head. May the fires of that judgment burn forever. May the name "Adolph Hitler" remain an execration to the latest generation. May this be the reward of all who walk in the footsteps of that madman. In the words of the Prophet Isaiah:

תּוֹלַעְתָּם לֹא תָמוּת וְאִשָּׁם לֹא תִכְבֶּה וְהָיוּ דֵרָאוֹן לְכָל־בָּשָׂר

Their worm shall not die, their fire shall not be quenched:
They shall be a disgusting sight unto all generations.
(Isaiah 66:24)

Throughout history there have been those who would rather die than forfeit their God-given humanity. Foremost among them is the American defender of Liberty, whose name and fame is well-known, whose fortitude and courage was the subject of Douglas MacArthur's farewell address at West Point. Against all odds, against storms of advancing tanks, against hails of artillery shells, against blizzards of machine gun fire, against Blitzkrieg and Kamikaze attacks, he has earned an everlasting reputation for himself. In a thousand campaigns, on a thousand battlefields, and around ten thousand campfires, he hath drained deep the bitter cup of war.

In the staggering columns of the first World War, slogging ankle deep through winter's mud, blue-lipped and frost-bitten. In the filth of murky foxholes, and in the slime of dripping dugouts. In the horror of stricken areas of war. In the bitterness of long separation from loved ones back home. Lo, see the American defender of Liberty. A teacher from Cleveland. A busdriver from Fresno. A farmer from Idaho. An appliance repairman from Detroit. An auto mechanic from Houston. A chemist from Albuquerque …

Pushing forward against hell and high water. Against the chords of Sheol and the torrents of Perdition. Onward and upward, in B-24 Liberators over the inferno of Ploesti. In B-17 Flying Fortresses on perilous daylight precision bombing runs over the submarine pens of Wilhelmshaven, easy pickings for German fighters. Three hundred and seventy-six Flying Fortresses left England on 17 August 1943. Sixty of them did not return. And those that did, told their harrowing stories—"flak so thick, you could get out and walk on it."

All eyes nervously peeled to the skies in the Flying Fortress *Memphis Belle.* Caliber 50 machine guns echeloned to the right and to the left, above and below, to direct concentrated cones of fire against enemy fighters. Pilot: Captain Robert Morgan, industrial engineer from Ashville, North Carolina. Co-pilot: Captain Jim Verinis, business administration student at the University of Connecticut. Radio operator and gunner: Sargent Bob Hanson, construction worker from Spokane, Washington. Navigator: Captain Chuck Leighton, chemistry student at Ohio Weslyian. Engineer and top turret gunner: Sargent Harold Loch, from Greenbay, Wisconsin. Tailgunner: Sargent John Quinlan of Yonkers, New York. Turret gunner: Sargent Cecil Scott of Rahway, New Jersey. Bombadier: Captain Vince Evans of Fort Worth, Texas. Left waistgunner: Sargent Bill Winchell of Chicago, Illinois. Right waistgunner: Sargent Tony Nastal of Detroit.

December 7th 1941. Day of infamy. One tranquil Sunday in December the Zeros and Vals swept over Pearl Harbor, leaving "blood, guts, burning oil and bursting shells" in their wake. But there too stood the obstinate endurance of the American defender of Liberty. On the other side of the globe, the same code of honor, the same ironclad imperative of discipline, the same indomitable American spirit, the same selfless sacrifice, the same uncompromising attack, the same swift and sure victory. On the decks of the carriers *Enterprise, Hornet, Yorktown,* and *Lexington.* On the wings of F-4 *Wildcats,* P-47 *Thunderbolts,* and P-51 *Mustangs.* At the battle of Midway, and on the sands of Iwo Jima. In rat-infested trenches in the Philippines. Guadalcanal. Leyte. Guam. Mindanao. Corregador. Tarawa. Battan.

There also stood the gaunt, gray, battle-weary American defender of Liberty, half-starved and almost out of ammunition. Through thick and thin. Through hell and highwater, never looking back. Onward and upward, through the bloody haze of the last reverberating shots, to decisive victory. And as the dust was settling they found a long pipe, stuck Old Glory's pole into it, and raised it atop Mt. Suribachi ...

Over here, and over there, he hath drained deep the bitter and horrible cup of war. In the four corners of the earth he gave his full measure of devotion. In the European Theatre. In the Pacific Theatre. In Korea. In Vietnam. At Omaha Beach and at Utah Beach; in the frozen forests of the Ardenne and at the Maginot Line; at Heartbreak Ridge and on Porkchop Hill; in the heat of the Tet Offensive and in the inferno of Dien Bien Fu; at Khe Sahn and at Da Nang; in the streets of Mogadishu Somalia, in the Persian Gulf, and in the desert of Afghanistan, he gave up his life to the obscenity of war, in order to stem the tide of elemental conformity.

What shall we say then, and how shall we thank these honored dead? In the words of Abraham Lincoln:

> The world will little note nor long remember what we say here, but it can never forget what they did.... It is rather for us to be here dedicated to the great task remaining before us—that from these honored dead we take increased devotion to that cause for which they gave the last full measure of devotion—that we here highly resolve that these dead shall not have died in vain, that this nation under God shall have a new birth of freedom, and that government of the people, by the people, for the people shall not perish from the earth.
>
> Abraham Lincoln, *Gettysburg Address*

What Abraham Lincoln describes as "government of the people, by the people, for the people," is the authentic and human convention that has stood in contempt of the derivative and tyrannical order since time immemorial. And so we publish it, with loud voice, and in a language as plain as A, B, C, saying that this is what we will fight for. Not to conquer and assimilate those who are different from us, or to go out in the world and set a table of fortune for ourselves, but to stem the tide of elemental conformity. To preserve the authentic humanity of Man created in the image of God.

Will there ever be peace on earth? Will there ever be a time when nations will beat their swords into plowshares and be done with the business of war? If we would answer "yes," we must understand the principle that has been productive of so much evil, violence and destruction on earth. Let us try to do that now, in the case of Bin Laden and "911."

THE DEVIL IN BIN LADEN

On 11 September 2001 terrorists under the direction of Osama Bin Laden hijacked and crashed four passenger jets, two into the World Trade Center in New York and one into the edifice of our Pentagon, killing thousands, changing the New York skyline, creating havoc, pandemonium, destruction, chaos and disorder of unprecedented proportions—massive increases of local entropy. What's this all about? Religion? Politics? Economics? Ideology? Or yet another anthropomorphization? Let us try to see what those terrorists did from the dispassionate point of view of a scientist or mathematician:

> New York before the terrorist attack: *lower entropy state.*
> New York after the terrorist attack: *much higher entropy state.*

This pattern of transformation, from lower entropy states to higher entropy states (from lower probability states to higher probability states) is the signature and modus operandi of the principality that we have nick-named "Cosmic Constable."

Let us start connecting the dots. Let us begin with the patterns of *complexity* that were the twin towers of the World Trade Center, housing thousands of human beings. When they were still standing, those towers embodied extremely low entropy states, having required massive amounts of energy, creativity, ingenuity, time, labor, resources, and funds to construct. Draw a circle around those towers and call it a *physical system.* Now increase the entropy of that physical system to near maximum. What would you expect to see happen? More or less what those terrorists accomplished, "death, destruction, twisted metal, a burned out mess of concrete and rubble," as one rescue worker described it.

The following generalizations assume a purely human convention, everything else being equal:

> The more ordered a system, the lower its entropy state.
> The more disordered the system, the higher its entropy state.

Thus a living organism would have a very low entropy state, a dead organism a high entropy state. A complex structure would have a low entropy state when standing, a high entropy state when reduced to rubble. Any such massive increase of local entropy would reduce living organisms into dead matter, structures into rubble.

How do terrorists like Bin Laden produce evil on earth? Arbitrarily? No, by serving as the Constable's submissive tools. By exploiting the social vulnerabilities of open societies to enable the Constable to move in for the kill and accomplish in a few hours what ordinarily would have required many years or centuries of natural corruption. Stated figuratively, devils like Bin Laden serve as "catalysts" or "accelerators" that speed up natural corruption and focus the activity of the Constable onto a local area on earth.

Shut down New York, cut off electricity, vacate the planet, and those twin towers would have eventually come down. In four score years they would have fallen into disrepair, windows broken and beams rusting. After a century or two of neglect, storm, rain, oxidation, earthquake, etc., they might have fallen down naturally. What Bin Laden did was to enable the Cosmic Constable to compress all of that natural corruption into a few hours. Terrorists like Bin Laden are the "catalysts" and "localizers" of the universal activity of the Cosmic Constable. They are the turncoats and Judases of the human race.

Notwithstanding the personal malice of Bin Laden himself, we are not looking at behavior that is authentic and human—we are looking at behavior that is derivative and elemental. We are looking at the behavior of matter and energy, mistaken for authentic human behavior. Was Bin Laden acting on his own "free will?" Do terrorists possess anything by way of "free will?" (Is a forest exercising "free will" when it is burning? Is a piece of deadwood exercising "free will" when it is floating downstream?) Is the behavior of Osama Bin Laden authentic? Or is it derivative? Is it "human?" Or is it a humanization of the statistical tendency to disorder internalized in flesh? Are we looking at the behavior of a human being doing the will of God? Or are we looking at the behavior of a mindless automaton working the increases of local entropy in defiance of the Law of God?

The question that we are asking is this: How much of the behavior of devils like Hitler, Stalin, Milosevic, Sadam Hussein or Osama Bin Laden can be said to be *authentic* and human, and how much *derivative* and elemental? Are we looking at something "human" in all of this death and destruction? Or are we looking at complicated physical systems moving from ordered to disordered states just like any other physical system in the cosmos? Are we missing something here? Is the dog wagging the tail, or is the tail wagging the dog?

In trying to show causality for the behavior of suicide bombers and terrorists like Osama Bin Laden, we should digress briefly and take a look at Freud's so-called *death instinct.* Freud may have been seduced by his own brilliance, but he was brilliant nevertheless. Greatly disturbed by the horrors of the war, he spent the remainder of his life trying to find a rational explanation for the destructive tendencies of man, stumbling onto something that he labeled *death instinct.* In a letter to Albert Einstein he described the *death instinct* as something in living things that is trying to return life to its original condition of inanimate matter. This is how he describes the "death instinct" in his *Outline of Psychoanalysis* (1949):

> We may suppose that the final aim of the destructive instinct is to reduce living things to an inorganic state. For this reason we call it the death instinct.[7]

There were rumors that Freud was drawing near to the concept of "entropy" just before he died. In a work entitled *Anatomy of Human Destructiveness,* the distinguished psychologist Erich Fromm considered the connection between Freud's "death instinct" and what scientists would call "equilibrium states," writing the following:

> If Freud was influenced by these physical theories, they would have seemed to imply that the death instinct was only one particular instance of general physical law....
>
> Whether or not Freud had in mind the connection between entropy and the death instinct does not matter too much. Even if he did not, the whole principle of excitation and energy reduction to the lowest minimal level rests upon the basic error that Dubos points to... of ignoring the fundamental difference between life and nonlife, between "organisms" and "things."[8]

What René Dubos described as a basic error, Freud himself may have described as the last pedestal of human arrogance. Erich Fromm's note of diffidence stems from the efforts of Dubos and some others, among them two English writers, R. Kapp (1931) and L.S. Penrose

(1931) to stonewall any attempt to factor "entropy" into human behavior. And surely this is something that Freud himself would have understood. We humans are arrogant and anthropocentric creatures, deeply hurt by the suggestion that we might not be "in full control." We are deeply insulted by the very suggestion that our material existence may, in some sense, resemble that of an automaton.

Some of the flawed arguments that were used to deny the relationship between entropy and human behavior in 1935 are still in use today. Those arguments may go something like this:

> Granted that matter and energy are oriented towards increasing entropy, but they also have unknown properties whereby they can transform themselves into living organisms. And when that happens, they reverse their orientations and become anti-entropic in nature. The devil in matter becomes a saint when it transforms itself into a living organism.

Chickens have lips, pigs can fly, and the emperor is wearing purple robes! The reality is, of course, otherwise—chickens don't have lips, pigs can't fly, and the emperor is naked. Matter and energy do not have "self-organizing" properties. We live in a universe in which life is in constant jeopardy of reduction *because* of the orientations of matter and energy. One unitary orientation underlies the physical constitution of "organisms" and "things" alike. The dichotomy assumed by Dubos and those English writers is a delusion. In the words of the Nobel physicist Richard Feynman:

> The most important hypothesis in all of biology, for example, is that everything that animals do, atoms do. In other words, there is nothing that living things do that cannot be understood from the point of view that they are made of atoms acting according to the laws of physics.[9]

Granted life requires highly specific combinations of matter and energy, but the orientations of matter and energy do not change in the transition from matter to living organisms. And they don't magically change with the use of the word "emergent" either (a pejorative and catch-all that some atheists invoke when they cannot reconcile the nature of physical reality with the *complexity* of living things). The so-called "emergent properties" of life are the products of Intelligent Design, having little or nothing to do with the orientations of matter and energy. It would be just as absurd to talk about the "emergent properties" of computer chips. Computer chips do not derive their orientation from the "emergent properties" of silicon atoms, they derive them from the intelligence of those who designed them.

We need to remind ourselves that living organisms are short-lived creatures. If it was indeed the case that the orientations of matter and energy could be *reversed* in living organisms, one would expect those organisms to live for ever. But they don't. They age and eventually die, regardless of the availability of graded energy. Matter and energy do not undergo mystical transformations in the course of abiogenesis. It is pure idolatry and nonsense to ascribe mystical properties to the atoms in living things, as though they were different from the atoms in non-living things.

One needs to understand these attempts at intellectual evasion in terms of what Freud himself would have called *the last pedestal of human arrogance.* This last pedestal of human arrogance has less to do with science and more to do with the root of depravity in human nature—the anthropocentric hubris that would claim exemption for human behavior by stonewalling any attempt to equate it with increasing entropy. The proud and pompous root of depravity in human nature has always tried to claim privilege and exemption for itself, at one time even claiming that the universe revolved around itself. This is the main problem and hurdle confronting the human race as we speak—pride and hubris. This is what we mean by the last pedestal of arrogance.

Whether we know it or not, whether we want to admit it or not, the cosmic running down process is acting like a gigantic behavioral field with respect to human behavior. We are made from the physics of this universe. The nature of our physical constitution is necessarily *derivative*, though the nature of our spiritual constitution need not be. If we would indeed lay the axe to the root of the problem, if we would say "never again" to the holocaust, and "never again" to 911, we must swallow our pride, smash that last pedestal of human arrogance and stop trying claim exemption for human behavior.

Like an internal governor, like a compass needle that is always trying to orient itself with the earth's magnetic field, our material existence is always trying to orient itself with the greater order of universal change. Much of the destructive behavior cataloged in human history is derivative. We are not looking at authentic human behavior in these acts of death and destruction, we are merely looking at complicated *physical systems* moving from ordered to disordered states. This is the natural behavior of physical systems. Absent any *special* worth or value that God may place on us as human beings, we are nothing but energy-driven systems—"just a bunch of neurons."

We are now in a position to comprehend what Freud and Fromm could only guess at 50 years ago, namely that the aim of the destructive tendency in man is to bring about local increases of entropy by reducing *complexity* into simplicity. Or as Freud would have put it, "by reducing [complex] life to its original [simple] condition of inanimate matter." The scientific term that describes the reduction process is *increasing entropy*. Where is the mystery in this?

The hard-nosed scientist will no doubt argue and say: "Fine! But show me the exact mechanism. Show me the exact mechanism by which the nature and orientation of the cosmos skews human behavior in the direction of disorder." The exact mechanism is subtle and difficult to grasp because it is not deterministic—it is statistical and probabilistic. The "exact mechanism" that the scientist would rightfully insist on is rooted in Causal and Cosmological principles. That mechanism derives itself from the energetic connection between man and cosmos, whereby the latter projects its nature and orientation onto the former. We know for example that even the blink of an eye requires energy, which is degraded upon use, which brings about an increase in the entropy of the entire universe. This establishes a connection between man and cosmos, suggesting that the nature and orientation of the cosmos is not something outside us—it is internalized in our flesh. We are indeed "cosmos-wired."

Sprinkle iron filings on a sheet of paper, position a strong magnet beneath and shuffle. The pattern of the iron filings will conform to the magnetic field. Sprinkle human elements onto the fabric of a cosmos in which entropy is increasing, and let history do the shuffling for you. The long-term behavior of those human elements will conform to the behavior of the cosmos by moving from ordered to disordered states. In the case of the iron filings the causal mechanism is deterministic. In the case of the human elements the causal mechanism is *probabilistic* and *statistical*, i.e., the relationship between cause and effect can only be observed in a "history" or a "large sample." The movement towards disordered states does not occur immediately. You don't need a microscope to see the causal relationship, you need a large sample—a sufficiently large number of cycles, permutations, decisions, events, changes. A sufficiently long span of time.

A good example can be found in the events that followed the Bolshevik Revolution. In 1917 Russia rejected God and reverted to the derivative order of existence. What was the result? The results that followed—reign of terror, purges of the Stalin era, twenty million dead from starvation, mayhem, iniquity, executions, Gulag labor camps,—took a few decades to render. Look at the former Soviet Union from the dispassionate perspective of a scientist or mathematician and you will see a physical system moving from low to high entropy states in those decades.

Extrapolate to "911" and you will see the devil in Bin Laden trying to achieve the same thing. But understand that the target of this devil is *any* pattern of complexity in the universe, not just New York. What this devil is really aiming for is e*quilibrium states*—the consummation of all life forms locally. In which case the "death instinct" of the terrorist, the fanatic, and the suicide bomber, may be an anthropomorphization as well. The tendency of physical systems to move towards "equilibrium states" is internalized in the material man. This tendency may, under extreme conditions, find outlets in terms of what we call "suicide." This would be the "entropic urge" latent/operative in the physical constitution of man, trying to unburden itself of the travail, difficulty and struggle of life's *complexity*, and return to the peace, rest and simplicity of dust .

Shakespeare describes the urge in *Hamlet.* Read between the lines and see a plain vanilla principle of physics expressing itself in eloquent words of William Shakespeare:

> To be or not to be...to die...by a sleep to say we end the heartache and the thousand natural shocks that flesh is heir to. It is a consummation devoutly to be wished. To die, to sleep...to sleep.

The second law of thermodynamics describes the natural way in which systems merge with their environments to consummate potential differences and move towards higher entropy (equilibrium) states. In their book *The Fundamentals of Physics* David Halliday and

Robert Resnick describe the second law as follows:

> A natural process that starts in one equilibrium state and ends in another will go in the direction that causes the combined entropy [disorder] of the system and its environment to increase.[10]

If this is true, then *the urge to merge with cosmos* would be internalized in all universal systems, flesh included. Why? Because cosmos is the ultimate "environment" in all cases. Eventually all universal systems merge with cosmos, becoming indistinguishable from it. This is exactly what happens when human beings die physically—"dust to dust, ashes to ashes." In death the matter and energy of the body becomes merged and integrated with the matter and energy of the cosmos, in a short while becoming indistinguishable from it (just like a wave dying on the surface of the sea). Which would suggest that the "death instinct" of the terrorist and suicide bomber may in fact be one particular instance of general physical law. The fact that Bin Laden and his band of murderers would try to justify and rationalize it by appeals to "jihad," is irrelevant. If it hadn't been "jihad," it would have been "Marxism" or some other excuse to destroy life and property. The culture of violence that took three decades to reify in Afghanistan has now taken on a life of its own, growing to a global monster whose behavior is no longer under the control of human beings per se. We are, once again, looking at the elemental inertia and monstrosity that Hanna Arendt referred to as *the banality of evil.*

We are deceived if we imagine the devil in Bin Laden to be a Manichaean fiend with horns and hooves. The devil in Bin Laden is nothing more than an *anthropomorphization* of the plain vanilla principle of increasing entropy. That this devil would obsess with "death" should come as no surprise. That this devil would instruct his fellows terrorists to "crave death" (Arabic instructions found by the FBI in one of the terrorist's belongings) should also come as no surprise. Look beneath the surface and you may see the outlines of a physical system yearning to move towards maximum entropy. Final consummation. The end of all energetic strivings. The peace of the dead.

The exodus of Abraham out of the pagan and derivative orders of existence spawned three sister religions—Judaism, Christianity and Islam. This is how most dictionaries have defined the word *pagan*:

pagan - one who is not a Christian, Moslem, or Jew.

These three sister religions stand in contempt of the pagan (derivative) orders of existence. The guiding principle of those who worship the God of Abraham is life and construction, not death and destruction. The idea that terrorists can go to paradise by blowing themselves up, crashing airplanes into buildings and murdering innocent women and children in cold blood is a perversion of Islam. The five pillars of Islam are faith, prayer, charity, self-purification and pilgrimage. The word *Islam* implies "submission to God," not "surrender to Satan," or "Cult of Death." We call upon all Islamic nations to turn to the one and only true God in complete dependence and humility and cleanse themselves of the false god and idol of Terror within.

לֹא־תַעֲשׂוּ עָוֶל בַּמִּשְׁפָּט בַּמִּדָּה בַּמִּשְׁקָל וּבַמְּשׂוּרָה׃
מֹאזְנֵי צֶדֶק אַבְנֵי־צֶדֶק אֵיפַת צֶדֶק וְהִין צֶדֶק יִהְיֶה לָכֶם
אֲנִי יְהוָה אֱלֹהֵיכֶם אֲשֶׁר־הוֹצֵאתִי אֶתְכֶם מֵאֶרֶץ מִצְרָיִם׃

You shall do no wrong in judgment, in measures of length, or weight, or quantity. You shall have just balances, just weights, a just ephah and a just hin: I am the LORD your God, who brought you out of the land of Egypt.

(Leviticus 19:35-36)

SECTION 5

Cosmos and Debt

Millennial Economics

The question we were asking was this: How much of human history is authentic, and how much derivative? Are the orders and systems of man authentic? Or are they by-products of the universe's statistical tendency to disorder internalized in flesh?

In this publication we describe the material nature of man as a function of the material nature of the cosmos itself, a cosmos in which entropy is increasing, a cosmos in which the greater order of change is flowing down the gradient that leads from complexity to simplicity, from heterogeneity to homogeneity, from ordered to disordered states. To help us sort things out we have set up a gestalt (a highly compressed teaching model) in which we posit a *principality* in lieu of the principle of increasing entropy, nicknaming it "Cosmic Constable."

In trying to move local systems from ordered to disordered states, this "Cosmic Constable" is exploiting human weaknesses, using vices such as greed, lust for power, etc., as tools to produce disorder on earth. Let us look again at the principle that the Constable embodies. The cosmos' statistical tendency to disorder, internalized in flesh, is always looking for *outlets* in terms of choices that may lead to disordered states here on earth. Given the infinite variety of choices confronting billions of human elements, any choice that might lead to disorder would tend to receive a statistical boost from the nature of physical reality, growing into a "habit" with the passage of time. Conversely, any choice that might lead to order would tend to receive the opposite (a statistical drag or restraint), fading with the passage of time. The surface appearances would make no difference. It would not matter to the Cosmic Constable if the disordered states were being produced by the choices of emperors, kings, pontiffs, politicians, central bankers, bioethicists, media moguls, social augurs, crime bosses, or derivative masses. The Cosmic Constable does not see these differentiations. He sees only physical states, numbers, patterns, arrangement of elements—entropy states. From the Constable's point of view *any* kind of human disorder would be an affirmation of the universal imperative of increasing entropy, and as such, deserving of statistical reinforcement.

Historically speaking, disorder has come in many different shapes and sizes. In the Dark Ages, for example, the Constable was able to produce centuries of disorder through a religious edifice of domination and control, using the tail of a derivative Christianity to wag the dog of human authenticity. Happily the Reformation exposed the falsehood and stripped the Constable of his religious disguises, bringing large numbers of the awakened peoples to the New World. Proceeding under Divine imperative, these settlers and pilgrims then set about the business of binding the Constable's hands down from further mischief by the chains of the Constitution. Perhaps the original intent of the Founders of America can be stated as follows:

> The tail shall not wag the dog.

But tell me, which is the tail, and which is the dog? Upon reflection it will be seen that all the insolent "tails" of history have owed their existence to something that they provided. They were *providers* of something that mankind had need of. They were "middle-men" or "go-betweens" of one sort or another, placing meters between mankind and the Providence of God. History is full of instances in which the derivative camel ended up in the tent because he was the *provider* of something that the master needed. The beast must find a human need to exploit. He can then use that need as an excuse to poke a toe into the tent, then a foot, then a leg, and then the whole carcass, crowding out the authentic owner. This is what we mean by the tail wagging the dog.

Perhaps one of the greatest lessons of history can be summed up as follows:

> No institution of tyranny can find ground to exist on if the people are free to produce and provide the same thing (that it produces and provides) for themselves. No institution of tyranny can perpetuate itself if the people have free and unencumbered access to the Providence of God.

The Founding Fathers of America were fully cognizant of the devil's stratagems in this respect. They did not wish to place meters between the Providence of God and the best interests of Man—they tried to remove existing meters and provide direct access. They labored diligently to indemnify posterity from involuntary dependency on all derivative providences, especially that of runaway government. In their *Declaration of Independence* they subordinated the institution of government to the God-given rights of Man:

> We hold these truths to be self-evident, that all men are created equal, that they are endowed by their Creator with certain unalienable rights, that among these are life, liberty and the pursuit of happiness. That to secure these rights, governments are instituted among men...

In the American scheme government is the tail, not the head. It only exists to protect the God-given rights of Man. The unalienable rights of Man cannot be granted or withheld by government itself. In a sense, the Constitution and the Bill of Rights were drawn up to prevent the Constable's "tails" from wagging the dog of human order and economy. Having just emerged from the Old World, these noble Founders succeeded in binding the Constable's religious tail from mischief in the New World. With his religious tail rendered impotent, the Constable went looking for alternate tails. He found what he was looking for in the sphere of money, banking and finance.

It was thought with a great deal of certainty that organized error had been dealt a death blow in the course of the American Revolution, and indeed it was a resounding blow that America's Founders were able to deliver into the ribcage of the derivative beast. Unfortunately what could not have been foreseen by them was the degree to which the ancient conflict would soon shift itself from the domain of religion to that of economics. They did not and could not have foreseen the extent of the industrial changes in the offing, and the extent to which the economy would emerge as a measure of human order and well-being. They could not have foreseen the degree in which the devil of Debt would begin to compete against the labor of Man and seek to deprive him of the dignity of his origins in God. They could not have foreseen the extent to which Money would combine into a global Leviathan with a power to grant or withhold credit to or from wholesale nations. Notwithstanding, Jefferson did issue a warning or two:

> I sincerely believe that banking establishments are more dangerous than standing armies, and that the principle of spending money, to be paid for by posterity, under the name of "funding," is but swindling of futurity on a large scale. [1]
>
> [T]he earth belongs to each of these generations during its course, fully and in its own right. The second generation receives it clear of the debts and encumbrances of the first, the third of the second, and so on. For if the first could charge it [the second] with a debt, then the earth would belong to the dead and not to the living....[2]

The idea that one generation ought not enslave the next by debt is a Biblical principle. The inscription on the Liberty Bell in Philadelphia is from the ancient book of Leviticus:

וְקִדַּשְׁתֶּם אֵת שְׁנַת הַחֲמִשִּׁים שָׁנָה וּקְרָאתֶם דְּרוֹר בָּאָרֶץ לְכָל־יֹשְׁבֶיהָ יוֹבֵל
הִוא תִּהְיֶה לָכֶם וְשַׁבְתֶּם אִישׁ אֶל־אֲחֻזָּתוֹ וְאִישׁ אֶל־מִשְׁפַּחְתּוֹ תָּשֻׁבוּ.

And you shall hallow the fiftieth year, and proclaim liberty throughout all the land and its inhabitants: it shall be jubilee unto you, and you shall return every man to his possession, and you shall return every man to his family. (Leviticus 25:10)

God's Law set aside a *Jubilee* every fifty years, granting the new generation a release from the debts of the previous. Perhaps this is why one of the symbols of America's freedom, the Liberty Bell, has a crack in it. The crack was repaired once but mysteriously reappeared. Without admitting of any superstition, we can only wonder if this has something to do with the indignation of the Supreme Judge of the universe towards a nation whose system of human economy is based on perpetual debt. A nation that writes *In God we Trust* on its money.

Whereas the religious disguises of the Constable are now footnotes to history, there is yet another disguise that has to be exposed before the derivative beast can be bound for a thousand years. This last disguise has to do with the world's system of *money creation*. For too long the subject of money creation has been left ill-defined and unresolved, to this day regarded an occult science hidden behind a cloud of mystery and technical jargon. Otherwise intelligent and thinking Americans do not know how their "money" is being created, or by whom, or at what cost. Americans have no idea why sound money is so scarce nowadays. They have no idea why the nation is facing bankruptcy, saddled with public and private debts that are augmenting themselves by geometric progression—literally undergoing astronomical increases by the day. Americans are at a loss as to why disorders such as debt, poverty, disease, want and crime should be found in such proportions in the most abundant land on earth, or why such things as "recessions" should ever *have* to occur here in the first place. This is a deplorable condition for any people to be in, let alone those who claim to be the freest on earth.

The problem is well camouflaged. It lies in the *system of money creation*. The world's system of money creation, specifically central banking, is still that of the old 17th century scaffolding work. The world's system of money creation is 300 years old. It is outdated and mortally flawed. This crumbling scaffolding needs to be torn down and rebuilt from the ground up. The old debt-system cannot be reformed. Bandaids won't fix things any more. Here too we are up against classical boundary conditions, which we defined as follows:

> You can't fix something that's broke on the basis of the same set of assumptions that made it broke in the first place—you will just bounce off the same walls and end up right back where you started.

The causes of global economic disorder are rooted in a 300 year-old system of credit based on the *unnecessary* creation and increase of public debt. The system whereby the money of the world is now created is of the old Malthusian paradigm of want and scarcity. It is a debt-creating, debt-compounding system with a built-in "catch-22" that precludes the possibility of reform. All of the "Money and Banking" courses offered by our institutions of higher learning teach a system of money creation that began with the charter of the Bank of England in 1694. They teach students of finance how the *old* system creates money in the form of debt, the foregone conclusion (the one that escapes all notice) being that this is the only way to create money on earth.

Before the charter of the Bank of England in 1694 the English system was more or less debt-free, coins and *tallies* being used from 1100 to 1694. First adopted by Henry I, fourth son of William the Conqueror, the *tallies* were made of hardwood, their sole value derived from their acceptability in payment of taxes. These *tallies* (short rods) were carefully marked and split lengthwise. One half was kept in the treasury and the other half was paid into general circulation when the Crown needed to buy something. When returned to the treasury (in payment of taxes) the outbound half was compared with the treasury half. If the two halves matched exactly, the treasurer would cry "tally ho!" and accept the returned half in payment of taxes.

No interest bearing public debts were incurred in the course of the many centuries in which tallies were used as money. When the Bank of England was chartered in 1694 there was the equivalent of about $70,000,000 in tallies in circulation. Everything changed at that time. The old debt-free system was gradually abolished and the new central bank became the sole purveyor of a debt-system of money creation. In 1830 the powerful Bank of England succeeded in outlawing the use of debt-free tallies altogether. Heaps of broken tallies were then confiscated and ordered burned in the government furnaces. Interestingly, a defective chimney resulted in a fire which completely destroyed the Houses of Parliament.

Prior to the charter of the *Old Lady of Threadneedle Street* (nickname given to the Bank of England) the English people had a debt-free medium of exchange. Not perfect by any stretch of the imagination, and much too cumbersome for use today, but nevertheless a viable credit concept used for seven centuries. The "value" of those wooden tallies was fully acknowledged by the governors of the newly chartered Bank of England—when the capital of the Bank was increased in 1697, $800,000 of the new capital was paid for with wooden tallies which were accepted at par.

The Bank of England became the first legal purveyor and executor of a nationalized Debt Money System. The truth be known all of the central banks of the world today, including our own privately owned Federal Reserve Banks, bear upon their gilded and marbled monuments the print, pattern, and spirit of the Bank of England. And in all this we are merely saying that the existing system of money creation is as old as the *Old Lady of Threadneedle Street.* We are not pointing fingers. Heaven knows, and as John Maynard Keynes might have said, "debt money is better than no money!" But regardless of any useful purpose that the debt-system may have served in the past, it is now anachronistic. It is now as obsolete as the old paradigm of human nature itself. It is time for a new system of money creation.

From the onset we should emphasize that we do not question the Free Enterprise System, or private property, or the private ownership of the means of production. If the dog of Free Enterprise could be set free to wag the tail of Money, (instead of the other way round), our economy would know no such things as astronomical debts, horrendous deficits, confiscatory taxation, and an insidious form of inflation. We hold the American system of Free Enterprise in high esteem. We lay great store by it, believing it to be the best scheme devised for the *production* of goods and services. The problem is this: the best method of production on earth will profit no man if the goods and services end up collecting dust on shelves because the people do not have access to sound money. It is the *debt-system of money creation* that is in question here, not American Free Enterprise, private property, or private ownership of the means of production. It is the system of money creation that we would now shed light on and investigate.

THE HARMFUL EFFECTS OF PUBLIC DEBT

Let us take a sober look at the effects of a 300 year-old system of money creation based on debt. Every nation is mired in debt, and none deeper than the United States. The wealthiest nation on earth is now facing the greatest debt crisis in her 200 year history, a crisis that would have made the very bowels of her Founding Fathers grate in horror and astonishment. The national debt of the United States has surpassed the *six trillion dollar* mark, a figure that is altogether incomprehensible. It is said that six trillion $1 bills placed end to end would pave a four-lane highway all the way to the sun and back. If Jefferson were to come back to life and see the actual numbers, he would have a heart attack and flee the realm of the living.

There has been a 90% decline in the purchasing power of the dollar since the passage of the Federal Reserve Act in 1913. Some older Americans can remember when they could have bought a veritable mansion for $10,000 and a brand new Chevy for less than $2000. Even with massive subsidies, farmers can barely keep their heads above water. On the heels of every hope, the threat of default and mortgage foreclosure. The plant is shut down, the plow is left in mid-furrow, the school house is empty, all for the want of sound money. Twenty million Americans are said to be living below the poverty line as Congress makes hypocritical apologies, raising the ceiling on the national debt so it can keep itself afloat for one more week, one more month. In the wealthiest nation on earth we are faced with poverty of soul, living from hand to mouth, robbing from Peter to pay Paul. Salaries are slashed, pension plans are looted, budgets are cut, veterans programs are scrapped. The sick cannot afford physicians. The laborer can no longer put aside a ransom for old age. The dream of the golden years has been replaced by the nightmare of poverty and the gloom of the geriatric war. Money has become the stumbling block of living itself.

Third World debt is exacting a ransom of life and limb from millions of poor and struggling peoples elsewhere. One needs to put flesh and blood on Third World debt figures to see the human cost of economic entropy. In many cases the interest payments that Third World nations are making to foreign banks are depleting the life-support equity of millions of young children, thousands of them dying of starvation daily. Many of the nations of Sub-Saharan Africa have been pressured into implementing the International Monetary Fund's debt-related austerity programs. To say that the results have not been good would be an understatement—the area has been gutted of natural resources, the overall standard of living plummeted, the foreign debt skyrocketed. Sudan is a living hell presently—tens of thousands dead from infighting, indescribable starvation and disease, money so scarce that human beings are reputedly bought and sold for $50 in some places. Benin, Burundi, Cameroon, Comoros, Congo, Cote d'Ivoire, Ghana, Guinea, Madagascar, Mali, Mauritania, Mozambique, Niger, Nigeria, Sao Tome and Principe, Senegal, Sierra Leone, Sudan, Tanzania, Togo and Zambia are strapped with similar straight jackets. Many of these nations are teetering on the edge of bankruptcy, living from hand to mouth, at the critical stage where they have to surrender 90% or more of their earnings to service foreign debt, leaving little or nothing to meet the domestic needs of their own people.

The situation is not too different in South America where debt-related disorder is a fact of life. Latin Americans regard the hemorrhage of money from their continent (in the servicing of foreign debt) as "the worst plunder since Cortez." They refer to the 1980s as the "lost decade." The economy of the sovereign people and government of Argentina is falling apart under pressure of debt-related globalization. To help service a snowballing foreign debt, Brazil's President Cardoso even started auctioning off chunks of the Amazon rainforest. The first parcel that went on the auction block was 2,500 acres in the northern Amazon state of Para. Thousands of acres of the Tapajos National Forest may be sold off to global logging interests.

The Amazon rainforest is a storehouse of God-created biological *complexity*, every nook, cranny, canopy and tree hollow literally pregnant with the exuberant variety of living things. Destroying such *complex* ecosystems is like hacking down a pregnant woman with a machete. The Amazon rainforest also happens to be one of the principle sources of the oxygen we breathe—one of the "lungs" of the human race. Why are Brazilians allowing it to be cut down? They have no choice. The devil of Debt has his foot on their necks. As Brazil's foreign debt mushrooms, Sao Paulo ends up having to sell off some of the most *complex* environs on earth to keep up her interest payments to foreign banks. Economic and environmental entropy go hand in hand. They are the children of a common parent.

Sao Paulo is Portuguese for "St. Paul." One wonders what Rav Shaul would have had to say about the economic predicament of a city named after him. Meanwhile the Central American nation of El Salvador is also wallowing in debt-related disorder. *El Salvador* is Spanish for "the Savior." One wonders what Jesus Christ of Nazareth would have had to say about the plight of the poor and destitute in a nation named after himself. (Fully half of Christ's parables were about money and stewardship.)

The global cost of money creation affects every man, woman and child on the planet. The idea that private citizens can avoid paying interest by avoiding personal debt is a misconception. In her book *Interest and Inflation Free Money* Margrit Kennedy reminds us that we all pay a price when money is created in the form of debt:

> [I]nterest is included in every price we pay.... The capital share in garbage collection amounts to 12% because here the share of capital costs is relatively low and the share of physical labor is particularly high. This changes in the provision of drinking water, where capital costs amount to 38%, and even more so in social housing, where they add up to 77%. On an average we pay about 50% capital costs in the prices of our goods and services.
>
> Therefore, if we could abolish interest and replace it with another mechanism to keep money in circulation, most of us could either be twice as rich or work half of the time to keep the same standard of living we have now.[3]

If we could abolish interest and replace it with another mechanism to keep money in circulation, perhaps Brazil wouldn't have to cut down the Amazon rainforest. Perhaps corporations wouldn't have to pollute the environment. Perhaps food processors wouldn't have to adulterate foodstuffs. Perhaps nations wouldn't have to lift up sword against one another. Perhaps human beings wouldn't have to behave like animals.

Consider the *moral* implications of a system of money creation based on debt. Where money is made scarce it increases the power of those who create and control it. Given the vices of human nature, money scarcity would be a foregone conclusion. Money scarcity leads to the love of money, which we know to be "the root of all kinds of evil," (1 Timothy 6:10). Many of the destitute nations of the world have been brought into a state of idolatry such as this, reduced to slaves of Mammon, forced to prostitute their own daughters, institutions, lands and God-given resources.

The overwhelming impression that one gets is that something has gone terribly wrong on earth and no one can do anything about it. The devil of Debt has taken on a life of its own and can no longer be restrained by mere mortals. It does not appear that any group of men or nations have a power to overcome the inertia of increasing economic entropy. The devil of disorder seems to have mankind over a barrel, able to demand a ransom in life and limb.

In his New York Times bestseller *Earth in the Balance* former Vice President Al Gore writes the following:

> The forces that shape and reshape our lives seem to have an immutable logic of their own; they seem so powerful that any effort to define ourselves creatively will probably be wasted, its results quickly erased by successive tidal waves of change. Inevitably, we resign ourselves to whatever fate these powerful forces are propelling us towards, a fate we have little role in choosing. [4]

In their international bestseller *The Global Trap* journalists Hans-Peter Martin and Harald Schumann try to make some sense of the banality of debt-driven globalization, documenting the inexorable slide of nations towards disordered states. The picture that they paint is that of an elemental world in which the tail is wagging the dog. An indifferent world in which masses mired in debt and poverty are drugged and pacified by media circus shows, nudity, and "tittytainment." A heartless world characterized by a surplus of gifted, skilled, undervalued and unwanted men and women. A psychotic world tortured by the insecurities that stem from the widening rift between the obscenely rich and the starving masses. A paranoid world in which 20% live in the opulence, luxury and self-indulgence of an *Alphaville* surrounded by armed guards, metal detectors and security cameras, while 80% slave in the barbed wire sweatshops of something falsely labelled "free market." Martin and Schumann paint a picture not too different from Fritz Lang's dreadful *Metropolis*—cinematic depiction of a world system in which human beings are reduced to cogs in a cosmic scheme of mediocrity and repetition.

Who is in charge of a world system such as this? Certainly not the sovereign nations themselves. Brought into a state of involuntary dependency, nations are no longer in full control of their destinies. They are as panhandlers begging for money, and beggars can't be choosers. Who then is steering the global economy? Multinational corporations? They too are global pawns, just like sovereign nations.

If capital costs are high, corporations must try to make up for it. How do they make up for it? By going overseas where there is cheap labor, or where they can avoid taxes. By polluting the environment. By cooking the books. By mergers and acquisitions. By exploiting every legal loophole their lawyers can dig up.

Who then is in charge of an indifferent world system such as this? Central bankers? The World Bank? The International Monetary Fund? Wall Street? The New York Stock Exchange? No, in a very real sense the "Cosmic Constable." Commenting on the bizarre events that led to a 30% devaluation of the Mexican peso in 1995, Martin and Schumann write the following:

> The government of the American superpower, the once omnipotent IMF and all the European central banks seemed to be guided by an unseen hand as they bowed to the dictates of a higher power whose destructive capacity they were no longer able to evaluate...[5]

Further on they write the following:

> Michel Camdessus, who, as head of the IMF in Washington, is a key link between the political world and the realm of money markets... leaves no doubt that Wall Street and its fund managers are the ones who call the shots: "The world is in the hands of these guys."
>
> "These guys," as he calls them, flatly reject his view. No, they argue, we are not in the driving seat either; no, we do not bear the responsibility either. "It is not us, it is the marketplace," comes the unanimous refrain...[6]

What then? What are we to think? Has the "marketplace" now become the tail that is wagging the dog of human order and economy? Is the "marketplace" competing against the labor of Man and trying to deprive him of the dignity of his origins in God? Was man made for the marketplace, or was the marketplace made for man?

Until recently we didn't know much about the agendas of the IMF and World Bank. Enter Davison Budhoo, a man of great conscience, integrity, and courage. Once a high ranking member of the IMF himself, Budhoo arrived at a point in his life where he could no longer look at himself in the mirror. He resigned, made his confession to the world, and died trying to reform the crumbling Bretton Woods scaffolding. Budhoo's now infamous *Letter of Resignation* has opened up the policies of the International Monetary Fund to public scrutiny. In the passage below Budhoo is lamenting the same measure of human failure that great poets and writers have lamented since time immemorial:

> Dear Mr. Camdessus,
>
> Today I resigned from staff of the International Monetary Fund after over twelve years, and after 1000 days of official fund work in the field, hawking your medicine and your bag of tricks to governments and to people in Latin America and the Caribbean and Africa. To me resignation is a priceless liberation, for with it I have taken the first big step to that place where I may hope to wash my hands of what in my mind's eye is the blood of millions of poor and starving peoples. Mr. Camdessus, the blood is so much, you know, it runs in rivers. It dries up too; it cakes all over me; sometimes I feel that there is not enough soap in the whole world to cleanse me from the things that I did in your name...
>
> But... I can hope that there is compassion and indignation in the heart of my world, and that people can stand up and take notice of what I have to say.... [B]ecause the charges that I make are not light charges—they are charges that touch at the very heart of western society and western morality and post-war inter-governmental institutionalism that have degenerated into fake and sham under the pretext of establishing and maintaining international economic order....
>
> The charges that I make strike at the very soul of man and his conscience. You know, when all the evidence is in, there are two types of questions that you and me and others will have to answer. The first is this: will the world be content merely to brand our institution as among the most insidious enemies of humankind? Will our fellowmen condemn us thus and let the matter rest? OR will the heirs of those whom we have dismembered in our peculiar Holocaust clamor for another Nuremberg....
>
> But beyond the question of guilt, there is a far more operational matter that bothers me; it is this: what devil is

> there in us that will allow us to go this far into a shame and an ignominy without screaming out a protest as human beings and as men of conscience?... When I ask myself that question I become disoriented because I cannot cope with the consequences of the answer that I know will surface one day.... It is the timeless story of human beings, faced with an exceptional opportunity to further the cause of mankind, turning around and destroying everything worth preserving because of some indefinable quirk in our Nature....
>
> I guess you can say that there was always a Mr. Hyde within me, and even as I did your Dr. Jekyl work I kept looking over my shoulder at his kind face. And one day he said to me: "Take stock of yourself; the image of the Beast is blotting out all else. Your soul is becoming shriveled up; you are becoming dispossessed of all traces of your humanity." And I replied: "It cannot be; I will never accept to be thus; I will fight tooth and nail to return to the Human Fold." This Letter is the start of my fight back to the Human Fold....[7]

Budhoo goes on to document many abuses. It seems that the IMF's shenanigans in Trinidad and Tobago were only the tip of the iceberg. It seems that the IMF has been wielding the same club over the heads of millions of poor and destitute peoples in Ibero America, the Caribbean, Eastern Europe, Africa, the Middle East, Russia and Asia. Is the agenda of the IMF authentic, or is it derivative? Who or what is the real choreographer of all of this debt, poverty, devaluation, marginalization, scorched earth and economic disorder?

That central bankers have "good intentions" is not in dispute. Doubtless many of them really do believe that they are administering "bitter but necessary medicine." But what is really going on here? Are we missing something? Are we looking at a human agenda in all this, or are we once again looking at the agenda of our friend the Cosmic Constable, mistaken for, and assuming the shape of a human agenda?

We said that if the Constable was endowed with the gift of speech his decree would be heard bellowing throughout the cosmos:

> Order! Order! Order in the universe! Consummate all the gradients! Reduce patterns of complexity to patterns of simplicity! Level down! Level down! Level down!

> Homogenize! Homogenize! Homogenize! Reduce, assimilate and absorb! Render everything the same! Arrest and prosecute all heterogeneity! Resistance is futile. You will be assimilated. Order! Order! Order in the universe!

Extrapolate this to the economies of 200 sovereign nations. What sort of demands would the Constable be placing on them? What would his *economic* edict read like? It might read something like this:

> Order! Order! Order in the universe! You must allow your local economies to be assimilated by the global economy! You must remove local restrictions on globalization! You must marginalize your local peoples and devalue your local currencies! You must take down your sovereign borders and let the foreign investors in! You must divest yourselves of political heterogeneity and merge with the global order! You must do as we say or we will cut off your credit and put you on the leper list. Resistance is futile. You will be assimilated. Order! Order! Order in the universe!

This is in fact quite typical of IMF conditionalities. The words may be different, but the spirit is identical. That the creed of the IMF is a homogenizing one is a foregone conclusion. Those dreaded SAPs (structural adjustment programs) are acid to political heterogeneity and solvent to national sovereignty. In the words of Davison Budhoo:

> [F]or the last five years we have been asking countries to transform themselves instantaneously, from whatever they were before, to a homogenized, new packaged brand of free wheeling capitalism, all elements of which are contained in our [IMF] programs...[8]

As far as the Constable's agenda is concerned, *homogenization* is the operative word. Take any pattern of heterogeneity and hand it over to the Constable. He will rearrange the elements in such ways as to work the increase of homogeneity. Begin with a low probability state, end up with a high probability state. Begin with a pattern of *complexity*, end up with a pattern of simplicity. Begin with a pattern of heterogeneity, end up with a pattern of homogeneity.

The globalist's cant of *opening up to free trade* sounds quite plausible until one realizes that the whole edifice of world trade is built around a crumbling 17th century scaffolding of money creation. No trade is possible without money, and no money can be created without going into debt. The nations that are now being asked to open their doors to "free trade" are in reality being asked to conform to an obsolete and crumbling system based on debt. All the dice are loaded. The devil that has vested interests in the unnecessary creation and increase of global debt is the devil that makes up all the rules of "free trade." You play by his rules or you don't play at all.

Let us put ourselves in the shoes of the Cosmic Constable and try to see how he might use global debt as a tool to produce massive increases of disorder (entropy) on earth. The connection between global debt and environmental entropy is unmistakable, as is the connection between public debt and social disorder. We human beings cannot survive without graded energy, and money is the medium that we need to purchase it with. Even by this measure the power to grant or withhold Money to nations would be a power to grant or withhold life itself. The connection between the availability of "money" and the survival of the human species is as obvious as the connection between global debt and the survival of many species now on the endangered list. That crumbling 17th century scaffolding is now placing the very survival of the human species at risk.

In trying to provide the reader with an intuitive understanding of "entropy," we said that a useful analogy might be found in a mortgage, where the interest accumulated for the duration of the loan would be analogous to entropy, and the equity analogous to graded energy. Human order and economy depend on the availability of graded energy (the opposite of entropy). Presently, "money" is the medium that human beings use to purchase graded energy (food, fuel, electricity, heating oil and the wherewithal of biological survival). If the devil himself wanted to move the human condition towards higher entropy states he could do no better than to take money out of peoples' pockets—by debt interest, by inflation, by legalized extortion, by confiscatory taxation, by hook or by crook.

MONEY CREATION

Economic systems need to be evaluated on the basis of some universal truth. Everything else being equal, systems that produce increases of life and *complexity* should be judged "good," and systems that produce the opposite judged "evil." Since money is the medium that people use to purchase the wherewithal of biological survival, the virtue of any monetary system should be evaluated on the basis of the degree to which it contributes to the survival and prosperity of the greatest number of people. The system that places the greatest volume of sound money at the disposal of mankind, thereby contributing to the survival and well-being of the greatest number of people, should be regarded as the most desirable. Any system that makes money scarce, or degrades the value thereof, should be rejected outright.

Fundamentally, money is nothing more than a medium of exchange. It is the tail, not the head. We need to emphasize this to arrive at a clear understanding of the subordinate role of money in the ordering of human affairs. We need to remind ourselves that money was introduced to facilitate the *exchange* of labor and goods. We need to go back to the historical place where bartering became well nigh impossible and money was first introduced as a concept device. That historical transition may be summed up as follows:

> Came the day when primitive society passed the stage of barter, there arose a need for a convenient medium of exchange. This need was fulfilled in the invention of the concept of "money."

The legitimate and useful function of money was and is to facilitate the *exchange* of goods and services. It is the solemn duty of every government to provide a just, fair and equitable medium of exchange to that end. Money provides human society with a unit of account, a means of facilitating transfers of credit, a means of establishing the exchange values of labor and goods in relation to one another. Money is a means to an end, and not and end in itself. In, of, and by itself, money has no inherent value. It is a unit of account, and not physical wealth. It has meaning only when applied to some object, just as the concept of the "gallon" has no meaning unless applied to some liquid. No one can buy or sell a "gallon" in, of or by itself.

Much of what we call "civilization" is built on trade and commerce. Without money there would be no trade or commerce—no civilization as we know it today. Money is a blessing as a medium of exchange. However when money is stored under a false pretext, when it is sought for itself, or when it is treated as though it was a commodity, it ceases to be a blessing and becomes a curse instead. The falsification of money gives rise to false values, and crooked institutions that profit by manipulating them. When government knowingly or unknowingly sanctions the misuse and falsification of money, it permits the rise of crooked institutions, not only within its own territorial boundaries but elsewhere in the world where those institutions may have their branches and subsidiaries. By allowing money to be falsified, government ends up condoning unethical practices throughout the entire world.

When money is falsified it vaunts itself on the head of society and begins wagging the dog of human order and economy. It needs no prophet's eye to see that this is exactly what has happened in the world today, where we see an array of financial institutions built on the assumption that money is *itself* a commodity that can be bought, sold, bargained for, speculated upon, exported, imported, etc.. On a daily basis we hear such expressions as *The Money Market*, for example, the global gambling casino in which the dollar has risen against the yen, or the British pound fallen against the euro.

Let us return to the analogy of the "gallon," for a moment. It would be absurd to hear an expression such as *The Gallon Market*, would it not? If the gallon is a unit of measure, common sense would require it to be a constant measure. Yet in the present world system it is as though the "gallon" itself had become a commodity, some days worth seven pints, some days eight, and some days nine!

We should point out that there is nothing wrong with the price fluctuation that result from the laws of supply and demand. The price fluctuations associated with supply and demand have been likened to harmless ripples that may exist on the surface of a lake. These ripples are the natural consequences of free trade and will exist as long as the free market exists. On the other hand the wholesale national ups and downs, that occur by reason of the fluctuations of global currencies, have been likened to giant unnatural tides that come and go, wreaking havoc on the internal price levels of different nations at different times. The wholesome laws that govern supply and demand will, by their natural restraints, determine the values of goods and services, allocate fair prices and equitable ratios of exchange. But as long as the "currency tides" keep altering the internal price levels of different nations, fairness will remain a charade and equity a pretense. As long as the tail of Money is allowed wag the dog of physical economy, fair trade will remain an idle dream and so too all our hopes of Millennial Economics.

When a government allows money to be treated like a commodity, the same thing happens to currency as to other commodities. If more speculators want to sell "dollar" than buy, the "dollar" will go down. If more speculators want to buy "dollar" than sell, the "dollar" will go up. Heavy "buying" of a certain nation's currency is the same as imposing an artificial "tide" on the internal price level of that nation. Conversely heavy "selling" of a nation's currency does the reverse. In this sort of context fair trade is very difficult.

Fluctuating currencies are like the ancient bag of deceitful weights. One of the greatest injustices that one nation could commit against another would be to agree on a price determined by the value of a currency at the time of a transaction, letting the people of another nation depend on that price when they take on obligations to import goods, and then allow the value of that currency to change so that when payment is due the purchasers are forced to pay two or three times more than what the original contract called for. Very often when transactions have been settled it is discovered too late that currency speculations going on at the time have created a situation in which each debt of $1000 can now be canceled by the payment of something less than that, much to the consternation of the exporting nation. Or conversely a situation in which each debt of $1000 must now be redeemed by something more than that, much to the horror of the importing nation.

Naturally this drives finance ministers and treasury secretaries to try all sorts of shenanigans in an effort to "shore up" their own currencies. Some of those shenanigans have backfired. "Derivatives," for example, started innocently enough as a hedge against currency fluctuation, but in a short time they grew into a global speculative bubble of obscene proportions. The derivative virus that brought down LTCM (Long Term Capital Management), and more recently Enron Corporation, is now making its way into the body and soul of wholesale economies, infecting everything from bank stocks to bond markets, mutual funds, pension and retirement funds. This is what happens when governments allow the concept of "money" to be falsified.

What are we saying? We are saying that the issue of *money creation* is pervasive, ruling on the dispositions of nations, their economies, stock markets, corporations, businesses, citizens, families, housing, health, nutrition, energy—the spiritual and material well-being of six billion human beings created in the image of God. An issue such as this cannot be trifled with. It can no longer be swept under a rug, or put off until tomorrow. The subject of *money creation* now demands the attention of the United States Congress.

A sovereign nation must have a *system* for creating its own money. When the Founders settled the American continent it was for the most part a wilderness. The nation was young then and the amount of money required by the first immigrants not too great. In the span of two hundred years the former wilderness has been transformed into the most productive civilization on earth, with a myriad of small and large companies producing everything from safety pins to wide-bodied jets. The amount of money needed to run the nation today is infinitely greater than what was required 200 years ago. It is easy to see that the volume of money has had to be increased to keep up with economic growth and development.

Throughout our history at regular intervals new money has had to be created and somehow *introduced into general circulation.* How does one introduce new money into general circulation? This is the question—and the stumbling block. The bone of contention centers around the *system* by which new money is introduced into general circulation. More than anything else, it is this *system* that gives money all of its characteristics, good or bad, and all of its qualities, desirable or undesirable.

Money is a lifeless thing, knowing no more good from evil than right from wrong. The money that is created at the Bureau of Printing and Engraving is not at issue. At issue is the system by which it is *introduced into the arteries of commerce*, after it has been created. What is that system? With a few minor exceptions, the world's system of money issuance has been based on debt. In this world, debt is used as the *occasion* to introduce new money into general circulation. What does this mean? Well, it just means that someone has to actually go and borrow the newly created money into circulation otherwise it will not enter the arteries of trade and commerce. This is what we mean by a *Debt-Money System.*

By *Debt-Money System* we do not mean private debt. Whereas every individual has a mind, conscience, and will of his own, we are not here to dictate what he or she should or should not do with his or her private finances. The bone of contention does not involve the voluntary borrowing of money (private debt), or the legitimate function of banking. If a private individual thinks that he can make borrowed money work for him, if he thinks that the dividends that he expects to receive on his labor and enterprise will exceed the cost of borrowing, that is his own business. The bone of contention involves public borrowing, not private borrowing.

A man who is bound in debt is sometimes called a *bondsman*. The person to whom he is bound is called a *bond holder*. The document that gives the latter a charge over the former is called a *bond*, and the association thus created is referred to as *bondage*. A citizen may choose to go into debt, which is one thing. A citizen may be placed in debt by government, which is another thing. When people are unnecessarily placed in debt by government, they must work to earn money, to pay taxes, to pay off their public debts. The term that we would apply to this business is *involuntary servitude*. Thomas Jefferson once said that the act of placing a debt on our children was the equivalent of enslaving them. We believe that most Americans would not think that they had the right to enslave their children. And yet this is exactly what a Debt-Money System does.

DEBT-MONEY SYSTEM

How does a Debt-Money System work? Basically it is a scheme in which governments print debt in the form of *bonds*. In essence they then take these bonds to central banks, deposit them as collateral, and say to the central banker, "Here is the collateral, now you print our money and lend it to us as 6% interest." This may be somewhat of an oversimplification, but it describes the basic way in which nations are financed through *bond issues*, using their national debts as a means of creating money. With rare exceptions, no new money can be created in a Debt-Money System without incurring additional public debts. It is a debt-creating, debt-compounding system. It exists on a foundation of bonded public indebtedness.

Now in case some folks are wondering about the excuse and rationale given to justify the necessity of such a system, the excuse and rationale might go something like this:

> Since no one will be able to get the cash too easily, and without paying interest on it, this will serve to restrain the greedy politicians from creating too much printing press money and fostering inflation.

This is the bogus argument that the camel has been using to keep the master out of his own tent for so long. Our legislatures have heard this argument so many times that they have been conditioned into believing that a national debt is an original idea, a basic principle of economics, a fundamental necessity, a tried and true law. The plain truth is that there is no such law. No nation has to *borrow* its own money into existence from autonomous banking institutions. There is no rule that forces a nation to go into debt in the course of creating its own media of exchange.

To hear the "experts" talk one would think that the people and Government of the United States were incapable of issuing their own money without destroying its value. Every time there is talk of a Debt-Free System these experts launch into tirades and issue dire warning about "printing press money," reminding us of the calamities that ensued when nations tried to create their own money free of debt and interest. These "experts" are very fond of reminding us of the hyperinflation that occurred in Germany in 1923.

When Germany fell in 1918 the Allies met in the mirrored halls of the Palace of Versailles to decide the terms of peace—to decide what the loser would have to pay. It was decided that Germany would have to pay a reparation bill of $132 billion in gold or pre-war marks, a staggering sum in those days. As it turned out, a few years later the Allies changed their minds and decided that Germany would be far more useful as a buffer against Stalin's Communism. In fact they began quietly lending money to Germany and looking the other way when she began to re-arm. In the financial chaos that paved the way for the rise of Hitler, the debt-laden German economy went into a tailspin, and hyperinflation was engineered to dispose of the obligations of Versailles. The German printing presses were kept going round the clock and the volume of paper money was increased at a rate bordering on the absurd until 1000 German marks which prior to 1923 would have bought $250 American dollars wouldn't buy a ten cent loaf of bread.

Those who have vested interests in the unnecessary creation and increase of global debt never miss an opportunity to wave the German hyperinflation scarecrow over the heads of nations, using anecdotes such as "taking a wheel barrow full of money to the supermarket to buy a loaf of bread." Americans have been brainwashed about "the evils of printing press money" to such an extent that it is not uncommon to find them throwing disdainful glances at Washington and making statements like this: "Those darned politicians. They just go down to the basement and print more money!" In the financial columns of America's newspapers one often runs across similar editorials, speaking about the "printing" of money as the blackest and most damnable of sins, warning that "government is fueling inflation by virtue of its uninhibited production of printing press money."

The question that we would put to intelligent and thinking Americans is this: If Uncle Sam could just go down to the basement and "print money," why would he be *six trillion dollars* in debt, and why would he be gnawing at the taxpayers' bones? The answer of course is that he can't "print money." He can only print debt. In this world system Uncle Sam is allowed to print dollar bonds. He is not allowed to print dollar bills.

Now we do not dispute the fact that "spending money" is a favorite pastime of politicians, heaven knows we don't. Given the flaw in human nature, we wouldn't even trust ourselves with the nation's purse strings. But this is why the Founders incorporated checks and balances into government. With proper oversight and accountability the American people *can* create their own debt-free money without destroying its value. To say that they shouldn't be allowed to, is to deprive them of true self-government.

Abraham Lincoln printed money free of debt and interest. The year was 1862 and the President was hard pressed for money for the Civil War. The bullion brokers, seeing that they had the President over the barrel, said they would loan out no money unless they were paid exorbitant interest. Lincoln refused to submit to such extortion. Turning to the Constitution, he directed the Federal Bureau of Engraving to print $450,000,000 in so-called "greenbacks" (called that because of their color). The Congress and the Supreme Court did not challenge his right, nor did the President himself see in the Constitution any limit to his issuing the money directly, without having to pay interest to some middle man.

By January 1863 $450,000,000 in authentic United States notes were *paid* into general circulation free of debt and interest. Those greenbacks stayed in the arteries of the nation's commerce for a hundred years (until 1965). Despite an initial depreciation, it has been estimated that in the century or so that they remained in circulation they changed hands enough times to facilitate the exchange and distribution of more than a trillion dollars in goods and services. What's more, for the length of time that they were used as money they saved the nation and several generations of its taxpayers about $50,000,000,000 in interest payments.

To echo the words of Andrew Jackson, "there are no necessary evils in government!" There is no law that compels a nation to *borrow* its own money into general circulation from a middle-man. Common sense would indicate that the people of a sovereign nation ought not be dependent on global banks for their media of exchange. A people cannot be both sovereign and subject at the same time. It is the Constitutional duty and responsibility of *representative Government* to create a just, fair and equitable medium of exchange for its people. It is not the duty, responsibility, prerogative, or privilege of private banks to do so. The founders of America said as much in Article 1, Section 8, Clause 5 of the U.S. Constitution:

> Congress shall have power....To coin money, regulate the value thereof....

Concerning Article 1, Section 8, Clause 5 of the Constitution, Jacques S. Jaikaran writes the following in his book called *Debt Virus* :

> If the federal government can create a dollar's worth of bond, why can't it create the dollar bill directly? Instead of getting a Federal Reserve note, why not use a United States note or dollar? How can the entire American citizenry be duped into believing that the privately created Federal Reserve notes, not backed by anything, are more valuable than a United States note, issued by the American government and backed by the integrity of the whole citizenry of America?
>
> The Federal Reserve Act of 1913 did not relinquish the power to create money to privately owned Federal Reserve banks, commercial banks, or thrift institutions. It would require an amendment to Article 1, Section 8,

> Clause 5, of the Constitution to do so. But this part of our Constitution was never amended; it is still the law of the land. What percentage of our elected officials today truly understand that Congress still has the right to create money? If they really do understand this, why do they allow a private corporation to create money out of thin air that they borrow at an interest charge that is passed along to United States taxpayers? There is neither rhyme nor reason in such an arrangement, which is the ultimate manifestation of the fundamental flaw plaguing our economy. [9]

Economic strength is an essential condition of Liberty and guarantee of peace. As far as industrialized nations are concerned, the prudent increase of the money supply for purposes of trade and production has *always* proved beneficial to the causes of Liberty and peace. Conversely every instance in which the supply of money has shrunk, has resulted in bondage, disorder, unrest, poverty, stagnation and mass misery. The truth (the non-contradiction) is that no nation has ever succeeded in restoring prosperity without placing adequate supplies of sound money at the disposal of its people. No greater, more solemn or urgent duty rests upon the United States Congress at this time than to do just that.

No, we are not suggesting that the government printing presses be let loose to litter the streets of America with $100 bills, or the secretary of the treasury go up in an airplane and "throw money out of the window." Neither are we suggesting that Uncle Sam resume borrowing himself into bankruptcy. What we do suggest is that our elected representatives give evidence of their sanity by understanding the difference between money that is created in the form of debt, and money that is created free of debt. Above all, we would have them stand their ground and stop bolting to the stampede at the first display of the old scarecrow—*Printing press money, inflation! Printing press money, inflation!* In short, we pray that God will open the eyes of the United States Congress so that the most august legislative body on earth should replace the crumbling 17th century scaffolding of central banking with a just, fair and equitable system throughout the earth. (Amen! May God open the eyes of the United States Congress!)

CLASSIC PRICE INFLATION

We said that in the broadest of philosophical contexts *entropy* can be said to be a type or simile of the universal principle of de-gradation. If human economies were physical systems, the Cosmic Constable would want to degrade them just like any other physical system in the universe. If money was a physical system, the Constable would want to degrade that as well. What would happen in that case? Money would undergo "inflation."

Inflation is an insidious evil that creeps up on a society and disembowels it without a single shot being fired. The devil of inflation seems to have plagued every civilization on earth. Circa 300 A.D., during the reign of the emperor Diocletian, the price inflation was so severe that it is thought to have contributed to the downfall of Imperial Rome. The severe inflation that seized Germany in 1923 paved the way for the rise of Hitler. In Russia it helped put the Bolsheviks in power. In China it was the prelude to mass social upheavals and the rise of Mao Zedong.

An old Elizabethan proverb goes like this: "Bad money drives out good." History confirms the proverb. Bad money drives out good money, spreading the red carpet before disorder, iniquity, injustice, and war. If the Constable wanted to produce such things on earth, he could do no better than to flood the earth with bad money. (During the American Revolution, British General William Howe tried to destroy the economies of the American Colonies by flooding them with counterfeit Continental bills.)

Today, in the wealthiest nation on earth, we have this thing called "inflation." Despite the fact that it has a historic reputation for devouring societies, no one in authority seems to know the real cause of it. The traditional cures are not working. The Federal Reserve policy of "raising interest rates" is not bringing *this* form of inflation under control. The degree to which the Fed restricted credit in past decades should have caused a tremendous fall in general prices—the same measure of credit strangulation would have brought prices down to a fraction of what they are today, had this been 1920. What is most disturbing is that prices continue their slow systemic rise, as though in express defiance of the law of gravity.

The CPI is the government's Consumer Price Index, and a "base period" is a year that the Department of Labor uses as a starting point in measuring price increases. Despite the fact that the base period has been moved up five times since 1913, the cold sober truth is that the purchasing power of the dollar has dwindled from 100 cents in 1913 to about 5 cents in 2000. The picture that comes to mind is that of a swimmer caught in an outgoing tide. He appears to be swimming toward the shore, but a strong undercurrent is taking him out to sea.

When a physician is confronted with a disease he must first diagnose it. Many diseases have overlapping symptoms. Some diseases, although quite different, have similar symptoms. If the symptoms include skin disorders, for example, they may be caused by a simple allergy or irritation. Or, they may be caused by a cancer. The correct diagnosis is very important. Inflation is like a disease, and here also correct diagnosis is the first step toward finding a cure. In this connection a certain truth is now emerging, namely that the physicians who have assumed charge over our ailing economy have not bothered to obtain a correct diagnosis. They have been treating the *symptoms* of inflation only. It is as though they have been applying ointments and bandaids to a systemic cancer.

There are different types of inflation. For here and now we will focus on two:

1) *Classic price inflation.*
2) *Systemic price inflation.*

Classic price inflation is caused by an imbalance between volume of money and volume of goods and services. The best way to understand classic price inflation is to think of the free market as an auction hall. What can we say about this auction hall? Well, for one thing we can say that there are no fixed prices in it. All prices are constantly changing, going slightly up or down according to the laws of supply and demand. In this auction hall sellers will try to get the highest price for their goods, and buyers will try to pay as low a price as they can. This is the very essence of what we call *free market.* If the seller is asking too much, the buyer will buy from someone else. If the buyer is offering too little, the seller will sell to someone else. Caveat emptor.

In this auction hall *effective demand* will determine the highest bid. If effective demand is high, the auctioneer will bid up the price. If it is low, the auctioneer will have to settle for something less. But what are we to understand by "effective demand?" For one thing we are to understand a basic desire on the part of people to buy whatever is being offered. The more they want something, the more they will pay for it. More importantly, however, effective demand depends on the amount of money in people's pockets.

Let us say the auctioneer is trying to sell a violin to interested buyers. At what price will the bidding start, and at what price will it end? Well, if the buyers have on average $10 in their pockets, we can assume that the bidding will begin at about $3 and end at about $9. But suppose everyone in the auction hall has on average about $100 in his or her pocket, what then? Well, again, it would be reasonable to assume that the auctioneer would attempt to bid up the price of the violin to somewhere around $90. And if everyone in the auction hall has on average about $1000 in his or her pocket, it would be reasonable to assume that the highest bid would be somewhere around $900.

Here is the point. The free market is much like an auction hall. Not only are there no fixed prices in it, but the prices that come and go are to a large extent determined *by the volume of money in general circulation.* The greater the volume of money, the higher the general prices; the smaller the volume of money, the lower the general prices. One doesn't need a degree from the London School of Economics to see the intimate relationship between the purchasing power of each dollar and the total number of dollars in general circulation. Because of this relationship, government has to keep an eye on the amount of money in circulation to try to avoid *classic price inflation.* The volume of money must be increased prudently and wisely, to reflect the volume of goods and services being auctioned in the free market. If it is increased too rapidly, a temporary imbalance will ensue between volume of money and volume of goods/services. Whenever this happens the auctioneers will succeed in bidding up general prices—classic price inflation.

Classic price inflation occurs when the nation's money supply is increased too rapidly, or when large pools of money enter the nation from outside. The temporary imbalance between the volume of money and volume of goods will bring about a *tide factor.* This tide will cause general prices to "float" upwards, as though by some spontaneous and unseen law. The reverse also holds true. If the nation's basic money supply is suddenly decreased, or if there is large capital flight out of the country, the "auctioneers" (manufacturers, retailers, etc.) will have to settle for a much lower price. In this case a *falling tide* will deflate general prices and cause them to stabilize at a lower level.

In light of the above it is reasonable to assume that classic price inflation can be caused by *industrial immaturity* as well. What do we mean by "industrial immaturity?" We mean the capacity of a nation to balance and offset any increase in money supply with the production of new goods and services. If there is only one violin for sale, the auctioneer will succeed in bidding up the price. But if ten more violins are quickly "brought to market," the price of violins would fall accordingly. Thus we arrive at one of the axioms of Classical Economics, or what is sometimes referred to as Supply Side Economics :

> If the supply of goods and services can be increased in relation to the volume of money, there will be a decline in general prices, which will restrain classic price inflation.

To recapitulate: Classic price inflation is caused by an imbalance between two things, 1) volume of money, 2) volume of goods and services. If these two things can be kept balanced there will be no classic price inflation. From this it can be seen that industrial maturity is the other half of the equation. If a nation has the capacity to quickly increase its production of goods and services, no reasonable increase in the money supply could lead to classic price inflation. Why not? Because the economy would speed up and crank out additional goods and services to match and offset the increase in the money supply. If a nation had the productive capacity to keep the two factors perfectly balanced, it would know no such thing as classic price inflation. For this reason one can argue that classic price inflation is more indigenous to the lesser developed nations of the world.

The inflation that was rampant in OPEC (Organization of Petroleum Exporting Countries) a few decades ago was for the most part classic price inflation. It was caused by an *imbalance* between the glut of oil money and available goods and services. Huge revenues from the sale of oil suddenly flooded the "auction halls" of the OPEC nations. Suddenly everyone in the auction hall had more money than he knew what to do with, so the auctioneers succeeded in bidding up the prices of what few goods there were sitting on the shelves. Those OPEC nations did not have the industrial capacity to offset, balance, and equalize the glut of oil money with rapid production of new goods and services. A temporary imbalance ensued, which brought about a tide effect, causing general prices to "float upwards" and stabilize at higher levels. And this is how economists derive their definition of classic price inflation—*too much money chasing too few goods and services.*

When the economic "experts" of this world speak about inflation, they mean classic price inflation. Evidently it has never occurred to them that there may be other types of inflation. Having never bothered to obtain a correct diagnosis, they claim that the lingering inflation in America is caused by too much money in people's pockets and not enough goods on the shelves. This is the rationale behind the Federal Reserve's tight credit policy. The "experts" believe that by raising interest rates and restricting credit they will reduce the amount of money in the proverbial auction hall and prevent the auctioneers from bidding up prices.

There is no denying that classic price inflation is to be avoided at all costs. It is detrimental to society because the increase in money supply does not filter down into all pockets equally, causing injustice, for instance, with respect to those who are on fixed incomes. It is bound to be injurious to world trade as well, because of the "tides" that it brings to bear, raising and lowering the internal price level of one nation against that of another. Yes, we wholeheartedly agree that classic price inflation should be avoided at all costs. Fortunately it not difficult to bring it under control. Classic price inflation is a fairly straight-forward phenomenon, each increase in the money supply seen to correlate with a proportional rise in general prices. It is not a self-augmenting—cancerous—affair. The increases in general prices are neither baffling nor difficult to explain.

One way of bringing classic price inflation under control would be to impose a temporary luxury tax. In this way government could take the excess money out of circulation quickly, while sparing the poor and needy classes that may yet exist in that nation. If inflation rears up its ugly head the rich will have a lot more to lose than the poor. A rich man who is also wise, would not mind the imposition of a temporary luxury tax, though the rich fool would complain like Scrooge. Using a temporary luxury tax to control classic price inflation would be a 4-step process:

1) Determine the excess in circulation.
2) Impose a temporary luxury tax.
3) Withdraw the excess money.
4) Repeal the tax and go back normal business.

This, and other means, including the raising of interest rates, would work if we were in fact dealing with *classic* price inflation. But are we? What sort of inflation are we looking at when we see the 90% decline of purchasing power since 1913? If it was classic price inflation then one could argue that the Federal Reserve approach of raising interest rates might bring it under control. Regrettably we are about to show the inflation in America is something altogether different.

SYSTEMIC PRICE INFLATION

By way of a grand introduction to the mechanism of *systemic price inflation* we would have intelligent and thinking peoples glance at the following table, familiarize themselves with the nature of compound debt, and notice the way in which it will inflate itself if both principle and interest have been left unpaid over the long run.

$1000 BORROWED INTO EXISTENCE
AT 6% COMPOUND INTEREST

Principal	Years	Amount Due
$1000	12	$2012
$1000	24	$4049
$1000	36	$8147
$1000	48	$16394
$1000	60	$32988
$1000	72	$66378
$1000	84	$133565
$1000	96	$268755
$1000	108	$540796
$1000	120	$1088188

From this table it can be seen that if both principal and interest are left untouched for 12 years it will take twice as much money to pay off the same debt-obligation. If both principal and interest are left unpaid for 120 years, it will take more than a million dollars in goods and services to pay off an original sum of only $1000.

Let us return to our auction hall and see if a debt-system will have any long term effects on the purchasing power of the dollar. Here we are, inside a brand new auction hall, the first in history. As of yet there are no "prices." As of yet no one has any "money" in his or her pocket. There is a central bank in the auction hall. The buyers and sellers (the body politic) go to the bank and borrow $1000 into general circulation at 6% compound interest. The auction is opened. The bidding starts. For the first time in history "prices" begin to seek their natural levels.

Question: In relation to what precedent did initial prices level themselves? Answer: $1000. How much money is in actual circulation? $1000. What is the obligation of the marketplace to the central bank? $1000. How many dollars in goods and services are required to redeem that obligation? $1000.

Let us now imagine that twelve years have come and gone and both principal and interest have remained unpaid. Question: How much money is in actual circulation? Answer: Still $1000. What is the obligation of the marketplace to the bank now? $2012. How many dollars in goods and services are required to redeem the obligation now? It will now take $2012 in goods and services to redeem the same obligation. Question: how can the people pay off their debt? Answer: By doubling their prices.

Let us look at that again. Twelve years ago the first "prices" leveled themselves off against $1000 in circulation. The volume of goods and services has remained unchanged. The actual amount of money in circulation has remained unchanged. But the original obligation has now swelled to $2012, and *that* is what prices must now level themselves against. So how is the auction hall going to compensate for what has changed? Answer: By allowing the only remaining variable—"price"—to float upward. Ergo *systemic price inflation.*

Our analogy may be crude, but the principle is consistent with reality. Long ago Uncle Sam gave up trying to pay off the principal on the Federal Debt, which has now swollen to something in excess of $6,000,000,000,000. Yes, Congress has been keeping up the interest payments, but the actual debt has been increasing by compound progression.

Systemic price inflation is also caused by an *imbalance.* Not an imbalance between volume of money and volume of goods and service, but an imbalance between volume of debt and volume of money. Not "too much money chasing too few goods and services," but *too much debt chasing too little money.*

The taxpayers must produce goods and services in order to earn dollars, in order to pay taxes, in order to service their public debt. The longer the public debt has been left to snowball, the more dollars in labor and goods it will take to service it. This is the imbalance that produces systemic price inflation.

Let us look at it holistically. Much the same way in which the cost of energy is an overhead of industry, the cost of money-creation is a fundamental but totally overlooked overhead of government and the private sector alike. What happens when that overhead increases? In order to keep itself afloat, the government will have to increase debt-related taxes. In order to keep themselves afloat the people will have to raise their prices. As the debt-overhead of the economy increases, the manufacturer faced with the increase in his own overhead will be forced to raise the price of his product or go out of business. Similarly the laborer faced with the increase in the cost of living will have to demand higher wages or declare bankruptcy. And so begins the insidious cycle.

As the imbalance grows, one or all of the following will have to take place in order to offset it: Prices will have to increase; taxes will have to increase; defense, social and other funds will have to be cut; the ceiling on the national debt will have to be raised. If none of the above is done the nation will be in default. The deeper the nation sinks into debt the greater the loss of purchasing power. As the compound debt snowballs it begins to outstrip and outdistance the nation's capacity to service it. The resulting deficit will drive more and more people out of business, out of work, out of house and home. The welfare and unemployment burden will increase, which will mean even higher taxes for those who have managed to stay in business, which will cause them to raise their prices still higher. With its liabilities skyrocketing, and its tax revenues plummeting, the ship of state will begin listing. When the process achieves critical mass she will roll and sink.

Let us take note of the fact that the principal on America's national debt is presently an astronomical figure in excess of *six trillion dollars*. Let us take note of increases in taxation since 1913. Let us take note of cuts in legitimate social programs. Let us take note of the fact that Congress has been regularly raising the ceiling on the national debt just to keep itself afloat. We would therefore submit to intelligent and thinking Americans that the 90% decline in the purchasing power of the dollar since 1913 is not a symptom of classic price inflation—it is beyond any shadow of a doubt a symptom of *systemic inflation.* It is built into the debt system of money creation.

Every economist worth his salt knows, or should know, that classic price inflation is easily identifiable by the presence of *high effective demand*—too many people with too much money wanting to buy too few goods and services. Is effective demand high in America today? Obviously not, otherwise economists wouldn't be calling it "stagflation!" How then can prices continue to rise in a stagnant economy? Only through systemic price inflation, identifiable by the presence of *low effective demand*—too much debt-overhead and not enough left over to buy all the goods and services collecting dust on the shelves. You would expect systemic price inflation to be indigenous to the debt-riddled economies of the industrialized nations. It is.

There is no glut of "unencumbered money" in the arteries of American commerce and industry. The Federal obligation alone is many times greater than the amount of money floating about in the big auction hall. How then can the "experts" be telling us that the inflation in America is caused by "too much money chasing too few goods and services?" Every sign would seem to be warning us that there is in fact a grave shortage of money in circulation. It is easy to see that there isn't nearly enough money in the auction hall, what with every remaining dollar stretched to the limit, every budget and fund being slashed, cities teetering on the edge of bankruptcy, everyone in debt, wives and husbands working three different jobs, Uncle Sam gnawing at the taxpayers' bones.

We don't have to waste time trying to show that there is not nearly enough money in circulation to meet the gargantuan needs of a nation such as the United States of America, a nation with several states that are among the highest ranking industrial entities in the world (California, for example, has been ranked 5th). Effective demand is low. The economy is growing at a snail's pace. In real terms factory orders for durable goods have been declining for years, automobile manufacturers offering huge incentives and cash rebates just to lure consumers into the auction hall. Unless one is blind, or in a state of denial, it is easy to see that our economy is in a highly *deflated* condition.

A nation is said to be "developed" when it has reached a certain plateau of industrial maturity beyond which the fluent production of goods is no longer an obstacle to material plenty. How in heavens name, we ask, can the "experts" claim that the United States is incapable of increasing its production of goods and services to offset a bucketful increase in money supply? How can it be said of a nation whose commercial market dominates world trade, whose productive and consumptive capacity is the king pin of the global economy, a nation that went from Kitty Hawk to a manned lunar module on the moon in seventy years, how can it be said of a nation such as this that it can't rev up its economy to offset a paltry increase in its basic money supply?

The economist's jargon, "too much money chasing too few goods and services," may have been applicable at the turn of the century when the horse and buggy were still in use. It may even have been applicable up to the time when old Henry was making Model A's one at a time. But is it applicable today? What we have here, folks, is a fantastic anachronism. How fantastic? Imagine drastically cutting the nation's supply of electricity, inducing blackouts from coast to coast, on the premise that "there are not enough incandescent bulbs in existence to warrant the output of this much electricity!"

The fact is that long ago ease of production ceased to be an obstacle to material abundance in America. Americans have not had any trouble producing for many decades now, and today their ability to produce knows no bounds. It is not the failure to produce that is causing America's cancerous inflation, it is the increasing cost of money creation pushing up prices.

The exponential growth of cancer usually leads to the death of the host. The exponential growth of debt can lead to recession, depression and catastrophic failure of human economies. When we treat skin cancer as though it was a minor blemish, we have gone a long way towards defeating ourselves. We can pretend that the cancer is just a blemish and try to control it by raising interest rates, but we will be fooling ourselves. The first and most important step towards curing inflation is correct diagnosis. Seeing only the outward symptoms, the experts are quick to administer bandaids and aspirin. Bandaids and aspirin may help the patient feel better, but they won't cure the cancer. There is no denying that the Fed's policy of "raising interest rates" is making Wall Street "feel better." With less money in the auction hall, the auctioneers will have to settle for lower prices.

But is this "curing inflation?" No, it is a clever way of imposing wage and price controls.

Raising interest rates to "cure" systemic price inflation is a contradiction so fantastic that it bears mentioning. Imagine if you will that there has been a terrible flood. And imagine a survivor of that flood, stranded waist deep in contaminated waters, suffering from exposure and thirst for many days. He sees the economic experts approaching in a rescue boat. Overjoyed, he cries out: "Water! Give me some water!" The experts survey his condition with a jaundiced eye. Then, with a great show of scholarship and wisdom, issue the following statement: "You want water? No! No! There is too much water in circulation already. It will worsen your condition."

THE SWAN SONG OF CENTRAL BANKING

We live in a world of cause and effect. Consider, for example, the effects of central banking in America. On 16 November 1914 the Federal Reserve Banks opened for business. America's national debt at that time was about $1 billion. In the course of ninety years it has snowballed to $6000 billion. The combined debts of Americans (both public and private) are now estimated to be many times that figure. There have been panics, crashes, recessions, booms and busts. These effects are not arbitrary.

Consider the effects of central banking on the economies of the rest of the world. Consider its effects on the poor and destitute peoples of the Third World. These effects are not arbitrary either. The marginalization of millions of human beings, poverty, hunger, disease, mass misery, degradation of ecosystems, pollution of rivers and oceans, the decimation of rainforests, destruction of species, depletion of resources and global warming, relate themselves to a 17th century scaffolding of central banking that is crumbling. This matter needs to be dealt with by all nations, and soon. Unless the old debt-system is replaced by a debt-free one, the world will carry the dead weight of the old order into the new millennium and there will be nothing in store but more of the same. More debt. More poverty. More disease. More marginalization. More reduction. More terrorism. More war. More Bosnia, Chechnya and Rwanda. More environmental degradation. More global warming. More human misery. The handwriting is on the wall.

God has given us the spiritual wherewithal to break free of the derivative orders of existence. Knowledge has increased by geometric progression. We now have the technology to clean up the oceans and rivers, to convert to clean energy sources, to replant forests, to build visionary cities, to restore man to the dignity of his origins in God. The gates of repentance are always open, and so are the gates of the Kingdom of God. All of the prime factors necessary for the creation of a truly advanced civilization are at hand. The Providence of God is inexhaustible. The material resources are all here. The jobs all need to be done. The labor is here. The know-how is here. The technology is here. But for some lifeless thing called "money," all of mankind's God-given creative faculties, talents, disciplines and resources would integrate to break the chains that bind.

MILLENNIAL ECONOMICS

The economic thinkers of our age seem to be suffering from some sort of mental block. And the few that are now calling for an end to central banking are sending mixed signals. While they are quick to condemn the flaws of the old model, they are slow to describe the one that might replace it. While they are eager to see the Federal Reserve System abolished, they are in disagreement as to what should take its place. Indeed some of the solutions that even they propose reveal as great a confusion of ideas and thoughts as one could imagine. This calls for a little clear thinking.

At a rudimentary level all human economies relate themselves to the laws of energy conservation and increasing entropy. Given a greater environment in which entropy is increasing, *conservation* and *economy* are ontological necessities. Hitherto all the economic systems of mankind have been flawed, reflecting the flaw in human nature itself. These flaws can now be corrected, pending the correction of the flaw in human nature. The world has now entered the Millennium. An old order has passed away, and a new one is upon us. It is time for a sea change.

Before we can begin to draw up the blueprints of *Millennial Economics*, we must journey back in time and take another look at why money was invented in the first place. We need to understand that "money" was never a preamble of economics. It was the tail, not the head. It was incidental to, and came after, the only preamble found in the entire history of economics—*exchange*. Money was never an immutable or indispensable artifact of history. God did not create money, man did. And man created it for the sake of expediency. He invented it for the sake of utility. It was never supposed to be an end in itself. It was never supposed to wag the dog of human order and economy.

Let us remind ourselves that "barter" had been for primitive society a natural and wholesome system of exchange. Bartering was decentralized, self-tending and self-limiting. No "middle-man" was involved. No "inflation" was possible. No one could barter with what he did not possess. There was no money to hoard, or speculate with or to manipulate. No one could incur an undeserved loss due to currency fluctuation. No one could obtain an unearned gain. And the love of money, said to be "the root of all evil," did not exist. Now in all this we are not saying that primitive society was utopia. We are merely saying that up to a certain point barter was a viable and wholesome system of exchange. Clearly, however, at a certain point mankind was obliged to enter into the next stage by inventing and using so-called "money." The causes that led to the creation of money can be summed up as follows:

> Came the day when primitive society passed the stage of simple barter, there arose a need for a convenient medium of exchange, a need that was fulfilled by the invention of "money."

Why did it become necessary for primitive society to make the transition from barter to money? The answer holds the key to Millennial Economics–

> because it became impossible to keep track of who owed what to whom!

Question: If primitive society had been blessed with information storage and transfer technologies, would it still have invented "money?" No, it would have had no need for it. Barter and all of its positive qualities would have continued down the ages, with tireless computers keeping track of who owed what to whom. And this is the whole key to *Millennial Economics*. With an old order passing away, the arrival of the information age is no coincidence. Millennial trade and exchange are now possible, using a global information utility. The tools that make *Millennial Economics* possible are already facilitating exchanges of billions of dollars worth of goods and services daily. The spadework has been accomplished already, thanks to trail blazers like Bill Gates and Tim Berners-Lee. The emergence of a global information utility means that the whole world can now engage in efficient exchange, letting the "slack" (limitations of distance and time between trading partners) be taken up by inanimate, efficient, accurate, and tireless computers.

Mankind is now in a position to replace the crumbling 17th century scaffolding of central banking with a Millennial system that is just, fair, equitable, self-tending, self-limiting, self-managing, self-regulating and self-stabilizing. And the electronic utility that would make that system possible is, for all intents and purposes, already in place. If this utility could be made a restrained creature of law, if it could be used in the context of a debt-free system, it would prove itself an unqualified blessing.

A reverence for the sovereignty of God should persuade us that beneath the surface clatter and commotion of this eleventh hour the technologies that are destined to serve mankind in the Millennium are materializing right on schedule. Notwithstanding, the American people must come to grips with what is now emerging, to dispose of potential hazards ahead of time. We don't have to spend all day trying to prove that a global utility such as this has a great deal of potential for good and evil. It can be a blessing, or it can be a curse. Whether it proves itself one or the other will of course depend on the laws that restrain it. The crossroads are before us. Which will it be? The blessing, or the curse? The outcome will depend on the American people and their elected representatives. Will they have the God-given wisdom to apply the lessons of history? Or will they stand by with indifference and allow this new tool to become yet another tail used by the Constable to wag the dog of human order and economy? The First Amendment of the U.S. Constitution reads thus:

> Congress shall make no law respecting an establishment of religion, or prohibiting the free exercise thereof; or abridging the freedom of speech, or of the press; or the right of the people peaceably to assemble and to petition the Government for a redress of grievances.

Who can calculate the sum of mischief that these few words have prevented in the last 200 years? Here are a few words written on a piece of paper, yet in all the pages of secular history you will not find a single blow more precisely and accurately launched into the ribcage of the principality that we have been calling "Cosmic Constable." So and likewise, a few additional words, written with providential and preventative foresight, will serve to indemnify future generations from untold mischief when it comes to the use of the nation's information utility. Members of the United States Congress would do well to earn the gratitude of future generations, just as the Founding Father have earned ours, by binding this new devil down from mischief ahead of time.

In 1913 the United States Congress placed its signature on a piece of preferential legislation that granted a monopoly of money-creation to the Federal Reserve Banks, for which prostitution of sovereignty the American people are now paying so great a price. To avoid the same sort of error, the nation's Information Utility must be protected by a Constitutional Amendment which may read like the First Amendment itself—*an Economic Bill of Rights*, if you will. Without presuming to dictate the exact wording, we submit the following facsimile:

> Congress shall make no preferential law respecting the nation's Information Utility, or applying usury to the use thereof, or requiring national identity cards in the use thereof, or hindering the free exchange of domestic labor and goods in the use thereof, or abolishing conventional moneys in the use thereof, or denying the right of the people to privacy in the use thereof.

An amendment along these lines must be made the law of the land or the American people will have no grounds to complain of the evils that may follow. Government must not be allowed to grant any banking institution a monopoly of the nation's Information Utility. That Utility must be used in the context of a debt-free system—the central banking system of the United States must be abolished. *Banks and financial institutions must not be allowed to charge interest on volumes of trade*, otherwise we will be right back where we started. The people must at all times be free to use other lawful media of exchange, such as cash, coins and notes, which usage embodies one of the basic freedoms of the American people. Government must protect, redundantly and comprehensively, the privacy of law-abiding citizens in the use of the Information Utility.

No national identity card will be issued by government, and no such abomination will be required to access the Information Utility. Neither shall any abomination be applied to human beings by way of permanent identification, whether of skin tattoo, or freeze marks, or any other mark, or chip insertions or any other insertion, in the use of the Information Utility. The "cards" that are used to access it should be limited in scope to the ATM-type debit and credit cards in use today, which may be issued by the banks of the private sector in the context of a 100% reserve banking system. Banks may charge interest on *loans* in this respect (someone using the bank's money to buy an appliance on time, for example), but they may not charge interest on *volumes of trade.*

So-called *smart cards* must likewise be made restrained creatures of law, otherwise the American people will have no grounds to complain of the evils that may follow. Here again, the way to safety lies in public disclosure and Congressional oversight. National security considerations notwithstanding, all Government issued smart cards and application specific integrated circuit cards must be subjected to Congressional oversight. Congress must routinely investigate and publish details relating to the following:

1) Intent
2) Components
3) Programming

Governments can easily protect the privacy of their citizens by means of personalized *public key* security codes or similar restraints. The invocation of these personal security codes by card holders would then exempt specified transactions from tracking and scrutiny. To quote the words of Daniel Webster: "Liberty exists in proportion to wholesome restraint." Through a little wholesome restraint, Congress *can* safeguard the privacy, liberty, and autonomy of individuals who are using the nation's Information Utility as a medium of exchange. These restraints must be incorporated into the Constitution of the United States to ensure redundancy. An addendum to the 4th Amendment might read as follows:

> Congress shall make no law establishing a system of computerized control and/or electronic eavesdropping over the privacy, property, or movement, of the people.

Addendi to Article IV, Section 2 of the Constitution might read as follows:

> Congress shall make no law restricting the mobility of law abiding citizens, or making the tracking and surveillance of their movements possible by means of the nation's Information Utility.
>
> Congress shall make no law establishing the linking of financial transactions with birth certificate records, employment records, health records, fingerprints, biometrics, voiceprints, palmprints, retinal scans, chromosome imaging, or other immutable marks of identification, in association with the use of the nation's Information Utility.
>
> Congress shall routinely publish the specifications relating to intent, components and programming of all related computers, software, encryption codes, telephone standards and communication protocols associated with the nation's Information Utility.

Once again, the charges incurred in the use of debit cards must be straightforward service charges, similar to those charged by other utilities (phone, gas, electric, etc.). *Congress must prohibit banks and financial institutions from charging interest on volumes of trade in such cases.* All such charges will consist of straightforwards fees, competitively structured—caveat emptor.

If this Information Utility is used as a debt-free medium of exchange, if it is protected by Constitutional Amendments containing redundant provisions that safeguard the rights of users, the system of economy heralded by it will prove a blessing surpassing the best that we can imagine. If not, it will end up being just one more tail that the devil of disorder will use to wag the dog of humanity. Should that happen, the American people will have no one to blame but themselves.

We now stand at the brink of the Millennium. Nature's forces have been harnessed to the service of man, not only releasing him from the original curse but also proving false the Malthusian premise of perpetual want and scarcity. Abundance of all good things is no longer a theory. It would be reality, were it not for an obsolete system that prevents equitable distribution of the Providence of God.

We are about to witness a sea change—an epochal Exodus out of the derivative orders of existence. The sudden increase in knowledge, and now the sudden arrival of the information age, make that Exodus practical. It could never have been done before. Only recently has technology reached the critical plateau where Millennial Economics becomes possible. No generation since the beginning of history could have put such a system into effect.

לֹא־תְאֻנֶּה אֵלֶיךָ רָעָה וְנֶגַע לֹא־יִקְרַב בְּאָהֳלֶךָ

There shall no evil befall you, neither shall any plague come near your dwelling.
(Psalm 91:10)

SECTION 6

Cosmos and Cancer

Millennial Medicine

We live in a unified creation governed by law. In this "cosmos," the greater order of change is flowing down the gradient that leads from low probability to high probability, from order to disorder, from *complexity* to simplicity, from heterogeneity to homogeneity, from non-isotropism to isotropism. This "flow" stamps the universe with an arrow of time and invests everything in it with a statistical tendency to disorder. The cosmos in which we live is oriented towards disorder. It has a nature and a property that make statistical selections in favor of disorder.

Universal systems are composed of elements which can be arranged in various ways, and they can be said to have order/disorder values depending on the entropy states of these arrangements. Everything else being equal, the lower the entropy state, the lower the degree of disorder; the higher the entropy state, the higher the degree of disorder; the more repetition, the higher the entropy state; the less repetition, the lower the entropy state; the higher the entropy state, the more probable the arrangement of elements within a system; the lower the entropy state, the less probable the arrangement of elements. In this cosmos disorder is more probable than order. In this cosmos ordered arrangements will tend to degrade into disordered arrangements.

Take any energy-driven pattern in the universe—a physical pattern, a behavioral pattern, an organizational pattern, a political pattern, an economic pattern, a biological pattern, a social pattern.

Look at the way in which its elements are organized and arranged. The more ordered, complex, dissimilar and heterogeneous the arrangement, the lower its entropy state. The more disordered, simple, repetitious, similar and homogeneous the arrangement, the higher its entropy state. In trying to move universal systems from lower to higher entropy states the Cosmic Constable must try to alter the organization of the elements within them, changing complex organizations into more simple ones, low-repetition arrangements into high-repetition arrangements.

The human body is an energy-driven system consisting of a large number of cellular elements. The average fully-grown human body consists of some 100 trillion cells of 200 different types. "Health" depends on a highly organized, highly ordered, and highly specific arrangement of these cellular elements. Give the Cosmic Constable a complex healthy arrangement such as this and he will try to increase its entropy state. And if he were to succeed in doing that, what would we end up with? We would end up with "disease."

The time has now come for scientists and physicians to nail down the universal provenance of disease. The plague principle is neither arbitrary nor local. It is universal. You would expect to find something called "disease" in a cosmos in which entropy is always increasing. In this cosmos, the ordered state that we call "health" is always in jeopardy of being reduced to the disordered state that we call "disease." The margins of health and disease are narrow. We walk a fine line, very fine indeed. The battle between health and disease is going on every moment of our lives, waged against the activity of the Constable by various arsenals of our bodies.

Throughout the cosmos the universal victim of corruption is *complexity*. In a universe in which simplicity is increasing, patterns of *complexity* are as fugitives and outlaws in constant jeopardy of reduction by the Cosmic Constable. The *complexity* of a healthy human body is precisely the sort of target to which the attention of the Constable would be drawn. As the Constable goes about the business of increasing the entropy of the universe, he is in effect behaving like a virus or a cancer, looking for targets of *complexity* to de-grade. The "plague" that would corrupt biological *complexity* is universal. The course of disease (pathology) flows along the universal gradient that leads from ordered to disordered states, from *complexity* to simplicity, from low-repetition to high-repetition, from low probability to high probability.

The human body with its trillions of cells is an energy-driven bio-cosmos wired into the fabric of the greater cosmos of matter and energy. The Constable is working to increase the entropy of the greater cosmos. Given the opportunity, he would also increase the entropy of the bio-cosmos. How? In the case of cancer, for example, via unregulated cell replication. Or in the case of AIDS, unregulated viral replication. The same plague-principle that is producing the increase of entropy in the universe of trillions of stars, would also produce the increase of entropy in the bio-universe of trillions of cells.

In a cosmic environment in which entropy is always increasing, the highly ordered state that we call "health" is a tenuous affair. In a cosmos oriented towards simplicity, biological *complexity* is as a candle in the wind. Biological life depends on myriad specific arrangements, all of them working in perfect harmony and orchestration. Any deficit, weak link, failure or compromise can throw the whole thing out of kilter, short-circuiting *complexity* into simplicity, health into disease, life into death. Life is a rare and *local* affair, requiring highly ordered, highly strung, highly tensed, highly stressed, highly unstable arrangements of material and energetic elements. And these are exactly the sort of complex arrangements that drive the Constable mad with rage. Suffice it to say that he would like to degrade the superlative order of life to the diminutive order of dust.

There is a contest afoot in the universe, one that pits the survival of enclaves of *complexity*, of which the living things found on earth are supreme examples, against the rising tide of simplicity, or what scientists call "increasing entropy." The tenuous nature of life, the fine line that separates health from disease, the rapid rate at which flesh will decay after death, all testify to the instability of life. All living things are struggling to survive the rising tide of increasing entropy. From the Constable's point of view they are as fugitives and outlaws that must be arrested and returned to dust. But for the overruling Providence of God, the Constable would have driven all of us into extinction long ago. For thus saith the Cosmic Constable:

> Dust to dust, ashes to ashes, and a hearty good riddance to all living things.

If God can be thought of as the Master Programmer, the *biologos* of life would amount to the "software" that was written by Him. *Biologos* implies "language of life," or what scientists are now calling *genome.* The human genome has sentence structure, and has been compared to a very long text containing some three billion encoded characters. All languages are made up of letter elements. The *biologos* is made up of four complex 3-dimensional letter elements—*adenine, guanine, cystosine, thymine* (AGCT). The "words" of the *biologos* are made up from the sequencing of these four letters.

The genome of a single human being has been compared to a book in which the sentences are various genes and the chapters, chromosomes. Each and every one of us consists of a unique biological text. Of the billions of humans that have lived on earth no two have had exactly the same text. Each one of us is unique, a one-of-a-kind event that cannot be found anywhere else in the universe. Each one of us is a genuine, original "Rembrandt" containing some 50-80,000 mind-bogglingly complex sentences that determine such things as height, bone structure, hair texture, eye color, voice, blood type, and myriad other differentiations.

Individual uniqueness notwithstanding, the *biologos* of God also specifies mind-bogglingly complex instructions that tell the cells of our bodies how to divide, differentiate, build, integrate and perform the myriad things that produce and sustain the pattern of *complexity* we call "health." A single misspelled or miscopied word might predispose a body to disease. To give perspective to the extraordinary *complexity* of DNA (deoxyribonucleic acid), let us note that the relatively bulky hard drive of a modern computer can store a few gigabites of information on inert media, whereas DNA can store millions of gigabites of information on strands so small that they can hardly be seen by the naked eye. DNA media contains enough complex specified information to produce everything from algae and bacteria to grass, tree bark, leaves, flowers, fish scales, dinosaur bones, insect eyes, eagle feathers, bear claws, elephant trunks, nerve fibers, blood platelets, human brain cells, neurons, etc.. The range of possible arrangements, differentiations and variations is truly mind-boggling.

But there is even more to it than that. This *biologos* does much more than provide complex "manufacturing" instructions. It also provides all the necessary *stop codes* that keep cells from reverting to elemental behavior—conforming to the Constable's dictum. Let us remind ourselves of the dictum of the Cosmic Constable:

> Order! Order! Order in the universe! Consummate all the gradients! Reduce patterns of complexity to patterns of simplicity! Level down! Level down! Level down! Homogenize! Homogenize! Homogenize! Reduce, assimilate and absorb! Render everything the same! Arrest and prosecute all heterogeneity! Resistance is futile. You will be assimilated. Order! Order! Order in the universe!

The human body with its trillions of cells and 200 different cell types is a living cosmos. Extrapolate the Constable's dictum to a bio-cosmos such as this and what sort of demands would he be placing on the cells? What would he be asking them to do? His *biological* dictum would read something like this:

> Order! Order! Order in the bio-universe! Reduce all patterns of complexity to patterns of simplicity! Replicate! Replicate! Replicate! Overwhelm the body with entropy and repetition! Homogenize! Homogenize! Homogenize! Consummate all cellular gradients! Wipe out all differentiation! Assimilate and reduce! Order! Order! Order in the bio-universe!

Fortunately the *biologos* of God includes redundant instructions that tell skin cells when to stop replicating, liver cells when to stop replicating, bone cells when to stop replicating, etc.. The living code contains myriad layers of checks and balances that regulate cell replication in healthy bodies and prevent the Constable from moving into the premises to work the increase of cellular entropy. "Thus far, and no farther," would be the essence of the stop codes that limit the division of healthy cells. Yes, cells have to be told how to divide and differentiate. But they have to be told when to stop as well.

To enable living cells to extract graded energy from foodstuffs, the *biologos* has to provide precise instructions that tell them when and how to open a limited window to the outside, an opening through which graded energy can be imported into the cell and degraded energy (entropy) exported. At the same time the *biologos* has to provide elaborate security instructions that tell the cell to keep all other doors and windows shut. The cell membrane has to be porous enough to let energy in, secure enough to keep the meddlesome Constable out. To obtain the energy it needs, the cell has to leave the door slightly ajar. Seeing the door ajar, the proverbial camel is going to try to get a foot in. This makes for the fine contest between health and disease.

The magnitude of the *complexity* that the Constable sees when he looks at DNA can only be guessed at. The situation can be likened to that of a nefarious thief gazing at the Crown Jewels, wondering how he can overcome the elaborate security arrangements. Suffice it to say that God has found it necessary to place the genetic code under lock and key, in an armored safe deep in the nucleus of each cell.

The cell is the sanctuary and "Fort Knox" of biological life. Israeli physicist Gerald L. Schroeder describes the nature and function of the cell in his book *Genesis and the Big Bang*:

> At each step as we go from simple to more complex compounds, we are in a sense swimming upstream in the flow of entropy....[H]ow is it that living organisms regularly produce complex compounds and do so in copious amounts? Life does it by working in the highly protected environment within its cells, by using catalysts that have the ability to select and concentrate the needed chemicals and to increase rates and extents of reactions, and by expending considerable energy to accomplish the tasks. The protected environment needed by life is found within life itself. [1]

The sanctuary needed by biological life is found within the cell. Outside that sanctuary the chances of finding life are miniscule. In order to build *complexity*, life needs a protected environment. Life must have a protected domain, a fenced off area, an enclosure in which to perform its work. Within this enclosure, it can then build up *complexity* by importing graded energy and exporting entropy. Enclosure is fundamental to life. Enclosure is also fundamental to many of the teachings of the Bible. In Genesis, for example, we note that "Eden" was a fenced off area. In the book of Job we find a type of the Cosmic Constable complaining about the protective "hedge" that God had built around His servant Job. During the 40 years in which Israel was wandering in the wilderness, the desert Tabernacle provided them with a "sanctuary." Later, the walled city of Jerusalem was their "sanctuary." Later, the Temple of Solomon was their sanctuary, the Holy of Holies the Sanctuary of sanctuaries.

God places protective "hedges" around nations, rendering them sovereign. Within nations He places protective enclosures around states. Within states He places enclosures around cities. God places a protective "hedge" around the institution of holy matrimony. He places a protective enclosure around the traditional family—the building block of Western society. The American dream of owning one's own home provides the family with a physical sanctuary. When one starts a business, the first thing one does is go down to City Hall and set up a legal "enclosure"—apply for a business name and license. With this legal area now fenced off, or as they would say in England, "limited," (Ltd.), one can then work to try to build up complex wealth. The file allocation tables (FATs) used by computer operating systems set up various enclosures, keeping files separate and distinct. If these FATs get corrupted, files may become "interlinked" and unreadable. (We are providing many different examples to drive home the point about the importance of the Biblical principle of enclosure.)

Earthly life has to be cell-based. Each cell is a fenced off area—an "Eden" in itself. From the simplest to the highest life form, if the cell fortification fails, the organism dies. To survive the universal activity of the Cosmic Constable life has to build a fortress around itself. In that fortress it can then follow the instructions of the *biologos* in relative peace and security, producing the hundreds of proteins necessary for orderly diversification and well-regulated growth. Even so, life has to keep an eye out for the Constable's shenanigans. The cell-fortification is designed to be very strong, its walls high and the moat deep, but the Constable has a few tricks up his sleeve as well—the siege mound, the battering ram, the catapult and the Trojan Horse. The Constable is in effect standing outside the castle wall issuing his decree: "Open up! You are in violation of the universal imperative. I have a cosmic warrant for your arrest." To which insult the healthy cell replies: "Go away! I am not violating the law of conservation of energy, or the law of increasing entropy." And so, for the time being, the healthy cell manages to keep the gate closed and the meddlesome Constable out.

The diseased cell, on the other hand, cannot keep the Constable out. Either its fortifications are too weak, or the wall too flimsy, or the draw-bridge failing, or the moat non-existent, or the castle gate carelessly left open. Somehow, by hook or by crook, the Cosmic Constable manages to wedge a foot in the gate, then a leg, then his whole carcass. Once he has invaded the sanctuary he flashes a warrant, seizes the assets and takes control of the assembly line. What happens then? Orderly growth and complex differentiation gets replaced by disorderly growth and unregulated replication.

In the bio-cosmos of trillions of cells, the state that we call "disease" can be triggered by any number of attacks launched by the Constable. He could use the Trojan Horse of a virus, for example, and there is much caution due here. The Constable would like nothing better than to use a virus to return the *complexity* of the human race to the simplicity of dust. Doubtless he sees more potential in the spread of anthrax, plague, H.I.V., Ebola and Lassa than in the advance of Nazi Panzer divisions. Using the Trojan Horse of a virus, the Constable can break and enter the cellular fortification like a thief in the night. Once inside, he can then steal from the host the genetic material he needs to crank out billions and billions of copies, flooding, overwhelming and choking the body with repetition. Using the Ebola virus, for example, the Constable can transform the *complexity* of a healthy body into the simplicity of a horrible corpse overnight. (Sleep not O sentinels of God!)

The attack may, on the other hand, assume the shape of a "cancer" that also sabotages the cellular assembly line. Once the assembly line has been taken over, it can then be used by the Constable to produce a hybrid of one body cell type. That accomplished, he can then crank out billions of stunted copies to overwhelm and choke all other body functions with repetition.

In order to sustain its pattern of *complexity*, a healthy body must produce and maintain a highly specific, highly ordered arrangement of 200 different cell types. These 200 different cell types are uniquely programmed to perform the different functions within the different organs in which they reside. Liver cells will not do for lung cells. Bone marrow cells will not do for kidney cells. Brain cells will not do for skin cells. When one stunted cell-type metastasizes and spills over into other parts of the body, the functions of those other part are encroached upon, choked and overwhelmed, in ways that may lead to death. This is the nature of cancer.

Cancer has three stages. The first is known as *initiation* or *invasion.* The second is known as *promotion* or *proliferation.* The third and final step is known as *progression.* Cancers that originate within the lining of organs are referred to as carcinomas. Those that originate within other tissues (muscle, bone, etc.) are referred to as sarcomas. Those that originate in blood cells are referred to as leukemias. But regardless of the outward disguise, we are dealing with the same unitary principle.

Cancer is an ancient disease, in some sense as old as the Cosmic Constable himself. The fossil record shows us that cancer has been around as long as animals have been around. Centuries ago the Greek physician Hippocrates (460-370 B.C.) was baffled by a growth in the breast of one of his patients. The growth was not going away, it was increasing in size. Hippocrates could see that in time it would encroach on other bodily functions. In examining the growth more closely he was astonished to find that his patient's body was actually supplying it with a network of new blood vessels. Hippocrates could see these new blood vessels radiating outward from the growth, looking like the arms and legs of a crab. He named the disease *cancer*, Latin for "crab."

The thing that baffled the father of medicine was this: why would the human body go to all the trouble of providing a deadly growth with a network of brand new blood vessels? Twenty four centuries later physicians continue to be baffled by the same thing, now referred to as *neovascularization* and *angiogenesis*. Both of these words describe the creation of networks of new blood vessels around cancerous growths, networks that divert food energy from the body and channel it into the gaping mouths of malignant tumors.

Why would the human body spread the red carpet before cancer like this? Does the body in all of its wisdom build new blood vessels around clogged arteries? No. Yet it builds brand new blood vessels around malignant tumors. The behavior of the body regarding its own best interests seems altogether irrational and suicidal. Why would the body do such a thing? To obtain a holistic explanation we have to journey to the cosmic side of the interface. We have to leave the realm of the human and cross over into the cold and indifferent realms of matter, energy and entropy—the dominion of the Cosmic Constable. Let us do that now. Let us broaden the scope of our inquiry to investigate the biological shape of entropy as it relates to the plague of the twentieth century—"cancer."

What is the human body fundamentally? Fundamentally it is an energy-driven system made from the physics of this universe. Whatever else the body does, it must first and foremost conform to the physics of the universe. The human body does that from cradle to grave. Every beat of the heart, every twitch of the nose, every blink of an eyelid, every motion of an arm, every movement of a muscle, every step of a foot requires graded energy, which is degraded upon use and converted into entropy, resulting in an increase in the entropy of the entire universe. We are made from the physics of this universe. We cannot violate its laws with impunity.

In utilizing energy, the body does not "expend" energy, it de-grades it. It *changes* it, from graded to de-graded form. The human body must conform to the universal imperative by changing graded energy ("food") into entropy (heat & waste). This is the basal *activity* that the human body performs from cradle to grave, and the term that describes it is *metabolism*, from a Greek word meaning "to change." *Metabolism* describes the breakdown of food energy that starts in the digestive system, ending up as heat & waste produced within the cells. We must always bear in mind that this metabolism (change) is taking place along a gradient common to the whole universe. The body's total set of chemical reactions is wired into the cosmic gradient that leads from ordered to disordered states, from low probability to high probability, from *complexity* to simplicity.

Although the *complexity* of a healthy body can be said to run against the grain of the cosmos, the metabolic activity of the body is very much in conformity with that grain. In some sense the human body is a glorified furnace that transforms food into heat & waste. We humans may enjoy feasting on a delicious dinner, but in reality "food" is nothing more than graded energy, our taste buds informing us of its *availability*. The branches and leaves that taste delicious to giraffes don't taste so good to human beings. This is because the bodies of giraffes are designed to feed on different grades of energy.

In order to comply with the universal imperative, the human body must degrade energy continually, in the bargain, being allowed to build a measure of *complexity*. The physical life of the body is rooted in the seamless continuity of its *basal metabolic activity*—the ongoing activity that de-grades energy. Right now, as the reader is reading these words, his or her body is converting graded energy (food) into entropy (heat & waste). Heat is continually produced by all the cells of the body through metabolic reactions. The BMR (*basal metabolic rate*) is an indicator of the rate at which energy is being de-graded. All BMRs are not the same. The BMR of a teenager will be far higher than that of grandma. Different species have different BMRs as well. The BMR of man is different from that of sheep, the BMR of mammals is different from that of cold-blooded reptiles.

Scientists use the same unit to measure the heat produced by chemical reactions as they do to measure the energy content of foodstuffs—the *calorie.* A calorie is the amount of heat needed to increase the temperature of one liter of water by one degrees Celsius. One gram of carbohydrate, for example, can be de-graded into 5.1 calories of heat. One gram of protein can be de-graded into 5.6 calories of heat. One gram of fat can be de-graded into 9.45 calories of heat. We mention these numbers to awaken the mind of the reader to the relationship that exists between the metabolic activity of the human body and the physics of the universe. God created us from the physics of the universe. The body's total set of chemical reactions cannot be isolated from the universal activity of the principality that we have nicknamed "Cosmic Constable." The Constable's incessant activity is not something that exists outside our bodies—it is internalized. The cells of the body are fully wired into the fabric of a cosmos in which entropy is always increasing.

Human bodies do not produce entropy (heat & waste) because they are "inefficient." Even the most efficient human body could not avoid producing entropy—it would die. All human bodies have to conform to the universal imperative by degrading food into heat & waste. That condition fulfilled, they are then, in the bargain, allowed to build a measure of *complexity*. In this universe it is not possible for a human body to transform 100% of food into *complexity*—doing so would violate the universal imperative. The Constable must be paid his entropy tax. The body must degrade energy in the process of producing *complexity*. It is not enough to be able to assimilate food. There has to be a mechanism for eliminating heat & waste. Malignant tumors do that more efficiently than healthy organs.

NEOVASCULARIZATION AND ANGIOGENESIS

Compared to a healthy organ of equivalent size and weight, a malignant tumor can produce far more heat & waste for a given amount of food energy. Why? Because the healthy organ has to allocate more of the same energy to the difficult task of producing *complexity*, and the tumor doesn't. Healthy cells and organs produce biological *complexity* in the process of degrading food energy. Tumors are simpler furnaces that degrade food energy into heat & waste more directly. Malignant tumors comply with the cosmic imperative to a greater extent than healthy organs.

An illustration may be sought in the different ways in which a toaster and a computer use energy. The toaster will degrade a given amount of energy into heat more or less directly. The computer, on the other hand, will degrade some of it into heat, but upgrade some of it into the patterns of complexity associated with *information.* Unlike the computer, the toaster does not have to perform complex tasks, meaning that it can degrade the same amount of electricity into heat directly. Question: given the choice between the behavior of the toaster and the behavior of the computer, which one will the Constable pick? He will pick the toaster every time! *This preference, on the part of the Constable, for shorter and more direct metabolic pathways, is the very essence of pathology.* Healthy organs would be analogous to the computer. Malignant tumors analogous to the toaster.

Healthy cells have to allocate more of their energy income to the creation and maintenance of *complexity*—genes have to be turned on and off in precise sequences, lines of code have to be read, rules, regulations and protocols have to be meticulously adhered to, all of which requires effort and energy. Malignant cells have it easy by comparison. They do not have to perform all the difficult and complicated tasks that healthy cells have to perform. This may be an oversimplification, but it serves to show the fundamental difference between healthy organs and malignant tumors. Because they don't have to perform all those other difficult and complicated tasks, tumors provide shorter, easier, more direct metabolic pathways for the flow of energy through and out of the body.

The "long-circuit" of health would embody a higher resistance metabolic pathway. The "short-circuit" of cancer would embody a lower resistance metabolic pathway. Given the choice between higher or lower resistance, energy will always flow along the path of lower resistance. Tumors provide energy with a path of lower resistance. Cancer can be compared to a "short-circuit" whereby the energy that was earmarked for healthy organs gets diverted into the furnaces of tumors where it can be converted into entropy (heat & waste) more directly.

Another illustration may be sought in an experiment in which equal amounts of water flow out of two containers separated by a baffle or partition. The water will flow out of the container with the large drain faster than the container with the tiny drain. Remove the partition and what happens? Most of the water will get diverted to the container with the large drain. In this illustration the container with the tiny drain would be analogous to the longer metabolic pathways of a healthy body, the container with the large drain analogous to the shorter metabolic pathways of a cancer-ridden body. Cancer has the effect of "removing the partition"—causing energy to drain out of the body along a path of lower resistance.

In all this one has to keep reminding oneself that the metabolic activity of the human body is not arbitrary. The transformation processes associated with the body's total set of chemical reactions are taking place along a gradient common to the whole universe. To try to understand cancer independently of that gradient would be to miss the forest for the trees. Let us take a few steps back and try to see the forest itself, using the gestalt that we have nicknamed "Cosmic Constable."

What is the Constable trying to do? He is trying to increase the entropy of the universe. Generally this means converting matter into heat. What is "heat?" There are many definitions, but in a broader context it can be said to be the lowest potential of pure and undifferentiated energy. Just as all rivers flow down the gradient that leads from high to low potential, likewise all the different forms of energy flow down the gradient that leads from matter to heat. In some sense heat is like a cosmic "sea level" or "low point" to which all forms of energy will eventually degrade. (The reader should not confuse "heat" with "temperature.")

The cells of the human body have to show deference to a cosmic "sea level" and "bottom line" such as this. By order of first importance, the human body must convert matter (food) into entropy (heat & waste). Naturally the Constable would prefer that this conversion take place along a path of least resistance. Tumors provide paths of lower resistance, but only if they are supplied with networks of new blood vessels through which the energy can flow. *Neovascularization* and *angiogenesis* supply tumors with those networks. Why does a diseased body build a network of new blood vessels around tumors? *Because tumors afford paths of lower resistance for the flow of energy though and out of the body.*

The body is an energy-driven system wired into the fabric of a cosmos in which entropy is always increasing. By order of first importance it must conform to the physics of the universe—allow energy to flow through itself along a gradient common to the whole universe. Tumors provide paths of lower resistance for this flow. Why does a cancer-ridden body build new blood vessels around tumors? Because it is an energy-driven system trying to conform to the physics of the universe! In the healthy state it can do this by making energy flow along a *long circuit*. In the diseased state it is forced to let energy to flow along a *short circuit*.

In a healthy body the breakdown of energy from food to heat has to take the *long circuit*. This would be the metabolic pathway of most resistance. Why? Because it has to wind through all the "energy dams" of the 100 trillion cells that are trying to produce biological *complexity*. In a healthy body the metabolic pathways of energy are necessarily long and circuitous, flowing through trillions of cells, each one of which offers something by way of resistance, adding up to considerable resistance in total. As it were, energy has to be "forced" through those 100 trillion cells. Imagine using a hand pump to force water through a myriad of long and narrow tubes—a difficult task. Naturally it would be easier to force the same volume of water through short and fat tubes. The metabolic pathways of a healthy body would be analogous to the long and narrow tubes. The metabolic pathways of a cancer-ridden body would be analogous to the short and fat tubes.

The metabolic pathways of a healthy body may be likened to the long and winding path of a river down mountains and valleys, driving the turbines of many hydro-electric power plants. We must remember, however, that the river would prefer to take the path of least resistance to the sea—burst all the dams and take a more direct route. In a healthy body, the river of energy is long and circuitous, necessarily so because it must flow through trillions of cells, turning their miniature "power plants" in the process. In a cancer-ridden body the path of the river to the sea is much more steep and direct, bypassing those "power plants" and starving healthy organs in the process. Imagine the path of the Colorado River as it flows down to the sea, powering many hydroelectric power stations. Now imagine a scenario in which the headwaters of the Colorado are made to fall straight down to sea level via a huge shaft created by bulldozers and dynamite, by-passing all those hydroelectric power stations. Cancer behaves like that "shaft." The flow of energy needed to sustain trillions of cells is increasingly diverted into the "shafts" of tumors, which grow rapidly, triggering the creation of more blood vessels. The deficit can only widen so much before healthy organs expire for lack of food—starve to death.

This "theft of energy" is a characteristic of many diseases. The process by which healthy cells starve because food energy is diverted elsewhere by disease, is in the medical establishment referred to as *cachexia*. Cachexia is the hallmark of a host of debilitating and chronic diseases whereby metabolic pathways are short-circuited, causing patients' bodies and minds to waste away due to a lack of energy. So when a physician says to a cancer patient "you have six months to live," he means this: "your metabolic pathways have been short-circuited by cancer: the healthy cells and organs of your body are not getting the energy they need because most of the food that you are eating is being diverted into tumors where it can be converted into heat & waste more directly. At the present rate of depletion, the remaining healthy cells and organs of your body will starve to death within six months."

Because energy flows from high to low potential, it can be used to generate electricity. Likewise, and for the same basic reason, energy can be used to power the "engines" of the 100 trillion cells in the body. But this requires a "gradient" for energy to flow along. Life cannot be sustained without energy. Energy cannot flow in the absence of a gradient. The metabolic pathways of a healthy body provide energy with a precise gradient, not too steep, not too shallow. The metabolic pathways of a cancer-ridden body are far steeper, far shorter, far more direct. What causes the body to switch from longer metabolic pathway to shorter? That is the big question.

WAR ON CANCER

On 23 December 1971 President Nixon declared war on cancer by signing into law the National Cancer Act. Since then untold billions have been spent in the attempt to find an elusive "cure," but the plague continues to grow in scope and dimension. In the United States one out of three Americans can now expect to get cancer in their lifetime. The number of Americans now dying from cancer is a single year is said to near the total battle deaths from all the wars in which all Americans have fought. This insidious plague has now spawned a gigantic world wide industry that depends on the Cosmic Constable for its annual revenues. It is now jokingly said that there are more people living off of cancer than dying form it.

The very word "cancer" is enough to strike terror in the heart of an elderly patient. It is as if he or she has suddenly ceased to be a human being and become so many pounds of flesh about to be processed through the meat grinders of orthodox medicine. When the verdict is "cancer," usually the patient has little choice but to surrender his/her body to the wisdom of the medical establishment, allowing the practitioners to attack it with debilitating poisons, surgical knives and/or radiation. One of the poisons used in chemotherapy, for example, was the deadly agent in the mustard gas used in World War I. Some of the side-effects of chemotherapy and radiation are truly devastating. In a publication called *Medical Alerts*, Dr. Julian Whitaker, long-time practitioner of preventative medicine, writes the following:

> It's a simple fact that radiation and chemotherapy simply devastate your immune system...allowing the cancer cells to multiply freely. It's like tearing down a fortress' walls to make it safer! You don't tear down the walls when you're battling a powerful enemy...you build them up so nothing can penetrate. [2]

Orthodox medicine attacks cancer by knives, poisons and radiation in the hope of defeating the monster. In truth, however, orthodox medicine really doesn't know what it is attacking. Even as we enter the Millennium orthodox medicine is still ignorant of the ontology of cancer. In 1987, Dr. Garth Nicolson of the Department of Tumor Biology at the M.D. Anderson Cancer Center of the University of Texas wrote the following in *Cancer Research*:

> The viewpoint that no unitary concept can give a satisfactory explanation of the intimate nature of cancer remains quite valid today. [3]

Is there a unitary scientific concept that can give a satisfactory explanation for the nature of cancer? Indeed there is. Cancer is a function of increasing entropy. Granted entropy does not increase in open systems, but that depends on the nature of the open system and the grade of energy being received from the "outside." The fact that the human body is an "open system" just means that it can draw on energies external to itself to maintain its low-entropy state a little longer than if it were a closed system. Even so, that depends on the grade of the energy that it receives. If it receives a high enough grade, it may succeed in maintaining it low-entropy (healthy) state for the season of a lifetime. If it receives a lower grade, cellular entropy may increase, paving the way for disease and premature death.

The inverse relationship between *complexity* and entropy can be inferred, as can the direct relationship between entropy and degree of repetition. Everything else being equal, a healthy body contains less repetition than a diseased body. As repetition increases, it can only do so at the expense of *complexity* and health. Granted the human body contains a great deal of cellular repetition already, but the margins are very narrow. There is a limit to how much additional repetition a healthy body can cope with before going over the edge. There is a threshold of repetition beyond which health will give way to disease. As a general principle, repetition (cellular entropy) can only increase so much before the onset of disease. Thereafter it can only increase so much before the onset of "death."

Cancer is a function of unregulated repetition. In reflecting on this truth let us take note of the fact that cancer does not originate where there is no mechanism of cell replication. In those tissues in which the mechanism is lacking (heart muscles and nerve fibers, for example) cancers are all but unknown. Human beings don't die of "heart cancer." The cells that form the muscles of the heart lack the replication machinery that can be shanghaied by the Cosmic Constable. Most of the other organs of the body can rebuild damaged muscle. Not so the heart. This is why heart attacks can be so devastating—the cells of the organ of the heart do not have the wherewithal to replicate and rebuild damaged muscle.

In the following exercise, the letter "c" stands for malignant cancer cells, and the other letters stand for healthy cells of different types. The letter patterns are arbitrary, made up by the author by closing the eyes and depressing keys at random (the reader should not obsess over the letters, as though they stood for actual cell types). The whole point of the philistine exercise is to show that the increase of entropy (unregulated repetition) goes hand in hand with the spread of cancer:

1: HEALTHY BODY

hlhklnbbcenpmcbslsehsnkcctatcfsehhbkbsclhmjhyrcpkwobjfhkx
cgjirwocplkwhfoivccnliwqpfuccnbosnfwizlfmsncicppqcnbvosiug
cckijjccmonospkllccyrwqssvvbpwlgflkscccisgrqwplmxncsiuyrwsc

2: CARCINOGENESIS (ONSET OF CANCER)

hlhklnbbcenpmcbslsehsnkcccccctcfsehhbkbsclhmjhyrcpkwobjfhkx
cgjirwocplkwhfoivccccccccccccccccccccccccfmsncicppqcnbvosiug
cckijjccmonospkllccyrwqccccccccgccccccccisgrqwplmxncsiuyrwsc

3: METASTASIS (ADVANCED CANCER)

cccccncccenpmcbslccccccccccccccccccccsclhmjhyrcpkwobccccc
ccjirwocplkwccccccccccccccccccccccccccccccccicppqcnbvocccc
cccccccccconospkllccycccccccccccccccccccisgrqwplmxncsiuyrccc

4: TERMINAL CANCER

ccccccccccccenccccscccccccccccccccccccccccccscccccccyrccccobccccc
ccgjirwcocccwccccccccccccccccccccccccccccccccccciccccncccccccc
ccccccccccccconosccccccccccccccccccccccccccccciscrccccccccncsiucccc

Look at the patterns as we go from 1 to 4, sliding from health to disease, from order to disorder, from low probability to high probability, from low repetition to high repetition, from *complexity* to simplicity, from heterogeneity to homogeneity. The change from health to disease is taking place along a gradient common to the whole universe. What we are looking at is a crude representation of the greater order of universal change itself.

The aggregate of the cells of a healthy body would resemble the 1st pattern. The aggregate of the cells of a cancer-ridden body would resemble the 4th pattern. We could change the letter "c" to "h" and the pattern of transformation would adequately describe the onset of disease via HIV. Or we could change it to "a" and it would adequately describe the onset of disease via anthrax. Or we could change it to "E" and it would adequately describe the rapid onset of death via Ebola. This is the *unitary* principle that gives a satisfactory explanation of the intimate nature of cancer.

Are we looking at a *universal* principle? Extrapolate to a plague of locusts and the underlying principle is the same (just change the letter "c" to "g" for "grasshopper"). Before Hitler came along, the arrangement of political, social and human elements in Europe looked something like the 1st pattern shown above. After Hitler did his thing, it looked more like the 4th pattern—just change the letter "c" to "N" for "Nazi." Extrapolate to "ethnic cleansing," and the legacy of Slobodan Milosevic becomes a cancer of sorts. Extrapolate to the behavior of Osama Bin Laden and it's the same plague principle—terrorists trying to reduce the whole world into copies of themselves. Extrapolate to the activities of some computer viruses and it's the same "disease" whereby patterns of *complexity* on the surfaces of hard disks are corrupted into patterns of garbled simplicity. This is what we mean by a *universal principle*—applicable to all spheres of human inquiry.

In the years to come physicians will be able to measure increases of cellular entropy with scanning devices. A century from now those devices might be mall hand-held instruments resembling the *tricorders* featured in the popular *Star Trek* series. How would the physicians of the 22nd century measure the health (*complexity*) of a human body? By measuring the reciprocal in terms of entropy and repetition. Likely the bio-scanners used by the physicians of the 23rd century will do that with extraordinary accuracy—say, up to ten decimal points. Such devices could be calibrated for different species as well.

THE REAL CAUSE OF CANCER

What keeps a healthy human body healthy? What keeps it from going over the edge and falling into disease? Layers of checks and balances written into the *biologos*. As long as the trillions of cells in the body can differentiate themselves according to complex instructions, intricate guidelines and highly regulated protocols, they can work together to produce the emergent quality that we call "health." When something goes wrong, when some weak link breaks, or when some defensive wall is breached, the Constable is able to take over the premises and we run into something that we label "disease."

The optimal *complexity* that we label "health" originates within the sanctuary of each cell, which has a terminal that is "plugged in" to the greater command and control centers of the brain and nervous system, providing for global communications, intruder alert mechanisms, immune activation and the general coordination that is necessary to survive an attack by the Constable. In this manner the cells of the body behave as one highly integrated castle-fortification, with defensive works, watchmen, archers and immune weapons.

How is this exquisitely designed fortress compromised? How are the walls breached? How does the Constable get inside?

Many a pathologist has observed the insidious compromise under a microscope. Pathology is a very important branch of modern medicine. In his book entitled *The Immortal Cell* pathologist Gerald B. Dermer provides us with the following insight:

> The condition of cells, the efficiency with which they carry out their tasks, determine the health of the entire organism. All disease is the result of damage to, or changes within, individual cells. [4]

The whole of the compromise that leads to disease takes place inside cells. As long as the cell is an impregnable fortress, disease is not an issue. But let there be a breach in the wall and the picture changes dramatically. Dr. Dermer:

> Cancer begins when one of the 100 trillion cells that make up the body becomes defective and stops obeying the rules that govern normal cell behavior. This cancerous cell does not develop, age, and multiply normally. The mechanisms that tell a normal cell to stop dividing are not functioning. Instead, cancer cells grow and multiply, eventually forming a mass of cells known as a tumor. [5]

What causes cancer? What triggers the insidious process? In his book *Cancer Prevention and Nutritional Therapies* Dr. Richard A. Passwater quotes a statement issued by the National Cancer Institute (NCI):

> Healthy cells that make up the body's tissues grow, divide, and replace themselves in an orderly way. This process keeps the body in good repair. Sometimes, however, normal cells lose their ability to limit and direct their growth. They divide too rapidly and grow without any order. [6]

Dr. Passwater then adds the following:

> The operative words are "unregulated growth of cells." What, then, causes cells to go astray? Whatever causes cell regulation to go astray is the cause of cancer. [7]

The devil that would cause cell regulation to go astray must first invade the sanctuary of the cell. As long as the sanctuary is whole, cancer is not an issue. It is only when the wall is breached that the devil of disorder can invade the sanctuary and cause cell regulation to go astray. But how is the wall breached?

The wall of the biological fortress can be breached by certain types of radiation. We know, for example, that airport x-ray machines can corrupt the information stored on photographic film, floppy disks and other sensitive media. Ordinarily the information contained in DNA cannot be damaged by small doses of x-rays, but it can be damaged by more potent types of radiation. Gamma rays, for example, are lethal to human beings—their frequency is so high and their wavelength so short that they can go right through the cell and knock blocks of information off the DNA helix. Fortunately gamma rays and other forms of deadly radiation are very rare on earth.

High doses of ultraviolet rays are also dangerous, being known to cause certain types of skin cancers. Our planet is constantly bombarded by lethal doses of UV radiation. Fortunately God has designed a marvelous shield in the form of an ozone layer. When deadly ultraviolet radiation strikes the oxygen in our atmosphere it forms ozone, which can screen out ultraviolet radiation while letting ordinary light get through. Although man has been tampering with the shield lately, the ozone layer is for the most part intact, still standing, still doing a good job of protecting the *complexity* of living things from sabotage and vandalism by the radiative arm of the Cosmic Constable. All things considered radiation cannot be the cause of the epidemic of cancer today, though it may be a contributing factor.

We must now consider the harmful effects of industrial pollution, chemical waste and environmental toxins. It is known that certain chemical agents can react with cell components to weaken and compromise the biological fortress. Carcinogens, for example, can damage cell structures, either directly, or by generating what are known as *free radicals*. Free radicals are unstable chemical molecules that have unpaired electrons. They are physically imbalanced and chemically unstable (highly reactive). They are like out-of-balance automobile tires—they wobble and shake as they spin, wasting a great deal of energy and running a' foul of one of the basic principles of nature. How can a free radical stabilize itself? The same way we balance the wheels of our automobiles. We add counterweights—the free radical adds an electron. But where does it get that electron? It steals it from a neighboring molecule. But the neighboring molecule is now out of balance, meaning that it too will try to pirate an electron. And so the vandalism may cascade in destructive chain reactions.

Free radicals can be compared to "shrapnel." The cell wall has membrane proteins (cytoplasm). The hail of free radical shrapnel can damage those proteins, breaching the wall of the biological fortification. The resulting cascade may then proliferate inside the cell, causing gene mutation and major security compromise. Granted, anti-oxidants like vitamins E and C can erect an interim defensive buffer to give the cell a chance to heal itself, but the long term effects of free radicals (brought on by excessive smoking, for example) may be more than what the body can cope with.

Notwithstanding, the human body has a wonderful ability to stand up to abuse. It can even take a great deal of exposure to carcinogens before being pushed over the edge. What then, is causing the epidemic of cancer today? Carcinogens, environmental toxins, PCBs, free radicals, industrial pollution, lead, carbon monoxide, pesticides, insecticides, tobacco smoke, alcohol, stress and the such may be significant factors, but they do not lead to disease in many cases. (Some people, for example, may smoke heavily all their lives without getting lung cancer.) There has to be an additional cause.

Is there an additional cause? Yes, and it has to do with basic cell nutrition. More than anything else, it is the junk that man puts into his mouth that enables the Constable to breach cell walls and invade the biological fortress. Simply put, the cell is not being built strongly enough. It's not getting the brick, mortar, cement, concrete, and steel that it needs to fortify itself—it is getting straw and mud instead. What sort of a fortification can the cell build with straw and mud? A very flimsy one, the sort that the Constable can blow down with one sneeze.

A host of critical components are needed to build and maintain healthy cells. What exactly are they and how does the body obtain them? They consist of numerous proteins, carbohydrates, amino acids, lipids, vitamins, minerals, trace elements, micro-nutrients and other building blocks found in healthy foods. Take, for example, the important roles played by trace elements like chromium, cobalt, copper, fluorine, iodine, iron, manganese, molybdenum, selenium, vanadium. Some are vital reactors, described as the very "spark plugs" of life. Others are catalysts, speeding up complex chemical reactions that would ordinarily require weeks. Most complex reactions in the body require specific enzymes. Trace elements can make up enzymes by joining themselves to protein. Trace elements also help the cells extract energy from food. Magnesium, for example, is said to activate more than sixty enzymes that enable cells to harness graded energy. Zinc, to give another example, is needed for the function of a host of other enzymes that synthesize proteins, facilitate nutrient absorption, regulate the genetic process, restore the structure of the DNA helix, metabolize vitamins, etc..

When it comes to "health," everything in the body has to work in precise coordination and synchronization with everything else. The operative word is "orchestration." It takes a very precise sort of orchestration to produce the pattern of *complexity* we call health. The musical score is the DNA. The conductor is the brain and nervous system. The musicians are the cells. The instruments are such things as proteins, micro-nutrients, vitamins, minerals and trace elements. Given well-tuned instruments, the cells of the body can produce the magnificent symphony of health. Otherwise you can count on cosmic noise, repetition and entropy—*disease.*

The human body with its trillions of cells is consummately designed and engineered for optimal health. The *biologos* written by God sees to it that all the fortifications and defense mechanisms are in place by the time of physical birth. If the body of a mother-to-be is supplied with its own nutritional needs well before the conception of new life, and if the level of those and other components are carefully monitored and maintained during pregnancy, at a time when the biological assembly line has a crying need for them, and at a time when the new life's "computer" is reading the intricate lines of code in the most exacting blueprint in the universe, we can confidently predict that when the baby is born he or she will have strong and healthy cells. And if the growing child's cells continue to receive the *exact* nutrition they need, we can also predict that he/she will stand a good chance of living a disease-free life. On the other hand if the mother's body is malnourished before conception, and/or starved of vital nutrients during pregnancy, her child may end up being susceptible to a host of diseases, not to mention birth defects and low IQ. The plan and blueprint of God is not wanting for the necessary fortifications. But it must have brick, mortar, cement, and steel to build those fortifications. You can't build strong fortifications with straw and mud. The colorfully packaged, sugar-coated, chemically adulterated, hydrogenated, over-refined, over-processed and over-simplified junk foods that line supermarket shelves will not do.

In 1 Corinthians 6:19 Rav Shaul describes the human body as *the temple of the Spirit of God.* If the devil himself wanted to desecrate that temple via disease, he could do no better than set up a world system in which food processors have to degrade the bread of Man to turn a profit. By making money scarce, the present world system actually encourages the adulteration, over-processing and over-simplification of foodstuffs. As we discovered in the previous chapter, the world's system of money creation is still that of the old 17th century scaffolding work—a debt-creating, debt-compounding system that thrives on money scarcity, creating all manner of perversions in the land. Where money is made scarce, it increases the power of those who create and control it. Given the debt-system, and the vices of human nature, money scarcity is a foregone conclusion. Money scarcity leads to the love of money, which we know to be the root of all kinds of evil—including disease.

In a world system in which the tail of Money is allowed to wag the dog of human health, disease is inevitable. In a world system in which life and death hinge on the disposition of the almighty dollar, in a world system in which health care has to be rationed to "cut costs," in a world system in which food production and processing have to conform to the quotas of some bizarre monetary expedient, it should come as no surprise to find half a million Americans dying of cancer every year.

One glaring example of over-processing can be found in the way in which Mother Nature's complex oils are degraded to make them "marketable." The degradation involves many steps and stages. The first step involves removal of such things as life-sustaining phosphatides, lecithin, complex carbohydrates, chlorophyll, calcium, iron, copper and magnesium. The second step involves the addition of caustic chemicals agents, wherewith the witch's brew is agitated at high temperatures. The third step involves the "bleaching out" of any traces of Nature's pigment and color, all of which are filtered and boiled out to provide the consumer with a colorless "clear oil." The fourth step involves "deodorizing" the oil via steam-distillation at temperatures of up to 518 degrees F. The fifth step involves the addition of synthetic chemicals to increase shelf-life. The final insult is a process called *hydrogenation*, whereby all the fatty acids are saturated with hydrogen under extreme pressure and temperature in the presence of metal catalysts. With all of its vitamins, minerals and micro-nutrients removed, this is the sort of degraded "clear salad oil" that millions of Americans put into their bodies daily. And then they wonder why they get sick.

Nature's complex oils (lipids) are vital to human health and nutrition. They play critical roles in metabolism, cell renewal and repair, brain and nerve functions. The human brain, the most complex system in the universe, contains tens of billions of neurons—as many stars as there are in our galaxy—all of which have to be able to communicate globally via long and short connections. The longer wire-like connections are usually encased in a substance called *myelin*, a fatty covering that expedites communication. The whitish, glistening appearance of the structure of the brain testifies to the presence of complex lipids.

Elsewhere essential fatty acids play vital roles in regulating chromosomes during cell division, for example, not to mention the formation of new cell walls. The entire sanctuary of the cell is enclosed in the somewhat fatty membrane of the cell wall. These cell walls are complex things in themselves, behaving like miniature "computer keyboards" by which complex instructions can be sent to the interior via inputs, stimuli and reactions. In order to function properly, the "micro-keyboards" of the cell walls require electron-rich lipids found in Mother Nature's complex oils.

Pure, rich, unrefined oils extracted from seeds, nuts and grains, can be worth their weight in gold. They are more potent than juices extracted from fruits and vegetables, and we all know how healthy those can be. Walnut, linseed, soy, and pumpkin oils contain many essential fatty acids along with umpteen other important ingredients. Properly used, linseed (flaxseed) oil is perhaps one of Mother Nature's most potent "food-medicines." It contains linoleic acid, for example, which the body needs to produce hemoglobin; it contains potassium, phosphorous, magnesium, calcium, sulphur, iron, zinc, sodium, not to mention manganese, silicon, copper, fluorine, aluminum, nickel, cobalt, iodine, molybdenum, chromium—minerals and trace elements vital to cell function. Imagine that! All of those ingredients in one tablespoon of linseed oil. Cold-pressed, dark green, extra virgin olive oil is likewise one of Mother Nature's potent medicines. If all the citizens of the world, all the restaurants of the world, and all the food processors of the world used it instead of the usual cheap hydrogenated abominations, the incidence of worldwide cancer might be cut in half within a decade.

A host of critical components is needed to build and maintain healthy cells. Man is supposed to get those ingredients in the form of food. But the food that man puts into his mouth has to be produced in a world system driven by debt and money-scarcity. In this world system agribusiness can't survive without taking shortcuts—relying, for example, on genetically-altered monocultures. In this world system the small farmer can't survive without depleting the soil of many of its nutrients. In this world system the corporate baker can't survive without reducing the complex bread of Man to the order of bleach-white simplicity. In this world system the conglomerate food processor can't survive without over-simplifying foodstuffs to the point of nutritional worthlessness, and then adding insult to injury in the form of artificial flavorings, chemical additives and other questionable substances. (We are not pointing fingers. We are merely describing the nature of a world system built on debt-money.)

Many of the minerals and trace elements that the farmer takes out of the soil play important roles in building healthy bodies. Many of the chemicals and additives that food processors put into food add insult to injury. But don't blame the farmer, or the food processor. Blame the United States Congress for legalizing a system of money creation based on the *unnecessary* creation and increase of debt. Usually the farmer is in debt up to his ears—a great portion of everything that he grows and harvests has to be set aside to make interest payments to the bank. He is on the cosmic treadmill, brow-beaten into over-exploiting the soil just so he can keep his head above water financially. He plants crop after crop after crop. The first crop is quite nutritious. The second crop less nutritious. The third even less. Many cycles later the roots of those successive crops have mined the minerals out of the earth and the soil has "played out." What does he do then? Does he go bankrupt in an effort to fully replenish the soil? No, in order to survive he must keep on planting non-stop. And he has learned how to shortchange the seventy or so nutrients found in rich soil for three. He has learned that by replenishing three (nitrogen, phosphorous and potassium) he can produce "bumper crops." The problem of course is that these so-called "bumper crops" are all quantity and no quality.

The sad truth, the one that every government must now factor into the cost of health care, is that after a century or so of intense agricultural planting and harvesting the world has now reached a watershed where most of the minerals and trace elements needed to build strong cells have disappeared from the soil itself. Governments must find within themselves the wisdom and wherewithal to remedy this deficiency, and soon. If they do, they will save untold billions that would have to be spent on "health care" after the fact. As the proverb says, "An ounce of prevention is worth a pound of cure." Hippocrates said it himself:

Let food be your medicine, let medicine be your food.

The plight of the farmer notwithstanding, the corporate baker and food processor have learned a dirty little trick or two as well. The survival game that they are forced to play has little to do with health and nutrition. This other game is called "processing, packaging, and advertising," also known as "how to turn a profit by fooling the consumer's taste buds." Food processors have learned how to survive economically by substituting saliva-inducing toxins and sugar-coated poisons for genuine nutrition. These include preservatives, dyes, stabilizers, artificial flavorings, bleaching agents, clarifiers, softeners, thickeners, hydrogenators, curing agents, fungicides, sweeteners, conditioners, alkalizers—all the things that make the food of man "creamy, crunchy, chewy, crispy." Round and round we go on Madison Avenue's treadmill to oblivion, wasting the balm of life in the vain pursuit of something called "money."

The incessant barrage of junk food commercials aimed at children and teens testifies to the wickedness of a world in which the tail of Money is allowed to wag the dog of human health and well-being. Many of the soft drinks being peddled to teens via "pop-culture-ads" contain *aspartame*, for example, an artificial sweetener made from aspartic acid and phenylalanine. In his book *How to Fight Cancer and Win*, William Fischer writes the following:

> What the ads don't tell you is that phenylalanine is toxic to brain tissue. It causes alarming reactions in some humans – symptoms like dizziness, headaches, epileptic-like seizures, eye pain and bleeding and menstrual problems.... Despite its known health hazards, aspartame is still widely marketed. [8]

Why is aspartame still being marketed? Why are our foods being laced with harmful chemicals? Why are so many human beings being slowly poisoned to death by the food they eat? Because of something called "money." Money, money, money!

When Pharaoh wanted to punish the Hebrew slaves he told them "Not only will you have to deliver the same quota of bricks, but from now on you will have to find your own straw as well," (Exodus 5:10-11). This, essentially, is what doctors and nurses are being told to do today—"from now on you will have to do more and more with less and less." Why has the Hippocratic oath been turned on its head? Why has the abiding principle of medicine—*first do no harm*—been replaced by health care rationing and the abomination of HMOs? Why has the lofty and noble discipline of healing been replaced by the banality of Wall Street medicine?

The answer to all of the above, of course, is "because of money." The marginalization of millions of human beings, disease, poverty, mass misery, compromise of ecosystems, degradation of nature's wholesome foods, the pollution of the water we drink and the air we breathe, all relate to an antiquated system of money creation based on debt. Many of the diseases that are ravaging the Third World are direct results of foreign debt. Even in the developed nations the causes of plagues such as cancer and heart-disease are as much economic as biological. Here too we are up against classical boundary conditions, which we defined as follows:

> You can't fix something that's broke on the basis of the same set of assumptions that made it broke in the first place—you will just bounce off the same walls and end up right back where you started.

It makes absolutely no sense to try to fix the broken health of mankind using the same Malthusian assumptions that broke it in the first place. Unless the United States Congress deals with the real cause there will be no end to cancer, heart disease, diabetes, AIDS and the host of unknown plagues that are now looming on the horizon. Unless the 17th century scaffolding of central banking is torn down and rebuilt from the ground up, the world will carry the dead weight of the old diseases into the new millennium and there will be nothing in store but more of the same. The handwriting is on the wall and facts speak for themselves.

An old order has now passed away. A new order is upon us. The era of dealing with disease after the fact is finished—the era of using toxic drugs, surgical knives, poisons and radiation has drawn to an end, and the era of *Molecular Medicine* has begun. What are we to understand by "Molecular Medicine?" Well, as we have already pointed out, it takes a host of precisely tailored nutritional components to build the pattern of *complexity* we call "health." Emphasis on "precisely tailored," because no two people are exactly alike. Human beings are endowed by their Creator with tremendous heterogeneity and polymorphism. Not only do they all look different, they are all biochemically and genetically different. The mathematically precise nutritional requirements of a 70 year-old grandmother will not be the same as that of a 20 year-old Olympic athlete. Happily the new science of Molecular Medicine can now fine-tune for both. This means that the precise nutritional requirements of each individual can now be assessed, monitored and fine-tuned by physicians with degrees in the millennial science of *Preventative Medicine.* It means a sea change. It means a tectonic shift. It means treating disease holistically. It means restoring sanity, dignity, respect and nobility to the lofty profession of Medicine.

MILLENNIAL MEDICINE

In recent years the increase of economic entropy has gone hand in hand with increase of medical entropy. Not only has the Hippocratic oath been turned on its head, but the culture of healing has also been transformed into a culture of death. Wesley J. Smith documents the backsliding in his book *Culture of Death*:

> Unbeknownst to most Americans, a small but influential group of philosophers and health care policy makers are working energetically to transform our nation's medical practice and health care laws. They are turning away from the "do no harm" model established by Hippocrates more than two thousand years ago, and towards a stark utilitarian system that would legitimize medical discrimination against —and even in some cases, the killing of—the weakest and most defenseless people among us.[9]

Smith goes on to list and catalog the nature of the emerging monstrosities. The leveling down of life, and leveling up of death. The leveling down of people into "beings" or "humans animals," and the leveling up of animals into the moral equivalents of human beings. The monstrous subversion of word and language in the effort to "redefine" life in certain cases (the unborn, the newly born, those suffering from cognitive disabilities and the terminally ill). The abomination that is now being called *Futile Care Theory*, allowing doctors to refuse wanted care on the basis of their own subjective assessment of the quality of patients' lives. Intentional killing of cognitively disabled people via dehydration (a horrible way of dying). The attempts to change the legal definitions of euthanasia and assisted suicide from "crimes" to "medical treatment." The attempts to rationalize and justify the macabre precedents of Dr. Jack Kevorkian—"Dr. Death." The attempts to glorify the practitioners and purveyors of death as "liberators." The attempt to elevate death and dying to the status of a religion. The attempt to associate death and dying with political correctness. It seems that the dictum of the Cosmic Constable has now become the "morality" of postmodern bioethicists. ("You have a duty to die. Resistance is futile. You will die! Order! Order! Order in the universe!")

The derivative culture of death is now trying to expand into new moral, ethical, and philosophical territories. Today "assisted suicide," tomorrow "a duty to die." Today a little infanticide, tomorrow Hitler's eugenics. Today a little "cloning," tomorrow chimeras. Today "non-heart-beating cadaver donors," tomorrow the organs farms portrayed in the film *Coma*. Inch by inch. Here a little, there a little. Push, push, push. Precedent by precedent.

It seems that the rider on the pale horse of the Apocalypse wasn't satisfied to come out of some closet in the Netherlands. The Grim Reaper, wielding the Dutch ethic of *death-on-demand*, is now coming out of closets in Oregon as well. Inch by inch. Precedent by precedent. As it is written:

יֵשׁ דֶּרֶךְ יָשָׁר לִפְנֵי־אִישׁ וְאַחֲרִיתָהּ דַּרְכֵי־מָוֶת

There is a way which seems right to man,
but the end thereof are the ways of death.
(Proverbs 14:12)

Where there are no absolutes there are no frames of reference. Where there are no frames of reference there are no guiding principles. Where there are no guiding principles there are no navigation aids. Postmodern culture has jettisoned all absolutes and all frames of reference; there is no ultimate ethical mooring; there is no reliable chart or compass. Medical ethics are now rudderless and adrift, blown in this and that direction. All motion and no direction; all form and no substance; all method and no content; all propriety and no morality. To whom nothing is sacred nothing is profane, not even the cold-blooded murder of fully grown babies or the killing of helpless elderly patients by dehydration. Once the sanctity of life has been violated anything goes. The principle, once admitted, there is no limit to its application. We see in all this the terrible price that man pays when he takes the smallest step away from God.

Forty years ago the modern age ended and the postmodern age began. Forty years ago we began to jettison all absolutes and embrace relativism instead. We said we didn't want to be governed by God any more. We thought we were freeing ourselves from "draconian restraints." But we ended up putting on the ball and chain of the Grim Reaper instead. Now we are paying the price of our folly. As it is written:

וְחֹטְאִי חֹמֵס נַפְשׁוֹ כָּל־מְשַׂנְאַי אָהֲבוּ מָוֶת

He that sins against Me wrongs his own soul:
all they that hate Me, love death.
(Proverbs 8:36)

We have become the lovers of death, counted as sheep for the slaughter. Death in our schools. Death in our hospitals. Death in our streets. Death in our cities. Death, death, death. Medical ethics have slid to hell in a handbasket. The "banality of evil" that Hannah Arendt ascribed to Nazi butchers has found its way into the halls of academia, medicine, and hospital wards. Babies living in the womb have been downgraded to "products of conception," thirty million of them aborted under the pretext of "choice." How did this happen? Two radical feminists, despising the so-called "patriarchy" and determined to "protect" women from "the male contamination," exploited the plight of a young woman named Norma McCovey. They picked Norma up when she was a naive and destitute young lady, used her to change the law, and then discarded her like so much garbage. In case Norma's real name doesn't ring a bell, her alias should—she is the "Jane Roe" in *Roe v. Wade*. An insider to the abortion industry, Norma came to see the profit motive of those who performed abortions, and the deceit of the so-called "pro-choice" propaganda. By the grace of God Norma renounced her involvement in *Roe v. Wade* in 1995, announcing her conversion to Christianity. Her story is another one of those dirty little secrets that the derivative and reprobate world would rather sweep under a rug.

In the meantime, of course, public morality and medical ethics have slid further down the gradient that leads to Hades itself. At this writing some 3000-5000 "D & X procedures" are being performed every year. "D & X" stands for "intact dilation and extraction," also known as *late term abortion*. What is it? It is the legalized, cold-blooded murder of helpless babies as they are pulled partly out of the birth canal, some of them kicking and struggling. Scissors are then inserted into the back of their heads and their brains vacuumed out. Their little bodies are then cut up and the various parts marketed to profit-seeking "medical research institutions."

There is an old saying: "Be careful what you ask for, you might get it!" Forty years ago we said we didn't want God, and we got what we asked for. And now the Grim Reaper is knocking at the door, demanding his pound of flesh. Is this suprising?

Is the situation hopeless? No, all of these dreadful trends can be reversed if we turn back to God. The gates of repentance are always open:

לְכוּ־נָא וְנִוָּכְחָה יֹאמַר יְהוָֹה אִם־יִהְיוּ חֲטָאֵיכֶם כַּשָּׁנִים כַּשֶּׁלֶג יַלְבִּינוּ
אִם־יַאְדִּימוּ כַתּוֹלָע כַּצֶּמֶר יִהְיוּ

Come, let us reason together, saith the LORD:
though your sins be as scarlet, they shall be as white as snow;
though they be red like crimson, they shall be as wool.
(Isaiah 1:18)

In a Judeo-Christian frame, Man is special because he is created in the image of the Absolute. In a pagan-derivative frame there are no absolutes. In a pagan-derivative frame the value of everything is relative, determined by its so-called "utility." Today some atheist bioethicists would ascribe more worth and value to a fully-grown animal than they would to unborn life, or newborn life, or some sick elderly person. Postmodern bioethicists do not ask, "Is such and such right or wrong in the sight of God?" They ask, "Is such and such expedient in a Darwinian/Malthusian world with too many people competing for too few resources?"

This is the nature of the conflict between the Judeo-Christian world view and the postmodern world view. In his 1982 address at Coral Ridge Presbyterian Church the late Christian philosopher Francis Schaeffer described the conflict in this way:

> I want to say to you, those of you who are troubled about the direction our society is going in, that we must not concentrate merely on the "bits and pieces"—permissiveness, pornography, the problem of the public schools, the breakdown of the family, abortion, infanticide, euthanasia, and many, many other things. We must understand that all of these dilemmas come as a consequence of moving [away] from the Judeo-Christian world view... into this other world view which is that the final reality is only energy or material, which has existed forever and which has taken its present shape by pure chance. [10]

In their Declaration of Independence the Founding Fathers of America stated that all men were created equal, endowed by their Creator with certain unalienable rights, among them life, liberty, and the pursuit of happiness. Were the Founders laboring under a terrible delusion? The derivative and pagan man would answer "yes." The argument of the derivative mind would read something like this:

> The Christian Founders of America were backward, superstitious, intolerant and patriarchal interlopers who for one fleeting second managed to defy the Cosmic Constable to his face. But now that they are dead and forgotten, we are free to revert to the derivative forms of existence and build a cozy little Sodom-commune for ourselves, over their graves.

The late Carl Sagan commenced his popular television series *Cosmos* with the following words:

> The Cosmos is all there is, all there has been and all there will ever be.

Statements such as this are the very essence of the postmodern zeitgeist (cultural mood). In a postmodern frame, we human beings are sub-microscopic slime on an insignificant planet whose galaxy would not amount to a speck of dust compared to the cosmos. In a postmodern frame, we are the result of purposeless and mindless processes that did not have our creation in mind. In his book *The Astonishing Hypothesis* scientist and Nobel Laureate Francis Crick writes the following:

> The Astonishing Hypothesis is that "You," your joys and your sorrows, your memories and your ambitions, your sense of personal identity and free will, are in fact no more than the behavior of a vast assembly of nerve cells and their associated molecules. As Lewis Carroll's Alice might have phrased it: "You are nothing but a pack of neurons." [11]

Do neurons have any unalienable rights? We have been saying all along that they don't. Take away the moral worth and value that God places on us, and we are nothing but physical systems moving from low to high entropy states. But this is where the derivative man wants to have his cake and eat it too. On the one hand he wants to be rid of God, and on the other he wants to claim cosmic privilege for himself.

Do we have any unalienable rights as human beings? Can we lay claim to any *absolute* worth or value as such? In Romans 5:7 Rav Shaul writes the following:

> Very rarely will anyone die for a righteous man, though for a good man someone might possibly dare to lay down his life. But God demonstrates His own love for us in this: While we were yet sinners, Christ died for us.

Let us remind ourselves of the words of *Yeshua* in John 15:13

> Greater love hath no man than this, that he should lay down his life for his friends. You are my friends...

If Christ died for us, how great our value and worth! We are in all respects persuaded, and believe, that the sacrifice of *Yeshua* at Calvary hath invested all men with *absolute* worth and value in the sight of God. We are persuaded, and believe, that all men are indeed created equal, endowed by their Creator with unalienable rights that cannot be withheld by emperors, kings, pontiffs, priests, potentates, central bankers, or "bioethicists."

It is time to restore Man to the dignity of his origins in God. It is time for the salt of the earth and the light of the world to take a resolute stand for the superlative order of Life, even as the derivative world reverts to the ways of death.

The First Amendment of the United States Constitution reads thus:

> Congress shall make no law respecting an establishment of religion, or prohibiting the free exercise thereof; or abridging the freedom of speech, or of the press; or the right of the people peaceably to assemble and to petition the Government for a redress of grievances.

Who can calculate the sum of mischief that these few words have prevented in the last 200 years? Here are a few words written on a piece of paper, yet in all the pages of secular history one would be hard-pressed to find a single blow more accurately launched into the ribcage of the devil that has been competing against the labor of Man and seeking to deprive him of the dignity of his origins in God. So also a few additional words written in a latter day Amendment will serve to indemnify future generations from untold mischief when it comes to the misuse of modern medicine. Without presuming to dictate exact wording, an addendum to the First Amendment of the United States Constitution might read as follows:

> Congress shall make no law respecting a definition of human life, or denying the equality of human life, or denying the personage or personhood thereof.

We say again: Like the Founders of America, we are in all respects persuaded, and believe, that all men are created equal, endowed by their Creator with unalienable rights that governments are instituted to protect. Life being one of those unalienable rights, which right physicians also are called upon to preserve, governments must now do their duty by reinstating an up to date version of the *Hippocratic Oath* by law, requiring that all physicians take it before receiving a license to practice medicine. Without presuming to dictate the exact wording, we may nevertheless submit the following draft, reflecting the spirit of the original Hippocratic oath (Circa 325 B.C.) and the revision of Louis Lasagna (1964):

HIPPOCRATIC OATH (MILLENNIAL)

I hereby swear, in the witness of God and Man, to fulfill, to the best of my ability and judgment, this covenant:

I will, henceforth and to my dying day, do hand-to-hand combat with my ancient adversary disease, so help me God.

I will preserve the sanctity of human life, abiding by the *primum non nocere* principle of the Hippocratic tradition, respecting the hard-won scientific gains of my peers, freely sharing such knowledge as is mine with those who are to follow.

I will apply dietic measures for the benefit of my patients, recognizing that an ounce of prevention is worth a pound of cure, remembering the words of Hippocrates—"Let food be your medicine, let medicine be your food."

I will neither administer a deadly drug to anyone who asks for it, nor will I make a suggestion to this effect. Similarly I will not give to a woman an abortive remedy. In the fear of God, in truth, and in purity, I will guard the integrity and sanctity of my profession.

I will not view any human life subjectively, nor make any presumption about the value thereof. I will not discriminate between my patients on the basis of race, gender, age, religion, culture, nationality, condition, or status. I will treat all human life as equally valuable.

I will not betray the trust of my patients. I will not violate

> the principle of physician-patient confidentiality. I will empathize and sympathize with my patients. I will always strive to preserve their God-given rights, dignities, and autonomies under all circumstances.
>
> If I remain faithful to this oath, God grant that my name be written in the Book of Life. Should I transgress it and swear falsely, may God strike my name from the Book of Life. Amen!

It is time for the salt of the earth and the light of the world to fulfill their destinies by using the virtues of the American political system to set things right *in due process of law.* As goes America, so goes the world. Let these wholesome restraints and lofty standards be set here in America, and the world will emulate in due course. Such measures of law must be established, and soon, otherwise the American people and the citizens of the world will have no ground upon which to complain of the evils that may follow.

The balm of life is precious. The *Complexity* of human existence is now under full-scale attack by a hidden enemy internalized in the physical constitution of man. The Adversary of mankind has thrown down the gauntlet and we are threatened by the rider on the pale horse of the Apocalypse. Let all believers—Christians, Jews, and Muslims alike—contend valiantly before the throne of the LORD, by faith, by prayer, by lawful and non-violent labor, and by their presence at the voting booths, so that all men, vanquished by the Spirit of God, should turn from Death towards Life.

וְגָר זְאֵב עִם־כֶּבֶשׂ וְנָמֵר עִם־גְּדִי יִרְבָּץ...
לֹא־יָרֵעוּ וְלֹא־יַשְׁחִיתוּ בְּכָל־הַר קָדְשִׁי כִּי־מָלְאָה הָאָרֶץ דֵּעָה
אֶת־יְהוָה כַּמַּיִם לַיָּם מְכַסִּים

The wolf shall dwell with the lamb, and the leopard shall lie down with the kid...
They shall not hurt or destroy in all my holy mountain:
for the knowledge of the LORD *will fill the earth,*
as the waters fill the sea.
(Isaiah 11:6-9)

SECTION 7

Cosmos and Sin

Understanding the Kingdom of God

Why is there so much evil in the world? Why do men seek affirmation in evil? Why does evil tend to get selected more often than good? Why is good more difficult to achieve than evil? Why is good so rare and short lived here on earth, and evil so pervasive and enduring? Why should disorder be so easy, and order so difficult? Why should war be so easy, and peace so difficult? Is there a scientific explanation for the paranoia and suspicion exhibited by all peoples towards those who are born different from themselves? Why can't all the different peoples of the world coexist peaceably without reducing one another? Why do human systems tend to interact in such ways as to destroy heterogeneity?

In analyzing physical situations it is customary for scientists to focus their attention on some event, arrangement, or pattern, which they separate in their minds and label *system*. Everything outside the system they label *environment*. They then try to investigate the way in which the system interacts with its natural environment. Universal systems tend to interact with their environments in known ways. The second law of thermodynamics predicts the outcome of such interactions thus:

> A natural process that starts in one condition and ends in another, will go in the direction that causes the combined entropy of the system and its environment to increase.

But does this law have *ethical* referents? Does it have *ethnic* referents? Can it be ruling on the fate of, say, a Kurdish system in the environment of Iraq, or an Armenian system in the environment of Turkey, or a Jewish system in the environment of Nazi Germany? Can it also be ruling on human interactions in such ways as to cause their outcomes to go in the direction of increasing entropy? Can the same law be reducing the racial, cultural and ethnic gradients of the human race by genocide, pogrom, holocaust, and ethnic cleansing? Can the same principle be at work among the diverse factions of humanity, consummating their potential differences by conquest and empire, by fagot and inquisition, by sword and Kalashnikov, by terrorism and suicide bombings? Can the same cosmic prejudice be at the root of such things as hate, bigotry, racism and antisemitism?

What is "right?" What is "wrong?" What is "ethical?" What is "unethical?" What is "good?" What is "evil?" What is "moral?" What is "immoral?" Is there an objective standard or measure? Can there ever be an objective basis to moral and ethical value judgments?

Having investigated the natural, pagan, religious, economic, and biological shapes of "entropy," let us now broaden the scope of our inquiry to investigate its moral, ethical, and political shapes as well. Let us begin by reviewing the twin premises of this publication:

1) Material reality is statistically oriented towards disorder.
2) Material human nature is governed by the same orientation.

One cannot begin to talk about morality and ethics without assuming something about human nature, and one cannot assume something about human nature without understanding a thing or two about the nature of the cosmos itself. Throughout this inquiry our goal has been to obtain an understanding of human nature that is consistent with the movement of the cosmos. In this publication we describe the material nature of man as a function of the material nature of the universe, a universe in which entropy is increasing, a universe in which the greater order of change is flowing down the gradient that leads from low probability to high probability, from *complexity* to simplicity, from heterogeneity to homogeneity, from order to disorder. To help the learning process we have set up a gestalt (a holistic framework) in which we posit a principality in lieu of the principle of increasing entropy, nicknaming it "Cosmic Constable," this being the adversarial entity that is directing every system in the universe towards disorder and dissolution. Let us see if we can use the universal activity of the Cosmic Constable as a holistic framework for moral and ethical calibrations.

MORAL AND ETHICAL CALIBRATIONS

From the Constable's point of view *any* kind of disorder would be an affirmation of the universal imperative of increasing entropy. Unjust wars, violence, destruction, reduction, corruption, degradation, marginalization, holocaust, ethnic cleansing, terrorism, racism, antisemitism, oppression, murder, larceny, bribery, extortion, blackmail, theft, lying, cheating, adultery, fornication, perversion, homosexuality and obscenity would all receive the Constable's stamp of approval and affirmation in varying degrees, these being behaviors that are condemned as immoral and evil by all civilized societies.

Let us strive for a holistic perspective, bearing in mind that our own brains, neurons and nervous systems are made from the physics of this universe, materially and existentially governed by the nature of the cosmos, as Scripture suggests:

> For all that is in the *world* [<Greek *kosmos*], the lust of the flesh, and the lust of the eyes, and the pride of life, is not of God, but is of the *world* [<Greek *kosmos*].
> (1 John 2:16, emphasis added.)

The lust of the derivative flesh is to *do* disorder; the lust of the derivative eye is to *see* disorder; the pride of the derivative life is to seek *affirmation* in disorder. The derivative desire of man is in conflict with the authentic desire of Man. Rav Shaul explains the nature of this conflict in the rhetorical discourse found in his letter to the formative church in Rome:

> I do not understand my own irrational nature. For I do not seem to be able to do what is good, but end up doing the very thing that I hate and know to be evil.... So then it is no longer I myself that is oriented towards evil, but something within my flesh. For I know that nothing good dwells within me, that is, in my flesh. I can will to do what is good and right, but I don't seem to be able to carry it out. For I do not do the good that I want to do, but the evil that I do not want to do, that is what I end up doing. Now if I end up doing what I do not want to do, then it is no longer I that do it, but sin which dwells in me. So then I find it to be a contradiction, that when I want to do good, evil lies close at hand. For I delight in the Law of God in my inmost [authentic] spirit and mind, but I see in my [derivative] flesh a contrary principle at war with the law of my mind, making me captive to the principle of sin internalized in my physical members.
>
> (Romans 7:15-23)

The derivative man is unconsciously aroused by the spectacle or prospect of disorder, real or fictional. The evidence for this is all around us. What, for example, is the derivative man aroused by when he watches vice, immorality, crime, shootings, car crashes and exploding buildings on television and in the movies? What devil is there in the flesh of man that would seek affirmation in the popular spectacle of violence, reduction, destruction and degradation that has come to be known as "extreme wrestling?" Why do the ratings go through the roof when there is a live police chase? Why are postmodern teenagers addicted to video games that glorify war, violence, shootings, killings and explosions? Why does the apostate media love to feed on vice, immorality, perversion, murder and corruption? Why are the most popular programs on television those that portray scenes of banality, immorality, and disorder? Why does the sitcom audience hoot and holler with pleasure at the very suggestion of nudity or fornication? These questions have never been answered scientifically.

Is there a scientific explanation? Yes, all of these behaviors amount to nothing more than local outworkings, expressions and *affirmations* of the universal imperative of increasing entropy. The unconscious arousal, the lust, the pleasure, the vicarious element, the enactment, the urge, the impulse, the violence, the injury, the perverse satisfaction and evil affirmation all derive themselves from the statistical tendency to disorder internalized in flesh. We are looking at *anthropomorphizations* of the cosmic process (transformation into human form of an impersonal principle of physics). A Freudian entropy show, in a universe in which entropy is increasing.

Matter and energy are oriented towards disorder. Flesh is constituted of matter and energy. As goes the behavior of matter and energy, so goes the behavior of the derivative man. Ultimately the urge to reduce, to consummate, to degrade and to destroy is not of human origin—it is elemental. The statistical tendency to disorder in flesh is always looking for outlets in terms of behaviors that may *produce* disorder. Given the infinite array of decisions and choices confronting billions of human beings, any decision or choice that might lead to disorder would tend to receive a subtle (statistical) boost from the nature of physical reality, registering derivative satisfaction and pleasure. Conversely, any choice or decision that might lead to order would tend to receive the opposite—a subtle drag, penalty or restraint, registering derivative dissatisfaction and displeasure. If one could label the former "immoral," and the latter "moral," then the Cosmic Constable would have to make selections in favor of "immorality." Not because he is immoral, you understand, but because he is a discriminating principle trying to move universal systems towards higher entropy states, using human elements as a means to that end. If immoral human behaviors are productive of higher entropy states, then that is the sort of behavior that the Cosmic Constable will have to affirm, sanction, support and encourage.

Are we saying behaviors that produce *decreases* of local entropy should be judged "good," and behaviors that produce *increases* of local entropy should be judged "evil?" No, one cannot universalize as such. The building contractor that destroys an old building cannot be said to be behaving immorally. On the other hand the terrorist that destroys the building *can* be said to be behaving immorally. Notwithstanding that the behaviors of both are productive of the same net increase in local entropy, there is a *moral* distinction to be made by civilized peoples between the behaviors of building contractors and terrorists.

Everything else being equal, a general distinction can be made between "good" behaviors that are on the whole productive of decreases of local entropy (on the whole supportive of life and *complexity*), and "evil" behaviors that are on the whole productive of the increases of local entropy (on the whole destructive of life and *complexity*). As difficult as the distinction may be in some cases, (the behaviors associated with the Boston Tea Party, or the American Revolution, for example,) mankind must endeavor to make rational and holistic judgments under God. The namby-pamby nihilism, limp-wristed irresponsibility and weak-kneed subterfuge that would refuse such judgments on grounds of "political correctness" deserves the contempt of rational human beings the world over.

There is an inverse relationship between entropy and *complexity*. Where entropy increases locally, it can only do so at the expense of local life and *complexity*. Everything else being equal, low entropy states are supportive of life and *complexity*, high entropy states injurious to life and *complexity*. The former would support the betterment of the human condition, the latter the detriment thereof. There being a relationship such as this, a distinction must be made between public laws, public doctrines, public principles, public choices and public policies that encourage human beings to conform to the nature of corruption (increasing entropy), and public laws, public doctrines, public principles, public choices and public policies that encourage human beings *not* to conform to the nature of corruption. Thus we stumble onto a Millennial template that is consistent with the Word of God:

> [Everything else being equal:] Public laws, public doctrines, public principles, public choices and public policies that encourage human beings to conform to the nature of corruption, to the extent of the encouragement, can be said to be evil. Public laws, public doctrines, public principles, public choices and public policies that encourage mankind to conform to the nature of Incorruption, to the extent of the encouragement, can be said to be good.

Is this guideline consistent with the Ten Commandments of God? Indeed it is. What are we to infer from the repetition of the words "You shall not... You shall not..." in the Decalogue? We are to infer a natural tendency to disorder internalized in all flesh. We are to infer an *evil inclination* that escapes man's conscious detection. We are to infer an internal urge or lust that, given free reign, would bring the course of mankind into alignment with the course of the cosmos, working the increases of local entropy in disorder, degradation, immorality, corruption and ruin of every kind. That which the derivative mind of man would naturally conform to, the Spirit of God cautions against by commanding "You shall not…"

The orientation of the natural man is the orientation of the cosmos itself—pointed towards entropy and corruption. Left to himself man will fall rather than stand, sink rather than rise. Left to his own devices man will conform to the way of cosmos itself, doing so naturally, unconsciously, automatically and existentially. This has been the way of the derivative man since time immemorial. To countermand this lower way, a higher way was given by God, beginning with the injunction against elemental conformity (idolatry). Having created the universe with foreknowledge, seeing the cosmic incline and all of its inclinations, seeing the *evil inclination* that might cause man to conform to the nature of corruption in idolatry, murder, adultery, theft, God gave the Ten Commandments through Moses saying, "You shall not commit idolatry… You shall not kill…You shall not commit adultery… You shall not steal…."

With all the subtlety with which the devil of disorder has been tempting man to conform to the nature of the cosmos, encouraging him to "slide down the incline," "go with the flow," and "do what comes naturally," God has etched on tablets of Sinai's stones a reciprocal Law, saying: "You shall not!" The Ten Commandments of God are based on truth, consistent with reality.

THE DERIVATIVE NATURE OF MAN: UNDERSTANDING THE EVIL INCLINATION

Granted that the increase of universal entropy does not translate into local determinism, but it does translate into the very things that the Bible speaks about—sin nature, evil orientation, evil tendency, evil desire, evil urge, evil lust, or what is in the Hebrew referred to as יֵצֶר־הָרָע—*yetzer ha-ra*, "the evil inclination."

The evil inclination in flesh is derived from the statistical tendency to disorder we have been describing. As such, it does not produce evil deterministically. The mechanism is subtle, probabilistic and statistical, meaning that it can only be seen in large samples—it becomes palpable, tangible, substantive and measurable only in the behavior of a sufficiently large number of elements. This does not mean that the principle of sin and death is not concrete. But even concrete needs time to set properly. If we may quote the words of the wise Solomon:

יֵשׁ דֶּרֶךְ יָשָׁר לִפְנֵי־אִישׁ וְאַחֲרִיתָהּ דַּרְכֵי־מָוֶת
There is a way which seems right to a man,
but the END thereof are the ways of death.
(Proverbs 14:12, emphasis added.)

Or words from the Sifré:

תְּחִלָּתוֹ שֶׁל יֵצֶר־הָרָע דוֹמֶה לְחוּט – סוֹפוֹ כַּעֲבוֹת הָעֲגָלָה.
The beginning of the evil inclination is like thread,
and the end like heavy rope.[1]

Or words from the Zohar:

הוּא שָׂטָן הוּא יֵצֶר־הָרָע
Satan is, in sooth, the evil inclination.[2]

Or words from the Epistle of James:

> Every man is drawn away by his own evil inclination and enticed. Then the evil inclination conceives and gives birth to sin, and sin, when fully matured, brings forth death.
> (James 1:14-15)

The material nature of man is cosmos-derivative—statistically oriented towards disorder. Unless restrained by the Spirit and Law of God, the derivative man will gravitate towards disorder. Absent the Ten Commandments, the derivative man will be governed by the orientation in his flesh. It is not within the capacity of the dust-formed man to direct his own steps towards the high plateaus of Order and Liberty. The nature of dust—the self-referential paradox, "blindness," and "catch-22" that we mentioned in the introduction to this publication—prevents him from doing so. As Scripture affirms:

יָדַעְתִּי יְהוָה כִּי לֹא לָאָדָם דַּרְכּוֹ לֹא־לְאִישׁ הֹלֵךְ וְהָכִין אֶת־צַעֲדוֹ

I have known, O LORD, that not of man [is] his way,
neither [in the capacity] of man to walk and direct his own steps.
(Jeremiah 10:23)

מֵיְהוָה מִצְעֲדֵי־גֶבֶר כּוֹנָנוּ וְדַרְכּוֹ יֶחְפָּץ
כִּי־יִפֹּל לֹא־יוּטָל כִּי־יְהוָה סוֹמֵךְ יָדוֹ

The steps of a [good] man are ordered by the LORD,
and He delights in his progress. Though he stumble,
he shall not perish, for the hand of the LORD will steady him.
(Psalm 37:23-24)

The low road and the high road are clearly marked in the Bible. The low road would work the spiritual and material defeat of mankind. The high road would work the spiritual and material victory of mankind. The low road is easy, derivative, and "natural." The high road is difficult, authentic, and "unnatural." As *Yeshua* affirms:

> Enter by the narrow gate. For wide is the gate and easy the road that leads to destruction, and those that enter through it are many. But narrow is the gate and difficult the road that leads to life, and those that find it are few.
> (Matthew 7:13)

Scripture informs us in as many words that man born of stardust has an affiliation with the nature of corruption. Howbeit Scripture also informs us that Man born of the Spirit of God has an altogether different affiliation. In studying Scripture we are given to understand that man has a lower affiliation and a higher affiliation, the former with dust made flesh and its predisposition towards corruption, the latter with the Spirit of God made living Way and its predisposition towards Liberty. The lower way is rooted in material trust and animated by the universe's statistical tendency to disorder. The higher way is rooted in Faith and animated by the Spirit of the God who is unaffected by space, time, matter, energy, nature, necessity, entropy and corruption, the Almighty Creator who is Eternal, Unchanging, Incorruptible, Imperishable and Blessed forever, Amen.

Time is like a river flowing towards higher entropy states. It is easy for the spirit of man to be carried downstream by it. It is difficult to resist the flow. Mankind is inclined to love that which is easy and hate that which is difficult. The Constable whispers: "Go with the flow!" The Spirit of God commands: "You shall not!" Two opposing forces are required to place the soul of man under tension, the imperative of God pulling in one direction, the decree of the Constable pulling in the other. By nature and by default the world would choose the Constable's way, sliding to hell in a handbasket. But God so loved the world that He sent his only begotten Son, to redirect the steps of man towards the high plateaus of Liberty. By nature and by disposition we once walked the path of spiritual and material ruin, swept downstream by the universal tide of increasing entropy. *Yeshua* came and rescued us, delivering us from the torrents of Perdition. As Rav Shaul affirms:

> And you has he made [spiritually] alive, who were once [spiritually] dead in trespasses and sins, wherein in time past you conformed to the course of this cosmos, according to the prince of the power of the air—the spirit that now animates the children of disobedience.
>
> (Ephesians 2:1-2)

NECESSARY VS CONTINGENT

In the history of ethics the general rule followed by all the great thinkers is that moral *prescriptions* should be based on *descriptions* of reality and human nature. By way of an analogy one might say that a *description* of the force of gravity must precede *prescriptions* relating to such things as building codes and public safety, elevator and bridge design, dam construction, architectural guidelines, public works, aviation safety, etc. The contractor who violates public codes by building an unsafe structure—one that gravity may cause to collapse, killing or injuring occupants—might then be judged unethical and have his license revoked.

If we could appropriate a little something from the great thinker Immanuel Kant, we might say that the difference between "ethical" and "unethical" boils down to the dichotomy between the *necessary* and the *unnecessary*, or as Kant himself might have said, the *necessary* and the *contingent*. When one asks "is such and such ethical," one is in effect asking "is such and such *necessary*?" But what are we to understand by the special use of the word *necessary* here? Ideally, the *necessary* would correspond to something real, something true under all circumstances, something objective, authentic and substantial—a real and true consciousness grounded in reality. The *unnecessary* would be the opposite, corresponding to a false consciousness based on something unreal, imagined or made up, something without truth anchoring, something subjective or circumstantial (its truth depending on circumstances), something misleading, deceptive, illusory, insubstantial, adventitious, accidental—something *contingent.*

Let us try to see the difference between the *necessary* and the *contingent* by way of a crude illustration. Let us imagine that, due to some strange madness, people are pushing one another off 40-ft. buildings. And let us say that we want to restrain this madness by instituting a public law that reads as follows:

"You shall not push people off the roofs of 40-ft. buildings!"

Would such a law be *necessary* in the sense defined above? Well yes, because it would be grounded in reality—it would be backed up by a scientific description of the force of gravity here on earth. But what if we are dealing with a human colony situated on the moon where gravity is weaker? Or what if we are building something in space where there is very little gravity? If you push someone off the roof of a 40-ft. building on earth he may die in the fall. If you push someone off the roof of a 40-ft. building on the moon he may land softly. If you push someone off the roof of a 40-ft. structure in orbit he may float away into space and perish out there. Three different *prescriptions,* grounded in scientific *descriptions* of gravity. What may be *necessary* on earth may be *contingent* on the surface of the moon. What may be *contingent* on the surface of the moon may be *necessary* on the surface of a space station.

What are we driving at and what are we saying? We are saying that *prescriptions* of ethics and morality need to be based on *descriptions* of the world and human nature. The determination as to what is *necessary* and what is *contingent*—what is ethically *right* and what is ethically *wrong*—cannot be based on zeitgeist, cultural mood, political expediency, political correctness or feel-good emotionalism.

Let us carry the analogy forward and apply it to the nature, property, and orientation of the cosmos itself. As *descriptions* of gravity had to precede *prescriptions* of law in the above examples, so also *descriptions* of reality and human nature must precede *prescriptions* of ethics and morality. What then? What shall we say about the prescriptions of Judeo-Christian morality? Are they *necessary*, or are they *contingent* (unnecessary)? Is the Judeo-Christian ethic true or false? Well, again, the answer would depend on descriptions of reality and human nature. If reality has no stable foundation, if cosmos is evolving gratuitously and chaotically, if human nature is completely "neutral," completely "unbiased," completely "transparent," then it could be said that the Judeo-Christian ethic is false and the prescriptions thereof *contingent*. But if reality has a stable foundation, if universal entropy is increasing, if the world is oriented towards disorder—and human nature a derivative thereof—then it could be said that the Judeo-Christian ethic is true and the prescriptions thereof *necessary*.

In retrospect we have to admit that some of the blackest and most damnable sins committed in the name of "religion" have had to do with this business of trying to make the *contingent* necessary. Recall that for 1500 years religious scholars tried to make adjustments to Ptolemy's model of the earth-centered universe. Was it *necessary*? No, it was a false consciousness based on human error and flawed cosmology. A damnable sin in itself? No, to err is human. But a damnable sin in that they tried to perpetuate the falsehood even after Galileo. The damnable sin was to use the authority of the Church to make the *contingent* necessary in the name of God.

Truth is the guiding principle of the Kingdom of God. It is a damnable sin to make the *contingent* necessary, elevating falsehood to the status of truth. The reverse is also a damnable sin. To try to make the truly *necessary* contingent, thereby degrading truth into falsehood, is also a damnable sin. Those who would organize politically to make the Ten Commandments of God *contingent* (unnecessary), would be committing a damnable sin.

Naturally this is what the political devil will try to do—make the *necessary* unnecessary and the *unnecessary* necessary by force of law. Which in essence is what the Bolsheviks did when they changed the laws, confiscated private property and communized human society in the former Soviet Union.

What then shall we say about the present culture war? Who is guilty of the damnable sin of violating truth? Who is guilty of trying to make the *contingent* necessary, and who is guilty of trying to make the truly *necessary* contingent? The present culture war pits the premises of Judeo-Christian morality against the assumptions of the postmodern zeitgeist. What are the assumptions of the postmodern zeitgeist? They might read as follows:

There are no absolutes.
There is no God.
Man is the measure of all things.
There is no objective reality.
There is no a priori reality.
Reality does not exist outside a scheme of human subjectivity.
Reality has no stable foundation.
Reality is a cloud of chaotic processes.
Reality has no bearing on morality or ethics.
Reality is contingent, relative and local.
Reality is socially constructed.
Human nature has no orientation.
Human nature is neutral.
Human nature is contingent, relative and local.
Human nature is socially construed.
There is no universal principle of corruption.
There is no such things as a sin-nature.
There is no such things as sin.
There are no frames of reference for moral/ethical calibration.
"Good" and "evil" are socially construed.
All moralities are socially construed.
All moralities are relative and equally valid.
There is no objective truth.
There is no hierarchy of truth.
All truths are socially construed.
All truth claims are subjective, relative, and equally valid.
Man enjoys a gratuitous existence in a chaotic universe.
Man is an autonomous and self-sufficient entity.
Man decides what is real or unreal.
Man decides what is truth or untruth.
Man decides what is good or evil.
Man decides what is right or wrong.
Man is his own god.

In the introduction to this publication we mentioned some of the chronic failures catalogued in history and said that the human race seems to be up against some sort of *classical boundary condition*, which we defined as follows:

> You can't fix something that's broke on the basis of the same set of assumptions that made it broke in the first place—you will just bounce off the same walls and end up right back where you started.

These are the deadly assumptions that man has been bouncing off since the foundation of the world. These are the "boundary conditions" that have kept mankind chained to systems of disorder and failure since the beginning of history. In aggregate, and as a system of belief, these assumptions might be referred to as *the devil's great lie*, as in the Genesis narrative where we find the serpent whispering to Eve: "You will become your own gods!" (Genesis 3:5).

The house of cards that has since come to be known as *postmodern culture*, sheltering within its walls what may be called *the liberal view of human nature*, is built on assumptions such as these. In part, or in whole, these are the irrational assumptions on which postmodern academicians, atheists, agnostics, nihilists, homosexuals, radical feminists, pornographers, abortionists, bioethicists and ACLU lawyers base their agendas and propaganda. In part or in whole, the above assumptions undergird and underwrite every policy statement issued by the devil of nihilism throughout history.

In his New York Times bestseller *Slouching Towards Gomorrah* former United States Acting Attorney General Robert H. Bork catalogs the events and legal precedents by which the devil of nihilism built his house of cards in America, producing in the span of a few decades the worst kind of moral deformity imaginable—a culture that is now in moral free fall with no bottom in sight, a culture in which the tail wags the dog, falsehood scoffs at truth, madness sits in judgment over sanity, perversion is "offended" by morality. A culture in which the devil of nihilism can dictate social policy through his control and manipulation of the media, academia, and judicial system. A culture in which the derivative man is given a free hand to distort the intent of the Founders, revise American history, vandalize the Constitution, pervert the First Amendment, subvert the English language, whitewash human nature, legalize the cold-blooded murder of helpless babies, legitimize perversion, dignify abomination, glorify immorality, legalize obscenity, restructure ethics, rearrange government, institutions of learning, medicine, marriage and family. A wholly derivative culture that lacks the spiritual strength to cope with reality, and so must degrade and dumb everything down to a fiction that *can* be coped with. A psychotic, neurotic and mattoid culture in which rationality itself is too difficult to deal with and therefore forbidden. As Bork indicates:

> Quite another form of irrationality afflicts portions of our intelligentsia: the astounding claim that rationality itself is neither possible nor legitimate. We have seen that some radical feminists make this claim... that what counts as rationality is socially constructed, that there are different ways of knowing, which means that reality has no stable content, not even in principle.[3]

Bork quotes the words of radical feminists who would dismantle the Judeo-Christian family if they could. Here are the words of a radical feminist who goes by the pseudonym of *Shere Hite*:

> "There is no such thing as fixed 'human nature.' Rather, it is a psychological structure that is carefully implanted in our minds.... Fortunately the family is a human institution: humans made it and humans can change it."[4]

Most radical feminists regard Judeo-Christian marriage as a form of "rape" instigated by what is to them the source of all evil on earth—the white, male, heterosexual, property-owning, religious, "patriarchy." In the above quotation, the words "carefully implanted" give a hint of the accusation leveled against Christianity and Judaism, not only by radical feminists, but by postmodern academicians, atheists, nihilists, homosexuals, liberal politicians, judges, abortionists, bioethicists, pornographers, the ACLU, apostate Hollywood, and other derivative organizations. If one were to put the accusation into words it would read something like this:

> The prescriptions of Judeo-Christian morality are contingent stuff and nonsense invented by the white, male, heterosexual, homophobic, bigoted, property-owning, religious, bourgeois patriarchy!

The propaganda aside, this is a serious charge, but it isn't new. In essence the same charge was leveled against Moses and Aaron by Korah's rebellious mob, accusing them of arrogating authority to themselves in the name of God (see the 16th chapter of the Book of Numbers). And in all ages the same sort of charge has been leveled against the seers, prophets, apostles and elect of God, accusing them of committing the damnable sin of inventing their own *contingent* morality and then elevating it to the status of the *necessary* in the name of deity. A few decades ago the same accusation was made by Marx and Engels in their *Manifesto of the Communist Party*:

> The selfish misconception that induces you to transform into eternal laws of nature and of reason the social forms springing from your present mode of production and form of property... this misconception you share with every ruling class that has preceded you.... On what foundation is the present family, the bourgeois family, based? On capital, on private gain. In its completely developed form this family exists only among the bourgeoisie. But this state of things finds its complement in the practical absence of family among the proletarians...

What then is the charge being levelled at Christianity and Judaism by the devil of nihilism today? The latest version would read as follows:

> You Christians and Jews are arrogating authority to yourselves in the name of your make-believe god, basing your legal opposition to such things as abortion, homosexuality and same-sex marriage on *contingent* truths that you yourselves have invented!

Is there any substance to the charge? If we have done a good job of laying down a framework, the fallacy of the above accusation should be obvious. All of the core truths of the Bible are based on an accurate model of reality and human nature. For thousands of years the Word of God has stood as a bulwark against the claims of paganism, pantheism, dualism, materialism, atheism, humanism, moral relativism, homosexualism, and the nihilism that would empty the human condition of purpose, content, design, and meaning. The Word of God resists the latest (postmodern) nihilism explicitly, declaring Man to be God's image and regent here on earth. What the Word of God has to say about such things as man's relationship with fellow man, woman, family structure, private property, individual liberty, morality, ethics, duties and esponsibilities, flows from a premise that is consistent with reality.

Throughout this inquiry our goal has been to obtain an understanding of human nature that is consistent with the movement of the cosmos. Having obtained such an understanding we suddenly find it to be consistent with the core truths of the Bible. Indeed when the scales fall from our eyes we discover that the core truths of the Bible have been consistent with reality all along. The "way" of the derivative man is the way of entropy and corruption. Sin, *as a nature and an orientation*, is something that we are all born with. Something that we inherit from the nature of the cosmos itself.

Knowledge is said to be *a priori* (literally, "prior to experience") when its validity does not depend on the evidence of experience, and *a posteriori* ("after experience") when it does. If the Judeo-Christian understanding of human nature was derived from a Biblical *a priori*, then its validity did not depend on the *a posteriori* of modern day science—the Biblical model of human nature precedes that of science by thousands of years. But if the *a priori* of the Bible can now be confirmed by the *a posteriori* of science, to whom can the truth thereof be attributed? There can be only one answer: to the God who created Man from the dust of the earth—from the physics of this universe. The prescriptions of Judeo-Christian morality are founded on a clear view of human nature as being oriented towards disorder, accepting the *necessity* of the constraints that God places on the liberties of man for man's own benefit.

How could the prophets, seers, apostles, disciples, rabbis, pastors and preachers have "invented" the prescriptions of Judeo-Christian morality? They could not have. They received these things from God on faith—*a priori*. They were not speaking on their own authority. In accusing Moses of speaking on his own authority Korah and his rebellious mob were challenging the Authority of God—sticking their fingers in the eye of God. For this reason the judgment of Korah had to be an unmistakable act of God (the well-excavated grave described in Numbers 16:11-33). When atheists, nihilists, homosexuals and radical feminists accuse Christians and Jews of "inventing" the prescriptions of Judeo-Christian morality, they too are sticking their fingers in the eye of God.

The foundations of Judeo-Christian morality are the building blocks of the Kingdom of God on earth. They were not derived from the wisdom of the Arm of Flesh. Christians and Jews didn't "invent" them out of whole cloth. To find fault with the foundations of

Judeo-Christian morality is to find fault with God, not man. To use lies, perversion, fraud, deceit, propaganda and media caricaturization to trash and vandalize the building blocks of American society is to insult God Himself. To feed on the moral capital of a nation whose institutions presuppose a Supreme Being, to misuse the virtues of the American system to make the *necessary* contingent, and the *contingent* necessary, is more than a damnable sin: it is to stick a finger in the eye of God. All who would stick their fingers in the eye of God would do well to repent and change course, lest their judgment end up being an unmistakable act of God as well.

JUDEO-CHRISTIAN MARRIAGE AND FAMILY

Marriage is a hotly contested issue in this evil age, the derivative devil trying to substitute his own bag of straw in place of a *complex* institution of God. To make matters worse most Christians and Jews don't seem to understand what God had in mind with marriage. Where then the provenance of Judeo-Christian marriage and family? Why must the institution of marriage *consist only of the union of one man and one woman* in order to be authentic and lawful?

Assuredly the Creator of the universe could have created three, four, or a dozen sexes had He so wished. Or He could have created only one sex, perhaps self-replicating. Why then did He choose to create them "male and female," (Genesis 1:27)? What do these two sexes represent? Is there a *profound mystery* hidden in their heterogeneity?

In order to answer the question we need to take a detour through the dualism that we mentioned in the second chapter of this publication. We said that the prophet Zoroaster, said to have come on the Persian scene around 660 B.C., conceived of a dualism that pitted the forces of the good god *Ahura Mazda* against those of the evil god *Ahriman*, and that in the centuries that followed different versions of this dualism spread throughout the existing world like yeast in dough, exerting more subtle influence on history than many other religions combined.

Zoroaster's dualism was the spiritual underpinning of the Persian Empire that at one time spread all the way to India on the east and Greece on the west. Circa 510 B.C., the Jews of the Southern Kingdom of Judah were taken captive into Babylon/Persia where some of them assimilated the dualism and later brought it back with them to Jerusalem. In the time of Christ the faction known as the *Essenes* was an extension thereof, mixing the Persian dualism with Hebrew traditions to embrace a fundamentally *apocalyptic* world view. Such world views, extant even today, deny the possibility of the redemption and transformation of evil elements, positing certain catastrophic events that will bring the world to a fiery end.

Standing in opposition to such dualism is the Christian Gospel that preaches the forgiveness and transformation of evil elements through the redemptive work of *Yeshua*. The New Testament is the antithesis of all such dualisms and doom sayings, substituting salvation and hope in place of fatalism and despair. The Christian Gospel does not try to separate the elements of light and darkness as though they were matter and anti-matter: it uses the light of God's truth to *dispel* the darkness of sin and error.

Two thirds of the New Testament was penned by Rabbi Shaul of Tarsus. Converted on the road to Damascus and known by gentiles as "Paul," Rav Shaul was given rare insight by God whereby he should fully understand, synthesize, and put in perspective the work of *Yeshua*. And having done so, to go and preach the Good News of a *reconciliation* between Heaven and Earth in the here and now, contrary to any dualism. Tarsus was an ancient city on the Cilician plain, the seat of a provincial governor when Persia ruled. Standing on the confluence of East and West, it was an eclectic place where the wisdom of the Greeks and the order of Rome merged with the dualism of Persia and mysticism of the Orient. Born and raised in Tarsus, young Shaul was given to draw from many cultures. Later he studied in Jerusalem under the auspices of the leading Jewish teacher of the time—the respected *Rav Gamaliel* referred to in Acts 5:34. Thoroughly imbued, disciplined and grounded in the principles and teachings of the Torah, Rav Shaul was at the same time a citizen of Rome, fluent in several languages, in all respects well-read and well-informed, familiar with all things religious, historical and philosophical—creation myths, Babylonian legends, Persian dualism, Greek Classics, teachings of Stoics, Epicureans, etc..

Thus, when we find Rav Shaul describing the institution of marriage as a *profound mystery*, we can be sure that something is up. Paul refers to this *mystery* in many places:

> To Him who is able to empower you, according to the Good News which I am preaching in my proclamation of Jesus Christ, concerning the *mystery* which had been kept hidden for long ages, but is now unveiled, through the writings of the prophets made known to all nations…
>
> (Romans 16:25-27, emphasis added)

> Unto me, who am less than the least of all of God's people, is this grace given, that I should proclaim among the Gentiles the Good News of the unsearchable riches of Christ; and to make all men see what is the fellowship of the *mystery*, which from the beginning of the world has been hid in God, the Creator of all things.
>
> (Ephesians 3:8-9, emphasis added)

> For this cause shall a man leave his father and mother, and be joined to his wife, the two becoming one flesh. This is a *profound mystery*, but I am applying it to Christ and the Church.
>
> (Ephesians 5:31-32, emphasis added)

What is this *profound mystery*? It is the union of God (Spirit) and Creation (matter) in the here and now, contrary to any dualism. The Christian Gospel demolishes dualism, Zoroastrian, Manichaean, or otherwise. It preaches the *marriage* of the Creator with His Creation, made possible through the redemptive work of *Yeshua* on the Cross. This is evident in the symbol of the Cross itself, where we find Heaven and Earth "kissing" in the intersection of two lines, the vertical line representing the Creator, the horizontal the Creation.

What are we driving at in all this and what are we saying? We are saying that there is far more to the institution of holy matrimony than what the derivative and reprobate world could possibly understand. The union of man and woman in holy matrimony is an *affirmation* of the Union of the Creator with His Creation, productive of the increases of life, *complexity*, wholeness, peace, prosperity, stability, progress, order and economy. Those who would devalue and pervert the institution of holy matrimony would devalue and pervert the relationship of the Creator with His Creation.

The heterogeneity of "male and female" is made to reflect the heterogeneity of God (Spirit) and Creation (matter), male being the analogue of God, female the analogue of Creation; the joining of the two celebrated in the joyous union of man and woman in Judeo-Christian marriage. In all respects the love affair between a man and a woman has its referents in the love affair between God and Creation. This is affirmed in the *Song of Solomon*, for example, where the love of the divine Bridegroom for His created Bride is projected in terms of Solomon's love for the Shulamite maiden, and her love for him:

דּוֹדִי לִי וַאֲנִי לוֹ

My beloved is mine, and I am his.
(Song of Solomon, 2:16)

There are other parallels. As the Nature of God and the nature of Creation are reciprocal but complimentary, so also the nature of man and the nature of woman are reciprocal but complimentary—*men are from Mars, women are from Venus*, to quote a popular saying. What goes on between husband and wife is a reflection of what goes on between God and Creation, the marriage contract a reflection of the covenants found in the Bible. It is, for example, the husband who initiates the union—the Spirit of God enters into the material Creation to impregnate and inseminate it with the seeds of life. As the Creation cannot enter into God, so also woman cannot enter into man, but man is given to enter into woman. And as God extends His hand towards the Creation, so also man extends his hand towards woman. And as the Creation assumes the name of God, so also the woman assumes the name of man, not the other way round. And as God takes care of His Creation, so also man is given to take care of his bride, not the other way around. And as God loves, honors, and provides for His Creation, so also man loves, honors and provides for his wife. Woman the pulchritude of Creation; man the strength of God.

Even as Eve is a figure of Creation, and Adam a figure of God, so also we find Eve being the entity whom the "serpent" approaches first. From which we can infer that the fall of mankind was not instigated by the failure of womankind per se, but by some limitation internal to the material Creation, of which "Eve" is made symbol and type in the Genesis narrative; i.e., in that narrative we are given to understand some profound truth about the subjugation of the Creation ("Eve") to the universal imperative of disorder ("the serpent").

What then shall we say about the *headship* of man over woman? Simply that it has its referents in the headship of God over Creation, there being neither blame, nor prejudice, nor superiority nor inferiority between the sexes per se. The primacy must always be given to the Creator, not the created thing. God is eternal. The Creation is transitory. This is why man is charged with the responsibility of being the "head" of the family. This is why the advent of Adam precedes and predates that of Eve in the Genesis narrative, just as the eternal and unchanging Existence of God predates and precedes the advent of the heavens and the earth. As David himself says:

הַשָּׁמַיִם מְסַפְּרִים כְּבוֹד־אֵל וּמַעֲשֵׂה יָדָיו מַגִּיד הָרָקִיעַ
The heavens declare the glory of God,
and the firmament bears witness to the work of His hands.
(Psalm 19:1)

Forasmuch as the Creation is the glory of God, likewise woman is the glory of man. And as God is not of the Creation, but the Creation is of God and for God, so also the male and female referents thereof. As Rav Shaul affirms:

> For a man indeed ought not to cover [deny] his head[ship], forasmuch as he is the image and glory of God: but the woman is the glory of the man. For the man is not of the woman, but the woman of the man. Neither was the man created for the woman, but the woman for the man....
> (1 Corinthians 11:7-9)

Just as God conceives the Creation out of Himself, (there being nothing else to conceive it out of), so also we find Eve being conceived out of Adam's "rib." And as the Creation proceeds from out of the Godhead, by whom all things were made and in whom all things have their being, so also we find Eve proceeding from out of Adam. And as God inserts His Spirit into the Creation to conceive of Life and *Complexity*, so also Adam is described as "knowing" Eve in the conceiving all of the families of the human race. And even as God steps out of Eternity to join Himself to His Bride-Creation as Husband and Savior ("Yeshua"), so also, "*for this cause*, shall a man leave his father and mother to be joined together with his wife," (Ephesians 5:31). Here is the Biblical origin and provenance of Judeo-Christian marriage.

Elsewhere God is described as a *husband* in numerous Biblical passages and teachings. For although God did not initially make Himself the contractual Husband and Savior of all mankind, yet He chose Israel as the model whereby He should describe Himself as such, the Mosaic Covenant serving as a prototype marriage contract:

כִּי בֹעֲלַיִךְ עֹשַׂיִךְ יְהוָה צְבָאוֹת שְׁמוֹ
וְגֹאֲלֵךְ קְדוֹשׁ יִשְׂרָאֵל אֱלֹהֵי כָל־הָאָרֶץ יִקָּרֵא

For your Maker is your husband, the LORD of hosts is His name,
and your Redeemer, the Holy One of Israel:
The God of the whole earth shall He be called.
(Isaiah 54:5)

Shall not the God and Redeemer of the whole earth also be the *Husband* and *Provider* of the whole earth? For although in the fullness of time God would make Himself the Husband and Provider of all mankind, initially He began His plan by making Himself the Husband and Provider of the twelve tribes of Israel. And when the twelve tribes became divided into two kingdoms, even then they were described as two sisters *married* to God, the Northern kingdom *divorced* and sown into the world in the Great Diaspora of 721 B.C., thereby making the whole world a potential bride of God also, awaiting remarriage and reunification in the fullness of time. (Doubtless this is another *profound mystery* worthy of investigation, but for now we are speaking about the institution of holy matrimony.)

That the Judeo-Christian institution of marriage is sacred and holy in the sight of God is born out by the Hebrew word for *marriage.* Hebrew words, derived from roots, are often grouped together. The letters that form a very common Hebrew root consist of ק–ד–ש. This root appears frequently in the Bible, its basic meaning being "holy," "sacred," "consecrated," or "set apart from the ordinary." The following are a few words formed from that root:

kiddushin—marriage קִדּוּשִׁין
kiddush—sanctification קִדּוּשׁ
kaddosh—holy, consecrated קָדוֹשׁ

keddushah—holiness, sanctity קְדֻשָׁה
koddesh—sacred, holy קֹדֶשׁ

That Judeo-Christian marriage is an institution of God is one of the core truths of the Bible. But can it be said to be *necessary* in a Kantian frame as well? Indeed it can, the principles and prescriptions of God being in all respects rational and consistent with reality.

Civilizations, nations and societies are composed of human elements which can be arranged in various ways. These arrangements have order/disorder values with far-reaching consequences. Ought not the Creator of the universe be concerned about the nature of these arrangements? Ought He not have come up with an optimal arrangement productive of life, liberty, and the pursuit of happiness? He has: the Judeo-Christian family.

Take any pattern in the universe—a physical pattern, a behavioral pattern, an organizational pattern, a political pattern, an economic pattern, a biological pattern, a societal pattern, etc.. Look at the way in which its elements are arranged. The more heterogeneous the arrangement, the more ordered the system. The more homogeneous the arrangement, the more disordered the system. In trying to move universal systems from ordered to disordered states, the Cosmic Constable must try to corrupt and degrade the organization of their elements, changing complex arrangements into more simple ones, heterogeneous arrangements into homogeneous ones, different-kind arrangements into same-kind arrangements.

The word "homogeneous" is a composite of the Greek *homo*, "one, the same," and *genus*, "kind." The word "heterogeneous" is a composite of the Greek *hetero*, "two, different," and *genus*, "kind." In this cosmos homogeneous arrangements are much more probable than heterogeneous ones. Absent the design of God there would be no heterogeneous Judeo-Christian marriage to speak of, only same-kind communes, cults, gangs, cabals, groupings, associations, unions and partnerships. Absent the prescriptions of Judeo-Christian morality the "familial" arrangements of human elements would conform to the mould of probability, flowing down the gradient that leads from complexity to simplicity, heterogeneity to homogeneity.

Where the *behavioral* patterns of man would conform to the nature of corruption in idolatry, murder, theft, etc., the *organizational* patterns of man would conform to the nature of corruption through same-kind unions, mergers, conglomerations, associations and partnerships. Therefore the God who commands "You shall not commit idolatry," also commands "Honor your father and mother, that you may live long and prosper," (Exodus 20:12). In that He says "father and mother," He confirms having created them "male and female," (Genesis 1:27).

What shall we say then of the perversions of this age? What shall we say of those who would degrade and pervert the institution of holy matrimony, substituting the banality of "domestic partnership" and "same sex marriage" in place of an institution of God? What shall we say of a homogenizing cult trying to lay claim to the rights of heterogeneity? What shall we say about attempts to infiltrate and degrade the church? What shall we say about *homo-sexuality*, this most divisive and corrosive issue of the postmodern era? The practitioners and purveyors of it have said it all, for they say: "It is our orientation!" Only a few decades ago homosexuality was listed among behavioral disorders requiring psychiatric treatment. With the advent of the postmodern delusion—and a few riots—it was taken off the list and reclassified "gay," "gayness" being now considered an immutable condition of existence. Is it? There are no scientific definitions for "gayness." What definitions that exist are societal and *contingent*—homosexuality is now declared to be an "orientation," and "being gay" a way of coming to terms with it. And this is the bill of goods that the Constable is now peddling to men and women on five continents, whispering in their ears: "This is your natural orientation. Don't try to fight it. Just accept and come to terms with it."

What then is this so-called "orientation" all about? Is it sexual? No, for according to many homosexuals there is much more to the "gay lifestyle" than copulation. Where then the provenance of the homophile lifestyle? Where the origin of this urge to merge in same-kind unions and partnerships? Whence this obsession with gender homogeneity? Why, for example, are transitions from heterosexuality to homosexuality instantly approved of in the apostate media and academia, but transitions from homosexuality to heterosexuality demonized and stonewalled as the blackest and most damnable of sins? The answer should be obvious.

We have been saying that greater order of change is flowing down the gradient that leads from low probability to high probability, from ordered to disordered states, from *complexity* to simplicity, from heterogeneity to homogeneity. We have been describing the nature of physical reality as a statistical ratchet mechanism that encourages movement in one direction and discourages movement in the opposite. This, in the final analysis, is the mechanism that governs the "morality" of the apostate media and academia when it comes to deciding what to allow and what to disallow, what to condone and what to condemn, what to applaud and what to scorn, what to dignify and what to demonize, what to tolerate and what to curse, what to include and what to exclude, what to publish and what to suppress, what to put in headlines and what to put on the last page.

The expression *zeit-geist* implies "spirit of the time." Upon reflection it can be seen that the spirit of postmodern "morality" derives itself from the orientation of the cosmos itself. Postmodern morality is wholly derivative, lacking any human authenticity. The postmodern bias towards homosexuality and homosexualism should come as no surprise. Having jettisoned all absolutes, having reverted to the rudiments of the perishable universe, postmodern culture is by nature and by predisposition *homosexualist*, supportive of and sympathetic towards the derivative behavior that has been trying to come out of the closet since time immemorial. The postmodern resurrection may hide behind the mantra of "brothers and sisters" and the propaganda of "political correctness," "inclusivism," "tolerance," "multiculturalism," "safe schools," but the whole of its agenda is elemental and derivative, the very mention of the words *gay and lesbian* a form of cosmic affirmation revered in postmodern academia—"gays and lesbians! gays and lesbians! brothers and sisters! brothers and sisters!" If the Cosmic Constable were endowed with the gift of human sexuality he would be found wearing women's apparel and marching in front of every "gay pride parade" down Main Street U.S.A., applauding and encouraging all the "brothers and sisters" who have "accepted" and "come to terms" with the orientation in their flesh.

Human nature is already oriented towards disorder, children all the more vulnerable. And do they need any encouragement in that respect? What then shall we say of those who would corrupt children for political purposes? What shall we say of those who would brainwash and indoctrinate innocent children with the rudiments of perversion? What shall we say of those who would flood the public school system with homosexual propaganda videos designed to encourage young children to accept the so-called "gay lifestyle?" Perhaps we should remind them of the words of *Yeshua* :

> Those who receive one such little child in my name receive me. But those who cause one of these little ones who believe in me to sin, it would be better for them to have a great millstone fastened round their necks and be drowned in the depth of the sea.
>
> (Matthew 18:5-6)

What shall we say of the related perversions of our day? What shall we say of the contagion of pedophilia and the gangrene of pornography? What shall we say when communications giants and media conglomerates reduce the sanctified union of man and woman into obscenity and peddle it to millions of households for filthy lucre? What shall we say of the sexual degradation of women for profit, rampant in the sewers of the apostate media and the internet?

What shall we say about the perversion of perversions—willful and methodical attempts to expunge the name of God from American society and force the nation to revert to paganism and immorality—on pain of a "Federal Hate Crimes" charge? What shall we say about the attempt to remove the words "Under God" from the Pledge of Allegiance? What shall we say of those who would use lies, deceit, fraud, propaganda and fetid emotional appeals to suppress and stonewall God's truth? Rav Shaul said it 2000 years ago:

> For the indignation of God is revealed from heaven against all the willful denial and wickedness whereby men suppress the truth. Because what can be known about God is self-evident, He Himself having made it quite clear to them. For since the beginning of creation men have seen earth and sky and all that God has made, in the design thereof inferring the existence and eternal power of an invisible Designer. So that they are without excuse. For even though they could infer the existence of God, they would not honor or thank Him, deluding themselves by vain rationalizations, their senseless minds confused. Professing themselves to be wise, they became fools, substituting in place of the glory of the incorruptible God their own idols.... Whereupon God gave them over to their own evil inclinations, allowing them to degrade one another bodily, punishing them for worshipping and serving the created thing instead of the Creator....
>
> For this perversion, God gave them up to all manner of perversions, their women substituting the unnatural for the

> natural, and their men doing the same thing, consumed by their lusts one towards the other, homosexuals, doing shameful things and receiving in themselves the rewards of their depravity. In that they willfully chose to deny and reject God, God gave them over to a reprobate mind and to immoral conduct, allowing them to mire themselves in unrighteousness, fornication, wickedness, covetousness, maliciousness, envy, murder, contention, deceit, malignity —whisperers, back-biters, haters of God, insolent, proud, boastful, inventors of evil things, disobedient to parents, without understanding, faithless, heartless, ruthless. Who, although knowing the Justice of God in regards to the sentence deserved by all who commit such deeds, not only keep doing these things, but even encourage and applaud others who do them as well.
>
> (Romans 1:18-32)

Many religious folks have been putting the cart before the horse, it seems. The immoral conduct that most fundamentalists rush to condemn as "sexual sins" are not the cause of God's wrath, they are the *effects* of God's wrath. In the passage above God is not angry because men and women commit sexual sins, He is angry because they deny His existence and suppress His truth, for which spiritual perversion He punishes them by *giving them over* to sexual perversions. As though to say: "If it is Sodom you want, Sodom you shall have. Bon appetite!"

The Justice of Almighty God is condign. Those who love and trust Him are granted access to His Kingdom and made to partake of Liberty. Those who hate and reject Him are denied access and made to partake of bondage—given over to a reprobate mind and allowed to mire themselves in falsehood, imbecility and degradation.

The perversions of this evil age notwithstanding, we would caution believers not to point Manichaean fingers at "sinners," nor try to take the law into their own hands. Now, more than ever, let the rule be "the sin, not the sinner." In terms of what believers call "spiritual warfare," the advice given by Josh McDowell and Bob Hostetler in their book *The New Tolerance* is consistent with the testimony of Scripture. Here are the words of Josh McDowell:

> Counter principles, not people. It is people, of course, who advance wrong thinking and behavior. But to be effective,

> you must attack immoral principles, not people. Stick to the issues; stand firmly for principles, but resist the temptation to attack your opponents.[5]

Now is the time for the salt of the earth and the light of the world to use the virtues of the American political system to redeem the times *in due process of law*. Now is time to restore marriage to the dignity of its origins in God by way of a Constitutional Amendment. Without presuming to dictate the exact wording, we submit the following facsimile:

> Marriage in the United States shall be defined as the lawful union of one man with one woman. Congress shall make no law respecting any other definition. Neither the Constitution of the United States, nor the constitution of any state, nor any state or federal law, shall otherwise confer marital status, or the legal incidents and privileges thereof, upon unmarried couples or groups.

UNDERSTANDING THE KINGDOM OF GOD: THE PREMISE OF THE BIBLE

The premise of the Bible can be found in the first Book of the Bible called *Genesis*. The promise hidden in the Genesis narrative is the premise from which the rest of the Bible flows. What is that promise? It might read as follows:

> If you choose to trust Me and do what I say, I will place My Spirit in you, to protect you from the devil of disorder and grant you access to Eternal Life. If you choose not to trust Me, and follow your own evil inclination, I will withdraw My Spirit, give you over to the devil of disorder and deny you access to Eternal Life. Trust Me and you shall partake of Life. Deny Me and you will partake of Death. The choice is your's.

Beguiled by the "serpent," our spiritual ancestors chose not to trust God, assimilating the great lie and falling from grace. Whereupon God turned them over to the rudiments of the perishable universe, and the common stock of their descendents have been "dying" ever since.

This has been the fundamental choice confronting mankind from the very beginning. There are only two options:

1) Trust God and choose His Way.
2) Deny God and choose the Constable's way.

This is the sum and substance of man's *free will.* God will not force the choice—only the consequences. The choice is simple. Abide by the Divine Principle and reap the benefits; violate the Divine Principle and reap the consequences. Trust in God enables the processes of life. Denial of God enables the processes of death. Everything flows from this Biblical *premise*, survival and extinction, life and death, blessing and curse, success and failure, victory and defeat hanging in the balance. The Biblical archetypes of the human race ("Adam and Eve") violated the Principle and suffered the consequences. Whereupon the human condition was allowed to default to the rudiments of entropy and corruption. In the foreknowledge of God, projecting as it were forward in time, the Genesis metaphor predicts the wholesale existential failure of mankind in alienation from God, instituting the sure plan of deliverance that is the subject of the rest of the Bible.

The prophet Habakkuk reduced all the precepts of God to one saying:

וְצַדִּיק בֶּאֱמוּנָתוֹ יִחְיֶה.
And the just, by his faith, shall live.
(Habakkuk 2:4)

Throughout the Bible trust in God has been the essence of the *justice* and *righteousness* summed up in the Hebrew word צֶדֶק (*tzedek*). Rav Shaul equates all the sins of the world with faithlessness:

For whatsoever is not of faith, is sin.
(Romans 14:23)

Flowing from the premise of the Genesis narrative, the words of Habakkuk are the central theme of the Bible, expanded by Rav Shaul in Romans 1:17 and Galatians 3:11. In these few words the Holy Spirit encapsulates the very essence of life and death. Trust in God brings spiritual empowerment and victory over the Constable. Privation of trust brings impotence, ruination, bondage, and defeat.

UNDERSTANDING THE KINGDOM OF GOD: SPIRITUAL EMPOWERMENT

God gifts His Spirit in return for faith. God invests a measure of His Spirit in those who trust and love him, and God-given *spiritual strength* is one of the Constable's greatest obstacles here on earth, resisting local movements towards disorder and corruption. By *spiritual strength* we do not mean spiritism or occultism—doing penances, performing austerities, rituals, seances, fasting, eating vegetarian, renouncing the world, becoming a recluse, striking poses, wearing robes, chanting mantras, meditating on charms, crystals, pyramids, mood-making, lighting candles, burning incense, etc.. By *spiritual strength* we mean the invincible wherewithal that can be traced to the Spirit of God, the moral strength and resolve that is productive of bravery, fortitude, enterprise, valor, stamina, backbone, determination, endurance, drive and tenacity. Those who are spiritually strong do not flinch or faint when confronted with the challenges of life. Trusting God, being fueled by faith, and being anchored to His Eternal power, they persevere, take risks, power through, drive forward, and overcome the seven thousand challenges that flesh is heir to.

The measure of the Spirit of God in man resists the activity of the Constable, promoting life, *complexity*, wholeness, individuality, heterogeneity, sovereignty, harmonious multiplicity, family, order, health, prosperity, progress—peace on earth and good will towards men. All these good things are enabled, not by the power or might or wisdom of the Arm of Flesh, but by the Spirit of the Living God. As it is written:

לֹא בְחַיִל וְלֹא בְכֹחַ כִּי אִם־בְּרוּחִי אָמַר יְהוָה צְבָאוֹת

Not by might, nor by power, but by My Spirit, says the LORD of hosts. (Zechariah 4:6)

The measure of God-given spiritual strength is the measure of Man's victory over the Constable. The measure of spiritual weakness is the measure of man's defeat. God gives of His Spirit freely, investing generous portions thereof in all who trust and love Him.

Figuratively, there are two "breaths" or "winds" blowing in the universe. Two different winds can blow upon the "sails" of the human condition, one powerful and Divine, the other persistent and cosmic. The cosmic wind is always blowing. The Divine wind is much more powerful, but can only be invoked through the exercise of faith. These two winds are thus given to drive the ship of man in opposing directions, one towards victory and safe harbor, the other towards defeat and shipwreck. The "wind" or "breath" of God would override the cosmic wind and propel man towards life and *complexity* (decreasing entropy). The "wind" of cosmos would overwhelm man and push him towards disorder and dissolution (increasing entropy). Within the imagery of the Genesis narrative we are given to understand that man will, by nature and by default, choose the latter.

Just as the exposure of a human body to a clean or toxic environment will gradually alter its structure for better or for worse, so also the exposure of the spirit of man to these two "winds" will gradually alter the disposition thereof for better or for worse. This is why the issue of the Bible is said to be *spiritual.* The Great Controversy found in the Bible revolves around the disposition of the *spirit* of man. The *spirit* of man (figuratively, the *sail* of his existence), may be propelled and steered by the powerful "breath" of the Creator, or it may be blown downwind by the nagging and insidious "breath" of the Constable. In trusting God, man chooses the former. In denying God he chooses the latter.

It is one thing for matter and energy to be corrupted by the breath of the Constable. It is another thing for the spirit of man to be corrupted by the breath of the Constable. The Constable has his proper place in the realms of matter and energy, allowed to demand his pound of flesh in material terms—processes whereby stars decay, mountains erode, bodies age, things wear out, etc.. But he must not be allowed to demand the same pound of flesh in terms of *spiritual* erosion—processes whereby civilizations decay, societies go to seed, the institutions of men are corrupted, nations are reduced to slavery, men and women reduced to serfdom, etc.. The prize is the *spirit* of man. But what are we to understand by *spirit*? By "spirit" we do not mean ghosts, goblins, poltergeists, disembodied entities and such things that move the morbid curiosities of superstitious folks. By "spirit" we mean something much more holistic, rational and down-to-earth, something on the order of heart, mind, attitude, temperament, disposition and orientation. As implied in many Biblical passages:

> For you have not received the spirit of bondage again to fear, but the spirit of adoption, whereby we cry, "Abba, Father!"
>
> (Romans 8:15)

What is it that undergoes displacement and registers emotion when we worship God, or when we hear the prayers that open a session of Congress, or when we participate in a joyous wedding, or attend a solemn memorial service? It is our *spirit*. What is there on the inside of us that gets uplifted when we observe the opening ceremonies of the games of the Olympiad, for example, or listen to a recital by a great symphony orchestra, or marvel at a Rembrandt, or smell a beautiful rose? What internal and incorporeal agency gets uplifted when one hears familiar notes of a John Philip Sousa march, or *Battle Hymn of the Republic*, or *The Star-spangled Banner*, or *God Save the Queen*, or *O Canada*, or *Ha-Tiqvah*? What changes within us when we hear the sound of bagpipes wailing in the Highlands of Scotland, or pan flutes singing in the valleys of the Andes, or accordions playing a polka in the Swiss Alps, or violins playing a Strauss Waltz in old Vienna, or trombones playing Dixieland in New Orleans, or trumpets blaring Mariachi on Oliveras Street, or a Caribbean steel band playing in Trinidad? What manner of internal states are these, and upon what incorporeal membrane or medium of our being do they impinge and resonate, evoking different moods as they do? They are *spiritual* states—modulations of the *spirit* within. We are *spiritually* inclined and motivated.

In the Bible the words translated into "spirit" are often the Hebrew *ruakh* (רוּחַ) and the Greek *pneuma* (πνευμα), the latter being used for the Spirit of God and the spirit of cosmos alike. That the cosmos (the world, the sum of physical reality) is endowed with a "spirit" of its own is born out by the testimony of Rav Shaul in his Epistle to the formative church in Corinth:

> Now we have received, not the spirit of the cosmos [<Greek *pneuma tou kosmou*], but the Spirit which is of God [<Greek *Pneuma toek tou Theou*], that we might know the things that are conferred on us by God.
>
> (1 Corinthians 2:12)

We are to understand the Hebrew *ruakh* and the Greek *pneuma* not as being analogous to stagnant air, but, as *ex-pulsions* or *ex-pressions* analogous to "breath" or "wind." In which case the spirit of cosmos—*pneuma tou kosmou*—would be an expression of the nature of matter, energy, space, time, entropy and corruption, whereas the Spirit of God—*Pneuma toek tou Theou*—would be an expression of the Nature of the God who is unaffected by cosmos, who is Eternal, Unchanging, Incorruptible, Imperishable and Blessed forever, Amen.

Man trusts God. For the measure of trust, God invests and empowers man with a measure of His own Spirit. The Spirit of God, applied to the spirit of man, changes the disposition thereof, resisting the pull of natural corruption. Man denies God. God withdraws His Spirit, allowing the spirit of man to default to the spirit of cosmos in entropy and corruption. How is this possible? How can two subtle, incorporeal, intangible and abstract causes be governing the disposition of man to the extent of enabling success or failure, good or evil, life or death, survival or extinction? The mechanism may be subtle, but we have the assurance of *Yeshua* that it is very real:

> That which is born of the flesh is flesh; and that which is born of the Spirit is spirit. Marvel not that I said to you, "You must be born again." The wind blows where it will, and you hear the sound of it, but cannot tell whence it came, or whither it goes: so it is with everyone who is born of the Spirit of God.
>
> (John 3:7-8)

An illustration. Sprinkle iron filings on a sheet of paper, position a strong magnet underneath and jiggle: an ordered pattern will emerge as the filings conform to the underlying magnetic field. Now remove the magnet and jiggle again: the pattern of filings will dissolve into disorder. Now sprinkle human elements onto the fabric of a cosmos in which entropy is increasing, position the Spirit of God underneath, and jiggle: an ordered pattern will slowly emerge as those elements conform to the Nature of Incorruption. Now remove the Spirit of

God and jiggle again: the ordered pattern will dissolve into disorder as those elements conform to the nature of cosmos. The changes may not be deterministic or "Newtonian," but they are very real, ruling on life and death, survival and extinction.

Remove the Spirit of God from the the human condition and you will be exposing the spiritual "sails" of the world to the cosmic wind (*pneuma tou kosmou*) by default, driving it towards higher and higher entropy states. What would change in that case? What would emerge? What would accumulate? What would you expect to see happen in the long run? You would expect to see the gradual accumulation of "entropy" on all fronts. You would expect to see all lines of separation being blurred, all distinctions, outlines, definitions, and differentiations dissolving and going out of focus. You would expect to see the spiritual muscles of man atrophy. You would expect to see the slow, systemic de-gradation of all of the institutions of man. You would expect to see the increase of disorder, corruption, reduction, pollution, marginalization, crime, malfeasance, vice, perversion, homosexuality, banality, mediocrity, imbecility and failure on every side. You would expect to see health give way to disease, wealth give way to poverty, peace give way to war, confidence give way to fear, hope give way to despair. You would expect to see *complexity* being reduced to simplicity, heterogeneity being reduced to homogeneity, the organizing principle of life being displaced by the disorganizing principle of death.

Imagine the results. Nation would rise up against nation. Diverse ethnos would be consumed by hatred of one another. Every cultural interface would become another "Bosnia," every ethnic interface another "Grosny." Every token of diversity a target of terrorism, every measure of security a candle in the wind, every felicity sacrificed on the altar of cosmic expediency. Every life lived in fear, every word a bitterness, every whisper a cursing. Every government an obscene leviathan, every politician a deceitful propagandist, every hamlet a paranoid *Alphaville*, every nation an Orwellian *Oceania* subjugated to the whims of Big Brother…

Every street a haunt of drug gangs. Every freeway a life and death gridlock. Every public entrance a metal detector. Every school a war zone. Every house a barbed wire compound. Every airport a maximum security search area. Every street lamp a surveillance camera. Every neighbor a suspect, every foreigner an enemy, every aircraft a target of terrorism, every cargo ship a potential weapon of mass destruction...

Every pasture a *lodebar*. Every crop a failure. Every cloud waterless. Every field a dust bowl. Every river a consuming flood. Every storm a category 5 hurricane. Every weather front a tornado. Every shaking seven points on the Richter Scale. Every species on the endangered list. Every stream a sewer, every ocean a waste dump. Every breath a lung full of toxic chemicals, every bite a mouthful of sugar-coated poison...

Imagine the outcome. Men indistinguishable from women, families devalued into "domestic partnerships," businesses swallowed up in "mergers and acquisitions," diverse economies assimilated in "globalism," sovereign nations reduced to "federal regionalism." Every marriage a divorce, every child an orphan, every mother a widow, every male "gay," every female "lesbian." Every hand and forehead stamped with the mark of the Constable. Every citizen a number, every worker a cog, every media a freak show, every publication an obscenity. Every nation broke and every enterprise bankrupt. Half the earth a dread penitentiary, the other half a police state run by ten thousand bureaucrats and trial lawyers burning incense to Beelzebub and chanting "we know what's best for you."

Let the present trends continue and we can be assured of all of the above. But let there be a Spiritual Revolution on earth and we will see a reversal of all these trends. The Spirit of God applied by faith, will displace the spirit of cosmos internalized by default. Apply the Spirit of God to the human condition and what would change? What would emerge? What would accumulate? What would you expect to see happen? You would expect to see the decrease of "entropy" on all fronts. You would expect to see the spiritual muscles of man restored to strength. You would expect to see all outlines grow vivid. You would expect to see the restoration of all of the upright institutions of man. You would expect to see the Love of God spread abroad like wildfire. You would expect to see the increase of goodness, mercy and compassion on every side. You would expect to see the return of morality, honesty, and decency on five continents. You would expect to see trust overcome suspicion, honesty overcome deceit, health overcome disease, wealth overcome poverty, peace overcome war, confidence overcome fear, hope overcome despair. You would expect to see the world being made whole, the organizing principle of life displacing the disorganizing principle of death.

Let there be a revival of faith. Let there be a spiritual revolution on earth. Let the nations turn to God in complete dependence and humility: Light will displace darkness, order will displace chaos, life will displace death, *complexity* will displace simplicity, heterogeneity will displace homogeneity, good will overtake evil, righteousness will overtake sin, spiritual strength will overtake spiritual weakness, success will overtake failure, decency will overtake immorality, excellence will overtake mediocrity, love will overtake hate, peace will overtake war, harmonious multiplicity will overtake the inexorable strife of all against all. Truth will become the guiding principle of nations, the earth will be restored to Eden, Man will be restored to the dignity of his origins as image and regent of God. Let there be a Spiritual Revolution on earth and we will spurn beneath our heels the dust of the elemental and put this veil of tears behind us. God Himself will wipe away every tear and reverse the evil tide of the world overnight. As He promises:

פְּנוּ־אֵלַי וְהִוָּשְׁעוּ כָּל־אַפְסֵי־אָרֶץ כִּי אֲנִי־אֵל וְאֵין עוֹד

Turn to Me and be saved, all the ends of the earth:
for I am God, and there is no other.
(Isaiah 45:22)

And as the *Yeshua* confirms:

> Seek you first the Kingdom of God and His righteousness,
> and all these things shall be added unto you.
> (Matthew 6:33)

We are not offering the peoples of the world "pie in the sky." We are offering them down-to-earth, practical wisdom, in the spirit of the Chinese proverb popularized by Premier Deng Xiaoping—"It doesn't matter if the cat is black or white, as long as it catches mice that's all that matters!" And if the cat that Heaven provides can rid the world of all the mice, why rage and complain? (Oh foolish controversy!)

לָמָּה רָגְשׁוּ גוֹיִם וּלְאֻמִּים יֶהְגּוּ־רִיק?

Why do the nations rage, and the people imagine a vain thing?
(Psalm 2:1)

What are we without God? Canon fodder for the Constable. A bunch of neurons trying to survive on a thin pie crust floating on an ocean of molten lava, our skulls protected from millions of incoming meteorites by nothing more than a thin layer of air. Irrespective of race, culture and nationality, we are all on the same boat, and the margins of our survival very narrow. A few minutes of oxygen deprivation and we suffer irrevocable brain damage. Twenty miles straight up and our veins explode outright. A three degree increase in the core temperature of our bodies and we suffer heatstroke. A three degree decrease and we succumb to hypothermia and death. A ten-foot fall and we are on our way to the hospital in an ambulance. A few beats missed by the heart and the undertaker is filling out another invoice.

The mantle of the earth, on which we build our proud cities, is composed of moving plates. Sometimes these plates hang up and the pressure may build, resulting in a devastating earthquake. Or, the pressure may vent gradually, resulting in a series of mild tremors. The quantum input of God can make all the difference between a devastating earthquake and a series of mild tremors. Man has no control over such things. God does, otherwise He is not God. The quantum labor that forestalls, lessens and mitigates natural disasters requires the Personal intervention and ordering activity of God.

Our very survival depends on a very intricate balance of natural forces. Normal operating parameters can be exceeded at the drop of a hat. Only a hairbreadth separates order from chaos, the ordinary from the catastrophic. God has to be there as Husband and Provider, on the job and ordering the blue planet for us—making the inputs that maintain the stability of weather patterns, for example. The slightest rise in the temperature of the sea can result in *El Nino*, causing vast areas of the earth to be reduced by droughts, hurricanes and typhoons. A little change in Monsoon patterns and parts of the Indian sub-continent are buried under flood waters. A little sneeze from a dormant volcano and thousands have to be evacuated from house and home. A little melting of the polar ice caps and entire cities will be submerged. A little steepening of the gradient between air masses and here comes the tornado, leveling everything in sight. Mobile homes are reduced to matchsticks in sixty seconds. School buses are thrown end over end like toys.

What regulates the intensity of solar flares and storms? What has kept millions of asteroids and comets from reducing the beautiful face of our planet? The quantum input of God! God somehow keeps us. Skillfully, lovingly, mysteriously, marvelously, miraculously. He builds a protective hedge around us. He stands the gap. He runs interference for us. He sustains our *complexity*. He makes us to lie down in green pastures. He leads us beside still waters. He restores our soul. Yea, though we walk through the valley of the shadow of death, we shall fear no evil, for He is with us. He prepares a table for us, in the presence of the Cosmic Constable. Only the Person of God can save and keep us, and the Bible assures us that He is ever faithful to do so, ever on the job, ever happy to do what it takes to keep the *complexity* of our blue planet from being reduced to the simplicity of dust by the Cosmic Constable.

Who causes the blessed rain to fall in due season, "to satisfy the desolate and waste ground, and to cause the bud of the tender herb to spring forth," (Job 38:27). How much annual rainfall does God have to allocate per hectare of rainforest to meet the needs of the exuberant variety of living things that call it home? How much on the African plains and Serengeti? How much to feed the multitude millions of China and India? What are the quantum needs of the Brazilian Matto Grosso, or Argentinean Pampas, or Australian Outback? How much grass do the cattle on ten thousand hills need to grow fat? "Who provides prey for the lions, to fill the appetite of the young lions? Who provides food for the raven, when his young ones cry unto God?" (Job 38:39-41). How much vegetation do the elephants of the world need to survive? How much food do the Caribou need to survive a harsh Canadian winter? Who feeds the blue whales? Who directs the salmon to swim up rivers to spawn? Who guides the snow geese on their annual migrations, their powerful wings carrying them aloft? Who regulates all the intricate and complex food-chains of the blue planet, providing sustenance for all creatures in due season? Who prevents beneficial insects from multiplying into plagues? Who oversees and sustains all the complex interrelationships that underlie the living Edens? אֵל שַׁדַּי —*El Shaddai*, the Almighty.

There are some things over which man has no control. There are areas in which man himself is wholly dependent on the Almighty. The seed that God gives will only yield its increase if rain and sun come at their appointed times. They may, or they may not, the livelihood of nations hanging in the balance. A few seasons of no rain and the earth is scorched—back to the dust bowl for the farmer in the Midwest. Too little rain, and the farmers in Japan can say sayonara to the bounty of the rice crop. An untimely frost in Mexico, and the strawberry crop that Jose Luis Andreu worked so hard to cultivate is destroyed. An unseasonable freeze in California, and billions of dollars worth of lemons, oranges and avocados are ruined.

A little hailstorm and millions are without power. A sudden shift in weather patterns and entire villages are buried under mudslides and avalanches. Three days of unremitting rain and half the state of Texas is underwater, houses and automobiles floating away, the proud businessman up a tree hanging on for dear life. Three days of heavy snow and the entire Eastern Seaboard is shut down. A spell of dry weather and California is a heated oven—"Los Padres is dry tinder! The hills above Montecito are ablaze with firestorms! Million dollar estates are going up in flames in Malibu!" Too much of this, and the Governor has to declare the whole state a disaster area! Too little of that, and we are undone, everything that we worked for is blown away—billions of dollars worth of labor and property sprout wings and fly away into yonder oblivion, never to be seen again. Natural disasters are costly, causing untold trillions of dollars in loss and damage that must be passed on to taxpayers.

We are not preaching religious rigmarole, we are talking about dollars and cents. At a rudimentary level all human economies depend on the ordering activity of God. There is no planetary stability, no agriculture, no infrastructure, no economy, no prosperity, no free enterprise, no free market, no stock market, no jobs, no employment, no house or home without the Providence of God. Even so, God is generous in the administration of His Providence, willing to keep His end of the bargain—seedtime and harvest, rain in due season, sun in due season, the blessing of the earth and the blessing of the sea, the blessings of the fields and the blessings of the orchards, the blessings of the vineyards and the blessings of the eternal hills, the blessings of the wombs and the blessings of the breasts.

Human prosperity is an exceedingly *complex* undertaking, requiring on-the-job critical inputs on the part of God. And Heaven help us if God walks off the job in disgust! The labor of Man must dovetail with the Labor of God to amount to something. The labor of man may be worth trillions of dollars, but the Labor of God exceeds the labor of man by many orders of magnitude. Even so,

God offers His Labor without charge, free for the measure of trust and faith. Our Heavenly Father is merciful and compassionate, slow to anger, gracious, patient, longsuffering, faithful, generous, loving and true, showing kindness to thousands, willing to forgive, overflowing with goodness, moved by the feeling of our infirmities. He is *happy* to order the blue planet for us, if only we will trust Him and walk in His truth.

UNDERSTANDING THE KINGDOM OF GOD: ABIDING WORLD PEACE

A world in which different peoples devour and destroy one another would be the most "natural" thing in the universe. A world in which different peoples live side by side in perfect harmony would be the most "unnatural" thing in the universe. The former would be conforming to the nature of corruption. The latter would be conforming to the Nature of Incorruption. The former describes the derivative orders of existence. The latter describes the Kingdom of God. In past ages the nature of man conformed to the nature of corruption. In the Millennium the nature of Man will conform to the Nature of Incorruption. In the former ages harmonious multiplicity was unheard of. In the Kingdom of God it will be commonplace:

וְגָר זְאֵב עִם־כֶּבֶשׂ וְנָמֵר עִם־גְּדִי יִרְבָּץ...
לֹא־יָרֵעוּ וְלֹא־יַשְׁחִיתוּ בְּכָל־הַר קָדְשִׁי כִּי־מָלְאָה הָאָרֶץ דֵּעָה
אֶת־יְהֹוָה כַּמַּיִם לַיָּם מְכַסִּים

And the wolf shall dwell with the lamb,
and the leopard shall lie down with the kid...
They shall not hurt or destroy in all My holy mountain:
for the knowledge of the LORD will fill the earth,
as the waters fill the sea.
(Isaiah 11:6-9)

Naturally, the wolf would devour the lamb, and the leopard would consume the kid. So Isaiah is not prophesying something "natural." It would have been easy to say "the wolf shall dwell with the wolf, the lamb shall dwell with the lamb, the leopard shall lie down with the leopard, the kid shall lie down with the kid." Where the prophet says "the wolf shall dwell with the lamb, and the leopard shall lie down with the kid," he is prophesying the antitype of natural conventions. He is prophesying something that runs against the grain of the cosmos itself.

In the Kingdom of God all the children of Adam—all the races, ethnos, cultures and nations of the world—will fellowship with one another as one family, the exuberant variety of their flags, standards and traditions complimenting, uplifting and enriching one another in emergent ways that we can scarce imagine today. In the Kingdom of God Palestinians and Israelis will dwell side by side in perfect harmony, respecting, valuing, affirming, and complimenting one another's cultural differences. Moreover they will do so willingly and spontaneously, without compulsion, without force, without fences, without tanks, without guns, without checkpoints. In the Kingdom of God Arabs will dwell in perfect harmony with Jews, Iraqis will dwell in perfect harmony with Kurds, Serbs will dwell in perfect harmony with Croats.

Hitherto what little peace the world chanced upon was either "here today and gone tomorrow," or it meant forced assimilation and compulsory homogenization—brotherhood by force and harmony at the point of a bayonet, as in the former Communist block. In the Kingdom of God the brotherhood of races, cultures and nations will be as spontaneous as the *Agape* shared by siblings, concerning which David composed that joyful song:

הִנֵּה מַה־טּוֹב וּמַה־נָּעִים שֶׁבֶת אַחִים גַּם־יָחַד
Behold, how good and how pleasant it is,
when brothers dwell side by side in harmony!
(Psalm 133:1)

Will there ever be a day when the whole earth is at peace and nations are dwelling side by side as true brethren? Isaiah prophecies it:

וְכִתְּתוּ חַרְבוֹתָם לְאִתִּים וַחֲנִיתוֹתֵיהֶם לְמַזְמֵרוֹת
לֹא־יִשָּׂא גוֹי אֶל־גּוֹי חֶרֶב וְלֹא־יִלְמְדוּ עוֹד מִלְחָמָה
And they shall beat their swords into plowshares,
and their spears into pruninghooks: nation shall not lift up sword
against nation, neither shall they learn war any more.
(Isaiah 2:4)

Isaiah is not describing some ephemeral "absence of war." He is not prophesying the artificial "peace" that has to be forced by the political sagacity of dissemblers sitting around the Machiavellian table of diplomacy and lies. No, this prophecy of Isaiah predicts a sea change in the *spirit* of the entire world, whereby it is taken out of alignment with the spirit of cosmos and brought into alignment with the Spirit of God. God Himself promises that He will put a new spirit in man:

וְנָתַתִּי לָהֶם לֵב אֶחָד וְרוּחַ חֲדָשָׁה אֶתֵּן בְּקִרְבְּכֶם
וַהֲסִרֹתִי לֵב הָאֶבֶן מִבְּשָׂרָם
And I will give them one heart, and I will put a new spirit within them;
and I will take the stony heart our of their flesh.
(Ezekiel 11:19)

וְהָיָה אַחֲרֵי־כֵן אֶשְׁפּוֹךְ אֶת־רוּחִי עַל־כָּל־בָּשָׂר...
And it shall come to pass in the latter days that I will
pour out My Spirit upon *ALL* flesh...
(Joel 2:28, emphasis added)

Joel's prophecy predicts the Exodus of all mankind out of the derivative orders of existence in concert. It predicts a wholesale spiritual transfiguration that will do away with the old business of war and render the harmonious coexistence of *different* peoples spontaneous. Joel is prophesying a transformation of universal significance—a fundamental change in the core nature of man, a transfiguration that will reconcile and reunite all the siblings of Adam in *Agape*. What are we to understand by *Agape*? By "Agape" we mean spiritual unity and kinship. In a single word, *love*, or rather *love of God and fellow man*. We mean the effortless and spontaneous observance of the two greatest commandments mentioned by *Yeshua*:

> You shall love the LORD your God with all your heart, and with all your soul, and with all your mind. This is the first and great commandment. And the second is like unto it: You shall love your neighbor as yourself.
> (Matthew 22:37-39)

What is *Agape*? An illustration might be sought in the selfless act of a fireman who risks his own life to run into a raging inferno and save some wayward children trapped inside. Thereafter those children and the fireman would be held together in the bonds of *Agape*—a spiritual tie that can never be broken. Such a fireman was *Yeshua* when he hung in agony on the Cross, and such wayward children were we.

Other illustrations may be sought in the selfless acts of soul-mates who fought side by side and saved one another's lives in Korea or Vietnam, thereafter united in the bonds of *Agape*. Another illustration might be sought in the plight of siblings separated at birth, for decades feeling the emptiness and hurt of separation. Thirty years later they find one another, and the television cameras are there to capture the emotional reunion, tears flowing in rivers of *Agape*. Concerning which we also have the testimony of *Yeshua* in the parable of the prodigal son—"and when the son was yet a great way off, his father saw him, and had compassion, and ran, and fell on his neck, and kissed him," (Luke 15:20). Another example of *Agape* can be found in the reunion of Joseph with his brethren in Egypt. They did not recognize him, having considered him long dead. But Joseph recognized them, and upon recognizing them he could scarce restrain his love for his younger brother Benjamin, and went and "sought a place to hide and weep," (Genesis 43:30). This is what the Heavenly Father wants from all of His children: *Agape*—a selfless amalgam of unconditional love and unfailing trust. The edifice of the Kingdom of God is built around such love and trust. The Kingdom of God is the sanctuary in which all the siblings of Adam, long separated in bitter and cruel ages of darkness, are reconciled and reunited before their Heavenly father.

What then is the stumbling block of world peace? The stumbling block is *internal* to each and every one of us and must be overcome on an *individual* basis. The external world can in no wise be transformed unless there is first an interior *spiritual* transformation of individuals. When enough individuals change internally, the external world will change, and not before. This is why God calls *individuals* to repentance. The transformation of the world calls for myriad *individual* transformations, which in aggregate will change the exterior world and remove stumbling blocks to world peace.

For we know that the exterior world has no arbitrary existence. What we call "world" is only the sum of the individuals that live in it, the exterior condition of the world being merely a reflection of the interior *spiritual* condition of the men and women who inhabit it. The "plagues" that are now reducing the world cannot be cured by the wisdom of the Arm of Flesh. This veil of tears cannot be fixed by duct tape and chicken wire, applied by the political sagacity of the "Princes of Zoan," (Isaiah 19:11). The disorder of the world cannot be transformed into order by smoke, mirrors, and a resort to material trust. The bandaid approach, the smooth talk, the Machiavellian diplomacy, the IMF's "structural adjustment policies," the World Bank's "generosity," David Rockefeller's "good intentions" and United Nations decrees will not do. Political Prozac and economic chemotherapy is no longer an option. All such evasions and shell games are now obsolete and must be discarded. History itself stands in judgment over them. All plans, policies, proposals, treaties, organizations and alliances patterned on the derivative model of human nature are now obsolete anachronisms.

The rising flood that is now working our ruin can in no wise be arrested unless there is a fundamental change in the core nature of man. Unless there is such a change, the rising tide will contaminate, degrade, corrupt, reduce and destroy everything in sight, notwithstanding the best efforts of all the king's men and all the king's horses. Unless there is a Spiritual Revolution on earth the world will continue in the same direction and its condition will deteriorate to the point where the whole of our prospect has invested itself with the character of Death and Hades. And yet this entire veil of tears can be reversed overnight. The whole of the human condition will change when enough human beings are changed inwardly. The world will be saved when enough people have been saved, and not before.

A thing is always the sum of its components. The world is the sum of the *individuals* who inhabit it. The condition of the earth is the sum of the spiritual condition of the men and women living on it. If men and women truly desire to change the world, they must first undergo the spiritual transformation described by *Yeshua.* Otherwise how can the exterior world change? How can there ever be an end to war and violence? How can there ever be peace and prosperity on earth? Without a core transformation of human nature the Constable will continue to degrade all things to the point where the earth will become unfit for human habitation. And yet the success of the Constable is made possible by the spiritual default of man. Man's spiritual default enables the Constable to degrade the *complexity* of the blue planet. Man's spiritual default enables the Constable to vandalize human wealth, degrade national economies, destroy ecosystems, decimate rainforests, oceans and rivers. Man's spiritual default provides the Constable with a legal holding, bond and mortgage, whereby he can rule it over the human race as cosmic creditor, oppressor, and dictator. Our spiritual default makes bond slaves out of us—it reduces us into submissive dwarfs and powerless victims.

But *Yeshua* removed the leaven of "entropy" from the spirit of man. With feather and spoon he removed the last crumbs, took them outside the city gates and burned them to ashes. With cruel lashes and a crown of thorns *Yeshua* dragged the spiritual "authority" of the Cosmic Constable to Calvary and there crucified it root and branch. The Constable's *spiritual* hold over man was broken 2000 years ago. All of the Constable's spiritual holdings in man were purchased back by *Yeshua* at Calvary—the cosmic bill was paid in full, the cosmic bond retired and the cosmic mortgage torn up. Where then the stumbling block to world peace?

It is now eleven fifty-nine and counting. Thinking men and women on five continents can sense the approach of a critical juncture beyond which "business as usual" will be the death of us. Thinking men and women of every race, nationality and culture can now sense that there is a discontinuity afoot, drawing nearer with each passing day. Even Mother Nature is now warning us that unless there is a Spiritual Revolution on earth unprecedented disasters lie ahead that even she will not be able to repair. Indeed this much is now certain: any continuation of the old order will lead to ruination. Throughout the world thinking men and women of conscience know this to be so, and are eager to throw their shoulders to the wheel to avert calamity and change the outcome.

For all who would throw their shoulders to the wheel, for all who would bid defiance to the real "enemy," for all who would get off the fence and bring about a sea change, *Yeshua* provides clear guidelines, teaching us that unless we undergo a spiritual rebirth we will not be able to enter into the Kingdom of God. This world can in no wise enter into the Kingdom of Peace without putting off the nature of corruption and putting on the Nature of the Incorruption. It is time to put down the derivative dwarf and raise up the authentic Man. It is time to come out of Babylon and enter into the Kingdom of God. When enough *individual* men and women enter into the Kingdom of God we will see abiding world peace, and not before. Until then we can cry "Peace! Peace!" until we are blue in the face, and nothing will change. As the prophet says:

שָׁלוֹם שָׁלוֹם וְאֵין שָׁלוֹם !

Peace! Peace! But there is no peace!
(Jeremiah 6:14)

In the Kingdom of God there will be forgiveness, pardon, mercy, reconciliation, reunification, renewal, restoration, help, recovery, healing, repair, *Agape* and genuine concern. In the Kingdom of God all of the siblings of Adam will be reconciled with one another in peace, which, like a Divine act of oblivion, shall bury in forgetfulness every former conflict and bitterness. What the stony heart of man has never conceived, nor his darkened mind imagined, we now preach in the Good News of the Kingdom of God on earth, persuaded that the preaching of *this* Gospel, throughout the world, shall be the signal for God to evict the derivative order of things and usher in the Millennium of Peace. As *Yeshua* affirms:

> This Good News of the Kingdom shall be preached in all the world for a witness unto all nations: and then the end shall come.
>
> (Matthew 24:14)

Let the reader understand: the "end" referred to by the Prince of Peace is not the end of the world itself, but the conclusion of the derivative orders of existence. That is, the end of the Constable's interventions in human affairs. And in this we are saying that there is now a *discontinuity* afoot in the affairs of the world. A derivative old order is drawing to a close, and an authentic new order about to dawn. The old man, the old nature, the old standard, the old rule of things is fast passing away and the Kingdom of God now imminent. The whole of the crisis before us has to do with a global transfiguration such as this.

Millennial Benediction
Restoring Man to Eden

בָּרוּךְ אַתָּה יְיָ אֱלֹהֵינוּ מֶלֶךְ הָעוֹלָם, אֲשֶׁר...

Blessed are you O LORD our God, King of the Universe, who…

transforms the things that are not, into the things that are,
who transforms darkness into light,
who transforms chaos into order,
who transforms entropy into information,
who transforms void into substance,
who transforms formlessness into form,
who transforms homogeneity into heterogeneity,
who transforms simplicity into complexity,
who transforms death into life,
who transforms matter into living things,
who transforms dust into Adam,
who transforms weakness into strength,
who transforms doubt into faith,
who transforms ignorance into knowledge,
who transforms bondage into liberty,
who transforms hate into love,
who transforms despair into hope,
who transforms fear into confidence,
who transforms swords into plowshares,
who transforms sickness into health,
who transforms poverty into wealth,
who transforms evil into good,
who transforms a sow's ear into a silk purse,
who transforms a sinner into a saint.

Blessed art thou O LORD our Sovereign, Ruler of the Universe, who brings Your Kingdom to fruition on earth!

Demolishing the Malthusian Gospel of Entropy

In this *Millennial Benediction* we will lift up the blue planet to God for sanctification and transformation, giving thanks to Him for having created this marvelous playground, this garden of delight, this haven of life suspended in the darkness of space, this mystical blue oasis, this priceless jewel, this citadel of *complexity*, this temple of life, this cornucopia, this plethora, this pageant, this legacy, this exuberant Eden. We will lift up the Bride to her rightful Bridegroom, in thanksgiving asking Him to deliver, sanctify and preserve her *complexity*, her priceless resources, her diverse peoples, her beauty, her grace, her majesty, her mystery, her charms, her pulchritude, her fruitfulness—her fullness.

We will lift this marvelous heritage up to the mercy seat of God, thanking Him for having created all the wonderful places that inspire us, places where snow-capped mountains pierce the clouds, where emerald seas meet white sand beaches, where fruited plain and purple mountain majesty lend tranquility to the mind, where green valleys uplift the spirit, where great deserts warm the soul. We will lift up this pageant of *complexity* as a witness to all nations, that they may understand the magnitude of the Love of the Creator, the greatness of His design and the majesty of His name. As David says:

יְהוָה אֲדֹנֵינוּ מָה־אַדִּיר שִׁמְךָ בְּכָל־הָאָרֶץ

O LORD our Lord, how excellent is thy name in all the earth!

(Psalm 8:1)

How excellent is the creative power of the Bridegroom, sculpting mountains, forming oceans, composing symphonies with earth, wind and fire, songs with sea and sky, portraits with rivers, gorges, valleys, deltas, plains and hills, filling the whole earth with the exuberant variety of flora and fauna, creatures great and small, creatures winged, furred, hooved and scaled. (May the Love that sustains all this *complexity* sustain us from generation to generation!)

We will lift up the Bride-Creation to the Bridegroom-Creator at this Millennial wedding supper, giving thanks to our Heavenly Father for the fullness of the earth, the fullness of her oceans teaming with life, the fullness of her plains, continental divides, forests, valleys and habitats filled with the exuberant variety of living things, the fullness of her peoples, races, ethnos, and nations, the fullness of their languages, cultures, flags, traditions, and good works.

We will lift up the pulchritude of earth's glaciers and Alpine meadows, the tranquility of her azure waters, atolls and barrier reefs, the places of her mountains, marshes, wetlands and ecosystems. We will lift up billabong and bayou, bog and turlock, marsh and cuyabeno, aquifer and arroyo, bluff and butte, caldera and canyon, cape and cavern, channel and cliff, crag and crevasse, delta and desert, sand dune and snow drift, escarpment and estuary, fjord and floodplain, geyser and glacial lake, gorge and grotto, gulf and gulch, headland and hill country, island and isthmus, lagoon and lake country, mesa and mountain, oasis and outcrop, pampas and peneplain, plateau and prairie, river rapids and rock ravines, satoyama and savannah, scrub and steppe, swampland and tidal pool, trade wind and monsoon, tributary and tundra, wadi and waterfall.

We will lift up the exuberant Edens to the throne of God in thanksgiving: The pastures of Bashan, Carmel and Gilead. Serengeti National Park in Africa, and Daintree National Park in Australia. Yosemite, Yellowstone, Zion Canyon National Park, Snake River, Grand Canyon, Grand Teton, and Monument Valley in the United States. The magnificent dunes of Death Valley, and the waves that crash against Big Sur. The white cliffs of Dover and the volcanic cliffs of Santorini. Lake Tanganyika, the most venerable lake on the planet, and Lake Titicaca, the highest. Rajastan and Bharatpur, among the finest wetland sanctuaries in the world. Denali and Patagonia, Shetland Isles and New Hebrides, Borneo and Bhutan, Glacier Bay and Kamchatka, Kakadu and Palau, Land's End and Shiri Toko, Cape of Good Hope and Tierra del Fuego. Newfoundland and Nova Scotia, Kashmir and Bengal, Honan Province and Szechwan Province, Carabobo and Maracaibo, Argentinian Pampas, Brazilian Matto Grosso, and Ecuadorian Igapo. Verdant isles, Caribbean seas, and Orinoco plains. The sands of Kalahari, and the snows of Kilimanjaro.

We will lift up the mountains of the earth, reaching up towards Heaven. The dews of beautiful Hermon, flowing down to refresh the mountains of Zion. Mighty Everest and remote Nuptse, overlooking South Col. Karakoram, towering Himalayan massif, crowned by infamous K-2. Annapurna, and mysterious Hindu Kush. Beautiful snow-covered Damavand, and rugged Zagros Mountains of Iran. Legendary Caucasus, and majestic Ararat. Royal Carpathians, and noble Apuseni Mountains of Rumania, overlooking the beautiful valleys of Transylvania. The majestic Alps and the legendary Pyrenees. The pulchritude of Mont Blanc and the chiseled symmetry of the Matterhorn. Tempestuous Stromboli and mysterious Etna. Ben Nevis of the Scottish Highland, and Benbulbin, austere flat-topped massif of Ireland. Great Saharan Atlas Mountains, and Aures Massif in Algeria. Ruwenzori Mountains of the Moon, and stately Table Mountain overlooking Cape Town. Majestic Mt. McKinley, forested Appalachians, picturesque Blue Ridge Mountains, the Alleghenies and the Ozarks, the Rocky Mountains and the high Sierras. Sierra Madre and her towering volcanic giants Popocatapétl and Citlaltépetl. The imperious majesty of the Andes, and *Illimani*, "glistening falcon," overlooking Bolivia. The awe inspiring granite peaks of Cerro Fitz Roy, overlooking Chile and Argentina. Hawaii's awesome twins Mauna Kea and Mauna Loa, the Philippines' perfectly shaped Mount Mayon, and Indonesia's bombastic Krakatoa. New Zealand's beautiful Mount Cook, or as the Maories would say, *Aorangi*—"cloud piercer." Japan's beloved Mt. Fujiyama, serene and lovely as a Christmas card. Beautiful Tien Shan, and Great Khingan ranges in China, Nan Shan and mighty Minya Konka.

We will lift up the waters that support the exuberant variety of living things on the blue planet. Oceans Pacific and Atlantic, Indian and Mediterranean. Brooks that babble, streams that gurgle, rapids that run, rivers that meander through incredibly beautiful places, waterfalls that roar, declaring the glory of God. We will lift up the river Jordan, beloved of the patriarchs, matriarchs, prophets, apostles and disciples. Legendary Tigris, noble Euphrates, and idyllic Shatt al Arab, flowing past a veritable Eden of palms, reeds, and lakes. Mighty Yangtze, born in the Tibetan highlands and spilling into the East China Sea at Shanghai. Mekong and sacred Ganges. The majestic Nile, flowing through the land of the Pharaohs—Thebes, Karnak, Luxor, Abu Simbal, Memphis, Giza, Heliopolis. Niger and Zambezi, Congo and Limpopo. Mother Volga, Lena, and mighty Amur. Tiber and Elbe, Don and Dnieper. Strauss's romantic Danube, and Smetena's brooding Moldau. Magnificent glacier-fed Aar river, cutting sheer-walled gorges through the Swiss Alps, and beautiful Semois River, winding through pastoral scenes of Belgium and France.

We will lift up venerable Thames and the pastoral Trent, not to mention well-bred Avon, blue-blooded Aire, royal river Clyde, and the fair river Shannon. We will lift up Canada's magnificent rivers—Yukon and Athabasca, Saskatchewan and Severn, not to mention the awesome beauty of the Saguenay River flowing into the vast expanses of the St. Lawrence. We will lift up Old Man River—mighty Mississippi and Missouri. We will lift up legendary Hudson and colonial Columbia, beautiful Potomac and industrial Ohio, breathtaking Colorado and legendary Rio Grande. We will lift up lofty Magdalena and magnificent Orinoco—*el orgullo de Venezuela.* We will lift up mighty Amazon and fair Sao Francisco, Rio La Paz and Rio Uruguay, Rio Negro and Rio Deseado. We will lift up the pulchritude of rivers down under—Darling and Murray, Flinders and Fitzroy.

We will lift up the roaring waterfalls of the blue planet, inspiring places where cascading waters cleanse the minds of men, lending wings to the spirits of poets, musicians, explorers and dreamers alike. Waterfalls of beauty and mystery, where sunlight, spray, rainbows and rainforests blend in perfect harmony. We will lift up Venezuela's Angel Falls, highest in the world, and Colombia's Tequendama Falls, most mystical. Magnificent Iguassu Falls in Argentina, and spectacular Kaieteur Falls in the remote forests of Guyana. Breathtaking Helmcken Falls and Hunlen Falls in British Columbia. The awe-inspiring roaring spectacle of the double cascade of Virginia Falls in the Canadian Northwest Territories. Legendary Niagara Falls on the border of Canada and the United States, and picture perfect Yosemite Falls. Breathtaking Staubbach Falls in the Swiss Alps, Iceland's mighty Dettifoss, Norway's regal Mardalsfoss and royal Voringfoss, said to have inspired the music of Edvard Grieg. Beautiful Maletsunyane Falls, Lesotho, and roaring Mandraka Falls, Madagascar. Spectacular Matakil Falls in the Central African Republic, and legendary Victoria Falls, Zimbabwe. Breathtaking Bahar-Dar Falls of Ethiopia, and pristine Tagbaladougou Falls of West Africa. And let us not forget New Zealand's picture perfect Sutherland Falls, spilling onto green forests from Lake Quill.

We will lift up all the places that move the spirits of explorers, wanderers, sojourners and visitors alike, marvelous, mysterious and enchanting places, remote wonders, fascinating hideaways, idyllic islands, natural bays and harbors, picturesque and charming fishing villages, scenic trails, magnificent rock formations, awe-inspiring seascapes... (let the reader understand that words cannot describe the beauty of these places, a picture being worth a thousand words, and a visit worth a thousand pictures).

We will lift up the spiritual beauty of *Aretz Israel*, the Land of Israel, the Holy Land, hallowed by God and sheltering the places of heart, places where the feet of the prophets stood, places where *Yeshua* preached the good news of the Kingdom of God. We will lift up the beauty of Gilead and the serenity of Galilee, the pulchritude of the Jordan Valley, Dead Sea, and Arava Valley. Places of old, places of renown, places where Abraham and Sarah, Isaac and Rebekah, Jacob and Rachel sojourned, places where the children of Israel encamped. We will lift up the magnificent places of the Negev, ancient and rugged places where David hid himself when he was being pursued by adversaries. We will lift up places of remembrance —Bethel, Hebron, the Brook of Eshcol, Gilgal, the valley of Achor, Ramathlehi, the valley of Berachah. Nazareth, Bethlehem and Bethsaida, Gethsemane and Mount of Olives, Gabbatha and Golgotha.

We will lift up the magnificent and fascinating places of the earth in thanksgiving and in witness to the common heritage of all mankind. Red hills, rock giants, great caverns, colorful formations, stone sentinels, great arches, dune deserts, remote volcanic lakes, diverse scenic wonders. Grottos and deep caves of Adonis in the Lebanon, Carslbad Caverns in New Mexico, fascinating Leviathan Cave in Kenya. Austria's Eisriesenwelt, said to be the largest ice cave in the world. Amesfrane Rock Wall in Morocco, and Ciudad Encantada in Spain. Mysterious Valle de la Luna in Argentina, and magnificent stone formations in ancient Thessaly. Strange Rock Forest of Yunnan Province in China, and the intriguing limestone domes of Kweilin Karst.

The wonder of Arizona's Giant Meteor Crater, and the wonder of Spain's ash-formed Montanas del Fuego. The wonder of Band-e-Amir in Afghanistan, where white, azure, turquoise and green lakes form at different elevations, flowing into one another. Framed by rugged mountains, walled by sheer rock cliffs and rock sentinels, Bande-e Amir looks like some mythical place found in science fiction. We will lift up Kilauea Crater on Hawaii, looking like landscape found on Mercury or Venus. We will lift up Ayers Rock and Olga Mount, great rounded sandstone giants that rise out of the Australian central dessert, as though rising out of the Cydonian region of Mars.

We will lift up Ross Ice Shelf of Antarctica, looking like the surface of Europa, and sun-baked Tibesti Soda Lake of Chad, looking like landscape found on Titan. We will lift up Tengger volcanic cone on Java, reminiscent of landscape found on Miranda, Oberon, or Ariel. We will lift up the tufa formations of Mono Lake in California, looking like a scene from another galaxy entirely.

We will lift up Greece, land for all seasons, the legacy of Athens and Attica. We will lift up ancient Macedonia, where the brethren once pooled their resources to help Rav Shaul. Ancient Thessalonica and Corinth, among the first to hear the Good News of the Kingdom of God. We will lift up Thrace, Crete, Cyclades, the Peloponnese. We will lift up jewels of the Mediterranean, Ionian, and Aegean Seas, islands bathed in charm and history, floating on a lazy, azure, idyllic, sun-drenched sea, places where time is suspended and cares are forgotten. The coastal beauty of Corfu, full of color and charm, and ancient Rhodes, boasting of the glory of her past. Kos, the island that gave us Hippocrates, and legendary Patmos, where the Revelation came to John. The Monastic beauty of the Dodecanese islands, Delos of renown, and Knossos, grandest of Minoan sites, 3500 years old. Santorini's austere volcanic cliffs, reaching down to the sea, harking back to a catastrophic explosion that rained rock and ash on Jason and the Argonauts, as legend would have it.

The cup of beauty runneth over—the cup of fascination cannot contain all the wonders of the world! Wonders in Asia, wonders in the Middle East, wonders in Europe, wonders in Africa, wonders in the Americas, and wonders in Oceania. Where shall we begin? Wonders in Ireland, where the mighty Tuatha de Danan once ruled, where mysterious mountains still brood, inspiring the pens of poets, bards, troubadours and folk singers. The lure of the Emerald Isle—Donegal and County Down, Limerick and County Galway, Wexford and Waterford to Bantry Bay, and the Twelve Bends that stretch across Connemara. Fortress Dun Aengus, Skellig Michael, and mysterious Aaron Islands. Dublin Town, Cork Harbor, and Dingle Bay—"All aboard... next stop America!" Land of the shamrock, land of the Fitzgeralds and the Kennedys, the McArthys, the O'Neals, the Clancys, and the seafaring O'Malleys.

We will lift up the wonders of Scotland and wonders of England, the wonders of Canada and the wonders of Australia, the wonders of France and the wonders of Italy, all of which would require many volumes to describe. The wonders of Germany and the wonders of

Austria, the wonders Sweden and the wonders of Norway, the wonders of Eastern Europe and the wonders of Russia. The wonders of ancient Egypt and the wonders of the Sudan. The wonders of Ethiopia, and the wonders of South Africa. The wonders of India, land of the tiger, the wonders of Nepal and Tibet. The wonders of China and Mongolia, the wonders of Sri Lanka and Burma, the wonders of Thailand and Cambodia. The wonders of idyllic Penang Island—gateway to the Edens of Malaysia. The wonders of Sumatra and Java, Bali, Timor, Borneo, Sarawak, Sabah, and Papua New Guinea. The wonders of Moorea, jewel of French Polynesia. The wonders of Tonga, Fiji, and New Caledonia. The serene wonders of the islands of Japan—Hokkaido, Honshu, Shikoku, and Kyushu.

We will lift up floral and faunal heritage of the children of Adam to God for preservation. We will lift up the beautiful oaks of Bashan and the tall cedars of Lebanon. The Baobab trees of Africa and the giant Sequoias of California. American elm, box, and conifer. Japanese maple and Burmese camphor, Italian cypress and sturdy English oak. Ponderosa pine and Norwegian spruce, larch, Joshua tree, and fragrant acacia. Resilient tropical palms that bend in the wind, and unyielding desert ironwood. Beautiful white bark birch and paper bark maple. Weeping willow and weeping hemlock. Ancient Tasman Huon tree, 3000 year-old Bristle Cone Pine, General Sherman sequoia, and Morton Bay Fig Tree. Regal Welwitschia mirabilis, legendary Tannenbaum, and precious Edelweiss. Beloved sycamore and esteemed beech, well-aged Bonsai and charming pygmy date palm. Myrtle and mimosa, American magnolia and Australian eucalyptus. People tree and giant banyan, African tulip tree, stately juniper, and Chinese yew. The fragrance of Bosnian pine, the beautiful flowers of the Tamarisk tree, and the pulchritude of giant wisteria—perfumed treasure of the Sierra Madre.

We will lift up the lily of the valley and the rose of Sharon. Rose of the Transvaal, rose Claude Monet and American Beauty, rose New Dawn, rose Rugosa, and rose Tropicana, red fantasia and yellow limelight, yellow Sutter's gold and the very fragrant Mr. Lincoln rose. We will lift up the scarlet hyssop that grows out of the wall, and the humble daffodil—herald of spring. We will lift up the carnations of Mother's Day, the geraniums of Memorial Day, and the Christmas poinsettias that are lovingly grown by the Ecke family of Encinitas, California. We will lift up hypericum and oleander, white begonia and lemon-scented pelargonium, Alpine rock jasmine and yellow flax.

Wild iris, lovely amaryllis and chincherinchee, California poppy, African agapanthus and the lovely Dutch tulips that grow near the windmills of Keukenhof—Weisse tulip, Berliner tulip, Astilbe, Monte Carlo, Thalia, Muscari, and Mr. Vander Hoef tulip. We will lift up South Africa's regal King Protea and royal blue Aristea. We will lift up Japanese allium and Spirea japonica. We will lift up Dahlia, spectacular jewel growing on the slopes of the Sierra Madre in Mexico, and the exquisite white flowers of the pearl bush growing in China. We will lift up serene lotus flower and magnificent harlequin glorybower, heirloom snapdragon, pink bougainvillea, and white azalea. Magnificent purple saritaea, and Iris germanica. Philodendron, marigold, and gladiola. Dianthus and verbena, yellow allamanda and red heliconia.

We will lift up mesquite and grape vine, climbing vine and honeysuckle, climbing hydrangea and caryopteris. Dwarf santolina, Peruvian ivy, and English lavender. The holly and the ivy, mistletoe, rosehips, and rustic beech hedges that crackle in the wind. Jacaranda, indigo bush and yarrow, Japanese andromeda and Spanish shawl. Fragrant chamomile, sweet woodruff, and the aromatic creosote bush that perfumes the desert air. The giant saguaro cactus that grows in the high Sonoran desert, alongside palo verde, aloe verde, bur sage, desert star aloe, aloe buhrii, aloe tauri, and aloe vera. Prairie drop seed and pampas grass, ocotillo, agave, bunch grass, sand love and zebra grass. Giant miscanthus and morning light, undine grass and silver stripe roland, 9-ft. tall molinia grass, and the manicured green grasses that carpet the cricket fields of England. Bluegrass and perennial rye, mint and Siberian ginseng, dill and cumin, cilantro and basil, parsley, sage, rosemary and thyme. Safron, calamus and cinnamon. Lemon grass, ginger, and watercress. Hungarian paprika, Madras curry, and Darjeeling tea.

We will lift up papyrus reeds that sway in the wind, sugar canes that grow on the beautiful slopes of Maui, tree ferns and green mosses that grow beneath forest canopies, pond reeds and native waterlilies, moss-covered rocks and vine-covered walls. We will lift up meticulously clipped hedges, white picket fences, Victory Gardens, rock pools alive with koi, Torii gates and exquisite Japanese tea gardens. Sunken French gardens in Versailles, English gardens with bird baths and sundials, legendary Edinburgh Botanic Gardens, Royal Kew Gardens. Gorki Park in Moscow, Volksgarten in the Vienna of Johann Strauss, Tivoli Gardens in Copenhagen, Hyde Park in London. Warm summer nights in the gardens of Spain, brought to life by the music of Manuel de Falla. Fragrant Exposition Park in Los Angeles, sporting 50,000 varieties of roses.

We will lift up the fullness of the sea to the throne of God for blessing and sanctification:

בָּרוּךְ אַתָּה יְיָ אֱלֹהֵינוּ מֶלֶךְ הָעוֹלָם, שֶׁעָשָׂה אֶת הַיָּם הַגָּדוֹל
Blessed are you O LORD our God, King of the Universe,
Maker of the great sea.

We will lift up the creatures that live in the great waters—the majesty of the blue whale and the song of the humpback, the magnificence of orca and the intelligence of dolphins. Fishes great and small, striped, painted and ornamented. Fishes that live in the depths of the sea, mammals that roam the shores. Blue shark and requiem shark, black tip and great white, hammer head and tiger. Ancient nautilus, wiley octopus, giant squid, and intelligent cuttlefish. The giant mantas that spread their wings in emerald seas, and the gentle manatees that swim up rivers. Flying fish that entertain visitors at Catalina Island, salmon that climb impossible waterfalls, and catfish that jump as high as the sky. Friendly loggerhead turtle and giant turtle, vagabonds of seven seas. Calico bass, angelfish, barracuda, garibaldi, and opaleye. We will lift up God's gift to the national fisheries—yellow fin tuna, striped marlin, sockeye salmon, mackerel, Icelandic cod, South African snook, Dungeness crab, New England lobster, Mexican shrimp.

We will lift up the winged creatures of the earth to God in thanksgiving. We will lift up the great white storks that sojourn in the land of Israel, and the bald eagles that soar above Yukon Territory. The cranes that fly over Rajastan, and the flamingoes that flock at Ngorongoro Crater in Africa. The magnificent sea eagles of Hokkaido, the majestic griffons of the Himalayas, and the sacred ibis of Egypt. Snow geese that fly with the moon on their wings, and herons that are made exceedingly happy by the flash of silver mullet. The superlative grace of the black-browed albatross, wheeling and soaring on air currents of the great Southern Ocean. Orange-billed white trumpeter swan, Cygnus buccinator, hooper swan, and the mysterious Black Swan of Tuonela, romanticized by the music by the Jean Sibelius. Bar-headed goose, Mandarin duck, teal, and mallard. Snowy egret, yellow-eyed Humboldt penguin, and Arctic tern.

Ostrich, rhea, and emu.

We will lift up the swallows that love to return to Capistrano in spring, and the buzzards that love to soar in the thermals above Mohave in summer. Magnificent frigate bird, master of aerobatics, and exquisite humming bird hovering motionless in the air. Mischievous wings galore—crows, blackbirds, rooks, ravens, magpies and chuffs, not to mention the most mischievous bird on the planet, the naughty kia. Exquisitely painted toucan and sulphur-crested cockatoo, African gray parrot, hyacinth, and magnificent military macaw. Jonathan Livingston seagull, kittiwake, shearwater, skua and storm petrel. Kiwi and peacock, blossom-headed parakeets, and the green pigeons of the Indian Monsoon forests. The yellow, orange and black feathers of the flamed bower bird. Red-knobbed hornbill and finch-billed starling, blue-winged kookaburra and brown lory, mockingbird and sanderling, blue-footed booby and pink-footed goose, pelican and kingfisher. Wallace's magnificent ribbon-tailed bird of paradise, the superb tail of the lyre bird, and the spectacular gyrations of the oropendula. Royal and regal quetzal, thought to be the most beautiful bird in the Western Hemisphere… (let the reader understand that words cannot describe the beauty of these winged creations, a picture being worth a thousand words).

We will lift up the humble pigeon, winged messenger and high flying tumbler. Carrier pigeon, barb pigeon, turbit pigeon, Jacobin, trumpeter, and fantail pigeon. We will lift up avocet and sandpiper, cormorant and himeu. We will lift up the song of the curlew, the mournful call of the loon, and the cry of the peregrine falcon echoing in canyons. We will lift up red-tailed hawk, barn owl and rooster, meadowlark and nightingale, woodpecker and turtle dove. The venerable puffins that love to make their nests on sea cliffs, and the white ptarmigans that love to play in the land of fire and ice. And let us not forget the humble birds that grace our gardens—cardinal and blue jay, precious sparrow, beloved goldfinch, cherished Kirtland's warbler, treasured indigo bunting, blessed house wren, esteemed scarlet tanager, adored eastern bluebird, and the dear American robin.

We will lift up the diminutive wings of the planet earth, untold hundreds of thousands of species that form part of the mosaic of earth's *complexity*. Where shall we begin? Bumble bees and honey bees, crickets that chirp in the summer nights, fireflies that flash in unison among the mangrove swamps of Borneo. Praying mantis and giant mantis, lady bug, damsel fly, swallow tail and the magnificent

Monarch butterflies that hazards long journeys across continents. Bombardier beetle, scarab beetle, and diminutive Samurai Helmet beetle—it is thought that some 200,000 species of beetles inhabit the planet earth, each contributing in its own way to the exuberant pageant of living things.

We will lift up creatures great and small to the throne of God in thanksgiving, creatures that run, creatures that migrate, creatures that hibernate, creatures that hunt, creatures that graze, creatures that laze about in the sun. We will lift up the king of the beasts, the royal African lion, and that most magnificent of endangered cats—the Bengal Tiger. We will lift up the grizzlies of Kamchatka, and *Nanuk* the polar bear. The red pandas of Central Nepal, the cunning snow-leopard of Tibet, sure-footed Himalayan ibex, and wiley arctic fox. Wolves that love to howl in the tundra, rabbits that love to run in the snow, wild mustangs that love to gallop on windy plains, elephants that love to splash in mud and water. Brown bears that love to feast on salmon, moose that love to snack on willow, sea lions that love to bask in the sun. Magnificent impala and graceful Thomson's gazelle, thundering caribou, wildebeest, springbok and buffalo. Stately giraffe, striped zebra, mighty bull elephant, cantankerous hippo, and stubborn rhinoceros. The superlative speed of the African cheetah, and the measured steps of Galapagos turtle. Kangaroo, wallaby, dingo, platypus, and the koala that love to feast on eucalyptus leaves. Coyote and prairie dog, chipmunk and squirrel, ringtailed lemur and slender-tailed meercat. Rock hyrax and giant anteater, Senegal bushbaby and slow loris. Ground hog, possum, porcupine, mischievous raccoon and industrious beaver. The mischievous chimps of Kenya, the magnificent silverback gorillas of the Congo, and the golden langurs of Bhutan.

We will lift up the cattle on ten thousand hills, and the sheep in ten thousand valleys. We will lift up all of man's animal helpers, from the venerable camel, ship of the desert, to the faithful horses that work on farms. Cutting horse, palomino, appaloosa, Shetland pony, rare Suffolk draft horse, the great shire horses of England, legendary Clydesdales, magnificent Arabians, and Royal Lipizzaners. We will lift up the rancher's treasured helper, companion, and best friend—the beloved border collie. We will lift up all of man's best friends to the throne of God in thanksgiving, among them dalmations, yellow labradors, golden retrievers, St. Bernards, Japanese akitas, great danes, Turkish akbashes, French pyreneans, old English sheepdogs,

German shepherds, Australian shepherds, bloodhounds, bulldogs, Italian greyhounds, French poodles, Mexican chihuahuas, Irish setters and Scottish terriers. And lest we forget, we will lift up all the domestic cats that have decided to tolerate us, among them silver tabby, Persian, red Abysinian, Siamese, and calico.

We will lift up the bounty of the earth to the throne of God for blessing and sanctification:

בָּרוּךְ אַתָּה יְיָ אֱלֹהֵינוּ מֶלֶךְ הָעוֹלָם, בּוֹרֵא פְּרִי הָאֲדָמָה

Blessed are you O Lord our God, King of the universe,
Creator of the fruit of the earth

We will lift up all the orchards and vineyards and farms of the blue planet. We will lift up the legacies of the farmers, growers, ranchers, vintners, packers and shippers of the earth, who by their labor transform the Providence of God into food that nourishes the body, and wine that gladdens the heart. Grapes from the Valley of Eschol, watermelons from Spain, pineapple from Costa Rica. The prolific bounty of California—the exuberant produce of the San Joaquin, Imperial, and Coachella valleys. The enduring legacy of Padre Junipero Serra, father of California agriculture, and the legacy of the McArthur family of McArthur, 4th generation California ranchers. The legacies of Walter and Cordelia Knott, of Knott's Berry Farm. The legacy of Nicaso and Maria Zoria, of Zoria Farms, and the legacies of all the growers and packers of the Sacramento Valley. Exquisite California olives, pride of Bob and Betty Graber, and extra virgin olive oil, pride of Angelo and Santa Bariani. Delicious peaches, pride of David Mas Masumoto of Fresno, and perfect pistachios, pride of grandma Lash, of Lash Farms of Carpinteria. Superlative medjool dates, pride of Bard Valley Medjool Date Growers, and exquisite Diamond Walnuts, "eighty years of agricultural excellence." Garlic of every kind, lovingly grown at the Christopher Garlic Ranch of Gillroy—"the garlic capital of the world." Legendary Alta Dena Dairy, producing highest quality healthy milk, buttermilk, kefir, cheeses, sour cream, yogurt, and cottage cheese for more than half a century. Delicious Fosselman's Ice Cream, in business since 1919.

How bountiful is the fruit of the earth, O LORD! Apples galore—red delicious, golden delicious, gala, Fuji, Granny Smith, Washington, Jonathan, McIntosh and Rome apples. Bartlett, basque and winter pears. Bing cherries and Georgia peaches, Persian pomegranates and Blenheim apricots. Passion fruit and mango, persimmon and fuyu, kiwi, strawberry, blackberry, scarletberry, and raspberry. Lemons and limes, oranges and tangerines. Delicious melons of all sizes and shapes, squash, zucchini, gourd, and pumpkin. Leak and cauliflower, iceberg, romaine, oak leaf and nancy lettuce. Nutritious beans of every description, perennial sweet peas, baby carrots and celery. Buttered corn on the cob, lentils, barley and rice. Mushrooms of every description, eggplant, breadfruit, Jerusalem artichoke and Idaho potato. Delicious red tomatoes ripened on the vine, and Maui onions lovingly preserved. Delicious cheeses of every kind, from Monterrey jack and Wisconsin cheddar to parmigiano reggiano, mozzarella, provolone and brie. Exquisite herb breads, pride of Jack Bezjian Bakery, and delicious Lebanese *baklava*, pride of Panos Zetlian Delicatessen. Exquisite chocolate, pride of Domingo Girardelli, and dark Belgian chocolate, pride of Barry Callebaut.

We will lift up the fruit of the earth's vines to the throne of God for blessing and sanctification:

בָּרוּךְ אַתָּה יְיָ אֱלֹהֵינוּ מֶלֶךְ הָעוֹלָם, בּוֹרֵא פְּרִי הַגָּפֶן

Blessed are you O LORD our God, King of the universe,
Creator of the fruit of the vine.

How excellent are the wines of the earth, O LORD! Legendary wines from Alsace, Bordeaux, Champagne, Loire Valley, Burgundy, and Provence. Dry sherry from Tuscany, sparkling cava from Catalonia, fortified wines from Madeira. Sancere and sauternes, pinot noire and cabernet sauvignon, California chardonnay and Australian Shiraz, Italian vermouth and Johannesburg riesling. We will lift up the legacies of the vintners of the world, among them Pétrus, la Romanée-Conti, Chateau Margaux and Chateau la Salle. We will lift up the legendary vineyards of California—Sanford and Benedict, Bien Nacido, Lane Tanner, Au Bon Climat, Costa de Oro, Di Bruno, Foxen, Firestone, Ojai, Qupé, and Zaca Mesa, not to mention the prolific vineyards of Napa, Mendocino, Tulare and Sonoma counties. We will lift up Barossa and Grange Hermitage in Australia, and we will lift up Los Boldos, the oldest vineyard in Chile. Have we mentioned them all? By no means. We would require many volumes to mention the contributions of all the vineyards and vintners of the earth!

We will lift up the legacies of the sons and daughters of Adam who became pioneers and explorers, legendary men and women of courage who ventured into the unknown, took risks, conquered the elements, discovered continents and opened up new territories. Hirkouf and Hanno, Polybius and Pytheas of Massilia, Zhang Qian and Xuan Zand, Eric the Red and Brendan the Navigator. Suleyman the Merchant, and Marco Polo. Ibn Battuta and Ibn Jubayr. Leif Eriksson and Vasco da Gama. Mary Kingsley, Mungo Park, Hugh Clapperton, David Livingston and Henry Morton Stanley. Roald Amundsen, Robert Falcon Scott, and Ernest Shackleton. Robert Edwin Peary, William Barents and Vitus Jonassen Bering. William Jansz and Abel Tasman. Vasco Nunez de Balboa, Ferdinand Cortez, and Francisco Vasquez de Coronado. Christopher Columbus, Amerigo Vespucci, and Sebastian Cabot. Captain James Cook and Louis Antoine de Bougainville. William Clark, Meriwether Lewis, and Zebulon Montgomery Pike. Sir Edmund Hillary the beekeeper from New Zealand, and Tenzing Norgay of the tribe of three-lunged sherpas. We will lift up the legacy of Jacques Yves Cousteau, guardian of seven seas, protector of the *complexity* of the oceans of the world. (Some say that when Jacques Cousteau passed away all the dolphins wept and all the whales mourned…)

We will lift up all the nations and peoples of the world to God for redemption, deliverance, transformation and sanctification, asking Him to protect their sovereignties, their languages, their customs, their traditions and their cultures from global assimilation:

> Afghanistan, Albania, Algeria, Andorra, Angola, Anguilla, Antigua and Barbuda, Argentina, Armenia, Aruba, Australia, Austria, Azerbaijan, Bahamas, Bahrain, Bangladesh, Barbados, Belarus, Belgium, Belize, Benin, Bermuda, Bhutan, Bolivia, Bosnia and Herzegowina, Botswana, Brazil, Brunei Darussalam, Bulgaria, Burkina Faso, Burundi, Cambodia, Cameroon, Canada, Cape Verde, Cayman Islands, Central African Republic, Chad, Chile, China, Christmas Island, Cocos (Keeling) Islands, Colombia, Comoros, Congo, Cook Islands, Costa Rica, Cote D'Ivoire, Croatia, Cuba, Cyprus, Czech Republic, Denmark, Djibouti, Dominica, Dominican Republic, East Timor, Ecuador, Egypt, El Salvador, Equatorial Guinea, Eritrea, Estonia, Ethiopia, Faroe Islands, Fiji, Finland,

France, French Guyana, French Polynesia, Gabon, Gambia, Georgia, Germany, Ghana, Greece, Greenland, Guadeloupe, Guam, Guatemala, Guinea, Guyana, Haiti, Honduras, Hong Kong, Hungary, Iceland, India, Indonesia, Iran, Iraq, Ireland, Israel, Italy, Jamaica, Japan, Jordan, Kazakhstan, Kenya, Kiribat, Korea, Kuwait, Kyrgyztan, Laos, Latvia, Lebanon, Lesotho, Liberia, Libya, Liechtenstein, Lithuania, Luxembourg, Macau, Macedonia, Madagascar, Malawi, Malaysia, Maldives, Mali, Malta, Marshall Islands, Martinique, Mauritania, Mauritius, Mayotte, Mexico, Micronesia, Moldova, Monaco, Mongolia, Montserrat, Morroco, Mozambique, Myanmar, Namibia, Nauru, Nepal, Netherlands, Netherlands Antilles, New Caledonia, New Zealand, Nicaragua, Niger, Niue, Norway, Oman, Pakistan, Palau, Panama, Papua New Guinea, Paraguay, Peru, Philippines, Pitcairn Island, Poland, Portugal, Puerto Rico, Qatar, Reunion Island, Romania, Russian Federation, Rwanda, Saint Kitts and Nevis, Saint Lucia, Saint Vincent and the Grenadines, Samoa, San Marino, Sao Tome and Principe, Saudi Arabia, Senegal, Seychelles, Sierra Leone, Singapore, Slovakia, Slovenia, Solomon Islands, Somali, South Africa, South Georgia and South Sandwich Islands, Spain, Sri Lanka, Saint Helena, Saint Pierre and Miquelon, Sudan, Suriname, Svalbard and Jan Mayen Islands, Swaziland, Sweden, Switzerland, Syria, Taiwan, Tajikistan, Tanzania, Thailand, Togo, Tonga, Trinidad and Tobago, Tunisia, Turkey, Turkmenistan, Turks and Caicos Islands, Tuvalu, Uganda, Ukrain, United Arab Emirates, United Kingdom, United States, Uruguay, Uzbekistan, Vanuatu, Venezuela, Vietnam, Virgin Islands, Wallis and Futuna Islands, Western Sahara, Yemen, Yugoslavia, Zaire, Zambia, and Zimbabwe.

We will lift up all the native peoples of the earth to God for sanctification and preservation. We will lift up the Bedouins that live in the desert, and the Berbers that make their homes in the mountains. Lemba, Zulu, Masai, Twareg, Shana, Bantu, Ashanti, Yoruba and Kikuro, Dogon, Mossi, Nuna, Nunuma, Winiama, and Bwa peoples of Africa. The natives peoples of Ibero America, the Maori of New Zealand, the Aborigines of Australia, the Huli and Morabe peoples of Papua New Guinea, the Dayak peoples of

Borneo, the Sarawak, Penan, Kenyah, Kayan, Kelabit, Lun Bawang and Iban peoples of Malaysia.

We will lift up Native Americans to the Creator of the Universe for sanctification and preservation. Aleuts and Algonquins, Apaches and Apalachees, Assiniboins and Aztecs. We will lift up the braves of the Cherokee, Cheyenne, Chickasaw, Chinook and Comanche tribes. We will lift up the great peoples of the Coyote stock, and the great peoples of the Cree, Crow, Dakota, and Delaware branch. We will lift up the Five Nation Federation of the Iroquois, whose founder was the great Hiawatha. We will lift up the Hopi, the Hurons, the Illinois, the Innuits, the Mandans, the Miami, the Micmacs, and the Minnesota. We will lift up the Mohave, the Mohawks, the Navaho, the Ojibaways, the Omahas, the Onandagas, the Piutes, the Pawnees, the Pequots, the Pueblos, the Seminoles, and the Senecas. We will lift up the swift arrow of the Lakota Sioux, and the discrete wisdom of the Suquamish people, whose leader was the great Chief Seattle. We will lift up the peoples of the Wichita, the Winnebago, the Wyandots and the Zuni.

We will lift up the legacies of the great leaders of the earth to God for sanctification, great men and women who established order, administered justice, conquered foes and paved the way for progress towards the Kingdom of God. ("All things work together for good to them that love God"—Romans 8:28). Where shall we begin? We will lift up the legacy of King David, a man after God's own heart, and King Solomon, the wisest of souls. We will lift up the legacies of the kings and queens of England—the legacy of her majesty Queen Elizabeth II, beloved daughter of God. May God save our gracious Queen! May God preserve the Crown of England from global assimilation! May God preserve and direct the leaders of Great Britain, Canada, Australia and New Zealand.

We will lift up the enduring legacies of the founders of America: Messrs. George Washington, John Hancock, Josiah Bartlett, William Whipple, Matthew Thornton, Samuel Adams, John Adams, Robert Treat Paine, Elbridge Gerry, Stephen Hopkins, William Ellery, Roger Sherman, Samuel Huntington, William Williams, Oliver Wolcott, William Floyd, Philip Livingston, Francis Lewis, Lewis Morris, Richard Stockton, John Witherspoon, Francis Hopkinson, John Hart, Abraham Clark, Robert Morris, Benjamin Rush, Benjamin Franklin, John Morton, George Clymer, James Smith, George Taylor, James Wilson, George Ross, Caesar Rodney, George Read, Thomas

M'Kean, Samuel Chase, William Paca, Thomas Stone, Charles Carroll, George Wythe, Richard Henry Lee, Thomas Jefferson, Benjamin Harrison, Thomas Nelson Jr., Francis Lightfoot Lee, Carter Braxton, William Hooper, Joseph Hewes, John Penn, Edward Rutledge, Thomas Heyward Jr., Thomas Lynch Jr., Arthur Middleton, Button Gwinnett, Lyman Hall, George Walton.

We will lift up the founders and leaders of America's neighbor to the south, the sovereign peoples and government of the Federal Republic of Mexico. (How good and how pleasant it is when nations dwell side by side in harmony!) We will lift up the legacies of Miguel Hidalgo y Costilla, Josi Marma Morelos y Pavsn, and Benito Juarez. As we would lift up the struggles of the heroes of the American Revolution, so also we would lift up of the heroes of the Mexican struggle for justice and freedom—Allende, Guadalupe Victoria, Venustiano Carranza, Emiliano Zapata, Francisco Villa. May God preserve the Aztec nation from global assimilation!

We will lift up the legacies of all who wrestled against the Cosmic Constable, fought for justice, strove for freedom and independence, established human rights, struggled to resist assimilation and homogenization. Where shall we begin? We will lift up the legacy of King Richard Lionheart of England, and we will lift up the legacy of his counterpart, Saladin the Great. Mighty Saladin, ruler of all Palestine, administrator of justice, defender of the widow and the orphan, patron of tolerance. It was Saladin the Great who issued decrees commanding that Christians and Jews be allowed to worship God in Jerusalem. We will lift up the leaders of the golden age of Islam, great ones who worshipped the God of Abraham, sponsored progress, scholarship, science and learning, who developed Arabic numerals, mathematics, algebra, medicine, art and architecture, who introduced new crops and agricultural methods, who built great palaces, places of worship, roads, bridges, schools, gardens and public parks, at a time when Europe was wallowing in the Dark Ages. Legends of Arabian Nights, rulers of Spain, rulers of North Africa, builders of Cordoba, builders of Alhambra—pinnacle of Islamic culture. Harroon Al Rashid, fifth caliph of the Abbasid dynasty, mighty ruler of Baghdad, patron of science, art and literature. Legends of the Ottoman Empire—Suleyman the Magnificent, who along with his great architect Mimar Sinan built 100 magnificent places of worship, 100 great schools and universities, hospitals, aqueducts, bridges, arches, baths, palaces and mansions, many of which still stand today.

We will lift up the memories of the great ones of Japan—forty-seven loyal Samurai, among them Oishi Kuranosuke and Nakayama Yasubei. We will lift up the struggles of Chinese leaders, from Sun Yat-Sen to Deng Xiaoping. We will lift up the struggles of Garibaldi, liberator of Italy, Mustafa Kamal Attaturk, founder of modern Turkey, Simon Bolivar, father of Venezuela, Colombia, Ecuador, Peru, and Bolivia. We will lift up the legacies of the founders of the modern state of Israel—Eliezer Ben-Yehuda, David Ben-Gurion, Khaim Weizmann, Yitzhak Ben-Zvi, Moshe Sharett, Levi Eshkol, Golda Meir. We will lift up the legacy of Hussein of Jordan, pilot-king, soldier, peacemaker, diplomat, educator, provider for the poor, protector of the widow and the orphan. We will lift up the struggles of the Egyptian peoples—the struggles of Jamal Abdel Nasser, Anwar Saddat, Hosni Moubarak. We will lift up the struggles of King Faisal of Saudi Arabia, and the struggles of Emperor Haile Selassie of Ethiopia, the struggles of Mohandas Karamchand Ghandi and Jawaharal Nehru, the struggles of Mrs. Indira Gandhi and her husband Rajiv Gandhi.

We will lift up the struggles of Martin Luther King, Aleksandr Solzhenitsyn, André Sakharov, Lech Walensa, Vaclav Havel, Nelson Mandella, Wang Dan, Aung San Suu Kyi, Gloria Macapagal Arroya, Frederick Chiluba, Caesar Chavez, Vicente Fox, Digna Ochoa—all who wrestled with the devil of injustice and tried to bring their peoples into the sanctuary of the Kingdom of God. We will lift up the legacies of the righteous who risked their own lives to protect others in harm's way, those who went out of their way to provide shelter and sanctuary for the persecuted. We will bring to remembrance the legacies of Harriet Tubman, Oskar Schindler, Raoul Wallenberg, Corrie Ten Boom.

We will lift up all the creative works of the sons and daughters of Adam to the throne of God for sanctification. As a father delights in all the creative works of his children, so also the Heavenly Father delights in all the creative works of Man:

בָּרוּךְ אַתָּה יְיָ אֱלֹהֵינוּ מֶלֶךְ הָעוֹלָם, עֹשֶׂה מַעֲשֵׂה בְרֵאשִׁית

Blessed are you O LORD our God, ruler of the universe,
Source of creative power.

We will lift up the wheel and the hammer, the furnace and the forge, the quill and the abacus, the spindle and the loom, the pulley and the gear, the axle and the flywheel. We will lift up the farmer's plow and the harvester's scythe, the woodsman's axe and the potter's wheel, the carpenter's saw and the stonemason's level, the blacksmith's anvil and the refiner's forge, the weaver's loom and the spinner's wheel, the baker's oven and the wine maker's still, the plumber's wrench and the electrician's pliers, the mechanic's screwdriver and the painter's ladder, the surveyor's theodolite and the prospector's drill, the accountant's book and the banker's ledger, the architect's drafting table and the shipwright's mallet, the sailor's compass and the astronaut's gimbal, the mathematician's sliderule and the scientist's bunsen burner, the physician's stethoscope and the dentist's probe, the teacher's blackboard and the coach's whistle, the music instructor's metronome and the conductor's baton, the poet's pen and the painter's canvas, the mailman's pouch and the fireman's hat, the marshall's truncheon and the judge's robe.

We will lift up the legacies of all the artists who defied the Constable, denied entropy, immobilized time and captured the essence of Man on canvas and other media. We will lift up the paintings of Man, ancient, classic, Byzantine, medieval, Gothic, renaissance, Flemish, romantic, realist. Cave paintings of Lascaux, Minoan frescoes, and the ancient art of Egypt. Greek sculptures, Etruscan amphora, and the priceless treasures of China. Celtic art, Anglo-Saxon Hexateuch, and Bayeux Tapestry. The Gothic art of Cimabue, Giotto, Pisano, Lorenzetti, and van der Weyden. The renaissance paintings of Masolino, Fra Angelico, Donatello, Bellini and Botticelli. Raphael's *School of Athens*, da Vinci's *Mona Lisa*, and Michelangelo's *David*. The art of the Flemish masters Rubens, van Dyck, Ruisdael, Rembrandt, Vermeer. Masterpieces of the Spanish baroque—de Riber's *St. Paul the Hermit*, and Velazquez' legendary *Las Meninas*.

We will lift up the rococo paintings of Tiepolo, Fragonard, and Boucher, the neo-classics of Sir Henry Raeburn and Sir Joshua Reynolds, the romantic works of Blake, Martin, Delacroix, and Goya, the realist masterpieces of Daumier, Abbot, and Fantin-Latour. Whistler's portrait of his mother, Homer's magnificent seascape *Breezing Up*, and Sargent's *Luxembourg Gardens at Twilight*. The impressionist art of Manet, Boudin, Degas, Caillebotte, Renoir, Pissarro, and Monet. The post-impressionist masterpieces of van

Gogh, Toulouse-Lautrec, Gauguin, Cézanne, and Rodin. *The Dance*, by Henri Matisse, and *Piazza d'Italia* by Giorgio de Chirico. Georgia O'Keeffe's *Lake George*, Salvador Dali's *Sleep*, and Pablo Picasso's *Guernica*.

We will lift up the musical instruments of the earth to God for sanctification. We will lift up all the drums of the world as they make a loud noise in the universe, announcing the beginning of Man's counteroffensive against the Cosmic Constable. Long drums and frame drums, kettle drums and timpanies. Legendary *bodhrán* of Ireland, gourds of Africa, *naqara* of Arabia, *tabala* of Yugoslavian, *dauli* of Greece, *timbales* of Latin American. Indian *jaltarang*, Hawaiian *hula ipu*, Guinean water drum, Russian *reshoto*, Turkish *tar*, Ugandan *ntenga* and Ethiopian *koboro*. The *panhuehuetl* drums of Mazatlan and the bongo drums of Cuba. The drums of Cambodia and the drums of Java. The Kodo drums of Japan, imitating the heartbeat of Man, the magnificent drums of Sado Island, fashioned from the wood of the beloved daiko tree—*tsuri daiko*, *o-daiko*, *taiko*, *da-daiko*. We will lift up the mighty drums of Africa, orchestrated by Nigeria's master musician Babatunde Olatunji, as they make a triumphant noise unto God. We will lift up the Shofars and the church bells that announce the victory of Man over the Cosmic Constable—"Awake you sleepers, for today is the day of your salvation! Hear the Shofar, and be born anew. Hear the church bells, and rejoice in the victory that God gives you!"

We will lift up the harp of David, making a pleasant sound unto heaven, and all the pleasant harps of the earth—Egyptian harp, Greek harp, Irish harp, Celtic harp, "Cythara Anglica," "Brian Boru," and modern Elysian concert harp. We will lift up all the musical horns of the planet earth—Greek *salphinx*, Celtic *carnyx*, Roman *cornu*, Finnish *paimensarvi*, Scandinavian *lur*. Cavalry bugle, military flugelhorn, marching cornet, sousaphone and herald trumpet. The *khen* mouth organ of Laos, the *sheng* mouth organ of China, and the *sho* mouth organ of Japan. We will lift up all the flutes of the planet earth—Indian *tikriti*, Chinese *ti-tzu*, Tibetan *gling-bu*, Yugoslavian *dvoynice*, Slovakian *fujara*, Basque *alboka*, Irish *tin whistle*, Moroccan double hornpipe, Tunisian *zummara*, South African *naga y lethlake*, and the panflute of the Andes. We will lift up French *musette*, Italian *zampogna*, German *dudelsack*, and Slovakian *gajdy*. We will lift up the bagpipes that sing in the Highlands of Scotland …

We will lift up the *ud* of Syria, the *santoor* of Iran, and the *sitar* of

India. We will lift up Russian *balalaika* and Ukranian *bandura*, Hungarian *mandola* and Neapolitan *mandolin*. We will lift up the guitars of the earth—medieval *gittern*, renaissance *vihuela*, and Italian *chitarra*. We will lift up the legacy of Antonio de Torres Jurado of Granada, the father of the classical guitar. We will lift up the legacy of Orville Gibson, founder of Gibson Guitars, and the creations of his associates Lloyd Loar, Les Paul, and Ted McCarty. We will lift up the legacy of C.F. Martin of Martin Guitars, the legacy of Clarence Leonidas Fender, designer of the electric guitar, and the legacy of Bob Taylor, father of Taylor Guitars. We will lift up the legacy of Thomas Delgado and Sons of Los Angeles, creators of exquisite handmade classic guitars, one at a time.

We will lift up all the stringed instruments of the earth—Apache fiddles of the Americas, Cape Breton fiddles of Canada, spike fiddles of the Middle East. Folk fiddles and banjos, Mongolian *morin-chur*, Japanese *ko-kiu*, Siamese *saw-thai*, Caucasian *fandur* and Bulgarian *gadulka*. Square fiddle from Ireland and *hardangerfele* fiddle from Norway. We will lift up the legacy of Cremona, Italy, the legacy of Andrea Amati, one of the first violin makers of Europe. We will lift up the legacies of his celebrated pupils—Antonio Stradivari and Andreas Guarneri. We will lift up the legacies of Theobald Boehm, the flute maker of Munich, Johann Christoph Denner of Nuremberg, the father of the modern clarinet, Jean Hotteterre IV of France, the father of many modern wind instruments, Hans Neuschel of Germany, the father of many brass instruments, and Rudolph Wurlitzer, the father of the magnificent Wurlitzer theater organ.

We will lift up the the legacy of Bartolommeo Cristofori of Padua, the inventor of the pianoforte. We will lift up the legacy of American piano maker Jonas Chickering—Abraham Lincoln had a Chickering piano. We will lift up the legacy of Dwight Hamilton Baldwin of Cincinnati Ohio, creator of legendary Baldwin pianos, and we will lift up the legacy of Henry Englehard Steinway, a testament to individual craftsmanship. The grand creations of Steinway and Sons, (sons Henry Jr., Albert, C.F., Theodore, and Charles), have since entered the realm of musical legend. There is genuine, authentic, original human wealth stored in the basement of New York's Steinway Hall at 109 West 57th Street, ready for shipment to the great concert halls of the world. We will lift up the legacy of Ignaz Bosendorfer of #12 Bosendorferstrasse in old Vienna, making legendary concert grands crafted from Bavarian spruce—"the pianos that even Franz Liszt couldn't wreck!" We will lift up the legacy of Torakusu Yamaha, maker of legendary pianos and keyboards that teach the universal language of music to children throughout the world.

We will lift up the composers of the world, legendary creators of symphonies, oratorios, overtures, masses, hymns, cantatas, operas, fugues, etudes, partitas, barcarolles, chaconnes, adagios, passacaglias, rhapsodies, rondos, nocturnes, waltzes, mazurkas, arias, tarantellas, polonaises, sonatas, ballads, caprices, etc.. Where shall we begin? Bach, Haydn, Handel, Vivaldi, Mozart, Beethoven, Brahms, Sibelius, Schubert, Mendelssohn, Mahler, Tchaikovsky, Wagner, Boradin, Rachmaninov, Shostakovich, Khachaturian, Mussorgsky, Prokofiev, Rimsky-Korsakov, Paganini, Strauss, Saint-Saens, Dvorak, Chabrier, Chopin, Debussy, Ravel, Grieg, Elgar, Vaughn Williams, Yanacek, Enesco, Scriabin, Respighi, Puccini, Massenet, Fauré, Honegger, Bartok, Balakirev, Copeland, Holst, Hanson, Britten, Bizet, Franck, Gorecki, Stravinsky, Duruflé, Rodrigo, Granados, Albeniz, de Falla, Villa Lobos, Segovia, Joplin, Gershwin…

We will lift up Bach's *Brandenburg Concerto* and Mozart's *Mass in C-Minor*, Beethoven's *Ninth Symphony* and Tchaikovsky's *First Violin Concerto*, Brahm's *German Requiem* and Vaughn Williams' *Sea Symphony*, Grieg's *Peer Gynt* and Dvorak's *New World Symphony*. Smetena's *Moldau* and Strauss's *Blue Danube*, Prokofiev's *Cantata Alexandre Nevsky* and Boradin's *In the Steppes of Central Asia*, Khachaturian's *Spartacus* and Bartok's *Hungarian Sketches*. Beethoven's beloved *Fur Elise*, Chopin's cherished *Waltz in C-Sharp Minor*, and Liszt's romantic *Libestraum*. Albinoni's bittersweet *Adagio* and Pachelbel's moving *Canon*. Kodaly's *Hary Janos* and Mussorgsky's *Pictures at an Exhibition*. Holst's *The Planets* and Britten's *Peter Grimes*. Copeland's *El Salon Mexico* and Rodrigo's *Concierto de Aranjuez*. Ravel's *Daphnis et Chloe* and Debussy's *Claire de Lune*. Scriabin's *Divine Poem* and Gorecki's *Symphony of Sorrowful Songs*. Sarasate's *Zigeunerweisen*, Kreisler's *Liebesleid*, and Massenet's *Meditation de Thais*. Marie-Joseph Canteloube's *Chants d' Auvergne*, and Heitor Villa-Lobos' *Bachianas Brasileiras*. Scott Joplin's *Maple Leaf Rag* and George Gershwin's *Porgy and Bess …*

We will lift up the concert halls of the earth where musicians rise to the occasion of *complexity*—Royal Albert Hall, Royal Opera House, Royal Festival Hall, Covent Garden, Berlin Philharmonic Hall, Beethoven Hall, Contcertgebouw, Salzburg Mozarteum, Musikverein,

Wiener Konzerthaus, Kurhaus, Brucknerhaus, Paris Olympia, Salle Pleyel de Paris, Campidoglio di Roma, La Scala, Arena di Verona, Teatro Real de Madrid, Megaro Hall, Bolshoi Theatre Hall, the Great Hall of the Tchaikovsky Conservatory, Grand Hall of the St. Petersburg Philharmonic, Suntory Hall, NHK Hall, Osaka Hall, Seoul Art Hall, Melbourne Blackwood Hall, Carnegie Hall, Lincoln Center, Orchestra Hall, Boston Symphony Hall, Avery Fisher Hall, Royce Hall, Abravanel Hall, Dorothy Chandler Pavilion, and magnificent Hollywood Bowl.

We will lift up the orchestras of the world—where shall we begin? Academy of St. Martin-in-the Fields, Bournemouth Symphony, English Chamber Orchestra, London Philharmonic, Orchestre de Paris, Jean-Francois Paillard Orchestra, Bamberger Symphoniker, Berliner Philharmoniker, Vienna Philharmonic, Budapeste Philharmonic, Hungarian Philharmonic, Czech Philharmonic, Prague Radio Symphony Orchestra, Polish Radio and Television Symphony Orchestra, Festival Strings of Lucerne, Camerata Zurich, La Orquestra Nacional de Espana, Israel Philharmonic, New York Philharmonic, Baltimore Symphony, Buffalo Symphony, Cincinnati Symphony, Milwaukee Symphony, Philadelphia Symphony, Utah Symphony—our cup runneth over and we would need many volumes to list them all.

We will lift up the maestros of the planet earth—where shall we begin? Arturo Toscanini and Serge Koussevitzky, Sir Thomas Beecham and Sir Malcom Sargent, maestros George Solti, Antal Dorati, Neville Mariner, Raymond Leppard, Paavo Berglund, Vernon Handley, Bernard Haitink, Jean-Francois Paillard, Eugen Jochum, Herbert Von Karajan, Lorin Maazel, Eliahu Inbal, Christoph Von Dohnanyi, Aldo Ceccato, father Mehli and son Zubin Mehta, Rafael Kubelik, Wolfgang Sawallisch, Paul Angerer, Karl Munchinger, Alfred Brendel, Janos Ferencsik, Raphael Fruhbeck de Burgos, Seiji Ozawa, Sergiu Comissiona, Robert Shaw, Josef Suk, Colin Davis, Thomas Schippers, Stanislaw Skrowaczewski, Dennis Russel Davies, Edo de Waart, Christopher Hogwood, John Williams, Erich Kunzel, Claudio Abbado, Maurice Abravanel, Gisèle Ben-Dor...

We will lift up the soloists, instrumentalists and recitalists of the earth—where shall we begin? Legends of the ivory keyboard Arthur Rubenstein, Ignacy Paderewski, Josef Lhevinne, Josef Hofmann, Sviatoslav Richter, Vladimir Ashkenazy, John Ogdon, Arthur Grumiaux, Arthur Schnabel, Michael Ponti, Ivan Moravec, Stephen

Kovacevich, Martha Argerich, Myra Hess, Cyprien Katsaris, André Watts, André Previn, Daniel Barenboim, Glenn Gould, Garrick Olson, Clara Haskil, Alicia de Larrocha, Ruth Laredo, Leon Fleisher, Krystian Zimerman, Zoltan Kocsis, Maurizio Pollini, Andras Schiff, Rudolf Serkin, Emil Gilels, Arturo Benedetti Michelangeli, Mitsuko Uchida, Rada Lupu, Robert Casdesus, Yevgeny Kissin…

We will lift up legendary violinists Yehudi Menuhin, Yasha Heifetz, Isaac Stern, Itzhack Perlman, David Oistrakh, Nathan Milstein, Salvatore Accardo, Zino Francescatti, Pinkas Zuckerman, Anne-Sophie Mutter, Nadia Solerno-Sonnenberg, Gidon Kramer, Annie and Ida Kavafian, Yang Liu, Sarah Chang, Siqing Lu, Sakura Tsai, Yumi Mai, Sally Kikuchi and Tim Braun. We will lift up the legacy of Mstislav Rostropovich of the Republic of Azerbaijan, who made the cello a beloved instrument on earth, and we will lift up the legacies of renowned cellists Pablo Casals, Jacqueline du Pré, and Yo-Yo Ma. We will lift up the legacy of the Chung family of South Korea—sisters Kyung-Wha Chung, Myung-Wha Chung, and brother Myung-Whun Chung. We will lift up the legacies of Andrés Segovia, and the royal family of the guitar—Celedonio, Celin, Pepe, and Angel Romero. We will lift up the legacy of the renowned organist E. Power Biggs, and the legacies of renowned flautists Jean-Pierre Rampal and John Galway.

We will lift up the great tradition of opera, from Bellini to Puccini and beyond. We will lift up Verdi's *La Traviata*, Wagner's *Taunnhauser*, Strauss's *Di Rosenkavalier*, and Puccini's *La Bohem*. We will lift up the legacies of the great voices of the world—Enrico Caruso and Maria Callas, celebrated tenors Carreras, Domingo and Pavarotti, legendary voices of Montserrat Caballé, Victoria de Los Angeles, Frederica "Flicka" Von Stade, Kiri Te Kanawa, Tatiana Troyanos, Jessye Norman, Marylin Horne, Kathleen Battle, Leontyne Price, Jan DeGaetani, René Kollo, Andrea Bocelli, Cecilia Bartoli.

We will lift up all the contemporary musicians of the earth—where shall we begin? Gilbert and Sullivan, Rodgers and Hammerstein, Irving Berlin and Cole Porter. We will lift up the voices of Fraulein Maria and the Von Trap children as they bring the hills of Austria to life with *The Sound of Music*. We will lift up the composers that brought the silver screen to life—Max Steiner, Miklos Rosa, Erich Wolfgang Korngold, James Horner, Alfred Newman, Lalo Schiffrin, Maurice Jarre, Hans Zimmer, John Williams, Jerry Goldsmith.

We will lift up jazz and popular musicians—the legacies of Duke Ellington, Glenn Miller, Benny Goodman, Count Basie, Woody Herman, Cab Calloway, Dizzy Gillespie, Shelly Manne, Billy Holiday, Harry Connick Jr., Lionel Hampton, Charlie Parker, Louis "Satchmo" Armstrong, John Coltrane, Art Blakey, Buddy Rich, Chet Atkins, Wes Montgomery, Gene Krupa, Charlie Bird, Milt Jackson, Ella Fitzgerald, Lena Horne, B.B. King, Herbie Hancock, Chic Corea, Les McCann, Ray Brown, Miles Davis, Jimmy Hendrix, Wynton and Branford Marsalis, Oscar Peterson, Stephane Grappelli, Pat Metheny, Henry Mancini, Nat King Cole, Bing Crosby, Harry Belafonte, Frank Sinatra, Richard Stoltzman, Ray Charles, Stevie Wonder, Otis Redding, James Brown, the Righteous Brothers, bob Dylan, Elvis the king...

We will lift up legends of country music—Grandpa Jones, Hank Williams, Billy Walker, George Jones, Johnny Cash, Merle Haggard, Charley Pride, Tammy Wynette, Kitty Wells, Patsy Cline, Loretta Lynn, Marty Robbins, Skeeter Davis, Jerry Lee Lewis, Statler Brothers, Roy Clark, Waylon Jennings, Governor Jimmie Davis, Buck Owens, Porter Wagoner, Willie Nelson, Boots Randolph, Garth Brooks, Randy Travis, Dolly Parton, Naomi and Winona Judd, the Oak Ridge Boys...

We will lift up the legacies of the bards and folk singers of the earth, from Hildegard von Bingen to Sting. Where shall we begin? We will lift up Fiona Ritchie's *The Thistle and the Shamrock*, showcasing Celtic legends from the ballads of the family O'Domhnaill to the tunes of Michael Coleman, James Morrison, John Ellis, Natalie MacMaster and Bonnie Rideout. We will lift up the legacy of Altan, "the heart and soul of Irish music," and the legacies of the beloved Chieftains—Paddy Moloney, Matt Molloy, Martin Fay, Seán Potts, Derek Bell, Seán Keane, Dave Fallon, Michael Tubridy, Peadar Mercier and Kevin Conneff...

From the four corners of the world we will lift up the legacies of Ravi Shankar and Ali Akbar Khan, playing the classical *ragas* of India, Theodor Bikel, singing Jewish folk songs, and the legacy of Umm Kulthum—"the voice of Egypt." We will lift up the legacies of Rentaro Taki, Masao Koga, Michio Miyagi, and Toru Takemitsu, contemporary bards of Japan. We will lift up the exuberant rhythms of the Gypsy Kings, and the vibrant tangos of Astor Piazzolla. We will lift up the lamentations of Bob Marley, the bard of *reggae*, and the legacy of Celia Cruz, first lady of *salsa*. We will lift up the legacies of all the popular musicians of Latin America, among them Gato Barbieri, Laurindo Almeida, Antonio Carlos Jobim, Paquito D' Rivera, Tito Puente, Pete Escovedo and daughter Sheila E, Julio and Enrique Iglesias, Gloria Esteban, Juan Gabriel, Selena, Lucero, Sergio Goyri, Ricki Martin...

We will lift up the exuberant dances of the earth—superlative affirmations of God-given Liberty. American square dance, Celtic folk dance, French *quadrille*, Viennese *waltz*, Swiss *polka*, Italian *tarantella*, Swedish *stegvals*, Norwegian *busserull*, Finnish *purpuri*, Hungarian *polka*, Polish *polska*, Romanian *alunelul*, Russian *korobushka*, Ukrainian *gopak*, Grecian *syrtos*, Spanish *flamenco*, Israeli *hora*, Syrian *bandee*, Lebanese *dabke*, Turkish *kelekvan*, Armenian *kher pan*, Indian *bharatanatyam*, African *sowu*, Mexican *jarabe tapatio*, Argentinian *tango*, Brazilian *samba*, Hawaiian *hukilau*, Philippine *tinikling*, Japanese *tanko bushi*, Chinese *ribbon dance*...

We will lift up all the dance ensembles of the earth arrayed in traditional apparel, among them the Aman Folk Ensemble, Ballet Folklorico de Mexico, Likha Philipino Folk Ensemble, Taipei Folk Dance Troupe, Bela Bartok Dance Ensemble, Krakusy Polish Folk Dance Ensemble, Karpatok Hungarian Folk Dance Ensemble. We will lift up the legacy of Igor Moiseyev and the legendary Moiseyev Dance Ensemble. We will lift up legends of classical dance, among them the Bolshoi Ballet, Kirov Ballet, Moscow Ballet, St. Petersburg Ballet, Royal Ballet, American Ballet Theatre. We will lift up the legacies of legendary dancers, choreographers, and artistic directors, among them Rudolf Nureyev, Margot Fonteyn, Anna Pavlova, Natalia Makarova, Mikhail Baryshnikov, Ruth Page, Alicia Alonzo, Alicia Markova, Nora Kaye, Vinogradov, Goleizovsky, Messerer, Kasatkin, Dowell, Robbins, Graham, Balanchine...

We will lift up the great authors and poets of the earth, their pens raised as a mighty weapon against injustice and human suffering. Where shall we begin? From Homer and Herodotus to Horace and Aesop, from Ovid to Omar Khayyam, from Plato and Aristotle to Kant and Hegel, From Virgil to Hume, and from Seneca to Disraeli, we would need volumes to list all of their names and works. Geoffrey Chaucer, William Shakespeare, Francis Bacon, John Milton, Alexander Selkirk, Daniel Defoe, Lord Byron, Percy Bysshe Shelley, Robert Burns, Alexander Pushkin, John Keats, William Wordsworth, Alfred Lord Tennyson, Charles Dickens, Hans Christian Andersen, Herman Melville, Fyodor Dostoevski, Leo Tolstoy, John Ruskin,

Ralph Waldo Emerson, Walt Whitman, Emily Bronte, Jane Austen, Alexandre Dumas, Lewis Carroll, Emily Dickinson, Henry James, Joseph Conrad, Arthur Conan Doyle, Rabindranath Tagore, Rudyard Kipling, Jack London, Robert Frost, G.K. Chesterton, Carl Sandburg, John Masefield, James Joyce, Agatha Christie, Boris Pasternak, F. Scott Fitzgerald, William Faulkner, George Orwell, Ernest Hemingway, John Steinbeck, Arthur Miller, Yevgeny Yevtushenko, Kenzaburo Oe, Kotaro Takamura …

How diverse are the works of the great writers of the earth, O LORD, striving for understanding! Where shall we begin? *Gilgamesh*, *Iliad* and *Odyssey*. *Shahnama* and *Rubaiyat*, *Canterbury Tales* and *Pilgrim's Progress*. Tales of *Hamlet*, *King Lear*, and *Macbeth*. Tales of *War and Peace*, *Pride and Prejudice*, *Crime and Punishment*. Of *Anna Karenina*, and of *Doctor Zhivago*. Of *Moby Dick* and of *Mutiny on the Bounty*, of *Robinson Crusoe* and of *Moll Flanders*, of *Eugene Onegin* and of *Boris Godunov*, of *Great Expectations* and of *Wuthering Heights*, of *Oliver Twist* and of *David Copperfield*, of *Anne of Greengables* and of *The Great Gatsby*, of *Farewell to Arms* and of *Death of a Salesman*, of *Grapes of Wrath* and of *Cannery Row*, of *Alice in Wonderland* and of *The Lord of the Rings*. Tales about the adventures of Tom Sawyer and Huckleberry Finn, tales about sleuths and villains, heroes and maidens in distress, tales of intrigue and controversy, tales of the triumph of right over wrong. Tales about the adventures of the Hardy Boys and Nancy Drew, Sherlock Holmes and Dr. Watson, Hercule Poirot and Inspector Hastings, Dixon Hill, and Perry Mason.

We will lift up the architectural legacies of Man to God for sanctification. Biblical Jericho and Petra, the Great pyramid of Cheops and the Great Sphinx of Giza, megaliths of Western Europe and monoliths of Easter Island. Pantheon, Parthenon, Areopagus, and Roman Colosseum. Ancient Constantinople (Istanbul), where the magnificent edifice of Justinian's *Hagia Sophia* still stands after fifteen centuries. Great Taj Mahal, most glorious monument to love between man and woman—gift of Shah Jehan to his beloved wife Mumtaz. Wall of China, Forbidden City, and Tiananmen—*gate of heavenly peace*. Angkor Wat in Cambodia, and Torii of Itsukushima in Japan. Sistine Chapel, Tempietto di San Pietro, and Notre Dame. Brandenburg Gate, Arc de Triomphe, Eiffel Tower, and Leaning Tower of Pisa. Teotihuacan, Machu Picchu and Chichen Itza in South America, Zimbabwe—*houses of stone*—in Africa. Edinburgh Castle, Westminster Abbey, Houses of Parliament and Buckingham Palace. Washington

Memorial, Jefferson Memorial, Lincoln Memorial, the Capitol Building, and the Lady in the Harbor with the torch of freedom ablaze in her hand. Empire State Building, Chrysler Building, Sears Tower, and the Petronas Towers of Kuala Lumpur. Falling Water, Palm House at Kew Garden, Pyramide du Louvre in Paris, and Crystal Cathedral in Garden Grove. London Bridge, Sydney Opera House, Getty Center, British Museum, El Prado, Smithsonian and Guggenheim.

We will lift up obelisks, minarets and onion domes. Charming old clock towers that chime in ancient cities, castles in Spain, villas on the French Riviera, beautiful estates in New England. Humble adobe, magnificent hacienda, and stately El Presidio. Vaulted ceiling and marble arch, cobblestone terrace and terra cotta roof, ornate column and spiral staircase, balcony and balustrade, walled courtyard and thatched roof, wrought iron trellis and vine-covered gazebo, fountains of Versailles, and fountains of Rome.

We will lift up the legacies of all the great master-builders and architects of the world, among them Andrea Palladio, Antonio Gaudi, Le Corbusier, Gustave Eiffel, Frank Lloyd Wright, Philip Johnson, Oscar Niemeyer, I.M. Pei, Richard Meier, Frank Gehry, Norman Foster, Tadao Ando, Aldo Rossi.

We will lift up the legacy of Brunel, master engineer of Queen Victoria's Empire, and James Buchanan Eads, master engineer and builder of the first bridge to span the mighty Mississippi. We will lift up the legacies of John Roebling and his son Washington Roebling, cable makers and bridge builders, constructors of the Brooklyn Bridge—"eighth wonder of the world!" We will lift up the legacies of Ferdinand de Lesseps and John Stevens, builders of the Panama canal. We will lift up the legacy of Robert Moses, New York's legendary highway commissioner, city planner, and master builder. We will lift up the legacy of William Mulholland, the man who brought water to Los Angeles. We will lift up the legacies of all the great city planners and mayors of the world, among them the honorable Richard Riordan, Mayor of Los Angeles, and the honorable Rudolph Giuliani, Mayor of New York.

We will lift up *Jeru-salem*, City of God, City of *complexities*, joy of all the earth:

אִם־אֶשְׁכָּחֵךְ יְרוּשָׁלָם תִּשְׁכַּח יְמִינִי׃
תִּדְבַּק־לְשׁוֹנִי לְחִכִּי אִם־לֹא אֶזְכְּרֵכִי
אִם־לֹא אַעֲלֶה אֶת־יְרוּשָׁלַם עַל רֹאשׁ שִׂמְחָתִי

If I forget thee, O Jerusalem, let my right hand forget how to function! Let my tongue cleave to the roof of mouth if I fail to make Jerusalem my chief source of joy!
(Psalm 137:5)

We will lift up the cities of the world to God for sanctification. How many, and how great are the cities of the sons of Adam, O LORD! We will lift up London, Liverpool, Belfast and Dublin town. Paris, Marseille, St. Nazaire. Lisbon, Oporto, Madrid, Barcelona, Valencia. Cordoba and Granada—mirrors of Andalusia. The beautiful cities of Italy and Sicily—Rome, Napoli, Milano, Turino, Genoa, Palermo and Salerno. Cities of renown, cities of commerce, Bern, Basel, Zurich, Munich, Frankfurt, Cologne, Dusseldorf and Hamburg. Brussels, Amsterdam, and wonderful Copenhagen—old girl of the sea. Prague in spring, where there is "beauty around every corner," Warsaw in the pleasant summer, and Budapest in the autumn, when leaves turn to gold. Hard working cities of Zagreb, Belgrade, Sarajevo, and Bucharest. Well-ordered Reykjavik, Oslo, Stockholm, and Helsinki. Odessa of old, Kiev, Minsk, Smolensk and Moscow. Athens, Istanbul, Ankara, Baku, Beirut, Damascus, Aman, Riyadh, and Aden. The magnificent walled city of Shibam in Wadi Hadramaut, Yemen, and the enchanting old city of Sanaa on the ancient spice route, where camel caravans rested on their way to Marib, Najran, Mecca, Petra, Gaza, and Jerusalem. We will lift up Tehran, Isfahan, Karachi, Jalal Abad, Lahore, Kabul, Kathmandu, Tashkent and Samarkand …

We will lift up Delhi, Bombay, Calcutta, Bangalore, and Madras—resting place of the apostle Thomas. We will lift up Beijing, Shanghai, Lanchow, Wuhan, Canton, Taipei, and Hong Kong. We will lift up Dacca, Rangoon, Bangkok, Seoul, Phnom Penh, Hanoi, Saigon, Kuala Lumpur, Singapore, Manila, Djakarta, Bandung, Port Moresby. We will lift up the cities of Japan—Sapporo, Sendai, Tokyo, Yokohama, Nagoya, Osaka, Kobe and Kyoto. We will lift up the cities down under, among them Darwin, Brisbane, Sydney, Canberra, Melbourne, Hobart, Adelaide. We will lift up Perth, city of lights—*God speed John Glen*! We will lift up the cities of New Zealand, among them Auckland, Napier, Palmerston, Wellington and

Christchurch. We will lift up all the cities of Oceania.

We will lift up all the cities of Africa to God for deliverance, sanctification and preservation, among them Cairo, Alexandria, Tripoli, Benghazi, Algiers, Oran, Rabat, Marrakesh, Las Palmas, Santa Cruz, Dakar, Bissau, Conakry, Freetown, Monrovia, Dabou, Accra, Lomé, Bamako, Ouagadougou, Niamey, Porto-Novo, Lagos, Ft. Lamy, Bangui, Yaoundé. We will lift up Khartoum, capital of the great Sudan, and Addis Ababa, *blossoming flower* of Ethiopia much beloved of God. We will lift up Mogadishu, Nairobi, Kampala, Kigali, Bujumbura, Kinshasa, St. Isabel, Libreville Brazzaville, Luanda, Lusaka, Zomba, Dar es Salaam, Lorenzo Marques, Salisbury, Gaborone, Windhoek, Pretoria, Johannesburg, Durban, Cape Town, Tananarive.

We will lift up all the cities of North America to God for sanctification, among them Halifax, St. John, Ottawa, Quebec, Montreal, Toronto, Winnipeg, Calgary and Vancouver. Portland, Boston, New York, Philadelphia, Baltimore, Pittsburgh, Washington, Raleigh, Charleston, Atlanta, Miami, Detroit, Columbus, Louisville, Memphis, Montgomery, Mobile, Jackson, Fort Wayne, Madison, Chicago, Minneapolis, Des Moines, St. Louis, Little Rock, New Orleans, Bismarck, Sioux Falls, Omaha, Wichita, Oklahoma City, Fort Worth, Dallas, Houston, San Antonio, Missoula, Cheyenne, Denver, Santa Fe, Boise, Salt Lake City, Phoenix, Seattle, Spokane, Portland, Salem, Reno, Sacramento, San Francisco, Los Angeles, Long Beach, San Diego.

We will lift up all the cities of Central America, the Caribbean, and South America to God for sanctification, among them Mexicali, Ciudad Juarez, Hermosillo, Monterrey, Matamoros, Mazatlan, Guadalajara, Mexico City, Puebla, Acapulco de Juarez and Veracruz. Guatemala City, Belize City, San Salvador, Tegucigalpa, Managua, San Jose, Panama City, Havana, Kingston, Port-au-Prince, Santo Domingo, San Juan, Fort-de-France, Port of Spain. Caracas, Maracaibo, Bogota, Quito, Lima, Belém, Recife, Salvador Bahia, Rio De Janeiro, Sao Paulo, Porto Alegre, La Paz, Asuncion, Montevideo, Rosario, Buenos Aires, Santiago, Valparaiso. (May God deliver all the cities of Man from the devil of debt and disorder, amen!)

We will lift up all of the earth's institutions of learning to God for sanctification, from the ancient halls of Cambridge, trodden by the feet of archbishops, astronomers, poets and princes, to the humble corridors of Unidad Educativa *Narciso Fragachan*, trodden by the feet of the children of Venezuela. (May God bring all of the schools, colleges and universities of the earth into a saving knowledge of His truth!) We will lift up Oxford, Sorbonne, Dortmund, Universidad de Madrid, University of Budapest, Hebrew University, University of Haifa, Ben-Gurion University of the Negev, University of Cairo, University of Zambia, University of Pretoria, University of Tehran, Calcutta University, Delhi Institute of Technology, Bombay Institute of Technology, Moscow State University, St. Petersburg University, Beijing University, Nanjing University, Shanghai Jiao-Tong University, University of Hong Kong, Hiroshima City University, Hokkaido Tokai University, Nagoya University, University of Western Australia, Australian Catholic University, Flinder's University, Queen's College, University of Sydney, University of Queensland, Universidad Nacional de La Plata, Universidad de Buenos Aires, Universidad Federal de São Paulo, Universidad de Brasília, Universidad de Los Andes, Universidad Distrital Francisco José de Caldas, Universidad Simon Bolivar, Universidad Central de Venezuela, Universidad de Panama, Universidad Nacional de Costa Rica, University of Mexico, University of Vera Cruz.

We will lift up the institutions of learning that produced many of the Founders of America. Harvard, whose motto hath been *for Christ and the Church*. Yale, which has seen God as *the giver of all wisdom*. Princeton, Dartmouth, King's College (Columbia) and Rutgers University, all founded on faith. We will lift up Amherst, Brigham Young, Cornell, Duke, Elmhurst, Florida State, Carnegie Mellon, Johns Hopkins, Stanford, Georgetown, Iowa State, John Brown University, Layola, Massachusetts Institute of Technology, Nazareth College, Ohio Wesleyan, Pepperdine, Purdue, Morhouse College, St. Olaf College, Quincy University, St. Mary's, Texas A & M, University of California, Vanderbilt, Wheaton. (May God deliver all the universities of the world from the tentacles of the Great Lie and the snares of "moral relativism!")

We will lift up all the scientists who brought man closer to an understanding of his relationship with the universe, great thinkers who unveiled the secrets of nature, inventors who bent the forces of the cosmos to the service of Man. Where shall we begin? Thales of Miletus, Pythagoras of Samos, Zeno of Elea, Heraclitus, Hippocrates, Archimedes, Socrates, Hipparchus and Ptolemy. Al-Khwarizmi, Ibn Ishaq Al-Kindi, Al-Battani, Al-Razi, Al-Farabi, Al-Sufi, Al-Idrisi, Ibn Al-Majdi. Leonardo da Vinci, Galileo Galilee, Johannes Kepler, Isaac

Newton, James Watt, John Dalton, Michael Faraday, Alfred Russel Wallace, Charles Darwin, James Prescott Joule, A.J. Angstrom, Heinrich Hertz, Dimitri Mendeleyev, James Clerk Maxwell, Hermann von Helmholtz, Lord Kelvin, Rudolf Clausius, Ludwig Boltzmann, Albert Michelson, Edward Morley, Thomas Alva Edison, Alexander Graham Bell, J.J. Thomson, Max Planck, Robert A. Millikan, Marie and Pierre Curie, Ernest Rutheford, Louis Pasteur, Dr. Walter Reed, Max Born, Albert Einstein, Niels Bohr, Werner Heisenberg, Erwin Schrodinger, Hans Geiger, Louis de Broglie, Wolfgang Pauli, Paul Dirac, Enrico Fermi, Jonas Salk, Richard Feynman, George Gamow, Carl Sagan, John S. Bell, Freeman Dyson, Stephen Hawking, Roger Penrose, Gerald Schroeder, Richard Dawkins, Francis Crick, Ian Stewart, Brian Goodwin.

We will lift up the legacies of those who installed wings on the feet of Man—brothers Wilbur and Orville Wright, Louis Blériot, Charles Lindbergh, Amelia Earhart, Howard Hughes. We will lift up the legacies of pioneers, barnstormers, courageous mail carriers, wartime fliers, pilots, and aces. Eddie Rickenbacker, Major General Curtis LeMay, General Jimmy Doolittle, Georgia O'Keefe, Jackie Cochrane. Chuck Yeager, the first man to break the sound barrier, Randy "Duke" Cunningham, America's ace, and John Cunningham, Britain's famed test pilot.

We will lift up the legacy of Dayton, Ohio, "the city that taught the world how to fly," and all the winged creations of Man flying at the Oshkosh Air Show. Legendary Wright biplane, Curtiss Jenny, Granville brothers' Gee Bee Model "A," Tiger Moth, Gypsy Moth, Dragonfly, bright yellow Stearman crop duster, Ford Tri-motor, Lockheed Vega, DeHavilland Comet, Aeronca "K," Luscombe Silvaire, Piper J-3 Cub, Beechcraft Bonanza, Mooney Mite, Cessna 195, Dornier DO-27, DeHavilland Beaver, Hawker Hurricane, Supermarine Spitfire, P-51 Mustang, P-47 Thunderbolt, F4 Corsair, Grumman Avenger, Grumman HU-16 Albatros, Catalina Flying Boat, Boeing B-17 Flying Fortress, Consolidated B-24 Liberator, Lancaster Bomber. We will lift up the legacy of the Blue Angels of El Centro, California, superlative precision on the wing, ambassadors of the United States Air Force to the world.

We will lift up the famous workhorses of aviation. Legendary Curtis-Wright Cyclone rotary engines, powering many Allied aircraft. Rolls Royce "Merlin" engines, powering many R.A.F. fighters. Pratt & Whitney R-2000 "long range" engines, powering many young airlines. Allison T-56 engines, powering many cargo aircraft. Reliable Lycoming and Continental engines, powering many smaller civilian planes. We will lift up the legacy of Frank Whittle of Rugby, England, father of the jet turbine, designer and builder of one of the first jet engines—the "WU." We will lift up dependable jet turbines made by Pratt & Whitney, General Electric, Rolls Royce, and Daimler-Benz, powering the silver birds that transport the children of Adam at high altitudes near the speed of sound.

We will lift up the aircraft that became reliable workhorses of aviation. Legendary Douglas DC-3 and DC-4, workhorses of the Berlin airlift. Legendary Lockheed Superconstellation of Howard Hughes fame, durable P-3 Orion, and dependable Lockheed C-130 Hercules—good old "Herc," sweet bird of mercy, long range troop transport, search and rescue platform, lifeline to Antarctica, faithful firefighter, workhorse of the Israeli raid on Entebbe. We will lift up Boeing 707 and 747, hardworking and dependable workhorses of commercial aviation the world over. We will lift up Europe's dependable Airbus, and ground-breaking Concord—first supersonic commercial transport.

We will lift up the legends of general aviation—Clyde Cessna, Willy Piper, Walter Beech, William Edward Boeing, the Lockheed brothers, Geoffrey DeHavilland, Claudius Dornier, Anthony Fokker, Donald Douglas, James McDonnell, Larry Bell, Glen L. Martin. We will lift up the legacies of Juan de la Cierva and Paul Cornu, progenitors of the helicopter, and the legacy of Jack Northrop, creator of the "flying wing." We will lift up the legacy of test pilot Glen Edwards, father of Edwards Air Force Base, and we will lift up the legacy of William Powell Lear, father of the corporate Lear Jet. We will lift up the legacy of Louis-Charles Breguet, father of Air France, and Sergei Vladimirovich Ilyushin and Andrei Nikolaevich Tupolev, fathers of Soviet aviation. We will lift up the legacy of Igor Ivanovich Sikorsky, genius, humanitarian, philanthropist, inventor, entrepreneur, designer of the first four-engined passenger plane.

We will lift up the legacy of Bernt Balchen, favorite son of Norway, one of the best pilots of the 20th century, little known but amazing individual who flew Admiral Byrd across the Atlantic and over the South Pole, who set up the supply lines for air drops to the Norwegian underground during WW II, and who later assumed a major role in the creation of SAS—Scandinavian Airlines System. We will lift up the legacy of Juan Trippe, visionary entrepreneur and founder of Pan American World Airways, for 41 years the driving force of commercial aviation, (Juan Trippe's association with William Allan of Boeing revolutionized commercial passenger travel with the introduction of the Boeing 707 and later the 747 Jumbo Jet). We will lift up the legacy of Jack Frye, first President of Trans World Airlines, in whose presidency TWA's fleet grew from a handful of Tri-motors to Super Constellations and emerged as a major world airline. We will lift up the legacy of genius and entrepreneur Fredrick Smith, founder, CEO, and chief architect of Federal Express, delivering goods to the sons and daughters of Adam by air—*the world on time.*

We will lift up all the Airlines of the world from A to Z, among them Aerolineas Argentinas, Aeronaves Mexico, Air Canada, Air India, Air Jamaica, Air New Zealand, Alaska Airlines, Alitalia, Aloha Airlines, BOAC, Braniff, British Airways, China Air Lines, Continental, Delta, El Al, Eastern, Egypt Air, Evergreen International, Japan Air Lines, KLM Royal Dutch Airlines, Korean Airlines, Laker, Lufthansa, Northwest, Ozark, Piedmont, PSA, Qantas, Royal Jordanian Airlines, Sabena, SAS, Saudi Arabian Airlines, Singapore Airlines, South African Airlines, Southwest Airlines, Swissair, TWA, United, US Airways, VARIG Brazilian Airlines.

We will lift up the legacies of those who installed rockets onto the feet of Man—Hermann Oberth, Konstantin Tsiolkovsky, Robert Goddard, Wernher von Braun, Vasili Mishin, Sergei Korolev. We will lift up the legacies of Marshall Flight Center, Dryden Flight Center, Cape Kennedy, and Baikonur Cosmodrome. We will lift up the legacies of Vostok, Soyuz, Voskhod and Mir. We will lift up the legacies of Friendship 7, Mercury, Gemini and Apollo spacecrafts. We will lift up the legacies of Yuri Gagarin, Alexei Leonov, Alan Shepard, John Glenn, Valentina Tereshkova, and Sally Ride. We will lift up the legacies of flight operations chief Christopher Kraft, and Houston flight director Gene Kranz, whose motto has been *failure is not an option.* We will lift up the legacies of the astronauts who first flew to the moon—Frank Borman, Jim Lovell and Bill Anders. We will lift up the legacies of those who finally planted the feet of Man on the moon—Neil Armstrong, Edwin "buzz" Aldrin and Michael Collins.

We will lift up the legacies of all who gave their lives to enable Man to soar among the stars on eagle's wings, among them Gus Grissom, Ed White, Roger Chaffee, and Vladimir Komarov. We will lift up the legacy of the crew of the Shuttle *Challenger* : Francis Scobee, Michael Smith, Judy Resnik, Ellison Onizuka, Ronald McNair, Gregory Jarvis and Christa McAuliffe. Let us say, in the words of President Ronald Reagan:

> We will never forget them, nor the last time we saw them, this morning, as they prepared for the long journey, and waved goodbye, and slipped the surly bonds of earth to touch the Face of God.
>
> President Reagan, 28 January 1986

We will lift up the legacy of the crew of the Shuttle *Columbia* : Rick Husband, William McCool, Michael Anderson, David Brown, Kalpana Chawla, Laurel Clark and Ilan Ramon.

We will lift up the rockets of Man, blasting off into space, taking the seeds of human *complexity* into the hostile dominion of the Cosmic Constable. Redstone, Jupiter, Atlas, Titan, Pegasus, Agena, Athena, Centaur, Delta, Taurus, and the mighty Saturn V that delivered a payload of 44 tons to the moon. We will lift up Russia's mighty RD-170, Soyuz, and Proton boosters. We will lift up China's Long March, France's Ariane, Japan's H-2, India's Polar Satellite Launch Vehicle, and Israel's Shavit. We will lift up the legacy of Morton Thiokol, and the legacies of the Space Shuttles *Challenger*, *Columbia*, *Atlantis*, *Discovery*, *Endeavor*, *Enterprise* and *Pathfinder*, the roar of their engines announcing the beginning of Man's counteroffensive against the Cosmic Constable. We will lift up the legacies of the men and women of JPL (Jet Propulsion Laboratory in Pasadena), nursing Man's formative steps into the solar system and beyond with Mariner, Voyager, Galileo, Pathfinder, Cassini-Huygens, Hubble, Odyssey, Mars Rover, Deep Space 1 and Deep Space 2. We will lift up the legacy of NASA administrator Daniel S. Goldin—a*d astra per aspera* ("it is a rough road that leads to the stars!")

We will lift up the maritime and seafaring legacies of the children of Adam, from Hiram to Brendan, from Leif Eriksson to Thor Heyerdahl, from Drake and Hawkins to Halsey and Nimitz, from *Castor and Pollux* to the *USS Enterprise.* We will lift up the legacies of the ancient boat-builders of the Chao Phraya River in Thailand, creating the seaworthy Dhow that has been crossing the Indian Ocean for thousands of years. We will lift up Arab *Dhow* and Chinese *Junk*, Egyptian *Felucca* and sturdy Cape Cod *dory*, Venetian gondola and Vietnamese *sampan*. We will lift up the double-hulled ocean-crossing canoes on which Polynesian navigators populated the islands of the Pacific. We will lift up Viking Longship, Knarr, Oseberg and Gokstad. We will lift up ancient Greek vessels and Roman galleons, stately English brigantine, Portuguese caravel, tall-masted windjammer, Yankee clipper, and "dirty British coaster with a salt-caked smoke-stack," (John Masefield). We will lift up *HMS Victory*, Nelson's flagship, and the Continental sloop *Providence* of John Paul Jones' fame, founder of the United States Navy. We will lift up the legendary *USS Constitution*, "old ironsides," the sight of whose billowing sails, it is said, would bring tears of joy to the eyes of all who prized freedom. We will lift up the memories of the dear old girls of the sea, dear *HMS Titanic*, dear *HMS Britannic*, and dear *RMS Lusitania*—may they rest in peace! We will lift up the legacies of the Victory Ships, Liberty Ships, and Troop Ships that delivered vital supplies to the Allies across the treacherous Atlantic, many of them falling victim to enemy submarines—may they rest in peace!

We will lift up HMS *Queen Mary*, HMS *Queen Elizabeth*, and record-breaking *SS United States*. We will lift up *Noordam*, *Maasdam*, *Statendam*, and *Rotterdam*, pride of Holland-America Line, epitome of Dutch quality and craftsmanship. We will lift up the magnificent ships of the White Star Line, Cunard Line, Abercrombie and Kent, Norwegian Cruise Line, Princess, Royal Caribbean, and P & O Orient. We will lift up the luxurious beauties of the sea, adorned in festival apparel, taking the children of Adam to marvelous vacation spots around the world: *SS Grand Princess*, *Carnival Destiny*, *Monarch of the Seas*, *SS Hanseatic*, *Crystal Symphony*, *Seabourn Legend*, *SS Europa*, *Royal Viking Sun*…

We will lift up the legacy of Captain William Matson and the ships of the Matson Navigation Company—*Emma Claudina*, *Wilhelmina*, *Manoa*, *Monterey*, *Mariposa*, *Lureline* and *Matsonia*. We will lift up the legacy of Aristotle Onassis and the ships that bore his name. We will lift up the legacy of Arnold Peter Moller, who with his father Captain Peter Maersk Moller founded the Maersk Steamship Company in 1904, (Maersk was engaged in Allied service under British/US flags in WW II). We will lift up the titans of the Maersk Line, giant container ships that deliver goods to the sons and daughters of Adam across great oceans: *Svendborg Maersk*, *Emma Maersk*, *Evelyn Maersk*, *Odense Maersk*, *Olga Maersk*, *Regina Maersk*, *Kate Maersk*, *Kirsten Maersk* and *Susan Maersk*. We will lift up the merchant vessels *Bremen*, *Astra II*, and *Columbus*, of the legendary shipping line of Hapag Lloyd.

On earth's seven seas we will lift up the ships of the Hanjin Shipping Company of Seoul, Korea. We will lift up the many Japanese shipping lines that deliver goods to the sons and daughters of Adam throughout the Pacific Rim, among them Kawasaki Kisen Kaisha and Nippon Yusen Kaisha. We will lift up the hard-working ships of Nippon Yusen Kaisha Line, among them *Jinsei Maru*, *Orion Diamond*, *Venus Diamond*, *Aquarius Leader*, and *Century Leader*.

We will lift up the legacies of "they that go down to the sea in ships, all they that do business in great waters," (Psalm 107:23). We will lift up the research vessels of the world, among them vessels of Woods Hole Oceanographic Institution and Scripps Institute of Oceanography, watchdogs of earth's *complexity*, their fingers on the pulses of the earth's oceans, their instruments measuring the entropy of blue planet. We will lift up *Calypso*, *Alcyon*, and *Calypso II* of Cousteau fame. We will lift up Coast Guard vessels, ice breakers, barges, tugs and workboats...

We will lift up the legacies of the fishermen who harvest the bounty of the sea for the table of Man. We will lift up the legacy of Gloucester Fishermen, thousands of whom have perished in gales on the Grand Banks and waters beyond, since the early 1600's. We will lift up all the names inscribed on the Wall of Remembrance at the Fisherman's Memorial in Gloucester, Massachusetts. The sea is a treacherous mistress indeed, but God hears the prayers of the fathers, mothers, wives, sons and daughters of commercial fishermen:

Eternal Father, strong to save,
whose arm hath bound the restless wave...
O hear us when we cry to thee,
for those in peril on the sea.
(William Whiting)

We will lift up the names of the fishing vessels of Man. Here are some of them: F/V *Sea Roamer*, hailing port Hyannis, Captain Arthur Davey at the helm. F/V *Holly* & *Michael*, hailing port Sandwich, Captain Marc Palombo at the helm. F/V *First Light*, hailing port Point Judith, Captain Michael Monteforte at the helm. F/V *Captain Gorman III*, hailing port Panama City, Captain Bobby Lucas at the helm. F/V *Ashly G*, hailing port Panama City, Captain Dennis Crosby at the helm. F/V *Arizona*, hailing port Galveston, Captain G.T. Bodiford at the helm (several generations of Bodifords have been fishing the Gulf of Mexico). F/V *Majestic*, hailing port Seattle, Captain Paul Clampitt at the helm. F/V *Kella Lee*, hailing port Comox, Captain George W. Newson at the helm. F/V *Arch Angel*, hailing port Juneau, Captain Clark B. Fay at the helm. We will lift up all the fishing vessels moored in various ports of the world, among them the ones moored in the harbor of Santa Barbara—the fishing vessels *Teresa Ann*, *New Hazard*, *Sashay*, *Donna*, *Samson*, *"C,"* *Alamo*, *Cecelia*, *Calogera*, *Kay-D*, *Mary-K*, *Princess Rachel*, *Vincent K*, *Spaniard*, *Miss Devin*, *Gloria Marie*, *Pieface*, *Victoria*, *Sal-C*, *Sea Brothers*, and the fishing vessel *Tytan* of the fishing firm of Burke & Sons.

We will lift up all the seagoing creations of Man, glistening sloops, cutters, ketches, schooners and yawls, sailing across vast oceans under mast, canvas, and grim determination, now beating against the gale with storm jib and trysail, now gliding before fair winds and following seas under spinnaker and pole. We will lift up the legacies of the great sailors of the world—John Claus Voss, Joshua Slocum, Vito Dumas, John "Hurricane" Guzzwell, Miles and Beryl Smeeton, Francis Chichester, Bernard Moitessier, Robin Knox Johnston, Eric and Susan Hiscock, Lin and Larry Pardey, Peter Blake, Florence Arthaud, Isabelle Autissier, Giovanni Soldini, Mike Golding, Debbie Druan. We will lift up the legacies of naval architects, among them Nathaniel Herreshoff, Richard Newick, Thomas Colvin, Carl Alberg, John Alden, Sparkman and Stephens, Robert Harris, Bill Crealock, Robert Perry, Nolan Atkins, Ted Hood, Bill Tripp, Ted Irwin, Bill Lapworth, Lyle Hess, Ted Brewer, Frank Parrish, J.J. Taylor. We will lift up the legacies of the great Multihull designers of the world, among them Arthur Piver, Norman Cross, Ed Horstman, Jim Brown, Walter Greene, Roger Simpson, Ian Farrier, Prout Brothers, Lock Crowther, James Wharram, Derek Kelsall.

We will lift up the legacies of the manufacturers of the world who bend steel, piston, and horsepower to the service of Man. We will lift up the legacy of George Stephenson, manufacturer of early steam engines and locomotives. We will lift up the legacies of all the railroads and trains of the world, from Rocket and Mallard to California Zephyr and Bullet Train, from Atchison, Topeka and Santa Fe to Burlington, Union Pacific and Orient Express. We will lift up the legacies of Bucyrus Erie and Ruston Bucyrus, manufacturers of the largest earth-moving machines on the planet—it took seventy-seven 90-ton Bucyrus steam shovels to excavate the Panama Canal. We will lift up the legacies of Benjamin Holt and Daniel Best, founders of Caterpillar Tractor Co., earth movers for the world. We will lift up the legacies of Robert and Cyrus McCormick, founders of the International Harvester Company, makers of farm implements, tractors, reapers, combines and threshing machines that plow, sow, and harvest the God-given bounty of the earth. We will lift up the legacy of American blacksmith and plow maker John Deere, founder of John Deere and Company, 5th oldest company in the United States, manufacturing tractors, harvesters, combines and agricultural equipment for farmers throughout the world. We will lift up the legacies of Messrs. Allis and Chalmers, producing the trusty Allis-Chalmers tractors that have benefited farmers the world over.

We will lift up the legacy of Henry Ford and his Highland Park Model T factory—"birth place of 20th century industry." We will lift up the legacy of William C. Durant, the carriage maker of Flint who went on to organize Buick, General Motors, and Chevrolet. We will lift up the legacies of Walter Chrysler, Lee Iacocca, and Bob Lutz, producing affordable and dependable transportation for the whole world. We will lift up the legacies of Soichiro Honda and Kiichiro Toyoda, founders of Honda and Toyota motors respectively. We will lift up all the automobile manufacturers of the world from A to Z, from Audi and Aston Martin to Volkswagen and Volvo. (Today the internal combustion engine, tomorrow fuel cells, superconductors, and private aerospace vehicles.)

We will lift up legacy of superlative speed, the legacies of Ferdinand Porsche and *Il Commandatore* Enzo Ferrari, Colin Chapman and Roy Lund. We will lift up the legends of Grand Prix, among them Juan Manuel Fangio, pride of Maserati, Tazio Nuvolari, pride of Alfa Romeo, and Jimmy Clark, pride of Lotus. We will lift up the memories of racing legends Stirling Moss, Graham Hill, Mike Hailwood, John Surtees, Richie Ginther, Dan Gurney, Mario Andretti—all them that have tamed the demons of horsepower.

We will lift up the legacies of the truckers of the world who deliver produce and goods to warehouses, stores and businesses throughout the earth, driving venerable workhorses made by Mack Truck, Peterbilt, Kenworth, Freightliner, International, Navistar, Western Star, GMC, Ford Truck, White, Sterling, Mercedes-Benz, Volvo, Isuzu, Mitsubishi.

We will lift up the legacies of the motorcycle manufacturers of the world, creators of marvelous machines that invest the sons and daughters of Adam with the powers of winged creatures on winding country roads. We will lift up legendary bikes, among them Ariel Square Four, BMW Boxer, Triumph Trident, Norton Commando, Ducati Desmo, Bultaco Metralla, Honda Hawk and Kawasaki Ninja. We will lift up the legacies of Messrs. William Harley and Arthur Davidson, founding fathers of Harley-Davidson—genuine, authentic, original American creation. We will lift up all the putt-putting bikes that transport the sons and daughters of Adam economically and efficiently across the crowded cities of the earth—Hondas, Yamahas, Kawasakis, Suzukis, Vespas, Lambrettas, Capris…

We will lift up the legacies of the millers that clothe the body of Man with cotton, worsted wool, fine knits, cashmere, polyester and synthetics fabrics, and who furnish the house of Man with lush carpets, elegant curtains and upholstery fabrics of every description. We will lift up the legacies of all the mills of the world, among them Evansville Mills, Guilford Mills, Mount Vernon Mills, and Burlington Industries. We will lift up the legacy of I. Merritt Singer, manufacturer of dependable sewing machines since 1853. We will lift up the legacies all the clothiers and tailors of the world, from Bavarian immigrant Levi Strauss to the world famous clothiers of Biela, Italy. We will lift up the legacy of Johann Birkenstock, fitting comfortable shoes to the feet of Man since 1774.

We will lift up the legacies of the manufacturers of home appliances—efficient and reliable refrigerators, ranges, ovens, washers, and driers from Amana, Whirlpool, GE, Kenmore, Maytag and Hoover. We will lift up the legacies of all the toolmakers of the world—Stanley, Black & Decker, Rigid and Craftsman. We will lift up the legacy of Aaron Montgomery Ward, whose motto was "satisfaction guaranteed," and we will lift up the legacies of Messrs. Richard Sears and Alvah Roebuck, providing the sons and daughters of Adam with reliable appliances, goods and services since 1890. We will lift up the legacies of all the department stores of the world, from Harrods of London in Knightsbridge to the friendly Radio Shack on Main Street USA.

We will lift up the legacy of Gerard Philips, producing everything from incandescent lamps and radio tubes at the turn of the century, to laser equipment, optical discs, telecommunications systems and the array of medical equipment that has been installed on the

International Space Station now orbiting the earth. We will lift up the legacies of Werner Siemens and Johann Georg Halske, producers of electrical, electronic and diagnostic equipment for the world. We will lift up the legacy of David Sarnoff and the Radio Corporation of America—RCA. We will lift up the legacies of Yataro Iwasaki, founder of Mitsubishi Industries, and Konosuke Matsushita, founder of Matsushita Electric. We will lift up the legacies of Yuma Shiraishi and Shizuo Takano, progenitors of the VHS video system that made the Japan Victor Company (JVC) a household name in America and throughout the world. We will lift up the legacies of Akio Morita and Masaru Ibuka, founders of Sony, and the legacies of Goro and Saburo Uchida, founders of Canon, creators of optics, cameras, camcorders and a host of precision tools and instruments. We will lift up the legacies of Carl Zeiss, Ernst Abbe, and Otto Schott, pioneers who made possible the modern era of microscopes, precision optics, and the host of instruments now used in hospitals, research labs and universities.

We will lift up Man's formative steps into the age of *information* and *complexity*. We will lift up the pioneering work of Charles Babbage and Alan Turing. We will lift up the legacies of Steve Jobs, Steve Wozniak, and Bill Gates. We will lift up the legacies of Microsoft and Big Blue, Apple and Intel Corporation. We will lift up the legacies of Xerox Park, Stanford University Network, and Silicon Valley. We will lift up the legacies of Bill Joy, Andrew Grove, Scott McNealy, Tim Berners-Lee, Gordon Moor, Bob Metcalfe, Peter Norton, Marc Andreessen, Jim Clark, Steve Case, Larry Ellison, James Gosling, Bill Hewlett and David Packard.

We will lift up the legacy of the genius, entrepreneur and philanthropist George Eastman, founder of Eastman Kodak. We will lift up all the cameras that have defied the Cosmic Constable, denied entropy and suspended time to capture the sons and daughters of Adam on film, from the legendary Hasselblad that Ansel Adams used to capture the essence of the Pueblo Indians to the Agfa with which grandpa took your picture on your fifth birthday—"say cheese!"

We will lift up the golden age of Hollywood, the creative legacies of Cecil B. DeMille, D.W. Griffith, Harry and Jack Warner, Louis B. Mayer, Samuel Goldwyn, Carl Laemmle, Harry Cohn, Jesse Lasky, Louis Zelnick, Darryl Zanuck, David O. Selznick, William Fox, Adolph Zukor, Hal B. Wallace, Charlie Chaplin, Alfred Hitchcock. We will lift up the creative legacies of Sergei Eisenstein, Stanley

Kubrik, David Lean, Stanley Kramer, Frank Capra, Ingmar Bergman, Vittorio De Sica, Carlo Ponti, Akira Kurosawa, Steven Spielberg, George Lucas. We will lift up legendary names of cinema—RKO, Paramount, Republic, 20th Century Fox, MGM, Columbia, Disney, Rankin Bass, British Pathe, Pinetree Studios, Dreamworks. We will lift up all the movies that have inspired and entertained the sons and daughters of Adam, from Cecil B. DeMille's *Ten Commandments* and D.W. Griffith's *Birth Of A Nation* to Steven Spielberg's *Indiana Jones* and George Lucas' *Star Wars*. We will lift up *Gone With The Wind* and *Mutiny On The Bounty*, *High Noon* and *Gunfight At OK Corall*, *Quo Vadis* and *Ben Hur*, *From Here To Eternity* and *The King And I*, *North By Northwest* and *The Third Man*, *Casablanca* and *The Maltese Falcon*, *Twelve O' Clock High* and *The Longest Day*, Gordon Pasha of *Khartoum*, and *Lawrence of Arabia*, *Ran* and *The Seven Samurai*, *Cyrano de Bergerac*, *The Bicycle Thief* and *Cinema Paradiso*, *The Hiding Place* and *Schindler's List*...

We will lift up the imaginative and creative inspiration of Gene Roddenberry, "to boldly go where no man has gone before," transporting us to undiscovered galaxies aboard the starship *Enterprise*. Legends of *Star Trek*, *Deep Space Nine*, and *Voyager*. Fascinating tales about James Tiberius Kirk and science officer Spock. Intriguing tales about insolent Klingons, treacherous Romulans, plaintive Bajorans, arrogant Cardassians and insufferable Ferengi. Tales about the holo-deck and the Klingon Home World, Ensign Crusher and Commander Data, Captain Picard and Ambassador Sarek of Vulcan.

We will lift up the legacies of all the great actors and actresses of world, from Douglas Fairbanks Jr. to Harrison Ford, from John Huston, "the voice of God," to James Earl Jones, the voice of Darth Vader, from Mary Pickford to Julie Andrews, from Deborah Kerr to Jennifer O'Neill. We will lift up the memories of Cagney and Lacey, Bogey and Bacall, Spencer Tracy and Katharine Hepburn, Richard Burton and Elizabeth Taylor, Cary Grant and Grace Kelly, Charles Boyer and Ingrid Bergman, Fred Astair and Ginger Rogers, Maurice Chevalier and Leslie Caron, Marcello Mastroianni and Sophia Loren.

We will lift up the legacies of all the distinguished actors and actresses that have graced the silver screen—Charlton Heston, Clark Gable, Jack Palance, Marlene Dietrich, Gary Cooper, James Stewart, Gregory Peck, Lawrence Olivier, Robert Taylor, Peter Ustinov, Yul Bryner, Kirk Douglas, Robert Mitchum, Paul Newman, Sidney

Poitier, Alec Guinness, Sam Jafee, Orson Wells, John Wayne, Ava Gardner, Julie Harris, Jean Simmons, Max von Sydow, Anthony Quinn, Marlon Brando, Omar Shariff, José Ferrer, Raul Julia, Antonio Aguilar, Pedro Infante, donna Maria Felix, donna Sarrah Garcia, Ricardo Montalban, Edward James Olmos.

We will lift up the legacy of the Ferret and the Rake—the legacies of the great journalists who ferreted out the truth and raked in the muck, comforting the afflicted and afflicting the comfortable, serving as the eyes of the blind, the ears of the deaf and the liberty of the oppressed. We will lift up the legacy of Samuel Morse, inventor of the telegraph, and the legacy of Paul Julius Reuter, who first used it to deliver news. We will lift up the legacies of those who formed Associated Press. We will lift up the legacies of the distinguished men and women of the news media, among them Edward R. Murrow, Fred Friendly, Walter Cronkite, Howard K. Smith, Edwin Newman, George Will and Bernard Kalb. The legacies of Chet Huntley and David Brinkley, Eric Sevareid, John Chancellor, Roger Mudd, Peter Jennings, Tom Brokaw, Dan Rather, Clete Roberts, Jess Marlow, Sam Donaldson, Britt Hume, Rush Limbaugh, Robin McNeil, Jim Lehrer, Charlie Rose, Bill Moyers, Helen Thomas, Andrea Mitchell, Diane Sawyer, Doris Kearns Goodwin, Carole Simpson, Cokie Roberts. We will lift up the standards of excellence established by great investigative journalists—the legacies of Don Hewit, Mike Wallace, and Lowell Bergman.

We will lift up all that the sons and daughters of Adam call sport and competition, from the sleds of the Iditarod to the kayaks of the Olympics. We will lift up team sports, track and field, swimming, skiing, skating, racing, sailing and everything in between. Where shall we begin? We will lift up the creation of Abner Doubleday and Alexander Cartwright, most genuine, authentic and original of American pastimes—*baseball*. We will lift up the legacies of the American fields of dreams: Fenway Park, Wrigley Field, Comiskey Park, Dodger Stadium, and the house that Ruth built—Yankee Stadium. We will lift up the legacies of Christy Mathewson, Honus Wagner "the flying Dutchman," fighting John J. McGraw, Mickey Mantle, Connie Mack, Joe DiMaggio "the Yankee Clipper," Hank Aaron, Nolan Ryan, Yogi Berra, Johnny Bench, Grover Alexander, Jackie Robinson, Walter Johnson "the big train," Tyrus Raymond Cobb "the Georgia peach," Casey Stengel and Henry Louis Gehrig, forever the gentleman of baseball.

We will lift up all the baseball greats from Ted Williams, Roger Maris, Pete Rose, Sandy Koufax and the great Roberto Clemente, to Mark McGwire and Sammy Sosa. We will lift up the legacy of Mr. Baseball himself, George Herman "Babe" Ruth. What shall we say about Babe Ruth, this icon of American baseball? The year is 1929 and we are at the bottom of the eighth inning at Yankee Stadium, the Washington Senators and the NY Yankees tied 2-2. A great hush descends over the stadium as the Bambino steps up to the plate, the smell of hot-dogs permeating the air. Here comes the pitch by Tom Zachary, followed by the crack of the bat, and the roar of the crowd. And there goes the ball... going... going... right out of the ball park.

We will lift up the legacy of Walter Camp, father of American Football. We will lift up the legacy of coach Vince Lombardi, inspiration and driving force of the legendary Greenbay Packers, leading them to five NFL Championships and two Super Bowls. We will lift up the teams of the National Football League—Arizona Cardinals, Atlanta Falcons, Baltimore Ravens, Buffalo Bills, Carolina Panthers, Chicago Bears, Cincinnati Bengals, Cleveland Browns, Dallas Cowboys, Denver Broncos, Detroit Lions, Jacksonville Jaguars, Green Bay Packers, Houston Texans, Indianapolis Colts, Kansas City Chiefs, Miami Dolphins, Minnesota Vikings, New York Giants, New England Patriots, New Orleans Saints, New York Jets, Oakland Raiders, Philadelphia Eagles, Pittsburgh Steelers, San Diego Chargers, San Francisco 49ers, Seattle Seahawks, St. Louis Rams, Tampa Bay Buccaneers, Tennessee Titans, Washington Redskins.

We will lift up the legendary gunslingers and matadors of the NFL. John Elway, the man who never knew the meaning of the word "quit," Roman Gabriel, Frank Ryan, Bert Jones, Charlie Conerly, John Brodie, Ken Stabler, Jack Kemp, Daryle Lamonica, John Hadl, George Blanda, Joe Namath. We will lift up the legacies of the royal quarterbacks who perfected the art of the passing game—Arnie Herber, Ace Parker, Bob Waterfield, Norm Van Brocklin, Bobby Layne, Bart Starr, Sammy Baugh—"slinging Sammy." We will lift up the legacy of Doug Williams, Joe Theismann, and Jim Plunkett—the Heisman Trophy winner who led the Oakland Raiders to a pair of Super Bowl triumphs. We will lift up the legacy of Phil Simms, who led the Giants to their first title in 30 years.

We will lift up the legacy of champion Steve Young, one of the greatest football players of all time, scoring six touch downs with deadly accuracy at the XXIX Super Bowl. We will lift up the legacies of quarterbacks Steve Grogan, Joe Ferguson, Jim Hart, Ken Anderson, Dave Krieg, and Boomer Esiason. We will lift up the legacy of Don Meredith—the driving force and inspiration of a Cowboys team that twice challenged the might of the Greenbay Packers in the NFL Championship. We will lift up the legacies of Warren Moon, Dan Fouts, Sonny Jurgensen, and Fran Tarkenton. We will lift up Y.A. Tittle's gallant quest for excellence, documented by his daughter Dianne Tittle de Laet. We will lift up the legacies of Bob Griese, Troy Aikman, and the legendary Otto Graham—the quarterback who led the Cleveland Browns to ten consecutive title games. We will lift up the legacy of Brett Favre, and the legacy of Roger Staubach—the NFL gunslinger who guided the Dallas Cowboys to a pair of Super Bowl titles. We will lift up the legacy of the invincible Terry Bradshaw, blasting the Pittsburgh Steelers to a 4th Super Bowl victory. We will lift up the legacies of Joe Kelly and son Jim Kelly, Dan Marino Sr. and Dan Marino Jr..

We will lift up the legacy of Pittsburgh native Johnny Unitas, legend of American football who led the Baltimore Colts to two world championships. We will lift up the legacy, courage, and resilience of another favorite son of Pittsburgh, perhaps the greatest gunslinger of the NFL, lightning fast on the draw and deadly with the aim, the living legend and inspiration that we have come to know as Joe Montana.

We will lift up the legacy of Eton College and the "Cambridge rules" that followed, creating the world sport of *football soccer*. We will lift up the legacies of the great soccer stadiums of the world, among them Old Trafford, Manchester, Wembley, Nou Camp, Barcelona, Azteca, Mexico City, Maracanã, and Rio De Janeiro. We will lift up legends of world soccer, among them Roberto Baggio, Franco Baresi, Franz Beckenbauer, David Beckham, Johan Cruyff, Alfredo Di Stefano, Eusebio, Garrincha, Ronaldo, Bebeto, Romario, Taffarel, Pagliuca, Oliver Kahn, Ruud Gullit, Diego Maradona, Stanley Matthews, Michel Platini, Marco Van Basten, Zico, and Zidane.

We will lift up the legacy of Brazil's invincible Edson Arantes do Nascimento, also known as *Pelé*. And what shall we say about Pelé, this living legend of football soccer? Shall we say, "Maracanã Stadium is filled to capacity… ?" Shall we say, "Pelé is running with the ball… he is driving towards the goal… ?" Shall we say, "aquí viene el disparo…?" Nay, we shall say, in the words of the Guyanan poet Grace Nichols:

Pelé kicked in his mother's belly!
And the world shouted:
Goooooooooooooooooooooooooooooal![1]

We will lift up the names of the players of the world-renowned Brazilian team of *Santos*, World Cup champions, beloved of God and coached by Luiz Felipe Scolari. Here are their names: Marcos, Edmilson, Lucio, Roque Jr., Cafu, Kleberson, Gilberto, Carlos, Ronaldino, Rivaldo, Ronaldo, Denilson, Paulista. We will lift up the legacies of all the great soccer teams of the world, among them AS Roma, Parma, Juventus, Inter Milan, AC Milan, Real Madrid, Atletico Madrid, FC Barcelona, Borussia Dortmund, Bayern Munich, Olympique Marseille, Olympic Lyon, Arsenal, Manchester United, Sheffield Wednesday, Nottingham Forest, Leeds United, Aston Villa, Crystal Palace, West Bromwich Albion, Liverpool, Sunderland, Newcastle United, America, Atlas, Cruz Azul, Chivas de Guadalajara, Leon, Morelia, Nexaca, Pumas, Tigres, Rosario Central, Union, Huracan, Lanus, River Plate… and last but not least, the young Leopards of Zanzibar—scoring "A" for effort.

We will lift up the legacies of great athletes, champions and thoroughbreds from among the sons and daughters of Adam. We will lift up the legacies of Jim McKay, Roone Arledge and Bud Greenspan—"the thrill of victory, and the agony of defeat." The four minute mile, the twenty-foot pole vault, gruelling triathlon and ephemeral 100-meter dash. We will lift up the legacies of baron Pierre de Coubertin and Avery Brundage, standards of excellence and depths of commitment associated with the quadrennial convention of the youth of the world at the Games of the Olympiad. We will lift up the hosts of the Summer Games (since 1948): London, Helsinki, Melbourne, Rome, Tokyo, Mexico City, Munich, Montreal, Moscow, Los Angeles, Seoul, Barcelona, Atlanta, Sydney. We will lift up the hosts of the Winter Games (since 1948): St. Moritz, Oslo, Cortina D'Ampezzo, Squaw Valley, Innsbruck, Grenoble, Sapporo, Lake Placid, Sarajevo, Calgary, Albertville, Lillehammer, Nagano, Salt Lake City.

We will lift up the memory of native American athlete Jim Thorpe, and the memory of black American athlete Jesse Owens, the poor sharecropper's son who put the best of Hitler's idols to shame. We will lift up all the legends of the Olympiad, among them Hannes

Kolehmainen, "the flying Finn," Johnny Weissmuller America's swimming hero, the incomparable Sonja Henie, the legendary Paavo Nurmi, the amazing Fanny Blankers-Koen, housewife and Dutch mother who won four gold medals in track and field in London in 1948. From the former Soviet Union, the legendary Alexander Medved, and mighty Vasily Alexeyev, "the strongest man in the world," (the first to lift 500 lbs.). Roger Bannister with the first 4-minute mile, Bill Toomey decathlon legend, Emil Zapotek of Czechoslovakia, Mustafa Dagistanli of Turkey, America's Bruce Jenner, Cuba's Teofilo Stevenson. Jack Kelly, the world's finest oarsman, daughter Grace Kelly cheering him on. Legendary African runners Abebe Bikila of Ethiopia, and Hicham El Guerrouj of Morocco. Kenya's hero Kip Keino, gold medal winner, local policeman, loving husband and father, guardian and caretaker of hundreds of Kenyan and Ugandan orphans and homeless children.

On Olympic track and field we will lift up all the sprinters, runners, jumpers, throwers and pole vaulters vying with time and entropy to push the envelope and break existing records. The great Eric Liddell and Sebastian Coe of Great Britain. Betty Robinson, streaking to victory in the 100-meter dash in Amsterdam in 1928, Gale Devers stealing the Gold at Barcelona in 1992. The great Carl Lewis and Edwin Moses of the United States, along with legendary sisters-in-law Florence Griffith Joyner and Jackie Joyner-Kersee. In the 400 meter track event, Australia's Kathy Freeman, "our Kathy," streaking to victory at the 2000 Sydney Games.

In the Olympic pool, America's gold medal winners Don Schollander, Matt Biondi, Mark Spitz, Lenny Krayzelburg, and Misty Hyman. Australia's Ian "the torpedo" Thorpe, Russia's legendary Alexander Popov, "the Russian rocket," the Netherland's Pieter van den Hoogenband, "the flying Dutchman," and South Africa's Terence Parkin. On the Olympic diving boards, legendary Klaus Dibiasi, Greg Louganis, Laura Wilkinson, Xiong Ni, Mark Ruiz, Fernando Platas.

On the parallel bars, uneven bars, horse, balance beam, and dance floor, Romania's legendary Nadia Comaneci, posting a perfect score (seven 10's) in Montreal. From Nadia's original home town of Deva, Romania, a gaggle of little girls vying for Gold with the more seasoned gymnasts of the world. From Czechoslovakia, gold medal gymnast and heroine Vera Caslavska. From America, champion Mary Lou Retton, catapulting to international fame at the 1984 Games in

Los Angeles. From Russia the legendary Aleksei Nemov, from China, gold medal gymnast Li Xiaopeng. From Japan, the great Naoya Tsukahara on the parallel bars, father Mitsuo watching anxiously.

On the Olympic basketball court the American dream team of Patrick Ewing, Karl Malone, Charles Barkley, Michael Jordan, Magic Johnson, Larry Bird, Clyde Drexler, Chris Mullin, Scottie Pippen, David Robinson, John Stockton and Christian Laettner…

On Olympic ice and performing the difficult jump called *axel* (named after the Norwegian skater Axel Paulsen), legendary figure skaters Irina Rodnina and Aleksandr Zaitsev, stealing Olympic Gold in the pairs competition at Lake Placid. Performing superlative manoeuvres, America's Brian Boitano, stealing the Gold at Calgary. Performing superlative axels and double-axles, the stars of Olympic ice—Peggy Fleming, Beatrix Schuba, Dorothy Hammil, Katarina Witt, Iksana Baiul, Nancy Kerrigan, Tara Lipinski. Excelling on and off the ice, America's favorite daughter Kristi Yamaguchi, flying with wings on her skates, inspiring the youth of the world to dare to pursue the paths of excellence with her Always Dream Foundation. On the speed-skating ring, Eric Heiden, "superlative speed on ice," and Bonnie Blair, "wonder woman on skates."

In the ice stadium we will lift up the legacy of the U.S. Olympic Hockey Team coached by Herb Brooks and led by captain Mike Eruzione, stealing Olympic Gold at Lake Placid—"one of the greatest upsets in the history of sports!" On the Olympic ski slopes we will lift up the legacies of France's legendary Jean-Claude Killy, stealing the Gold in the Alpine Downhill at Grenoble, and Austria's legendary Franz Klammer, stealing it at Innsbruck. On the 70-meter ski jump, Japan's hero Yukio Kasaya, flying like a bird to steal the Gold at Sapporo.

So shall we lift up all the sons and daughters of Adam who have striven for excellence, endured hardship, overcome the obstacles of life, achieved great things, reached for the stars, and pressed towards the mark for the prize of the high calling of God. Have we provided an exhaustive list of their names and accomplishments in this book? By no means! We have only provided meager and random samplings. There are so many great athletes, so many great sportsmen, so many great journalists, so many great actors, so many great entrepreneurs, so many great industrialists, so many great architects, so many great scientists, so many great poets, so many great authors, so many great musicians, so many great leaders, so many great names, so many great legacies, so many great accomplishments, so many great works, so many great disciplines, so many great pursuits, so many great professions, so many great pastimes, so many great institutions, so many great buildings, so many great cities, so many great places, so many marvels in the world, so many wonders on earth, so many living Edens, so many species, so many oceans, so many rivers, so many hills, so many mountains, so many valleys, so many forests, so many scenic wonders—so many that if they should be mentioned every one, I suppose even the world itself could not contain the books that should be written.

Now at this point some religious windbag will no doubt complain and say: "You are mad! You have gloried in the things of the world! You have boasted of sinners! You have boasted of infidels, foreign leaders, pagans, capitalists, industrialists, politicians, members of the secular media, rock and roll artists, and even communist astronauts! Why have you not boasted of the great ones of the Church? Why have you not mentioned the Reverend Billy Graham, for example, or Mother Teresa?" What shall we say then, brethren? Are them that are whole in need of physicians? And what saith the Great Physician concerning this plaintive world? This is what he says:

> For God so loved *THE WORLD*, that He gave His only begotten Son, that whosoever believe in him should not perish, but have everlasting life. For God sent not His Son into the world to condemn the world, but that the world through him might be saved.
>
> (John 3:16-17, emphasis added)

What saith *Yeshua* concerning any that may have lost their way and strayed from the Truth? This is what he says:

> What do you think? If a man has a hundred sheep, and one of them has gone astray, does he not leave the ninety nine and go into the mountains to find the one that has gone astray? And if so be that he find it, truly I say to you, he rejoices more for that sheep, than for the ninety and nine which did not go astray.
>
> (Matthew 18:12-13)

Does God plan on giving up on the multitude millions that have lost their way and gone astray? Did He bring them into a world such as this to abandon them to the rudiments of the perishable universe? Has the Potter indeed decided to toss to hell the luckless pots that He marred in the making? Has He made up His mind to invite only those who consider themselves "righteous?" If any would think themselves "righteous," they would do well to remember the parable of the Marriage Feast:

> Then said the king to his servants, "the wedding feast is ready, but them that were invited are undeserving. Go, therefore, into the highways, byways and streets of the city and compel any and all that you come across to come to the marriage feast, so that my house may be filled." So his servants went out into the highways and streets, and gathered together all, as many as they found, both bad and good. And the wedding was furnished with guests.
> (Matthew 22: 8-10)

Now the spirit of religion will argue and say: "You are mad! It is the world that is unworthy of the Kingdom of God! This world has not earned enough merits to enter into the Kingdom of God!"

What shall we say then, brethren? Who is "worthy," and who has earned enough "merit?" Are men worthy because they have earned enough merit in the sight of God? If any would think themselves "worthy," they would do well to remember the admonition of the Holy Spirit:

> By grace are you saved through faith, which also is a gift of God and not something that you earned through your own merit. For this Salvation is the free gift of God, and not a reward for any good that you yourselves have done, nor anything that you yourselves can take credit for. For we are His workmanship, and not our own, fashioned in Christ Jesus to do His good works according to the way that was prepared of God from the foundation of the world.
> (Ephesians 2: 8-10)

Does the salvation of God require any addition on the part of man? Are they that are saved, saved because they have performed the necessary deeds and earned enough "merit points?" What then? Was the sacrifice of *Yeshua* on the Cross insufficient to redeem the whole world, requiring that men add something to it by way of their own "merit" and "righteousness?" What shall we say then, brethren? That the price paid at Calvary was insufficient? That the price paid by *Yeshua* fell short of the sum, requiring that men should add their own two cents worth in order to be saved?

The *faith* that we boast of was imputed of Christ, and the *righteousness* that we boast of is also God's. Therefore let us not place "merit-meters" between the world and the Kingdom of God, as though to boast of our own "score." Granted that "many are called, but few chosen," (Matthew 20:16), but He that chooseth is God, not man. God will choose. God will judge. God will separate the wheat from the chaff. God will punish and reward accordingly. God will do all these things, for He is God. Let us therefore leave the judgment of the world in His capable hands.

If we have been "boasting" of the accomplishments of men in this Benediction, we have not done so beyond proper limit, but within the limits permitted by God, that we may encourage and inspire all men, at a time when the universe itself would seem to be putting them down. We have been presenting all the good things of the world to God, that He may preserve and protect them, as only He can. We have been invoking the Power of the Holy Spirit to wrest the things of the world out of the hands of the "Cosmic Constable" and place them into the capable hands of God. And this is no sin, for Scripture itself says:

לַיהֹוָה הָאָרֶץ וּמְלוֹאָהּ תֵּבֵל וְיֹשְׁבֵי בָהּ

The earth is the LORD's and the fullness thereof,
the world, and they that inhabit it.
(Psalm 24:1)

But let it be known that the whole of this fullness, this *Complexity*, this birthright, this priceless legacy, this marvelous playground, this garden of delight, this cornucopia, this plethora, this living pageant, this exuberant multiplicity, this veritable Eden is now in jeopardy of reduction by the principality that we have been calling "Cosmic Constable." Let it be known that the Constable has now placed the whole of our human *Complexity* in his cross-hairs, intending to return it to the order of dust. What then? What shall we do? Roll over and play dead? Let him have his way? Shall we take this birthright, this cornucopia, this legacy, this history, this labor, this priceless wealth, this *Complexity*, this burden born by our fathers, this difficult and uphill climb of the centuries, all our accomplishments, all our hopes and aspirations, put them all on a silver platter and surrender them to the Constable in exchange for two cents worth of cosmic affirmation and evil pleasure? (Oh, sorry trade!)

That which is now in jeopardy of reduction is everything that we have fought for, struggled for, worked for, hoped for and striven towards—everything that we embody and stand for as human beings. The question that we would now put to all the sons and daughters of Adam is this: how much ground are you willing to concede to the devil in terms of a postmodern default? How much in terms of spiritual and material Liberty? How much in terms of righteousness and morality? How much in terms of life and property? How much in terms of health and prosperity? How much in terms of safety and security? How much in terms of futurity and posterity?

At the dawn of the Millennium we stand at the brink of a vast new era. Limitless objectives and transcendent horizons are now within reach, the magnitude of which makes our spines tingle with anticipation. An entire galaxy lies open for exploration, and we are persuaded that God would have us take possession of this New Canaan. For He did not bring us through the difficult centuries to suddenly abandon us on the brink of the Millennium. Assuredly God is with us, on our side, and rooting for us. How then shall we fail? The Spirit of God is willing, and the spirit of Man is willing, but the flesh is still weak. Notwithstanding, failure is not an option. Failure now would spell the ineffable sadness—*tristesse absolue*—of man's defeat by the Constable. Final and penultimate defeat, despite the long, hard, bitter, uphill struggle of the centuries.

The Gospel is Man's Declaration of Independence from spiritual slavery. No Declaration of Independence is an end in itself, but a prologue to Revolution. It is time for a *Spiritual Revolution.* Today is the day to break free of the Constable's yoke spiritually. Tomorrow may be too late. The whole of the issue boils down to this: does Man have occasion against the Constable? Have the peoples of the world had enough? Do the congregations of humanity have it in them to bid defiance to this devil and claim the Liberty prepared for them from the foundation of the world? Are the races, cultures, nations and ethnos of the world now ready to tell this devil to vacate the premises of the earth? Or have they resigned themselves to failure and defeat? We are persuaded that their faith will shortly triumph. As Rav Shaul affirms:

> Nay, in all these things we are more than conquerors through him that loved us. For I am persuaded, that neither death, nor life, nor angels, nor principalities, nor powers, nor things present, nor things to come, nor height, nor depth, nor any other created thing, shall be able to separate us from the love of God, which is in Christ Jesus our Lord.
>
> (Romans 8:37-39)

The victory of the sons and daughters of Adam is not a matter of fate: it is a matter of restored *faith* in the God who created the heavens and the earth. The Exodus of nations out of the derivative orders of existence awaits a spiritual revival such as this.

Endnotes

Introduction

1. Stephen Hawking, *A Brief History of Time* (Bantam Books, 1990), p. 12.
2. Michael Ignatieff, *Blood and Belonging* (New York: Farrar, Straus and Giroux, 1993), pp. 44-45.
3. *Ibid.*, p. 244
4. Quoted in *The Great Quotations* compiled by George Seldes (New York: Pocket Books, 1976), p. 921.

Section 1

1. Johannes Dogigli, *The Magic of Rays* (New York: Alfred A. Knopf, 1961), p. 33.
2. Ian Stewart, *Nature's Numbers* (Basic Books, 1995), p. 110.
3. Derek Kidner, *Genesis, an Introduction* & *Commentary* (Inter-Varsity Press, 1967), p. 47.
4. Stephen Hawking, *A Brief History of Time* (Bantam Books, 1990), pp. 168-169.
5. Augustine of Hippo, *Confessions* (Translated and edited by Albert C. Outler, 1994), 7.12.18.
6. Charles Darwin, *The Origin of Species* (New York: Modern Library Paperback Edition, 1998), p. 109.

Section 2

1. Joseph Davydov, *God Exists* (Schreiber Publishing, Inc., 2000), p. 91.
2. Huw Price, *Time's Arrow and Archimedes' Point* (New York: Oxford University Press, 1996), pp. 168-9.
3. *The Oxford Companion to Philosophy*, edited by Ted Honderich (New York: Oxford University Press, 1995), p.58.
4. Edith Schaeffer, *Christianity is Jewish* (Tyndale House Publishers), p.23.

Section 3

1. Charles Darwin, *The Origin of Species* (New York: Modern Library Paperback Edition, 1998), pp. 648-9.
2. Quoted by J. Horgan, "In the Beginning...," (*Scientific American*, February 1991), p. 117.
3. Charles Darwin, *The Origin of Species* (New York: Modern Library Paperback Edition, 1998), p. 244.
4. Stephen Jay Gould, *Full House* (New York: Harmony Books, 1996), p. 169.
5. Gerald L. Schroeder, *Genesis and the Big Bang* (New York: Bantam Books, 1990), pp. 49-52.

6. Charles Darwin, *The Origin of Species* (New York: Modern Library, 1998), p. 72
7. *Ibid.*, p. 406.
8. *Ibid.*, pp. 87-9.
9. *Ibid.*, p. 21.
10. *Ibid.*, p. 209.
11. *Ibid.*, p. 141.
12. *Ibid.*, p. 141.
13. *Ibid.*, p. 160.
14. *Ibid.*, p. 639.
15. *Ibid.*, p. 5.
16. *Ibid.*, p. 82.
17. *Ibid.*, p. 170.
18. *Ibid.*, p. 193.
19. *Ibid.*, pp. 208-9.
20. *Ibid.*, p. 227.
21. *Ibid.*, p. 491.
22. *Ibid.*, p. 534.
23. *Ibid.*, pp. 608-9.
24. *Ibid.*, p. 629.
25. *Ibid.*, p. 636.
26. *Ibid.*, p. 638.
27. *Ibid.*, pp. 227-8

Section 4

1. John Adams, *Dissertation on the Canon and Feudal Law* (Boston: Brown, Little, 1856), Vol. III.
2. Adolph Hitler, *Mein Kampf* (Boston: The Houghton Mifflin Company, 1971), p. 55.
3. *Ibid.*, p. 127.
4. *Ibid.*, p. 56.
5. *Ibid.*, p. 123.
6. *Ibid.*, pp. 244-5.
7. Quoted in *The Great Quotations* compiled by George Seldes (New York: Pocket Books, 1976), p. 253.
8. Erich Fromm, *The Anatomy of Human Destructiveness* (New York: Holt, Rinehart and Winston, 1973), pp. 476-7.
9. Richard Feynman, *The Feynman Lectures on Physics* (San Francisco: Addison-Wesley, 1963), Vol. 1, pp. 1-8.
10. D. Halliday and R. Resnick, *Fundamentals of Physics* (New York: John Wiley & Sons, 1970), p. 415.

Section 5

1. Thomas Jefferson, *The Writings of Thomas Jefferson* (Memorial Edition, Washington, D.C., 1903-04, Lipscomb and Bergh, editors), 15:23. 888
2. *Ibid.*, 888
3. Margrit Kennedy, *Interest and Inflation Free Money* (Philadelphia: New Society

Publishers, 1995), pp. 24-5.
4. Al Gore, *Earth in the Balance* (New York: Houghton Mifflin Company, 2000), p. 239.
5. Hans-Peter Martin & Harald Schumann, *The Global Trap* (London:Zed Books, 1997), pp. 45-6.
6. *Ibid.*, p. 189.
7. Davison L. Budhoo, *Enough is Enough* (New York: Apex Press, 1990), pp. 2-3.
8. *Ibid.*, p. 107.
9. Jacques S. Jaikaran, *Debt Virus*, (Glenbridge Publishing Ltd., 1992), p. 167.

Section 6

1. Gerald L. Schroeder, *Genesis and the Big Bang* (New York: Bantam Books, 1990), p. 109.
2. Julian Whitaker, *Medical Alerts*, Vol. 11, No. 4, (2002), p 12.
3. G. Nicolson, "Tumor Cell Instability, Diversification, and Progression of the Metastatic Phenotype: From Oncogene to Oncofetal Expression," *Cancer Research* 47 (1987), pp. 1473-1478.
4. Gerald B. Dermer, *The Immortal Cell* (New York: Avery Publishing Group, 1994), p. 13.
5. *Ibid.*, p. 19.
6. Richard A. Passwater, *Cancer Prevention and Nutritional Therapies* (Keats Publishing, 1993), p. 22.
7. *Ibid.*, p.23.
8. William L. Fischer, *How to Fight Cancer & Win* (Fischer Publishing, 1994), pp. 231-2.
9. Wesley J. Smith, *Culture of Death* (San Francisco: Encounter Books, 2000), p. ix.
10. Francis Schaeffer, quoted in *Impact*, (Coral Ridge Ministries, April 1977), p. 3.
11. Francis Crick, *The Astonishing Hypothesis* (New York: Simon and Schuster, 1995), p. 3.

Section 7

1. Quoted by Reuven Alcalay in *Words of the Wise, an Anthology of Proverbs and Practical Axioms* (Israel: Modan Publishing House, 1997), p. 135.
2. *Ibid.*, p. 426.
3. Robert H. Bork, *Slouching Towards Gomorrah* (Reagan Books 1997), p.164.
4. *Ibid.*, quoted on p. 205.
5. Josh McDowell and Bob Hostetler, *The New Tolerance* (Wheaton: Tyndale House Publishers, 1998), p. 150.

Millennial Benediction

1. Grace Nichols, *A Caribbean Dozen* (Cambridge, MA: Candlewick Press, 1994), p. 24.

Index